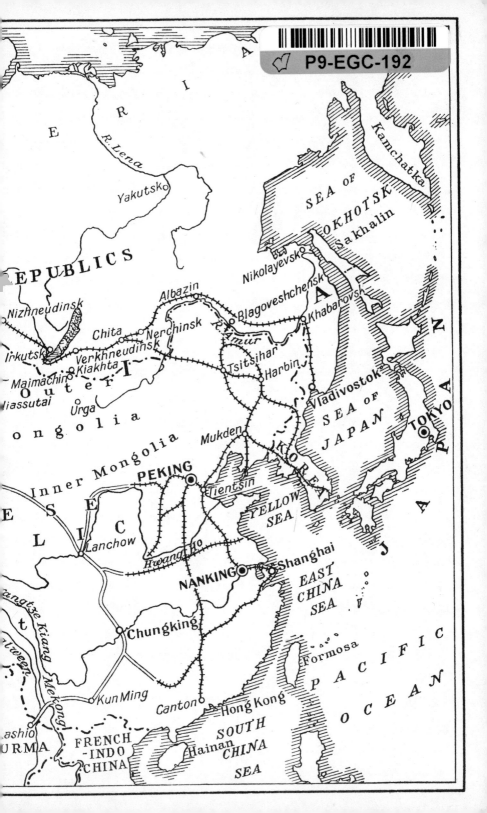

CHINA AND THE SOVIET UNION

CHINA AND THE SOVIET UNION

A Study of Sino-Soviet Relations

by

AITCHEN K. WU, Ph.D. (London)

Formerly Chinese Consul-General at Vladivostok;
Professor of International Relations at Yenching
University and West China Union University

KENNIKAT PRESS, INC./PORT WASHINGTON, N. Y.

CHINA AND THE SOVIET UNION

First Published in 1950
Reissued in 1967 by Kennikat Press

Library of Congress Catalog Card No: 67-29610

Manufactured in the United States of America

FOREWORD

IT is to me a genuine pleasure to introduce the author, already well known to the reading public, and to say a few words on the subject dealt with in the book. Mr. Aitchen K. Wu has had much experience in foreign affairs, having been at home Special Delegate of the *Waichiaopu* in the provinces in charge of such matters and abroad our Consul-General in Siberia. He resided also for some time in Chinese Turkistan as Commissioner of Foreign Affairs, and as such acquired direct knowledge of the relations between that far-off Chinese province and the Soviet Union. His interesting and authoritative book, *Turkistan Tumult*, gives a very full account of conditions in that province, its recent history and his personal experiences there.

In the present book he deals in a painstaking manner with the larger aspects of Sino-Soviet relations in recent times, and brings their history up to date—a task which has not yet been undertaken by any other writer, but is of the greatest importance. He has a thorough acquaintance with this vast subject, of which he here provides an excellent bibliography; and, moreover, he writes from personal experience and direct observation both as our Consul-General in Siberia and as a frequent visitor to Moscow. He has also discussed privately certain aspects of the question with the high personages who were entrusted by our government with negotiations with the Soviet authorities. Thus what he has now put on record attains as far as is at present possible to historical accuracy, and often possesses the degree of authenticity only to be had from direct contact with officials ultimately responsible.

He has expressed himself with much frankness at times and has not hesitated to make fair comment. He believes, as many people do, that it is necessary and helpful between good friends to tell each other sometimes the unvarnished truth. No reasonable Chinese can fail to realize that, with a common frontier of many thousands of miles and with diplomatic and commercial relations dating back to an earlier period than those between China and other nations, the Chinese and the Soviet peoples should and could not be anything but the best of friends, and this idea runs like a thread throughout the length of the book.

With these few lines I commend the book to the large number of readers interested in international relations.

W. W. YEN,
Former Chinese Ambassador to the U.S.S.R.

PREFACE

IT was in 1939—when I came to London from the U.S.S.R. to write my first book, *Turkistan Tumult*—that I began specific research into the subject of Sino-Soviet relations. This work was, unfortuantely, interrupted by the war. Leaving London, I settled in Hong Kong to continue my writing, and later I flew to Chungking, not only to gather additional materials but also to seek an opportunity to return to London for the further research necessary for the completion of the book.

Though I made many efforts to get sent to London on official missions, the abnormal circumstances of the times deprived me of success. Eventually, as the unhappy political situation showed no signs of becoming more favourable to my project, I resigned my post in Formosa and came to London quite independently, arriving in the autumn of 1949.

It had been my custom during ten years of intensive study of my subject to scan carefully all relevant books in public libraries and private collections, hoping to find useful information. I was doing this amongst the libraries and Chinese Government archives in Chungking even when there were frequent air raids. In the course of these, by the way, the only thing I always took to the air-raid shelter was my manuscript. I consider myself most fortunate to have been able to preserve it intact through such tumultuous times of war.

Since my arrival in London I have been kept busy in such places as the British Museum and Chatham House checking and revising my past work as well as bringing the whole book up to date.

Notwithstanding my regret that the publication of this book has been delayed some ten years, I trust that this delay has not proved detrimental but has been beneficial, as during this time I have had ample opportunities to add more materials and render the work as comprehensive as possible.

Being descended from five generations of Chinese scholars, I naturally love books, and, having pored over so many English ones that have enlightened me, it seems only fair that I should myself try to write something useful in the spirit of 'one good turn deserves another'. It is for this reason that I have undertaken so much drudgery outside my peculiar interests. It is far from being a business proposition to publish such a book as this. If, however, it can be accounted a slight contribution to world history in the making, or serve to foster better relations in the Far East, then the author will deem such recompense more than he deserves.

The book is in three Parts, and arranged in both geographical and chronological order. The first Part consists of five chapters, furnishing the historical background of relations between China and Tsarist Russia. This is of prime importance because history often repeats itself. The influences of geographical propinquities and traditional thought, are constant regardless of changes in administration and governments. The second Part comprises six chapters, and deals with relations between China and the Soviet Union from 1917 to 1930. The third Part consists of eleven chapters, in which all events occurring from the Manchurian Incident of 1931 to the Sino-Soviet Treaty of Friendship, Alliance and Mutual Assistance of 1950 are fully discussed. The last two decades have, indeed, been outstandingly eventful.

It seems that the world is now split into two camps—Capitalist and Communist—and this presents a world-wide problem that every human being has to face. This problem goes beyond the scope of Sino-Soviet relations, yet the destiny of the world will depend upon it.

As I have been at work on this book for the last decade, it is almost impossible for me to acknowledge all those who have either read the manuscript or furnished valuable materials. However, I must mention just a few.

I am much indebted to Professor C. W. A. Manning of the London School of Economics and Political Science, who has constantly given encouragement and advice in the completion of the task. The Librarian of the Chinese International Library in Geneva was good enough to let me borrow numerous Chinese books to take to China with a promise to return them after use.

Dr. W. W. Yen, a veteran diplomat and former Chinese Ambassador to Moscow, read most of the manuscript, and provided inside information as well as contributing a foreword. His lamented death occurred while I was reading the proofs, and I regret being thereby prevented from presenting the finished book to him.

Among those who have read my manuscript, I particularly wish to mention Mr. Kuo Ting-I, Professor of History of the Central University at Chungking, who was kind enough to check up the dates relating to early Sino-Russian diplomatic history. The late Sir Eric Teichman of the British Embassy in Chungking provided well-informed counsel. Mr. Richard Price was also good enough to read through the narrative while he was a refugee in Chungking. Dr. Agnes Chen, Professor of Political Science in Yenching University is another who has been very helpful.

Coming to London in August 1949, I met my old friend, Mr. M. Urban, by chance in the Oriental Students' Reading Room of the British Museum, and his untiring service in the work has bound us anew in friendship. Sir Alwyne Ogden, an old colleague of mine in China as far back as 1924, has kindly read some chapters and made candid suggestions. Mr. Guy Wint, whom I had the pleasure of meeting in Chungking during war-time, has carefully gone over the manuscript with helpful results. I have also benefited by several discussions with Mr. G. F. Hudson, of All Souls College, Oxford, who is an authority on this particular subject. An old-time friend, Mr. Clifford Troke, has rendered some assistance. Miss K. T. Kuo has done much clerical work and helped in making the index. Last but not least I consider myself fortunate in having the expert assistance of Mr. Richard W. Eland in the reading of the page proofs. In respect of the whole of the book, I alone accept responsibility for any defects and shortcomings, many of which may be due to the use of a language not my own.

I cannot help adding here that my wife, who accompanied me to London, passed away after a long illness at the very time I was finishing my writing. Though this was to me a tragedy and an irretrievable loss, nevertheless I do not regret coming to London to complete the task, whatever sacrifices have been involved, if only the book can be of any service to the reading public.

Primrose Hill, London   AITCHEN K. WU
June 1950

CONTENTS

Part III

CHINA AND THE SOVIET UNION: 1931-1950

PART I

CHINA AND TSARIST RUSSIA
1618-1917

Chapter I

INTRODUCTION

SINO-SOVIET relations entered upon a new phase with Moscow's repudiation of the Nationalist Government in Canton and the simultaneous recognition by Moscow of the Chinese People's Republic in Peking on October 1, 1949. The Nationalist Government, in answer to this, severed connections with the Soviet Union two days later.

Canton's fall to the Reds completed the transformation. Sun Yat-sen had set up his government in that city during 1921, and from there had started his northern drive with the help of Soviet advisers. Less than thirty years later, the Chinese People's Republic, headed by Mao Tse-tung, made a victorious drive towards Canton, again with the alleged help of the Soviets. The wheel had gone full circle.

The Chinese People's Government was established on September 30, 1949, and it received official Soviet recognition almost immediately. The Soviet Government could not have forgotten the Treaty of Friendship and Alliance made with the Nationalist Government in 1945, nor was it unaware that such a 'right-about face' would antagonize the United Nations, especially the Security Council on which the Nationalist delegate holds the power of veto.

After the fall of Chungking and Chengtu, the Nationalist Government retreated to Formosa and set up its new capital in Taipeh. This was the fifth Nationalist capital within a period of eight months. Such swift surrender is unprecedented in Chinese history. It seems clear that, whenever there are two rival parties in China, the one

I

backed by the Soviets always has the upper hand. It was for this reason that the Nationalist Government were able to drive out the old warlords and, in the same way, the Chinese Communists have gained the victory over the Nationalists to-day. This only goes to show what a mighty influence the Soviet Government has over China.

Since Russia extends over both Asia and Europe, she forms a bridge between East and West. Although the bulk of her population is found west of the Urals, and her economic as well as cultural life is far more western than eastern, Russia is nevertheless more like an Asiatic nation with interests in Europe than a European nation with interests in Asia. This is even truer to-day than in the past as a result of the Soviet policy of furthering the 'self-determination of peoples'. To this end, the Soviet Government encouraged the Asiatic races in Siberia to set up their own independent governments which would form part of the Union of Soviet Socialist Republics. There are eight Asiatic Republics in the Soviet Union; the other eight are European. Stalin, himself a native of Georgia, once bluntly said to Matsuoka, the then Japanese Foreign Minister: 'I, too, am an Asiatic.' This goes to show how quickly a great European nation such as Russia can become 'Asianized'.

It was the firm belief of Lenin that for the revolution to be successful in Russia it must be enlarged and expanded into a world revolution. This policy, however, failed not only through the retreat of the Red Army at Warsaw, as a result of the help given by France to the Polish forces, but because of the recovery of the capitalistic powers, especially Germany, after the 1914 War. After this set-back, Lenin sought friendly terms with capitalist countries. This was the object of the 'New Economic Policy'.

Stalin held that though the capitalist countries, to his surprise, had turned out to be stable, the Soviet Union, too, had become tranquil, stable and peaceful, perhaps even more so than they. Indeed, he went so far as to say that the Soviet Union could continue to make progress by herself and within her own borders without bothering about a world revolution.

Nevertheless, it is doubtful whether the Comintern or later the Cominform has given up its basic policy of world ferment. The advance guards of the world revolution may have been temporarily halted. But if Russia's attention has been diverted from Europe, it has been directed towards Asia. Further, Russia has adopted the 'national policy' of helping all oppressed nations in the Far East to throw off the shackles of imperialism, thereby weakening the capitalist hold on the Orient. China, in particular, is seen as a power that will play the chief role in this drama. As China has one-fifth and Russia one-tenth of the world's population, the union of these two peoples in a common understanding must have the utmost significance to all mankind.

China is now in the throes of a great social upheaval which involves millions of people. Everything is in a state of flux, and conditions are changing almost hourly, so that it is hard to foresee what will happen. Nevertheless, it would seem that the Communist régime with its headquarters in Peking has come to stay. The Nationalist forces degenerated through bad morale and not through the Communist onslaught, for there were few serious military encounters, and the casualties of the war had been low. After the collapse of the Nationalists, there remained only one possible government, the Chinese People's Republic.

In matters of foreign policy the Chinese people do not speak with one voice. Some are pro-American, others are pro-Japanese, while great numbers are pro-Soviet. The failure of Wang Ching-wei's puppet régime, following the surrender of Japan, proved a sharp lesson to pro-Japanese opportunists. The pro-Americans were disillusioned by the Yalta Secret Agreement. Thus only the pro-Soviet group escaped being discredited.

With the establishment of the People's Republic of China in Peking, relations with the Soviet Union became much easier as compared with those under the Nationalist régime. The Soviet Union is in ideological sympathy with the People's Republic of China, and would like to see the new régime stabilized. But this is certain only if the Soviet Union respects China's sovereignty and integrity. Only then can the People's Republic of China strengthen itself by winning the confidence of the people.

It should benefit New China to adopt a 'closed door' policy towards the outer world for a certain length of time, since she has suffered so much during the last decade. It is probable that all unnecessary imports will be cut down with a view to stabilizing the monetary system. The door may be shut temporarily to put the house in order until such time as business with the outside world can be placed on an equal footing. In a few years' time, China will have recuperated and become financially sound, to the advantage of the rest of the world. 'Hands off China', refers to all countries. However, it would not do to shut the front door and leave the back door wide open. In this connection, there will certainly be considerable international controversy, and this may even be a prelude to another world war. Manchuria, for instance, has been a bone of contention for the last century.

It is for these reasons that Mao Tze-tung went to Moscow and later was joined by Chou En-lai in the attempt to revise Sino-Soviet relations. It seems that China gained some success in the negotiations. At least Stalin was persuaded to give up, not later than 1952, the treaty rights which he gained in 1945. Both parties agreed upon mutual military or other assistance to prevent any further aggression by Japan alone or in co-operation with any other state.

Fear of renewed Japanese aggression may be premature. But what worries the Soviet Union most is the possibility of some other State linking up with Japan. All the difficulties which Russia placed in the way of the taking over of Manchuria by the Nationalist régime were due to the fear that the influence of some other State would penetrate Manchuria right up to the Soviet border. Because of this fear, Russia was indifferent to the Nationalist Government. Because of this fear, Russia favoured the Communist régime. The consequence has been the abrogation both of the Sino-Soviet Treaty of 1945 and the Yalta Secret Agreement. By these steps, initiated by the Soviet Union, the peace of the world should be strengthened.

The writer has been twenty-five years in the Diplomatic Service. He is non-partisan and tries to record diplomatic history in an unbiased but uncompromising way. He has spent four periods of his life in the Soviet Union. On the last occasion he was Chinese Consul-General in Siberia for three and a half years. He loves the country, and particularly the people, who are kind and great-hearted. Travellers find no racial prejudice in the Soviet Union, where all men are deemed equal. Hence, it is the writer's aim to make an analysis of Soviet interests in the Far East, starting with an account of Tsarist rule in the days gone by, passing on to an interpretation of the present position of the Soviet Union, and offering finally a reasonable forecast of the future.

Chapter II

EARLY DIPLOMATIC RELATIONS BETWEEN RUSSIA AND CHINA

CHINESE diplomatic relations with other countries overland began before maritime foreign relations. Since the spread of the Chinese race has been from north to south, relations with the regions that are now Russian Central Asia and Siberia can be traced back for many centuries. To study Sino-Soviet relations with a clear understanding, it is advisable, at the outset, to trace the early direct diplomatic relations between China and Russia.

1. First Sino-Russian Official Contacts

The first real attempt to reach China from Russia took place in 1608. Russian knowledge of China, at that time, was confined to the belief that 'the Chinese Kingdom has a stone-built town and courtyards in that town wherein there are temples, and in them a great ringing of bells'.[1] The first officials to reach China by an overland route were two Russian Cossacks named Petlin and Mundoff, who made their appearance in the year 1618.[2] These two Cossacks were then sent by the Tsar during the Ming Dynasty and were instructed to seek information as to the kingdom of China and the customs and languages of the people. They seem to have reached Peking by way of Kalgan, but they failed to obtain an audience of the Emperor Wên-li, not only because they brought no 'tribute' wherewith to pay respects to the Celestial Empire, but also because His Imperial Majesty did not consider these two agents of a little-known Tsar to be of sufficient consequence. They were dismissed by a letter and consequently returned empty-handed to Russia, except for bringing back to the Tsar a map of the provinces

[1] Baddeley, John F., *Russia, Mongolia, China*, London, 1919, Vol. II, p. 34.
[2] ibid., pp. 65-86, signifying the pretended journey of 1567 by Petroff and Yalicheff.

of China. It was said that no one at the time could make out the contents of the imperial epistle at Moscow. It was not interpreted until 1676, when it was taken back to Peking to be translated by a Jesuit priest.

During the reign of Shun-chih of the Ching Dynasty, another Russian mission under Theodore Isakovich Baikov arrived at Peking in 1656 with a small caravan of government goods, after being well-nigh two years on the journey. He was ordered to make enquiry as to how far it was possible to reach China either by water or overland, and what arms the Chinese had; what goods were to be bought in China; what Russian merchandise should be sent there.[3] It so happened that Baikov reached the Chinese capital simultaneously with a Dutch Embassy under Goyer. His Imperial Majesty asked both missions to present their 'tribute' and to perform the kotow ceremony, namely, the bow of servile allegiance to the Chinese Emperor forming part of Court etiquette. The Dutch Envoy acquiesced, and an audience was, in consequence, granted him. The Russian Envoy, however, would only present the complimentary address in a standing position, according to the usage of his own country, and refused to kneel or kotow. He was not admitted to audience, and accordingly his tributary gifts were declined.

After that, envoys sent to China by the Tsarist Government were chosen from among merchants going to China with caravans of goods. It was then a very strict rule of the Chinese Court that an audience could only be granted after performance of the kotow ceremony, otherwise the tribute would be rejected, though the Envoy concerned might still effect sales in the capital. The year 1659 witnessed yet another embassy, this time under Perfiliev and Ablin, who carried with them gifts together with a letter from the Tsar. An audience was granted them, so, apparently, they had fulfilled the requirements of the Chinese Court. Before departure, they were handed a letter to the Tsar by the Chinese Emperor saying, 'The tribute thou didst send we have accepted, and in return we send thee our gifts and favours.'[4] Among the gifts was tea, but Perfiliev sold all the tea in Peking as it was an unknown and unwanted article in Russia.

2. Spathary's Mission

The first real Ambassador sent by a Tsar was Nicholas Spathary

[3] Baddeley, op. cit., Vol. II, p. 132.
[4] ibid., p. 168.

in the year 1675. It was the custom of the Chinese Court that all missives from any kingdom should first be taken and perused by the Board of Ceremony before they could be presented to the Emperor. To this, Spathary raised the objection that if ambassadors could be received by the Chinese Emperor, why not the letters of their masters. He was warned that, if he refused to take the Tsar's letter to the Board, his labour would be in vain, and he would have to return, like Baikov, empty-handed. When this condition had been complied with, another dispute arose concerning the performance of the Court etiquette, to which Spathary at first objected, although he later gave way when he was brought to Court. Spathary made the complaint: 'When I bowed I knew not to whom, the Khan being invisible.'[5] He was then cordially received by the Emperor, tea and fruits being served. Ere long, he was dismissed because of the bad conduct of his Cossacks, who beat the Chinese guards and roamed around outside the city walls. He was allowed to receive the Emperor's gifts for the Tsar without following the usual custom of kneeling, thus safeguarding the honour of his master.

In the early part of the seventeenth century, Russian influence gradually spread to the Amur. Although the Manchus had established their dynasty in Peking, they were kept busy for some years in suppressing the San Fan Rebellion (Three Border Rebellion), which affected many provinces of China. It was only after considerable turmoil that victory came to the imperial forces, thus making it possible to consolidate and set about the task of establishing peace. As the new Manchu Dynasty, reigning in Peking, was not yet half a century old, it was obvious that, if diplomatic means could secure the necessary safeguards on the Amur frontier, it would be better not to resort to arms against the Russian newcomers.

In the year 1667 a Tungus prince by the name of Gantimur fled to Russia. Thereupon the Emperor Kang Hsi sent one of his nobles to Nerchinsk to request the surrender of Gantimur. Such a request was not complied with, but Kang Hsi sent the Tsar a letter in 1677. This letter remained unanswered for the reason that it was written in Manchu, a language unknown to Russians. The Chinese troops were then actively besieging Albazin on the Amur frontier, which had been previously occupied by the Russians as a reprisal against China. The siege in question was carried out under the pretence of hunting, whereas, in fact, it was an attempt to drive out the Russians.

[5] Baddeley, op. cit., Vol. II, p. 362.

China had little, if any, need for commerce with Russia. Her material civilization was incomparably higher and she supplied her own requirements within the confines of her extensive empire. She did, nevertheless, desire good relations with Russia, for she had already begun, in spite of the paucity of information concerning that country, to foresee that here was a neighbour likely not only to grow more dangerous with time, but one that would not hesitate to exploit the tributary states and tribes on China's frontiers. The Chinese Emperor accordingly sent two letters in Latin to the Tsar dated May 6, 1683, which were received in Moscow as late as November 15, 1685, after having taken fully two and a half years to reach their destination. 'These letters referred to many earlier ones from China that had remained unanswered, requiring the evacuation of Albazin, but giving indications of a disposition to be conciliatory.' Russia at the time was likewise anxious to settle the constant friction created by her settlers, in trading between the two countries. Any friction was liable to start reprisals that might lead to war on a large scale. Therefore, as soon as Russia received these two letters, she decided to send an embassy to China and try to come to a prompt decision with the Peking Government. The embassy was entrusted to Nikifor Veniukoff and Ivan Favoroff in advance of the Russian plenipotentiary, Golovin, to Peking, to announce his coming. They brought a letter from the Tsar to the Chinese Emperor asking for pardon for past misunderstanding and for a suspension of hostilities in Albazin.[6]

3. Activities of Golovin

It was Peter the Great who selected Theodore Alexeivitch Golovin as his 'High Ambassador Plenipotentiary'. The major questions he was to bring to the notice of the Chinese Emperor, Kang Hsi, were those concerning the frontier and the trade problems along the Amur and its tributaries. Golovin, while on the way to China, was instructed to meet the leading Mongolian Prince and endeavour to persuade him to side with the Russians, holding out, as a bait, the promise of favourable commercial relations. There could be little doubt that he had secret instructions to put out feelers to ascertain the attitude of the various influential non-Chinese peoples with

[6] Cahen Gaston, *Histoire des Relations de la Russie avec la Chine, sous Pierre le Grand (1689-1730)*, Paris, 1912, p. 35. See also Baddeley, op. cit., Vol. II, p. 242 and N. 2.

whom he would be coming into contact and, if feasible, to encourage them to look to Russia for support. Another task set him was to acquire all possible information regarding the river routes into China.

Golovin was to lay special stress on the Tsar's desire to regularize trade as well as to induce the Chinese to send to Moscow, through their own agents, precious stones, silver, velvets, damasks and spice. He was also to invite merchants to bring ingots and silk which, he said, the Russian treasury would buy immediately. This is significant, as it was a proof of the Tsar's intention of making trade with China a government monopoly.

On January 26, 1686, Golovin and his mission left Moscow with a military escort on its long journey. He spent nearly two years in various parts of Siberia. It was the first time such a high official had been despatched to survey the new territories annexed during previous decades. Peter the Great was much more energetic than his immediate predecessors, having a decidedly broader vision so that he could foresee tremendous possibilities in these yet little-known lands.

The two advance agents, Veniukoff and Favoroff, left Moscow on December 20, 1685, and reached Peking on October 13, 1686, where they remained but a short time. The Chinese Emperor, Kang Hsi, after learning of Russia's peaceful intentions, sent orders that the siege of Albazin, which had been going on for some time, should be raised. The Russian agents, pleased at this initial success of their mission, headed by Golovin, straightway sent couriers to inform him of their safe arrival as well as give news of this friendly gesture.

On the return journey, they carried two letters from the Chinese Emperor. One was written in Mongolian, briefly acknowledging the messages the Tsar had conveyed through his agents, while the other was in Latin and dated the 16th day of the 10th moon of the 25th year of Kang Hsi (November 21, 1686)[7].

The following is an extract from Kang Hsi's letter:

'The officials to whom I have entrusted the supervision of the sable hunt, have frequently complained of the injury which the people of Siberia do to our hunters on the Amur and, particularly, to the Chucheri. My subjects have never provoked yours nor done them any injury; yet the people of Albazin, armed with

[7] According to Baddeley the date should be July 17, 1687.

cannons, guns and other fire-arms, have frequently attacked my people, who have no fire-arms and were peaceably hunting. Moreover, they have given shelter to our deserters, and, when my Superintendent of the Chase followed some deserters of Kandagan to Albazin and demanded their surrender, Alexei, Ivan and others responded that they could not do this but must first apply to the Changa Khan for instructions. As yet, no answer has been vouchsafed to our enquiries, nor have the deserters been given up.

'In the meantime, my officers on the frontier have informed me of your Russians having carried off some peaceful hunters as prisoners. They also roved about the Lower Amur and injured the small town of Genquen and other places. As soon as I heard this, I ordered my officers to take up arms and act as occasion might require. They accordingly made prisoners of the Russians roving about the Lower Amur. No one was put to death, but all were provided with food. When our people arrived before Albazin and called upon it to surrender, Alexei and others, without deigning to reply, treated us in a hostile fashion and fired off cannon and muskets. We did not put anyone to death. We liberated our prisoners, but more than forty Russians, of their own choice, preferred remaining amongst our own people. The others we exhorted earnestly to return to their own side of the frontier where they might hunt at pleasure. My officers had scarcely left when four hundred and sixty Russians returned, rebuilt Albazin, killed our hunters and laid waste their fields, thus compelling my officers to have recourse to arms again.

'Albazin was consequently beleaguered a second time, but orders were nevertheless given to spare the prisoners and restore them to their own country. Since then, Veniukoff and others have arrived in Peking to announce the approach of an ambassador and to propose a friendly conference to settle the boundary question and induce the Chinese to raise the siege of Albazin. On this, a courier was at once sent to Albazin to put a stop to further hostilities.'[8]

The *Peking Gazette* at the time reported: 'The 6th day of the 4th moon of the 26th year of Kang Hsi (May 16, 1687) our troops withdrew 20 verst from Albazin to the place known as Djakan . . . and on the 11th of the 7th moon (August 18) the Emperor gave

---

[8] Putnam Weale, *Manchu and Muscovite*, p. 34. See also Baddeley, op. cit., pp. 425-7.

orders for retirement to Ninguta.'[9] This item coincides with what was stated in the letter of Kang Hsi.

These imperial messages were received in Moscow on July 17, 1687, but the Russian Government had already come to the decision that further steps should be taken to conciliate the Chinese. On June 24, 1687, fresh secret instructions were despatched to Golovin.

Golovin was to cede Albazin (perhaps we should say 'vacate' it as it was not Russian territory) in exchange for satisfactory commercial relations. He was to avoid, except in case of dire need, any bloodshed (this did not mean much as Albazin was about to fall): and if all his efforts should fail, he was to request that another embassy be permitted to visit Peking at a convenient date.

The two Russian agents, in the meantime, returned to Moscow and were partly instrumental in making their government realize that their so-called 'concessions' were of no particular consequence to the Chinese. The government decided, some months after the issue of the special letter of instructions to Golovin, to furnish him with a new authority enabling him to act on behalf of the Russian Court at any conference which the Chinese Emperor might desire to hold. This official document was dated October 29, 1687, but Golovin was told not to leave Siberia until Ivan Loginoff, who was bearing him the new instructions, had first been sent to Peking for the purpose of providing Kang Hsi with copies of them as proof of Russia's goodwill and anxiety to reach a peaceful settlement. Golovin was also instructed to obtain, if possible, the services of the Hutukhtu, or Living Buddha, the important Mongol religious leader, as a sort of diplomatic liaison officer between Russia and China.

Golovin had since the close of 1686 already attempted to win the favour of the Hutukhtu, then residing at Urga, but with little success. The latter was suspicious of Russian overtures, and knew that too intimate relations would place him in the bad books of the Chinese.

While these tremendously long journeys were being undertaken from Peking to Siberia and thence to Moscow and from Moscow back again, Ivan Vlasoff, Governor of Nerchinsk and simultaneously a member of Golovin's suite, received information in October 1687 that the siege of Albazin had been raised and that hostilities had come to an end.

Korovin, an agent sent by Golovin to Kang Hsi, arrived at Peking

[9] Cahen, op. cit., p. 38, N. 5.

on March 14, 1688, and did not leave till April 17, 1688. He brought back a message from the Chinese Emperor designating Selenginsk as the town for a conference between representatives of the two countries. The Chinese delegates departed from Peking on May 29, but on July 22 they abruptly discontinued their journey on account of war in Mongolia, and, after despatching a letter through couriers to Golovin, announcing that they wished to delay the conference till the following year, they returned to Peking.

It was later agreed by China that the postponed conference should take place at Nerchinsk, a more suitable venue in view of the trouble with the Eleuths (Oirats). The Chinese envoys, consisting of Prince So San (also known as Son-go-to), and Tang Kwo-kang, maternal uncle of the Emperor Kang Hsi, Ah Erh-ni, President of the Lifan Yuan (Colonial Office), Ma Tsi, Ma La, accompanied by two Jesuits, Gerbillon and Pereira acting as interpreters, left Peking on June 13 and arrived at Nerchinsk on July 31, 1689.[10] A few days later, the Russian delegates, headed by Golovin and Vlasoff, arrived at Nerchinsk.

The Chinese delegation was supported by an army of ten thousand men with a fleet of boats and cannon. The Tungus and the Buriats of the district were definitely pro-Chinese and could be counted on as a material factor in case of need. The Russians had, at the back of them, a thousand troops, not including about five hundred of their countrymen at Nerchinsk capable of bearing arms.

The meetings were begun on August 12. The delegates on both sides sat in their tents, one over against another, without any superiority on either side. The Russians alighted first and advanced a few steps to meet the Chinese, inviting them to enter the tent first. They sat on benches opposite each other with a table in between. The interpreters sat at the upper end of the table and retinue stood by. In the opinion of Gerbillon, the Chinese showed themselves so exacting that the discussions were quickly broken off, and it was due to the efforts of the two Jesuit interpreters that the negotiations were carried through. The Jesuits favoured China, and when the Russian envoy tried to speak directly with the Chinese in Mongolian, the Jesuits opposed this on the ground that they were the official interpreters, and that they alone held the office of intermediaries. The Russians tried to bring the Jesuits to a better frame of mind

[10] Ho Chiu-Tao, *The Strategy of Conquering the Russians* (in Chinese), Vol. IV.

by means of promises for their society, but the Jesuits refused to do anything that might be considered harmful to China. On the other hand, they would not press the Russians to a rupture.[11]

The Chinese delegates demanded that the frontier be placed at Nerchinsk. The Russians refused to agree to this. For two whole days they argued, neither side willing to give in to the other. The Chinese then threatened to break up the conference, and this had the effect of making Golovin more tractable. And when, on August 16, the Jesuit interpreters intervened in an effort to settle the impasse by introducing some minor concessions and naming Gorbitsa as the boundary, Golovin was ready to meet them more than half-way. After the boundary settlement, the question of repatriation was brought up, particularly on the surrender of Guntimur. It was learned that Guntimur had left for Moscow, accompanied by his father, to join the Russian Orthodox Church. At this point the matter was deemed closed.[12] Thus, the Treaty of Nerchinsk was concluded in 1689.

4. Activities of Ides

In 1692, Peter the Great sent Everard Ysbrand Ides on a mission to Kang Hsi for the purpose of exchanging ratifications of the Treaty of Nerchinsk and of improving the commercial relations between the two countries. On March 14, that same year, Ides left Moscow with a caravan of some four hundred men for China. He was a foreigner, being a Dutch or German, though born on Danish soil, and he had been trading extensively in the Sea of Archangel since about 1677. It was he who obtained the consent of the Russian Court to head a trade mission to Peking. As it was not unknown in those days for merchants to be charged with certain diplomatic tasks, Ides was designated Envoy in contradistinction to Ambassador, which would have implied the possession of a considerably higher authority for the negotiation and discussion of international affairs.

Ides, apart from his personal trade interests, was charged with two tasks, one political and the other commercial. As to the former, he was told to heed Chinese Court ceremonies so as to ascertain from the Chinese Emperor his personal views concerning the recently concluded Treaty and, in general, the Chinese attitude to Russia's

---

[11] Cahen Gaston, op. cit., p. 46.
[12] Chen Fu-kwang, *Sino-Russian Relations during the Ching Dynasty* (in Chinese), p. 28.

Far Eastern Policy. Among the other minor diplomatic instructions he received, was one to try and obtain a site in Peking for the building of a Russian Orthodox Church, the expenses of which the Tsar would pay out of his own pocket. With regard to the commercial aspect of his mission, he was enjoined to persuade the Chinese to send their merchants to Moscow with ingots of silver, precious stones, spices and other native products, and to make detailed enquiries as to the kind of goods Russia could sell profitably in China.

It took Ides eleven months to reach Irkutsk, where he sojourned about a month until March 7, 1693. He set out again and arrived at Peking on November 3, by way of Nerchinsk and Manchuria. He was fittingly received, and after delivering his credentials obtained his first imperial audience on November 14, 1693. On the day following the first audience, the letter from the Russian Tsar as well as the gifts were returned to Ides with the remark that the titles of the Chinese Emperor had been written below those of the Tsar. This was in itself considered a discourteous act, and the opportunity for any further discussions between Ides and the Emperor's ministers could easily have been refused. Happily, however, the Chinese statesmen reasonably deemed that while he could not be officially acknowledged as a diplomatic representative of the Russian Court, his mission would nevertheless be a useful medium for a better understanding between the two countries.

From the date of his arrival at Peking until his departure on February 19, 1694, Ides had four audiences, which were of a ceremonial nature, and provided little or no opportunity for business discussion. The mission, while not producing the results expected by the Russians for a closer political and commercial understanding, was not altogether fruitless. Ides, as we have already remarked, was not a fully accredited plenipotentiary of the Russian Court, and it would have been too much to anticipate that the Chinese Emperor would consider him as such. Permission for a Russian church to be built in Peking was refused, and this certainly could not have been deemed an affront. While Kang Hsi did not officially ratify the Treaty of Nerchinsk, Ides was given to understand that he looked favourably upon it, and had nothing but friendly intentions towards the Russians. What was of first-rate interest to them was Sino-Russian trade. As to this, the Chinese Emperor saw no reason why it should not be continued to the mutual benefit of China and Russia so long as the latter did not encroach upon Chinese territory.

On February 1, 1695, nearly a year after his departure from Peking, and three years after leaving Moscow, Ides arrived safely home.

5. First Chinese Envoy Appointed

The first Chinese Envoy ever despatched by Kang Hsi to the Khan of the Torguts was Tu Li-shen, whose mission lasted from 1712 to 1716. In his book *Yi Yu Lu* or *Journal of a Mission Abroad*, we have, for the first time, a Chinese account of Siberia. He left Peking on June 23, 1712, and arrived at Selenginsk by way of Mongolia on August 24. He was instructed by the Imperial Edict that he should go to St. Petersburg and have an audience with the Tsar. He was accorded Russian military honours when he reached the Russian frontier. On arrival at Tobolsk, August 13, 1713, where he had a conference with Prince Gagarin, the Russian Governor-General of Siberia, he was informed that Peter the Great had been apprised of the mission but regretted being unable to receive the envoys from the Celestial Empire in Moscow. This was in all probability due to his wars with Sweden which were then taxing all his resources and taking up all his time. They were, however, impressed with the fact that Russia had nothing but the most friendly feeling towards them.

The Chinese Envoys, continuing their journey, reached Kazan and sailed down the Volga to Saratov, whither the Torguts had migrated from their homes. They received two audiences from Ayuki, Chief of the Torguts, at Manutokhai, where they stayed a fortnight. At the first audience, Ayuki was thanked for the presents one of his officials had conveyed to Peking, and was informed that his nephew Arabjchur, not having been able to return home after a sojourn in Tibet because wars with the Kalmuks had forced him to take refuge in Peking, had not yet been escorted on his way home, owing to the hazards of the journey. In the second and last audience several days later, Ayuki, evidently suspecting that the Chinese were utilizing this as a pretext to hold his nephew as a hostage, stated that while it was indubitable that the southern route was closed on account of the conflicts with the Kalmuks, the northern route through Russian Siberia was dependent upon the goodwill of the Tsar. This was a broad hint that if the Chinese did not meet Torgut aspirations half-way, the Torguts would be not altogether unwilling to side with the Russians who had been constantly angling for some such alliance.

It is improbable that this Embassy was sent for the sole purpose of considering some safe route by which Arabjchur, an unimportant prince, could return to his relatives. More likely, it had, as its underlying motive, a study of Russia's political, military and economic strength in Siberia and her relations with the Torguts and other peoples, forming a barrier between the two countries.

At the end of some days of feasting, the Chinese Embassy set out on the return journey, after final expressions of goodwill by both parties. On April 30, 1715, the mission reached Peking by the same route it had come.[13]

6. Ismailoff's Mission

Thirty years after the Treaty of Nerchinsk, Peter the Great decided to send Leon Vasilievitch Ismailoff on an embassy to Peking. Ismailoff was a soldier possessing a certain amount of diplomatic experience. After some service with the Imperial Guards, he was despatched to Denmark on a diplomatic mission. This experience, together with the Tsar's personal faith in him, rendered him a suitable person to head a mission needing delicate handling.

Ismailoff's suite was made up of a first secretary, Laurent Lang, a second secretary, Ivan Glazunoff, a number of scientists, interpreters, servants, soldiers and, curiously enough, an English adventurer, or rather, a Scottish physician by the name of John Bell. A representative of the Ministry of Commerce, Nicolas Khristizii and, at Irkutsk, the archimandrite, Antony Platkovakii, were later to join the Embassy. The value of religious workers for gathering political and other information was no doubt appreciated by Peter the Great, as is shown by the despatch of a churchman with Ismailoff to Peking. Ismailoff's instructions were in three parts. In the first place, if the Chinese insisted upon it, he was strictly to observe Chinese Court etiquette, that is, perform the kotow and other ceremonies. In his credentials, the proper method of addressing the Chinese Emperor was implicitly followed. Secondly, Ismailoff was to do all in his power to persuade the Chinese to extend trade relations. The Ministry of Commerce had high hopes of this. In the instructions to Ismailoff, consisting of sixteen articles, precise tasks were prescribed. The most far-reaching was to ask for complete liberty to trade, on reciprocal terms, throughout the whole of both empires.

---

[13] See Tu Li-shen, *Narrative of the Chinese Embassy to the Khan of the Torgut Tartars* (entitled *Yi Yu Lu*), translated into English by G. T. Staunton, London, 1821.

It was hoped that Russians, in restricted numbers, would be permitted in river and maritime ports to purchase gold, silver, precious stones, silks, etc., for export without duty, and likewise to sell or barter their own products, furs and other articles without taxation of any kind.

Russia desired the appointment of a consul-general in Peking who, besides his ordinary offices, would have a commercial depot and would be empowered to place vice-consuls or sub-agents in the provinces. Like privileges would be given to the Chinese. A commercial tribunal would be established to adjudicate upon all points where merchants of either country differed. The Russian Consul-General, aside from looking after the diplomatic and commercial interests of his country, would be charged with the function of acting as judge over his own nationals, except in cases having to do with the murder of Chinese or other foreigners, under which circumstance they were to be handed over to the Chinese tribunal. The above were the main points of commercial and political interest.

The third part of the Embassy was of a military nature. Ismailoff was instructed to inform the Chinese Emperor that the Russian forts along the Irtysh and elsewhere in Siberia had been built for protection against unruly Cossacks and adventurers and against the Jungars, but were by no means designed for aggressive purposes towards the Chinese. Ismailoff was told, of course secretly, to study China's military resources and fighting power in general.

Ismailoff and his suite left St. Petersburg on July 16, 1719, and faring by way of Moscow, Kazan and Irkutsk, reached Selenginsk on May 28, 1720. It took them about a year and a half to reach the Chinese border where they were welcomed by imperial officials especially despatched for the occasion. They entered Peking on November 18, after travelling through Kalgan. A number of incidents threatened to prevent the Embassy from reaching its destination, but despite various difficulties a give-and-take policy was finally adopted by both Chinese and Russians, and all misunderstandings were smoothed out.

On arrival at Peking, Ismailoff at first refused to carry out the kotow ceremony on presenting his credentials, but he finally agreed on condition that when the Chinese Emperor sent his envoy to Russia that envoy would be instructed to perform the self-same ceremony at the Tsarist Court. This was gladly accepted, as the Chinese Emperor at the time had not the slightest idea of sending a delegate to any 'barbarous' country whatsoever. It is rather interesting to read John Bell's own statement as to his unforgettable experience:

'During this part of the ceremony, which was not long, the retinue were standing without the hall; and we imagined, the letter being delivered, all was over. But the master of the ceremonies brought back the ambassador; and then ordered all the company to kneel and make obeisance nine times to the Emperor. At every third time we stood up, and kneeled again. Great pains were taken to avoid this piece of homage, but without success. The master of the ceremonies stood by, and delivered his orders in the Tartar language by pronouncing the words "morgu" and "boss", the first meaning to bow and the other to stand; two words which I can never soon forget.'[14]

From November 18, 1720 to March 2, 1721, Ismailoff sojourned in Peking. He was received most graciously, and in the dozen audiences Kang Hsi was pleased to give him, he was treated with the utmost friendliness.

When Ismailoff and his suite set out on the return journey, he left behind his first secretary, Laurent Lang, as an agent 'for the business that the Ambassador Ismailoff had proposed'. A list of ten Chinese claims and wishes were presented to him to carry back to the Russian Court. Among other things, they referred to the question of the Mongol frontier which still remained unsettled, despite many Chinese requests; and to the regulation that Russian merchants would only be permitted to enter China upon presenting one of the hundred seals or credentials exchanged with Ismailoff; and that, since the Kalmuks had now been defeated, a common meeting-ground could be established on the Irtysh.

On January 13, 1722, Ismailoff reached Moscow, thus concluding his homeward journey. He felt he had largely succeeded in his mission. The Chinese, while çautious of taking any hasty steps towards enlarging Sino-Russian trade, were nevertheless not unsympathetic to Russian ambitions in this respect. It was too much to expect them to take the very radical step of permitting free trade with foreigners throughout the Empire since that would straightway permit Russian agents and consuls to reside in the provinces; but Lang was permitted to remain in Peking at least until a partial fulfilment of their projects had been effected. Time was needed to

[14] John Bell, *Travels from St. Petersburg in Russia to Diverse Parts of China*, Vol. II, p. 7.

dispel Chinese suspicions that Russia had other than purely commercial interests in China. (As matters turned out, however, Peking was never for a moment taken in by Russia's friendly promises.) Ismailoff succeeded in making Kang Hsi sanction the building of a Russian church in Peking. Another point causing constant friction was that the Kalmuks and others were deserting Chinese territory to enter the Russian realm. The Russians had not abided by the agreement to return such offenders. Ismailoff was requested to bring this matter to the notice of the Tsar who, it was hoped, would send the needed instructions to his officials in Siberia to deliver such people to the Chinese authorities.

Lang, who remained in Peking, practically accomplished nothing. Two things hindered him. First, the Chinese distrusted Russia's good faith which had never been held in high esteem because of decades of depredation in Siberia and along the Amur as well as secret efforts to inveigle the Torguts and other peoples to side with her against China. Second, there was the unfortunate voluntary transfer of Mongols to Russian sovereignty. The fact that China refused to allow caravans into Peking, and that she had much less need of Russian trade than Russia had of hers, was no reason for the prevention of an amicable understanding. Lang was strongly guarded and was watched by soldiers constantly stationed at the entrance to his residence on the pretext of being there for his protection. He wanted to rent a house near the Russian quarter on his own behalf, but was flatly turned down by the Chinese authorities. He was, at the time, so grossly insulted that he even threatened, so soon as His Tsarist Majesty had finished the war with Sweden, that nothing should prevent the Tsar from turning his arms to this side.[15] His threats did not move any of the Imperial Court, and he was finally compelled to leave the capital after many months' uncomfortable stay, during which he had been treated like a prisoner of the Chinese Government.

On January 20, 1724, after the death of Kang Hsi, Lang and Glazunoff appeared as commissioners to settle the frontier question. Lieutenant-Colonel Bucholz was sent with an escort of a thousand cavalry and a thousand Siberian infantrymen.[16] This display of armed force was most injudicious. It belied Russia's claims to friendly intentions and served to increase Chinese suspicions that the Russians had motives other than commercial.

[15] See Laurent Lang, *Journal of Residence at Peking*, Vol. II, p. 300.
[16] Cahen, op. cit., p. 186.

7. Count Vladislavitch Raguzinsky's Embassy

An Imperal 'Ukase' of August 11, 1725, appointed Count Sava Vladislavitch Ruguzinsky 'Envoy Extraordinary and Minister Plenipotentiary' to the Court at Peking. It was felt by the Russians at the time that another ambassador should be sent to speed up diplomatic and commercial relations with China. What is more, Vladislavitch was far better qualified than his predecessors for the task given him. At the time of his appointment he had reached the ripe age of sixty. Years of experience as a merchant and a secret agent in various parts of Europe on behalf of the Russian Government, as well as a number of transactions he had successfully fulfilled for Peter the Great, made him a trusted and highly suitable agent.

The death of Peter the Great in January 1725 and the accession to the throne of the Tsarina Catherine the First, was an appropriate occasion for an embassy to China. Both China and Russia were eager for good relations. China was anxious that Russia should not side with the Eleuths, who were a constant thorn in China's side and danger to her northern frontiers. Russia wanted money from trade which she needed to fill her coffers. Superficially, the problem was easy of solution. Russia's Siberian ambitions, however, dictated a 'wait and see' policy vis-à-vis the Sino-Eleuth quarrel, and the latent hope that she might yet prove militarily stronger than China caused her to postpone, under the flimsiest of excuses, the demarcation of frontiers and the question of the extradition of subjects of the Chinese Empire who, whether rebels or criminals, had sought refuge in Russian territory.

Ill-defined frontiers would, at some future date, allow of encroachment upon Chinese territory. The non-extradition of Chinese elements (mainly Kalmuks and non-Chinese peoples) would encourage them to rebel against the Chinese Empire which, it was hoped, would tend to weaken China and make her more susceptible to Russian pressure for the purpose of territorial gain or trade advantages.

On March 3, 1725, Lang, then in Selenginsk, after realizing the futility of remaining in China, was advised of the desire to send a new embassy to Peking, and he, in turn, quickly passed on this information to the Chinese authorities.

Vladislavitch was given Lang as an experienced adviser in Chinese matters, diplomatic as well as commercial. A number of scientists, linguists, etc., made up the complement of his suite. In short, after a year or more of careful preparation, he possessed the best-equipped embassy ever sent to China. As usual there was no lack of choice European articles as gifts for the Chinese Emperor and his officers of state. The presents the Russians had previously received were munificent. Though a diplomatic mission, the time factor caused them to bring along commodities, mainly furs, to sell to or barter with the Chinese merchants.

The Embassy proper, consisting of nearly one hundred persons, and a military escort of 1,500 soldiers, reached Peking on October 21, 1726, after nearly thirteen months of travel and sojourns at several stopping-places.

According to Cahen, Vladislavitch was charged with four principal tasks. (i) The Ambassador should conclude a commercial treaty or renew those commercial relations that had been intercepted; (ii) he was to fix the frontier in accordance with a map to be compiled as quickly as possible, and the work was to be done by a joint Russo-Chinese commission; (iii) as for deserters, the Ambassador was to refer to an 'Ukase' of Peter the Great dated July 22, 1722, which ordered such persons to be sent back to China; and (iv) he was to try to obtain a piece of land on which to build a church, the expense of building to be defrayed by the Tsarina, and finally he was instructed to ascertain the military strength and resources of the Empire.[17]

The Ministry of Commerce provided Vladislavitch with the same instructions as furnished to Ismailoff in 1719, with a number of important additions. They related to the ascertaining of the different means of transport in Siberia, and of any improvements that might be accomplished, trade conditions in Mongolia, the state of affairs existing between the Chinese and the Dutch, English, French and Portuguese merchants then trading at Canton, and the possibilities of trade at this port.

Vladislavitch stayed in Peking from October 21, 1726 to April 13, 1727, that is, six whole months. His breadth of vision together with his training in the school of commerce, diplomacy and spying, made him a worthy opponent of the Chinese officials who were highly cultivated men and skilled diplomats. He displayed more tact, good taste and patience than any other European previously visiting the Court had seemed to possess. These qualities, in themselves, were a strong recommendation to the Chinese Emperor and his ministers.

[17] Bantysh-Kamensky, *Diplomaticheskoie Sobranie Diel Rosiiskim Kitaiskim Gosudarsivami s 1616-1792*, pp. 424-6, and 456 (in Russian).

Vladislavitch, too, had no compunction in using spies to further his ends. By holding out a promise to assist the Jesuits, then in Peking, to enlarge their missionary work, he struck a favourable bargain. Père Parrenin, head of the Italian Jesuits in Peking, provided him with secret information and acted furthermore as a liaison officer between the Russians and the members of the Chinese Court,[18] thereby keeping him fully informed of the sentiments of the Chinese ministers. This was naturally of inestimable value to Vladislavitch.

Later on, Vladislavitch enlisted in his service a Mongol, Galdan by name, but not connected with the famous Eleuth warrior prince, who, for certain sums of money, was to keep him informed of Chinese wishes concerning demarcation of the frontiers.

The Chinese, no novices in the art of espionage, an imperative necessity in conjunction with matters diplomatic as well as military, undoubtedly employed various people for this specific purpose.

However, as both China and Russia were pacifically inclined, a long and intricate diplomatic tussle could only reach a peaceful conclusion. Threats and counter-threats courteously uttered, but with no genuine intention of using force, were freely used as pawns in this patient game of diplomatic chess. The troublesome Eleuths were once again up in arms and, therefore, a useful card to use against the Chinese. Russia was, at this time, at peace with her European neighbours, but she did not contemplate a possibility of using military measures against China, at least not for some years to come. It would take her a long while to recover from the financial and economic difficulties she had incurred in her recent wars.

Vladislavitch, it is highly interesting to note, some months after his return to St. Petersburg in December 1728, handed over to the Tsar, Peter II (Catherine I had died while he was away), a number of maps and documents, one of which related to the possibility of conquering the whole of China. This extraordinarily ambitious scheme was the inspiration of Russian aggression in the second half of the nineteenth century, but, by then, there were other European powers no less anxious to become masters of a part, if not the whole, of the vast Chinese Empire.

This ex-Ambassador said that the following points were essential for the conquering of China. (i) Peace in Europe. This would allow the Russian Government to devote time and money to the undertaking as well as to despatch large forces to Siberia and the Amur.

[18] Cahen, op. cit., pp. 173-6, and 209, N. 1.

(ii) A decade of steady planting and reaping of crops in Trans-baikalia. This would be sufficient to provision the frontier troops. (iii) Fifty regiments of regulars and twenty regiments of irregulars to contend against the Chinese forces. A Russian force of this size would be victorious as he, Vladislavitch, had observed that the Chinese people were not a fighting race, and the Manchus who ruled the country were not only numerically far fewer than the Chinese, but alien to the country, so that the natives would, in case of defeat, rise against their rulers. (iv) A Sino-Russian war would have the effect of encouraging the Eleuths, Mongolians and other non-Manchu peoples to seize the opportunity to strike for independence. This combination of factors, he considered, would so divide the Manchu forces that they would succumb to Russian attacks and leave the way open to a speedy conquest of China.[19]

Vladislavitch's bold dream was never realized for a variety of causes. We need mention but two. Vladislavitch grossly under-estimated the fighting strength of the Manchus while overestimating their authority in China, which was ruled as a whole not by the Manchus, but by the Chinese themselves, with the tacit consent of the Manchus. China, with a vast and highly civilized population, could not be conquered by the Russians as the semi-nomadic tribes in Siberia had been. The Mongols and Manchus, both powerful fighting peoples, had flung tens of thousands of troops into China, but the forces of Chinese civilization had in time conquered them. And these two peoples were racially akin to the Chinese. Swift to see the wisdom of following Chinese ways and the Chinese system of government, their emperors were able to sit on the Chinese throne. When, however, they attempted to rule by force, they were in time overthrown by the Chinese people. A Russian governor-general in Peking, ruling the whole of China, was a dream impossible of accomplishment. Russian ways were utterly alien, and would have appeared brutally unjust to every farm-house and city-dwelling throughout the length and breadth of the Chinese Empire.

We will next turn once more to the outcome of the Sino-Russian negotiations with which Vladislavitch had been entrusted.

Before leaving Peking on April 23, 1727, he succeeded in coming to an understanding upon the following points: The frontier, from the Uda to the Stone (Kamennyi) Mountains in the east, was to remain undecided as in the Treaty of Nerchinsk, owing to the lack of definite topographical information concerning these regions, but

[19] Cahen, op. cit., p. 224.

everywhere else it would be determined by a joint Sino-Russian border commission. Deserters would henceforth be strictly extradited. A Russian caravan of two hundred merchants would be permitted to come to Peking once every three years, and on the· frontier two centres where trade might be permanently and continuously carried on would be established. Passports would still be required, but ambassadors, diplomatic agents and official messengers would be received without hindrance.

On June 14, 1727, Vladislavitch reached Bura near Selenginsk. Another three months were needed for the conclusion of a general treaty, and a year for its final ratification. On June 23, 1727, a series of meetings was held to consider the marking of the boundary. Vladislavitch was assisted by Lang and two other experts. The Chinese commission consisted of Longotu, an uncle of the Emperor, Yung Cheng, the head of the commission, and Tu Li-shen, a member of the embassy to the Torguts already referred to. The Russians, who were reasonably well informed of the topography of the regions under discussion, were able to draw up the frontiers to their advantage. Longotu did not give in regarding the boundary marking, and he even threatened to break off the conference. Vladislavitch, however, retorted that as Russia had ended military operations in Europe, she was now free to deal with the Far East. Ere long, Longotu was recalled by the Emperor to replace Prince Thailing. This was due not only to dissensions but, according to Vladislavitch's statement, to secret assistance rendered by Galdan and Parrenin as well as a Chinese official, Ma Tsi, who had accepted bribes from Vladislavitch.[20]

The display of arms at the frontier by Lieutenant-Colonel Bucholz also helped the Russian situation. Shortly after the arrival of Prince Thailing, two delimitation agreements, known as the Treaty of Bura, were signed on October 12, 1727, by the two parties. Later, Vladislavitch received a duly ratified treaty from Peking dated October 21, 1727, in full accordance with the conclusions reached by the joint commission as well as the agreements arrived at during his sojourn in China. This was named the Treaty of Kiakhta, from the town wherein Vladislavitch was then residing, and which included a fort built by him. This treaty remained in force until June 1858. It thus lasted over a century and a quarter, and gained renown for being one of the most long-lived treaties in world history.

[20] Cahen, op. cit., p. 65.

In 1737 Russian caravans were no longer allowed to call at Peking but stopped at Kiakhta—a more suitable rendezvous for trade purposes—and this town continued to be the focal point of commerce for both countries.

The Tushetu Khan was, *ex officio*, the superintendent of trade, but in 1772 he was relieved of this post, and two imperial officials were stationed at Urga for the purpose of supervising foreign trade. It was decided that one of them should be a native of Outer Mongolia, as the people there were considerably interested in trade with the Russians. Commercial relations were, on the whole, satisfactory, and only on three occasions, namely in 1764, 1779 and 1785, did the Chinese Government temporarily suspend trade in order to rectify certain misunderstandings. This boycott of Russian goods always proved salutary. It is not uninteresting to note that neither side charged any customs duty.

Two treaties of minor significance were signed during the reign of Chien Lung. The first, at Kiakhta in 1768, defined more clearly the procedure concerning the extradition of deserters, and the second, signed in 1792, between the Governor of Irkutsk and Chinese frontier authorities, aimed at the better regulation of trade at Kiakhta and other points along the frontiers.

In 1805 a Russian Embassy under Count Golovkin was sent to Peking with a large retinue. His refusal to conform to Chinese Court etiquette, combined with the fact that China was then much disturbed by internal troubles, made his presence unwelcome. He departed without bettering Sino-Russian relations.

In the following year, two Russian ships arrived at Canton, South China. It was only after certain sales and purchases were made that the Chinese authorities at Canton received instructions from Peking that Russians be forbidden to trade by sea as they had already obtained the privilege of trading by land. They were asked to leave Macao without delay.

The news of British manœuvres in China and the Treaty of Nanking signed in 1842 apparently awakened the latent dreams of Tsarist imperialism for a share of the Chinese spoils. This giant of the Far East had been defeated by a small fleet, and several thousand troops transported from a great distance. But Russian struggles with Turkey at the time, and after that the Crimean War with England and France, prevented her from carrying out any openly aggressive measures in the Far East.

The Treaty of Kiakhta was, in the main, entirely satisfactory, as is evidenced by the fact that no further treaty was signed between China and Russia for over a hundred and twenty-five years. It was an agreement signed by two sovereign powers. Neither side had been compelled to concede anything likely to endanger its position as an independent state. Above all else, there existed during the period a mutual wish to maintain peaceful relations. The Treaty of Kiakhta held good until the situation changed, which was not till 1858, when China was compelled to sign a most humiliating treaty known as the Treaty of Aigun, whereby the relative strength of the two countries was radically altered.

Chapter III

RUSSIA'S RELATIONS WITH OUTER MONGOLIA

Russia and China first made contact in Outer Mongolia at the time of the Tatar invasion, though it is stated that the Russians and Mongols came together as early as the eighth century. Temuchin won his western campaign in the thirteenth century and made himself 'Emperor of all men' with the title of 'Genghis Khan'. This put dread in the heart of all Europe. It was through him that Russian and Chinese contacts were made.

Harking back to the very dawn of Russian history, we find the forest zone in the north inhabited by scattered Finnish tribes as early as the third century. These helped to build the first powerful empire in Russian history. As to the southern zone, this was successively invaded by Asiatic tribes for several centuries. On the bounds of Persia and China, two great and civilized countries lying along the southern border of the Eurasian plain, there dwelt a vast and scattered mass of Turko-Mongol tribes, always deemed dangerous on account of their ruthless and warlike nature.

China, then under the Han Dynasty, was already a powerful nation. About 100 B.C., a noted Chinese Envoy, Su Wu, was sent by Emperor Han Wu-ti to offer peace and goodwill to the Khan of Hsiung-Nu (believed of Turkish origin)[1] in Mongolia. Unhappily the mission failed in its purpose, and the poor Envoy was imprisoned by the Hun ruler and only released after nineteen years, living the while in exile upon the shores of Lake Baikal until the restoration of peace. The nomad tribes, pressed by the Chinese, began to move west, but met with stubborn resistance from the Persians who, also at the expense of the Turko-Mongols, were expanding in the opposite direction. Pressed by the simultaneous advance of the Chinese and the Persians, they had to follow the line of least resistance by marching north into the great wastes and into Russia.

[1] Baddeley, op. cit., Vol. I, p. 29.

1. Tatar Invasion

Having achieved a power greater than that of the ancient Hsiung-Nu Empire, Genghis Khan made his first conquest of China, and by 1224, four years before his death, the Mongolian invasion had swept over all Asia as far as south-eastern Europe. His son, Ogoday, came to the throne and finally overcame the Kin Dynasty, ruling China north of the Yellow River in the year 1234; it was not, however, until 1264 that Khublai Khan proclaimed himself Emperor of China, thereby setting up the Yuan Dynasty with Peking as capital, after overcoming the Sung Dynasty in Central and South China. Ogoday started his European drive and sent his nephew, Batu, with 600,000 well-trained troops to Russia in 1237. It was not a wild horde, but a regular army far superior to European forces. The march on Europe went with such force and rapidity that the army penetrated the very heart of Russia. So bloody and cruel was the onslaught, so great the massacre, that Europe shuddered at the approach of the ruthless conquerors.

The story is told of a certain Russian prince who sent deputies to another prince informing him that his country was being invaded by a strong and cruel tribe called Tatars, 'strange-looking men with brown faces, eyes small and wide apart, thick lips, broad shoulders and black hair'. The deputies went so far as to warn the prince in these words: 'To-day, they have seized our country and to-morrow they will seize yours if you do not help us.'[2] The prince, though without sympathy for the other, immediately came to the rescue for fear his own turn might come next.

The all-conquering invaders devastated an enormous area including Moscow, but having almost reached Novgorod in 1238, they suddenly wheeled round and disappeared. Thus came to an end the first visit of such unwelcome strangers.

In 1240 they came back and renewed their activities, occupying and demolishing the city of Kiev. Then they divided themselves into two armies; one raided Hungary and the other entered Poland. They advanced even as far as the Adriatic, pillaging and murdering, and their attempt to fare farther west put all Europe in alarm. The panic even swept through England for a time, putting a stop to the herring fishery on the coast.

Pushing west, they at last met with stubborn resistance in Bohemia. Hearing of the death of Ogoday Khan, they finally

[2] Mackenzie Wallace, *Russia*, p. 223.

retreated and turned back towards the Lower Volga to which place the Russian princes were summoned to do homage to the victorious Khan. The princes came, not daring to make another attempt to combine together against the common foe. Nearly all the principal towns had been burnt and the inhabitants slaughtered or carried off as slaves. At first, the Russians had only a vague idea of what their enemy was. 'For our sins, unknown peoples have appeared', and 'Only God knows whence they came and whither they went'[3] were the general remarks among the people. Some even thought they were God's chosen people and could only be known by those deeply read in books.

How did the Mongols keep themselves so strong and march with such amazing rapidity? To answer this question, we have to explain their way of living. They needed no base of operations. They just took along with them their flocks, tents and other worldly goods. All they wanted was the grass steppe to feed their flocks, which in turn, of course, could feed the men. Further, the manure or argol of the flocks served as fuel, giving out a great heat. So they made their home wherever pasture and drinking water were to be found. Instead of diminishing in force as is usually the case when advancing from the base of operations, they on the contrary increased in numbers and kept as strong as ever on their thrust forward. Thus 'the man of gigantic stature' led his army west, it being his ambition to conquer the whole world and make himself the sole ruler on earth in the same way that God is the one ruler in heaven.

Undoubtedly Genghis Khan was an administrative genius. For this reason, he succeeded in creating a colossal empire, which was entirely by conquest; but it lacked an organic life, and this, coupled with the desire of the conquered peoples for independence, meant that his supremacy over Russia could not be long retained. After his death, despite the fact that his descendants were still able to maintain their military authority, local rulers rapidly tried to free themselves from the centralized administration. The colossal power he had created began to wane and, less than fifty years after his death, the great Mongol Empire gradually weakened and fell to pieces.

2. Golden Horde

Nevertheless, eastern Europe at this time was far from being out of danger. A grandson of Genghis Khan established himself on the

[3] Lobanov-Rostovsky, A., *Russia and Asia*, 1933, p. 20.

Lower Volga as the ruler of what was known as the Golden Horde, and built a new capital called Sarai, a very populous and beautiful city. Here lived the Khan of the Golden Horde, which kept Russia in subjection for over two centuries.

Mongol administration, after the conquest of Russia, is also interesting. They had no ambition to possess the land overrun, since they already had plenty to spare. Annexation was entirely foreign to them. All they cared for was movable goods to enable them to enjoy nomad life. They simply sent officials into the country to collect tribute in proportion to the population. Not only was no occupation or confiscation of land put into practice, but even the existing Russian political organization, under different independent princes, was left undisturbed. They had no idea whatever of denationalizing the Russian people. They were satisfied as soon as the Russian princes took oath of allegiance and the people were willing to pay a certain amount of tribute. Russians were also allowed to retain their lands, use their own language and worship according to their own religion. Moreover, the Tatar invaders never settled in Russia proper, and were never assimilated by the native population, nor did they try to assimilate them. The Russians remained Christians, and the Mongols remained Shamanists or Buddhists, although later they became Mohammedans. When the Horde adopted Islam, the difference in religion raised an impassable barrier between them.

As a matter of fact, the princes at first tried in every way to sap the Khan's power. Finding this of no avail, they thereupon endeavoured to gain favour by the frequent bestowal of rich presents on the Mongol Suzerain. Some even used this favour to extend their possessions at the expense of neighbouring princes and, to this end, did not hesitate to call in Mongol assistance. The Khans, however, made no complaint so long as tribute was not neglected.

The Khans, instead of keeping the Russian princes on the same level, thereby rendering them all weak, were often bribed into giving special favour to one who soon became more powerful than the others. The most successful of these was the Prince of Moscow who, realizing the danger of arousing suspicion of growing power, assumed an attitude of complete submissiveness to the Khan. 'Having discovered that the distribution of money at the Mongol Court was the surest means of gaining favour, they lived parsimoniously at home and spent their savings on the Horde.' It was said that the arrival of the Prince of Moscow was always welcomed at Sarai on account of his rich and costly presents. This cunning policy was so effective that he soon won favour and was given the title of Grand Prince. What is more, he was permitted to collect taxes in the neighbouring principalities for the Golden Horde. When Novgorod refused to pay tribute, and when the people of Tver rose against the Khan's authority, the Grand Prince of Moscow immediately received 50,000 horsemen from the Khan to meet the situation. This not only gave the Muscovite supreme power over others, but induced him to invade and finally annex the territories of his neighbours.

Successive Moscow princes stuck to the 'wait and see' policy. They were so obsequious that they pretended 'to love the Mongols beyond measure'. This humble and submissive attitude, however, only lasted as long as the Golden Horde remained in power. When Moscow found itself strong enough it turned abruptly against the Mongol Court and threw off the galling yoke that had proved so burdensome and humiliating. It was the Grand Prince Dmitri Donskoi who openly challenged the Golden Horde by refusing to pay tribute. The ruling Khan, Mamai, prepared to deliver a crushing blow, though quite aware of the seriousness of the revolt. After some encounters, the Tatars suffered a drastic defeat, an evidence of Moscow's newly acquired military strength. The Golden Horde, though defeated in battle, was still strong enough to start another offensive a few years later with a newly organized army. Until then, the Russians had been on the defensive, but thereafter they took the offensive which carried them right into Asia.[4]

This eastern drive is an important landmark in Russian history. In the fifteenth century, the Golden Horde finally fell to pieces, thanks chiefly to Tamerlane, ruler of Samarkand, who attacked from the rear. Tamerlane, apparently a new world conqueror, marched into Russia, destroyed Sarai and then marched on to Moscow. Before reaching it, he changed his plans, being now fired with the ambition to conquer China. So he turned back to Samarkand, but died on the way to China. This was the last Tatar invasion of Russia.

3. Russia's New Era Under Ivan IV

In the middle of the fifteenth century, the Tsar, Ivan II—successor of the Grand Prince of Moscow—continued with conspicuous ability

[4] Labanov-Rostovsky, *Russia and Asia*, p. 29.

and success the great work of ' gathering together the Russian lands '.
He refused to obey a summons to go to the Tatar Court. Thus, the
last link in the chain of dependence was broken. However, it was
not until the reign of Ivan IV (known as ' the Terrible' on account
of his incredible cruelties and countless executions), who succeeded
his father Vasili III in 1533, that there took place the capture of
the Volga towns, Kazan (1552) and Astrakhan (1554), both deemed
Tatar strongholds. The Crimean Tatars took revenge by burning
Moscow in 1571, sparing only the Kremlin.[5] After that, Mongol
and Tatar prestige sank for ever. Then began Russia's new era of
relations with Asia through the channel of the Volga during the
half-century reign of Ivan the Terrible.

This changeover of Mongols and Russians was due to the reversal
of positions. The former conquered the latter because they were
united under a strong leader. When the latter at last came to be
united under a powerful dynasty, the Mongols, as a result of growing weakness and disunion, were completely beaten and remained
thenceforward but a name.

Mongol domination, though little affecting the life and habits
of the Russian people, had a considerable influence on the political
development of the nation. The policy of the Khans helped to
facilitate unification and growth and went so far as to create that
autocratic power so characteristic of the Tsars. It should be known
that the Mongols themselves in the first instance were influenced by
Chinese practices during their reign in China. They followed
Chinese tradition in building their own empire, and we cannot be
very wrong in saying that, through the medium of the Mongols,
Chinese influence actually reached Moscow and helped in the building of an imperial dynasty. The first Tsars of Muscovy were the
political descendants, practically speaking, neither of the old
independent princes nor of the Mongol Khans, but of the Celestial
Empire of China. Therefore, it is safe to say that autocratic power,
a most important factor in Russian history, was created by the
Mongolian domination influenced by Chinese practices.[6]

4. Eastward Drive of the Eleuths

The Mongol reign in China, known as the Yuan Dynasty, was
rather short-lived, lasting scarcely a century. It was superseded by

---

[5] Baddeley, op. cit., Vol. I, p. 56.
[6] George Vernadsky, *Political and Diplomatic History of Russia*, Boston, 1936,
p. 20.

the Ming Dynasty in 1368. The Khans then divided what was left of their empire among their heirs and created three main, separate principalities, namely those of the North-Khalkhas, those of the south, and those of the West-Oirats, known as Kalmuks or Eleuths.[7] The Kalmuks or Eleuths comprised four main sections or tribes, viz., the Sungars, Derbets, Torguts and Khoshotes. When the Yuan fell, the Kalmuks grew stronger and separated from the Mongols, and for a time became supreme in Mongolia.[8] During the days of Hung Wu of the Ming Dynasty, Inner Mongolia was brought under Chinese control. Owing to its geographical advantages, Inner Mongolia was again subjugated by the Manchus, who had already conquered China in 1644. The Manchus, having conquered China, fought against their former allies and brought the southern Mongols under their control. The Eleuths took the initiative against the Manchus longer than the other western Mongols, and caused some worry to the Manchu Government. During the period under survey, they inhabited three principal regions: (1) the steppe of the lowest part of the Volga basin round about Astrakhan; (2) Zungaria, Kuldja and the adjacent territories of Chinese Central Asia; (3) Tsaidam, Kokonor and other parts of north Tibet and south-west Mongolia.[9]

In Trans-Baikalia, a Mongol known as Ayuki, a Torgut, succeeded in uniting under himself all the tribes of Astrakhan and the Urals. The Russians endeavoured unsuccessfully to bring these people under their tutelage. On the further extension of Russia into Siberia, the Mongols held a sort of general conference at Khurien-Beltchir in 1686 and decided that, as they were too weak to resist aggression at the hands of their neighbours, they should voluntarily throw themselves under Chinese protection. This decision was made only just in time. The Eleuths, a hardy fighting people, headed by ambitious chiefs, began an eastward drive. They controlled the routes from Siberia to the south and those from China to the west, and this inspired them with the hope of becoming the sole masters of all central Asia. Having already defeated the Bukhariots, they made themselves protectors of Tibet, supporting Lamaism against Chinese Buddhism. The challenging attitude of the Eleuths, a force by no means contemptible, thus made them an enemy to be dispelled by force or weakened by diplomatic strategy. As the Mongols had so opportunely decided to side with the Chinese, it was impera-

---

[7] Yakhontoff, Victor A., *Russia and the Soviet Union in the Far East*, 1932, p. 75.
[8] Baddeley, op. cit., Vol. I, p. 43.
[9] Yakhontoff, op. cit., p. 5.

tive to consolidate the link. This did not present any serious obstacle as the northern Mongols feared domination by the Eleuths, and all that was required was to treat them with fairness. The Torguts, themselves a branch of the Eleuths, were later to throw in their lot with the Chinese for a very plausible reason: the old-time animosity between the Torgut and the other Eleuth chiefs. The question to be settled was: Could and would the Eleuths and Russians combine together against the Chinese?

The Eleuths desired it. An alliance with Russia would have strengthened them in preventing Chinese interference with their establishment of a hegemony in Central Asia. This was a magnificent ideal well worth fighting for. Cunningly, they made overtures to the Russians through their diplomatic agents, the Bukhariots, whom they had conquered. Even before the Russians had been given time to consider these overtures, they had spread subtle rumours of the establishment of a pact between the two peoples.

The Chinese, past masters in diplomacy, were not to be deceived so easily nor inveigled into taking steps which might cause friction with the Russians. They felt they held the best cards in this three-handed game. Chinese spies were on the watch for any Russian acceptance of Eleuth proposals. The first definite signs of closer ties between the two would have resulted in a rupture of relations with Russia. China would have put a stop to any trade with the latter, an act of little significance to her but damaging to Moscow. Of this the Tsar was fully cognizant.

Russia had practically nothing to gain by an equitable alliance with the Eleuths, and she was certainly in no position to wage a national war with China. China would have welcomed a struggle between the Eleuths and the Russians, but neither of them could be manœuvred into a fight. It would, in any case, have been indecisive (for Russia was not then able to throw in sufficient forces to conquer even the Eleuths), and thus the result would only have weakened both sides. In addition to all this, it would eventually have brought China into the orbit of Central Asia, and thus have served as an inducement to an attempted expulsion of the Russians from Siberia.

5. Galdan's Ambition

Now let us return to the events of a serious war which the Eleuths started in Mongolia. Galdan, an Eleuth prince, after a series of spectacular intrigues, assassinations and battles against his blood-brother princes, established himself as the sole master of the Eleuths or Kalmuks. Not content with this, between 1680 and 1685 he brought Turkestan under his sway by a number of bold moves.[10] This only served to whet his appetite for power. As he had once lived in Tibet where he had taken initial steps to enter the Lamaist priesthood, he astutely utilized this fact to arrogate to himself the role of representative of the Dalai Lama. In this capacity he claimed precedence over all Mongolian princes, and therefore claimed the right to be ruler of Mongolia.

The Khalkha Mongols of Outer Mongolia were, naturally enough, unwilling to accept Galdan as their overlord. In 1688 he left Zungaria with a large army to establish his position by right of arms. At a place called Ologoi, the Khalkha Mongol princes challenged him. After a fierce battle, lasting three days, he emerged victorious. His opponents fled, some south towards Inner Mongolia and China proper, and others north into the Trans-Baikal regions in Siberia. It was about this time that the Sino-Russian conference at Selenginsk was to have taken place. At this conference, Golovin was to have represented the Russians, but the Chinese delegates suddenly discontinued their journey and returned to Peking on account of the victory of Galdan and the Eleuth Mongols over the Khalkha Mongols who, though recognizing the suzerainty of the Chinese Emperor, prevented his envoys from travelling to Selenginsk, as explained in the foregoing chapter.

The Mongols who were seeking refuge in Trans-Baikal, unaware of the negotiations to be opened, attacked the Russian delegate, Golovin, who had already arrived at Selenginsk. This was in answer to many years of ruthless, hostile acts by Russians against the Mongols and local Siberian tribes like the Buriat Mongols with which the Khalkha Mongols were bound by ties of racial affinity, culture and religion. Golovin succeeded in breaking out of Selenginsk, and six months later, after considerable military preparations, made a sudden attack on the Mongols on the banks of the Khilok, a tributary of the Selenga River. He defeated them, and after many aggressive moves, forced them to acknowledge Russian suzerainty in a treaty signed on March 12, 1689. Kang Hsi, the then Emperor of China, had devoted his attention to eliminating the Eleuths since they were a menace to the northern territories. Later, Galdan became so strong that he entered Inner Mongolia and threatened to march to the very gates of Peking. The Emperor himself played an important military

[10] Cahen, op. cit., p. 43.

role in the following six years, ending in the extermination of Galdan and his supporters. Their lands in northern Sinkiang, which had served as a physical barrier between the Torguts and the Chinese, were annexed. More than half a century later, Chien Lung, grandson of Kang Hsi, thoroughly defeated the remaining Mongols of Sinkiang. It was at this time that a large part of the Torgut tribe, who under Eleuth (Jungar) pressure had migrated to the Volga, returned to Sinkiang. Who can but admire their stand for freedom for so long a time in face of Russian arms and Russian political machinations? The sad fate of so many other Siberian tribes undoubtedly served as a constant warning to them. To be under China was indeed far preferable, for the Chinese, while nominal masters, used no brute force. A certain loss of independence would be compensated for by benefits that would accrue to them from immediate contact with a people enjoying a far higher material and cultural civilization.

6. Influence of Lamaism

Lamaism, a religion characterized by meditation and acquiescence, permeated the daily life of the Mongols, gradually weakening and disintegrating them. True it is that the Kalmuks were converted to Lamaism in the early seventeenth century. Nevertheless, they were still a menace to China even in the middle of the eighteenth. Suffice it to say that, though the Mongol race had been weakened to a great extent through belief in Lamaism, it was the Chinese emperors, namely Kang Hsi, Yung Cheng and Chien Lung who incessantly and untiringly fought the decisive battles to a finish over a period of eighty years from 1608 to 1688. This creed was introduced while the Yuan or Mongol Dynasty held sway in China. On the fall of the Yuan Dynasty, the Mongols retreated to Mongolia, whereupon Lamaist Buddhism suffered a serious decline. It witnessed a revival at the beginning of the sixteenth century, when it became of great political significance. The western Mongols, bordering on Tibet—the home of Lamaism—gladly accepted Lamaist teachings and thereupon sought to establish a hegemony over all other Mongols. The Manchu Dynasty, seeing danger in all Mongols uniting into one body, tried to make the Mongol Church more powerful than the State. By this means, with the coming into power of Buddhism, China was once and for all relieved of the fear of the nomads that had haunted her for over two thousand years. The Emperor, Chien

Lung, once remarked: 'The Mongols are fallen and have grown feeble, thanks to the influence of the Lamas.' A modern Chinese writer says: 'The powerlessness of the Mongols is a blessing for China, and the governance of Mongolia by means of Buddhism is one of the most important of China's political calculations . . . the feeling of mercy has conquered in them (the Mongols) the lust of slaughter; the belief in future reward and punishment has tamed their ferocity. This is the triumph of Zunkava by which not only China but other nations benefit.'[11]

It would be appropriate to add here a short résumé of the previous intercourse between the Mongols and the Lamas. Genghis Khan and his ancestors were followers of Shamanism—a religion which prevailed among the Tunguses and many Siberian tribes. It remained the state religion of the Mongols, although Buddhists, who lived in the Kin Empire, must have secured some converts among the Mongols. The type of Buddhism that existed in Tibet was known as Lamaism. It is stated that Genghis Khan once sent an Envoy to the chief of the Lamas in Tibet asking him to follow his counsel and become the lord and protector of the faithful, thereby combining the practice of religion with the government of the State. The Dalai Lama consented to this, and Genghis excused the whole priesthood of Tibet from the payment of taxes.[12] When Khublai Khan came to power, he gave firm support to the Lamas. Lamaism thereupon became the national religion of the Mongols, and spread among those who were of the opinion that Lamaism was necessary for the good of this life and also of the future.[13]

The Tibetan Lamas persuaded the Mongol princes to become Lamaists and acknowledge the grand Lama as their spiritual head, as well as to send their sons to Tibet for education. This suggestion was gladly accepted by many princes who sent a son to Tibet to become a Lama.[14] Afterwards it became customary for each Mongol family to have one of its sons become a priest, thus greatly weakening the empire as a whole.

7. Treaty of Kiakhta

Notwithstanding that Galdan's ambition was completely thwarted by the powerful and untiring efforts of Kang Hsi, the Eleuths were

[11] Baddeley, op. cit., Vol. I, p. 83.
[12] Howorth, H. H., History of the Mongols, Vol. I, p. 504.
[13] ibid., p. 405.
[14] ibid., p. 501.

not brought to submission. The Peking Government was very much concerned about the close contacts between the Eleuths and the Russians, fearing the latter might spread into the Mongolian territory and brew further trouble. This was the main reason why China wished to keep on good terms with Russia during the early eighteenth century. The request for the demarcation of Russo-Mongolian frontiers was therefore frequently made to Russia in order to create a better understanding between the two countries.[15] Lang, who stayed in Peking as a liaison officer, also petitioned the Russian throne, stating that two Chinese officials with a plenipotentiary had reached Selenginsk, north of Kiakhta, for the purpose of taking up the frontier problem with Russia.

Later, Tu Li-shen was sent by the Chinese Emperor to negotiate with the Russian Envoy who had been sent to the spot to settle the demarcation based upon the Treaty of Bura known as the Treaty of Kiakhta, signed on October 21, 1727.

The Treaty of Kiakhta contained eleven articles. All the frontier was to be marked, except the section lying to the east of the Gorbitsa, which was still unmapped. The Russians were requested to settle this matter speedily, as it was conducive to much trouble. All deserters were in future to be extradited and punished, but all were to remain where they were at the time of the Treaty. A caravan of two hundred men was to be admitted triennially to Peking. Kiakhta, being near to Selenginsk, was to be made a trading centre and a market for the exchange of commodities. Ambassadors, official messengers and letters were to be received and transmitted without let or hindrance, and any obstruction was to be taken as good cause for the rupture of commercial relations. In Peking, a permanent Russian church was allowed to be established, thus enabling Russians to worship God according to their own religion, while a priest, three curates and five language students were also allowed entrance into the house of the Ambassador.

Analysing this treaty, we note that Russia made three distinct gains. She had the frontiers marked to her advantage, a matter the Chinese discerned but were nevertheless willing to grant; she secured extension of trade; she received permission to erect a church and for nine of her nationals to be stationed permanently in Peking. She failed to get permission for a Consul-General or any commercial or political agent to remain in China. However, the Russian church-

[15] Chen Fu-kwang, *Sino-Russian Diplomatic Relations During the Ching Dynasty* (in Chinese), p. 52.

men were to act as observers. Hopes of establishing trade relations in Chinese river and maritime ports, however, did not materialize.

China, on her side, succeeded at last in having the troublesome frontier question finally settled. This she was anxious to do, as she wanted to be able to keep a watchful eye on Russia and to put her in the position of not being able to affirm the non-existence of a definite boundary as an excuse for extending her territory. The agreement to extradite 'rebels' meant that malcontents in Chinese territory would no longer find Russian territory a refuge. Finally, the ill-defined clause regarding the delay in the reception of officials, etc., could easily be utilized by the Chinese as a pretext for breaking off commercial relations wth Russia. This was a weapon China would not have the slightest hesitation in wielding, should Russia act detrimentally to her interests.

After the signing of the Treaties of Bura and Kiakhta in 1727, between China and Russia, Russia's main attention was directed to the West, while her advance in the Far East and her struggle with Turkey were more or less neglected. Again, after 1760, the struggle for the Baltic gave place to the one for the Black Sea, Russia finding herself too busy to pay attention to the Far East.

8. Russian Manœuvres in Mongolia

In the middle of the eighteenth century, Trans-Baikalia was opened as a field of colonization by adventurous Cossacks, and later was entered by new settlers coming from European Russia. From Trans-Baikalia, the Russians spread into nearby Mongolia and traded with the Mongols at Kiakhta. By penetrating into Outer Mongolia, friendly relations were maintained for some time between Russia and China.

The colonization of eastern Siberia was going on before the Russo-Japanese War in 1904-5, though it had been neglected during the Russo-Turkish War of 1877-8. This slow progress in colonization was chiefly due to lack of communications prior to the construction of the Trans-Siberian Railway.

Russia's humiliating defeat in the Russo-Japanese War not only put an end to the exploits of Russian adventurers but actually terminated Russian penetration in the Far East. Her influence in China being greatly impeded, she now changed her policy and acted in co-operation with Japan. On July 30, 1907, Russia signed a secret convention with Japan, wherein it was stated that the Japanese

Government would recognize the special privileges of Russia in Outer Mongolia and guarantee not to interfere with them. On July 4, 1910, Russia signed a second secret pact with Japan, reaffirming the convention of 1907 which concerned the construction of a direct railroad from Siberia to Peking.

Trouble soon came when the Mongol ruling princes desired to free themselves from China. Naturally it was a golden opportunity for Russia to establish her hegemony over Mongolia. Russia had in mind the important trade routes along which the best tea was brought to her from China. It was the intention of the Russian Government to establish a strong influence over Outer Mongolia and leave Inner Mongolia to the Chinese. Though the attitude of aggression towards Outer Mongolia by the Tsarist Government had been made clear, the Chinese authorities blundered somewhat in dealing with Mongolian affairs. At the end of the Manchu Dynasty, it was considered that the Chinese Government should retain its sovereignty over Outer Mongolia in view of the constant unrest along the frontier. A scheme for immigration and an increase of Chinese garrisons in Outer Mongolia were instantly effected. Further, some stringent administrative reforms were also put into practice. This caused great dissatisfaction among the Mongol princes, so the Russians seized the opportunity to instigate them to work for full independence, meaning, of course, emancipation from the Chinese yoke. In June 1910, a secret meeting was held among the princes whereat it was unanimously agreed that independence should be declared. So in May 1911 a powerful prince, Hanto, was sent as a special Envoy to St. Petersburg to ask for assistance. About two months later, shortly before the Chinese Revolution broke out at Wuchang, a Tsarist force arrived at Urga.

It is worth stating here that as early as 1881 Russia had signed a very advantageous treaty with China, securing many privileges along the Mongolian frontier. By the terms of that treaty, Russian Consuls were to be appointed to Outer Mongolia, and Russian merchants were to be permitted to purchase houses, shops, etc., and a zone was to be established along the Russo-Chinese frontier within which all imports and exports were to be duty free. The treaty lasted for ten years, whereafter it was renewed twice, first in 1891 and again in 1901. On its third renewal becoming due in 1911, however, the Peking Government hesitated about the matter. The Russian Government has since constantly reminded the Chinese Foreign Office of the necessity for its renewal. The Russian Minister at

Peking was duly informed that the treaty only provided for renewal if such were desired by both contracting parties. The Chinese Government could not agree with the Russian request that the treaty be renewed as a whole. Instead of declaring its renewal due on August 1, the Chinese officials began to levy customs duties. There then began riots and troubles in Mongolia, and the Chinese accused the Russians of instigating them. Realizing the danger of Russian encroachment, the Manchu authorities adopted more vigorous measures to make Mongolia a Chinese province. Chinese emigration was encouraged by the Mongolian Bureau of Colonization, and Chinese settlers flocked into Mongolia in great numbers.

China was not afraid of the Mongols, but feared the neighbouring powers working behind the scene. She became more suspicious of the relations between the Mongols and the Russians, and was naturally greatly alarmed by the increasing number of Russian troops on the borders of Mongolia. To check the Russian advance, the Manchu authorities decided to station a strong military force in Urga, the capital of Mongolia, as well as in other important cities. Barracks with a capacity of more than two thousand soldiers had been constructed in different localities before the Revolution broke out in Wuchang, an uprising that ultimately spread all over China.

9. Mongolia's Independence from China

When the Mongol princes learnt that the Manchu Dynasty in Peking was going to abdicate in December 1911, they held a meeting in Urga declaring that their obligations to the Manchus to whom they had pledged their loyalty were ended, and therefore they declared their secession from China. They were in close touch with the Russians, and chose the Hutukhtu of Urga, who was a pro-Russian, to be the Mongolian Emperor.

The young Chinese Republic refused to recognize Mongolian independence, insisting that, for centuries, Mongolia had been a province of the Chinese Empire, and that it would not permit Russian infringement upon the sovereignty of China. Russia addressed a note to the Chinese Government on September 6, 1912, stating that the treaty of 1881 was in force for another ten years, at the same time putting up some further demands including the abolition of the privileged zone on the Russian and Chinese side of the frontier.

Shortly after the news of the Wuchang outbreak came to Urga, the Hutukhtu addressed a note which was, in effect, an ultimatum to the Chinese Amban, Santo, asking him to leave Mongolia within three days with all his officers and soldiers. Santo had only a body-guard of two hundred with him, so he could hardly do otherwise than comply with the demand. All Chinese merchants had to follow suit, suffering untold losses at the hands of Mongolian and Russian soldiers.

When Yuan Shih-kai came into power and was made the President of the Chinese Republic, he despatched a telegram to the Hutukhtu urging him to cancel the declaration of independence. A reply was received from the Hutukhtu some while later. It ran:

'The declaration of independence and autonomy was effected before the abdication of the Manchu Emperor. Such proclamation has been made to the world, and I am not at liberty to make any alteration. If you insist on doing so, please consult with the neighbouring country to prevent any objections that might arise.'[16]

The so-called 'neighbouring country' meant, of course, Russia. From all this it seemed clear that Mongolian autonomy was entirely under Russia's influence. When China's troubles had subsided a little, it was decided to start a campaign to terminate Mongolian independence, which was regarded as mere child's play. The Russians, knowing Mongolian troops to be unreliable, feared the annexation of the newly organized independent state to the Chinese Empire as a result of the Chinese campaign. The Russian Government had already lodged several protests, stating that if China sent troops to Mongolia, Russia could not be indifferent to this violent change which would affect the peace of the border and ultimately endanger the cordial relations between the two countries. On receiving this threat, the Chinese began to realize that the matter was much more complicated than had hitherto been supposed, and that intrigues behind the Mongolian stage were something to be considered. The Russians had insisted on the employment of Russian military officers for the training of the Mongol troops. Large quantities of second-hand ammunition had been sold to the Mongols as part of the equipment of their army. The Four Leagues of Outer Mongolia were requested to conscript ten thousand men each, to be trained by Russian officers. It was agreed that Russian military officers should, while thus employed, have authority to command the

[16] C. L. Chu, *The Last Ten Years of Russo-Chinese Relations* (in Chinese), p. 138.

Mongol troops in the case of war breaking out with China. A loan of two million roubles was granted to the Mongols for military purposes, for which the mines of Mongolia were pledged as security. The employment of Russian economic advisers, who actually supervised the expenditure and even had the right to exploit industry, was provided for by the terms of the agreement. A government bank was set up by Russian capitalists, and the use of Russian bank-notes was enforced upon the Hutukhtu. After some military preparations, the Russian officers commanded the Mongol troops to occupy the city of Kobdo, and simultaneously the Russian army also occupied Urianghai, the north-western extension of Outer Mongolia.[17]

On November 3, 1912, Russia sent an envoy to Urga and signed a special agreement with independent Mongolia stating that Russia would assist the Mongolian Government to maintain the *status quo* and the training of troops to prevent the Chinese army from coming into Mongolian territory. In return, the Mongols promised all sorts of privileges to the Russians, including freedom of travel and navigation, freedom to open banks and exploit the land and industries, extra-territoriality for Russian subjects, Russian consular and postal service, freedom from customs duties and the right to buy land.[18] The Mongols further agreed that if their Government should find it necessary to conclude a treaty with China or any other power, the new treaty would in no way infringe the clauses of the present agreement, and also that the Russo-Mongolian agreement could not be modified without the previous consent of the Russian Government.

The Mongolian Government was soon compelled to conclude another secret treaty with Russia by which the Russians were permitted to develop mining industries in Mongolia and also to concede to Russia the right to build railways and construct a telegraph line from Irkutsk to Uliassutai.[19]

In view of the easy terms extorted by the Russians, the whole economic power of Outer Mongolia was put under Russian influence. Indeed, although Outer Mongolia was declared to be an independent state, it actually was under Russian domination. In answer to protests from the Chinese Government, the following remarks were passed by Sazonov, then Russian Minister of Foreign Affairs.

[17] Liu Kwei-han, *The Past and Future of Outer Mongolia* (in Chinese), The Eastern Miscellany, February 16, 1935.
[18] Korff, S. A., *Russia's Foreign Relations*, 1922, p. 72.
[19] Liu Kwei-han, op. cit.

'If China agrees not to send troops to Mongolia, not to colonize Mongolia and not to interfere with the internal politics of Mongols, then some agreement may be reached between the two governments. Otherwise, Russia has to maintain the Russo-Mongolian Agreements.'

Sazonov also mentioned in his speech in the Duma on April 13, 1912, that if Mongolia were left alone, she would again come under Chinese domination, to which Russia could not be indifferent on account of her national interests.[20] It was clear that Russia, though not firmly insisting upon Mongolian independence, certainly would not give up her political influence nor the privileges already gained in Mongolia.

10. Signing of Tripartite Agreement

The Chinese campaign against Mongolia was hindered by Russia, and direct negotiations were likewise turned down by the Hutukhtu. It was generally feared that if Mongolian affairs dragged on like this, things might go from bad to worse. So China was compelled to take up the matter with Russia. Three successive Foreign Ministers took a hand in the negotiations as firmly as ever, and no change of policy could be induced. On November 5, 1913, an exchange of notes took place between Peking and St. Petersburg. It was agreed that Russia should recognize China's nominal suzerainty over Outer Mongolia. China further agreed not to interfere with the internal administration of Outer Mongolia, not to send troops there, and to abandon the policy of colonization. It was stated that China could appoint an envoy to be stationed at Urga, and that delegates could be sent to other important cities of Outer Mongolia.

Regarding questions of a political and territorial nature, the Chinese also agreed to consult with the Russian Government, in which negotiations the Mongolian authorities should be allowed to participate. Though China's suzerainty over Outer Mongolia was acknowledged in this mutual agreement, it was merely a matter of saving China's face. In reality, Outer Mongolia became a protectorate under Russia and China.

According to the exchange of notes, the appointed representatives on both sides held numerous meetings in 1914 at Kiakhta. The conference, however, which lasted ten months, was deadlocked on

[20] Weigh, K. S., *Russo-Chinese Diplomacy*, p. 176.

several occasions, and there was constant danger of negotiations being broken off. It was due to China's concessions that a tripartite agreement was signed between China, Russia and Mongolia on June 7, 1915. Briefly, the tripartite agreement was as follows:

1. Outer Mongolia recognizes the exchange of notes between China and Russia and also recognizes Chinese suzerainty, agreeing in return to abandon her independent sovereignty.

2. China and Russia recognize the autonomy of Outer Mongolia and also the latter's right to sign commercial and industrial treaties with other powers; although autonomous, Mongolia has no right to conclude any treaties of a political or territorial nature.

3. The Chinese Envoy and his associates shall be stationed at Urga, Kobdo and Kiakhta respectively. Further appointment of associates to the different localities may be effected with the approval of Outer Mongolia.

4. The Russo-Chinese Protocol of 1912 is recognized to be still in force.

5. Chinese and Russian merchants are to be exempted from customs duties on importing goods into Mongolia.

6. Chinese residents are to be under Chinese jurisdiction, Russians under Russian jurisdiction, while in Russo-Mongolian mixed cases, the law as stipulated in the Russo-Mongolian Protocol of 1912 shall be applied. In Russo-Chinese cases, special mixed courts shall be established on the model of the Russo-Chinese mixed court then established on the Chinese Eastern Railway.

The treaty was drawn up in four languages, namely, Chinese, Russian, Mongol and French. The French text is authoritative in case of dispute arising in regard to the treaty.

After signing of the tripartite agreement, all Russian privileges gained in Outer Mongolia were formally recognized by China. Outer Mongolia, though a part of Chinese territory, was turned into a protectorate with merely formal respect for 'China's suzerainty'. Russia, politically speaking, had as much power as China, and economically had more power to dominate autonomous Mongolia. The Mongolian Government was given the right to sign treaties with foreign powers concerning questions of a commercial and industrial nature, but the distinction between commercial and political treaties was so vague and obscure that it was very easy for the inexperienced Mongol rulers to fall into the trap set by the Russians who wanted to dominate the whole scene of affairs. Therefore, it is safe to say that Outer Mongolia was a Russian Protectorate rather than a part of the Chinese Empire.

The tripartite agreement was the basis of relations between China, Russia and Mongolia until the Russian Revolution broke out in 1917, when the Mongol princes, fearing future danger to themselves, voluntarily abandoned their autonomy and immediately sought Chinese protection. Thus Outer Mongolia became, practically as well as formally, part of Chinese territory.

Chapter IV

RUSSIAN EXPANSION TO THE AMUR

Russia's drive east in the sixteenth century put dread into the hearts of the many tribes dwelling about the Asiatic borders who saw their race and religion endangered. Face to face with a new invader, they had forthwith to make up their mind whether to give in or fight the foe. At the time, Russia was too weak to expand west where she had Sweden, Poland and Turkey for neighbours. So she took the line of least resistance. Vast lands in the east were hers for the taking. By the end of the sixteenth century, Russian pioneers had crossed the Urals, ultimately penetrating north.

1. Causes of Amur Expansion

In the middle of the sixteenth century, the Tatar Khan sent envoys laden with gifts of sable and squirrel skins to congratulate the Tsar on his victories, imploring him to add Siberia to his realm and to defend all who were willing to pay tribute on the spot. A Muscovite Envoy accordingly returned the visit the following year. This man was the first to bring back from Siberia tribute in furs. Ivan the Terrible, in a letter addressed to King Edward VI of England, and dated 1554, gave himself the proud title of 'Lord of all Sibir'.[1]

In spite of the rich lure of sable and other valuable furs, south-eastern Siberia was slow to be explored. It was the Cossacks who served in the fell work of overcoming the Siberian aborigines by plunder, murder and rape, after having first got word of the fat Amur plains, from the Tunguzians of the Aldan River.[2]

Early Russian expansion eastward was mostly the work of hunters, trappers and other adventurers on the look-out for the fur-bearing game then so abundant in Siberia.[3] Stroganoff, a rich merchant adventurer, petitioned the Tsar in 1558, asking for a far and thinly

[1] Baddeley, op. cit., Vol. I, p. 57.
[2] Putman Weale, op. cit., p. 15.
[3] Yakhontoff, op. cit., p. 5.

47

populated region to be conceded him to develop and exploit, with all the needful protection from outside encroachment. The Tsar, because of the very difficult situation, consented thereto, and, moreover, bestowed various trade privileges together with the right of administration and the power to levy troops.

2. *Historical Invasion of Yermak*

The year 1581 saw Yermak's historic invasion. He began as a highwayman, but, ere long, his gangs waxed strong in number, getting so notorious and troublesome that government troops found it necessary to act against them. Yermak's men went to Strogonoff's settlement, but were not welcomed. Strogonoff hinted that he would be willing to give the needful provisions and ammunition if Yermak with his followers would cross the Urals into Siberia and conquer the natives. To this Yermak assented, and with 800 Cossacks reached the Irtysh by way of the Tobol River. He met with some resistance from the Kuchum Khanate, remnants of the Mongols on the upper part of the Ob River, and in 1583 he captured Sibir, the capital, which gave its name to the vast land now known as Siberia.[4]

Arrived there, he forthwith sent a delegation to Moscow, telling of the newly won territory. The delegates bore a rich tribute of furs to lay at the feet of the Tsar in the fervent hope that the death doom passed on Yermak for bygone lawlessness would be set aside. Thereupon, Yermak was brought back to Moscow, and taken before the Tsar, who not only gave the culprit a full pardon, but went so far as to reward him richly for his loyal services.

Hailed as a great hero, Yermak then went with a body of Cossacks on yet another expedition in an endeavour to win even more lands for the Tsar. On this expedition he was drowned by the weight of his armour in the Irtysh while harrying the Tatars.[5]. The deceased was even honoured with a sacred title by the Russian Patriarch. Although this rover-explorer's sudden death brought his projected 'Conquest of Siberia' to an end, it was only a matter of time before all these vast lands fell beneath the sway of Moscow. Siberia's bitter winters, and the dangers and hardships to be borne so far from civilization, made yet more wonderful the tales of fabulous wealth to be won in domains farther south still to be discovered by them.

[4] Yakhontoff, op. cit., p. 6.
[5] Wright, G. H., *Asiatic Russia*, 1902, Vol. I, p. 131.

These simple native tribes, half agricultural, half nomad, showed the Cossacks some of the fruits of Chinese civilization. Garments of fine silk and soft cotton; gold, silver and jade ornaments; copper vessels, porcelain dishes and what not; all such treasures soon fired the imagination of the Russians. These last pictured a land with towns and fields far richer than any before seen, and all waiting to be won. Just as they flogged with raw-hide whips the kindly Siberian tribes that so hospitably welcomed them, so they flogged their imagination into dreaming of still greater loot.

From that mushroom town and fast-growing fur mart, Yakutsk, a number of Cossack expeditions were sent forth to explore the unknown lands that promised so much. One of the most fortunate, after a perilous journey by boat and sleigh, managed in 1643 to sail the Dzeya River which joins the Amur near Blagoveshchensk. The high-handedness of the Cossack rovers soon antagonized the natives. One illustration will suffice.

'The pangs of hunger forced the leader of this expedition to despatch a lieutenant with some men to forage, and orders were foolishly issued that they were to entice the native chiefs out of their villages and hold them as hostages until provisions were forthcoming. . . . No such stratagem was required, for in every case the simple native chiefs went of their own accord and greeted the Russians as friends, offering them their services. But the lieutenant, instead of at once realizing that the first instructions could be disregarded, followed them to the letter. He brutally seized the chiefs, and as a result of this overbearing conduct, provoked the inhabitants to an attack. The Daurians resolutely sallied forth from their villages, and after a short fight drove the Russians into the woods where they were surrounded. Matters then seem to have arrived at a deadlock, for we read that in four days the adventurers were able to escape and that they arrived back in a state of utter collapse. The failure of this foraging expedition entailed great suffering on all the Cossacks, and half of them succumbed before relief came.'[6]

Poyarkov, who was sent by the Russian Governor at Yakutsk to the Cossack expedition, at length reached the mouth of the Dzeya and entered the Aldan River, where dwellings were erected along the bank for winter. He led his men farther south by crossing the

[6] Putnam Weale, op. cit., p. 17.

mountains, and maybe was one of the first Russians to sight the Amur. Soon after, he discovered the Sungari. By force, he made the surrounding tribes pay tribute. In 1646, after three years' hard exploring, the expedition returned to Yakutsk. Very few of the party were lost, thanks more to the peace-loving population than to armed superiority. By now, Russia was bent on annexing this great territory.[7]

The Muscovy Government, busy with home troubles as well as involved with its neighbours Poland, Sweden and Turkey, was not in the mood to direct the policy of its subjects in Siberia. The tremendous distance from Moscow, coupled with the fact that the means of communication were so complicated and hazardous, resulted in the Russian local authorities, particularly the one stationed in Yakutsk, carrying out a more or less independent programme of expansion at the cost of the native Siberian tribes. Lack of control from the capital was in no way a deterrent, but on the contrary it acted as an impetus to the Russian pioneers to bring more territory under their jurisdiction. They anticipated that the fruits of their endeavours would be correspondingly greater as a result of their initiative.

3. Under Manchu Lenient Control

The native tribes paid taxes and tribute to the Manchu authorities, but Manchu control never appeared to be onerous. They hunted and fished, grew grain and tended their cattle, much as they pleased. The wellnigh limitless territory which was theirs to settle upon or to use for grazing cattle was conducive to peaceful living as a general principle within each tribe and between one tribe and another. It was largely because of this that they were so ill equipped to defend themselves against the marauding Cossacks and other Russian adventurers.

The Manchus, skilled horsemen and excellent warriors, dwelt in what are more or less the three provinces of Manchuria. Being numerically and militarily much more powerful than the Siberian tribes, they took the latter under their control. This, as we have already seen, was far from harsh. The Manchus were content to exact a certain amount of taxes and tribute whereupon the subject tribes were left free to do pretty much as they pleased.

The southern neighbours of the Manchus, the Chinese, were, how-

[7] Ravenstein, *The Russians on the Amur*, pp. 9-13.

ever, an infinitely more populous and richer people possessing a remarkably high culture and ancient civilization. It was a constant temptation and spur to the Manchus to attempt to make an inroad into China. In 1644, the Manchu or Ching Dynasty, after overcoming a number of difficulties, began its reign in Peking.

For roughly four decades, the new Imperial House had its hands full, at times persuading, and at others coercing by force of arms rebellious Chinese into acknowledging allegiance. When Kang Hsi ascended the throne on the death of his father in 1661, the assimilation of the Manchus by the Chinese was already taking place. This was inevitable on account of the superiority of the cultural as well as the material civilization of the latter. We must, in honour to the virile, war-like Manchus, recognize that in place of utilizing the right of victors to subject the defeated to their rules and laws, they wisely and resolutely determined to follow the advanced Chinese civilization.

We should be right in maintaining that China, almost from the very commencement of the new régime, was jointly ruled by the Manchus and the Chinese. Furthermore, the Manchu element suffered considerable decrease through absorption with the passing of time. Despite the good intentions of Shun Chih, the first Ching Emperor, and of his son, the illustrious Kang Hsi, it was impossible to bring the whole of the vast Chinese Empire under control without utilizing force. The defeat, however, of the rebels in 1680 enabled the empire to be consolidated, and the Emperor to set about the complicated task of bringing peace and plenty to the land. Until the death of Ch'ien Lung, the renowned grandson of Kang Hsi, in 1796, the Chinese Empire prospered and had no fear of threats from without.

4. Khabarov's Notable Expedition

Let us now return to the events taking place in Siberia in the middle of the seventeenth century. The Manchus, who were in duty bound to protect the various native tribes in Siberia, were, as already pointed out, in the throes of a gigantic struggle to gain control of the Chinese Empire. This taxed their resources to the full. It was precisely for this reason that they were incapable of despatching sufficient military forces even to the Amur region, the northern boundary proper of their territory, to cope with the depredations of the Cossacks.

Quick to take advantage of this state of affairs, the Cossacks continued with impunity to deprive the Siberian natives of their land, to despoil them of their goods and to murder and enslave them. It was unhappily remarked that when they received the Cossacks with open arms in their willingness, nay, eagerness, to offer them hospitality, they exposed their breasts to the bullets of the new-comers.

In 1648, within two years after the return of the Poyarkov expedition to the Amur, information was received that there existed a shorter and less difficult route to the Amur. It was approachable by travelling south towards the east banks of Lake Baikal.

Khabarov, one of the leading Russians in Siberia, no less thrilled than the hundreds of other adventurers hastening from the western domains of the state of Muscovy at the prospect of amassing fortunes in vast but little-known territories, had no trouble in obtaining the consent of the Russian Governor of Yakutsk to his taking upon himself the task of annexing for the imperial government whatever new lands he might discover. Having received the good wishes of the Governor, he departed with a strong escort of Cossacks.

In 1650 this expedition arrived at the western section of the Upper Amur. News of the deeds of the Russians had already spread up and down the land. As a result, their appearance meant the disappearance of the natives. Even a number of forts were deserted, as the soldiers of the native princes realized that, being armed only with bows, arrows and swords, they could not defend them against invaders armed with guns.[8]

On one occasion when four horsemen were sent by the Tungus chief, Prince Lavkai, to ask why the expedition had come, Khabarov said that it had come solely for the purpose of trade. They declared that they had been told by a Cossack that the Russians had come to enslave the country. Khabarov bluntly announced that he would be content if some slight tribute were paid on behalf of the Russian Tsar, who would thereupon take all the natives under his protection. They were permitted to depart unmolested. The Russians themselves had confirmed that they were about to make them subject people, and this, combined with their previous experience of Cossack actions, only seryed to heighten their fears.

Those of the natives who were not in a position to escape on the advance of Khabarov's expedition, were compelled to pay the tribute exacted of them and submit to being plundered. The Russians then

[8] Putnam Weale, op. cit., p. 20.

settled along the River Yaksa, and a town was founded named Albazin (called Yaksa by the Chinese and the Tatars). After that, the Russians held the fort of Albazin as their headquarters.

Khabarov returned to Yakutsk. His first adventure convinced him of the prizes to be won by dominating the Amur; but this required a force far stronger than what he had taken with him at first. Once again showered with official blessings and now with a large armed force, he returned to the Amur. In the summer of 1651, with a makeshift fleet, he sailed down the river. This was the signal for a hasty evacuation of all the villages he passed.

After some days, he reached a line of fortifications built in all probability to stem the Russian invasion. In the fierce fight that ensued, some six hundred and sixty Daurian natives were killed and nearly four hundred women and children taken prisoner. The Russian losses, once again due to superiority in arms, were only about fifty killed and wounded. The booty included, among other things, three hundred and fifty horses and cattle and rich stores of grain.[9]

The Cossacks had fought without giving quarter, and we can well imagine the fate of the captured natives. This ferocious action on the part of the Cossacks heralded a series of deeds more dreadful than anything that had occurred in previous years.

The Achan natives (a different tribe of the Tungus), realizing the utter futility of coping with the Russian voyage of piracy and plunder on the Amur, were driven to call upon the Manchu authorities for aid. The Manchu Governor at Ninguta with a force of some two thousand horsemen, armed with bows and arrows, swords and spears, a number of cannon and a few matchlocks, attacked on March 24, 1652, the Achanskoi Gorod fort which Khabarov had built for the winter quarters of his expedition.[10]

Once again the Russians proved victorious, inflicting a terrible defeat upon the Manchus, who had seven hundred killed to the ninety or so Russians killed and wounded. This can only be accounted for if we bear in mind the fact that almost the whole of the available Manchu forces had been transferred to China, and that the majority of the men who had attacked the Russians were in all probability untrained soldiers with poor fighting equipment.

Khabarov, with the number of his Cossacks seriously diminished, saw every reason to make haste to leave his fort before the Manchus and local inhabitants had time to recover and make another attack.

[9] Ravenstein, op. cit., p. 17.
[10] ibid., p. 19.

He hurriedly departed on his barges and was fortunate enough to escape being attacked by another force of six thousand Manchus and natives which had gathered to destroy him. In the upper reaches of the Amur, he was reinforced by additional Cossacks despatched from Yakutsk, and this increased his forces to about three hundred and fifty men.

Aware that in future he would have to contend not only with the badly armed natives but with Manchus who were now determined to prevent any further inroads into the Amur regions, Khabarov decided that it was opportune for him to return to Yakutsk. Experience had shown him that he could no longer count on a few hundred Cossacks conquering the Amur, but he estimated that a permanent force of about six thousand men would be sufficient for this purpose. There were not enough men for this at the time, and the Governor of Yakutsk, in view of the great prizes at stake, urged the Tsar, through messengers sent for the specific purpose, to support him with men and money for the attempt to dominate the Amur.

In this decade of semi-official exploration, the Russians made themselves felt all along the Amur. With the comparatively small number of some five hundred or so Cossacks and civilians, they sacked village after village, plundering and killing the natives even when they were hospitably received.

Russian merchants in Siberia, as well as freebooters, profited as a result of this ruthless method of colonization, which had already begun to take on the aspect of annexation of foreign territory. So when the Moscow Government realized the full potentialities of a region so fertile and rich, it decided that it was high time matters were put under its immediate control.

There were reasons why this was deemed necessary. First, because the government saw no reason why private individuals alone should tap such vast resources and pocket all the rewards when the government might, by despatching a few thousand properly equipped and commanded troops, wrest still more territory and simultaneously direct the major part, if not the whole, of the economic life of the area for the benefit of the Russian exchequer. Russia was, we must bear in mind, very much an autocracy, and this consequently meant that the Tsar, the imperial family and the nobility would have the lion's share.

Khaborov was royally welcomed in Moscow by the Tsar. As if to substantiate his reports on the Amur regions, he brought with him to the Court a number of Siberian natives. The Tsar looked upon them as the citizens of a new colony, and in anticipation, no doubt, of the future, was pleased to give them many presents before he dismissed them. When they returned home, it was hoped, they would speak favourably of the powerful emperor, and because they had basked in the light of his presence, they would forget that they had been torn from their homes.

Three thousand troops were sent to Siberia. It was no simple task for such a large force to travel through such extensive and scarcely mapped regions. Local governors and other government officials were few and far between. Also, even the officials themselves were not at all well acquainted with the areas of which they were supposed to be in charge. Furthermore, they were, to a large extent, dependent upon uneducated and uncouth Cossacks and adventurers for much of their information.

5. Ambitious Adventures of Stepanov

In the meanwhile, a man by the name of Stepanov, much after the fashion of his predecessors, Poyarkov and Khabarov, but on a still more ambitious scale, began his adventures on the Amur. He followed in the footsteps of the latter, taking control of the settlements he had founded and which still existed.

In the spring of 1654 we find him at the mouth of the Sungari. Here he met a large force of natives and Manchus prepared to give fight. Undaunted, he decided to withstand them. Once again the Russians were victorious. The manifest determination, however, of the local inhabitants to prevent further destruction of their homes and their hatred of the invaders who had come to subject them, warned Stepanov that in future he would have to tread more warily. By winter, he had built a strong fort manned by about five hundred men at the mouth of the Kamara River on the upper Amur.

When spring came, several thousand hostile troops, armed with a number of cannon and many matchlocks and siege weapons, made a fierce onslaught on the fort. They were still not a match for the Russians, and despite their furious efforts, failed to dislodge them. Therefore, for the following two years, Stepanov roved the Amur like a pirate chief, exacting tribute and taking by force whatever was not forthcoming swiftly enough to suit him.

The local forces, despairing of any definite material aid from the Manchus, who, although they were reigning in Peking, were still harassed by many difficulties within the Chinese Empire itself, gathered together another force ten thousand strong to put an end to Stepanov's depredations. Having learnt many lessons from previous defeats, they made certain this time of victory. In 1658, forty-five boats, heavily armed, met Stepanov below the Sungari. All his five hundred men, except those who deserted him when they saw the superiority of the enemy and when the battle was going against them, were either destroyed or made prisoner. He himself was also killed. Thus, for a time, the native tribes were able to live in peace.[11]

While Stepanov was temporarily master of much of the Amur, some hundreds of miles away to the west on the Shilka River, Pashkov had in 1656, with the help of six hundred Cossacks, settled in Nerchinsk. Owing to the peculiarities of Russian officialdom, he was simultaneously appointed Commander-in-Chief of the Amur, although at that time the annihilation of Stepanov's forces had not yet leaked out to the outside world. Pashkov, when the time came, ascertained that he had no one to carry out his instructions on the Amur. Aware of the hazards that would confront him if he were to divide his forces between the Shilka region and the still larger Amur, he decided to entrench himself where he was.[12]

For ten years there was peace on the Amur. The old tribes returned to their previous abodes and lived much as they had lived before the advent of the Russian Cossacks and adventurers. They thought that a new and happier phase had arisen. But they were soon disillusioned. This period of tranquillity was to be followed by yet greater violence.

6. Siege of Albazin

Siberia had for long been a refuge not only for those who were discontented with the Tsarist Government but also for criminals eager to escape the law and find fresh fields for their nefarious schemes. In 1669 a Pole named Chernigovsky, a fugitive from justice, with a company of nearly a hundred other desperate men, after overcoming many difficulties, managed to establish himself as master of Albazin. After the fort of Albazin had been retaken, Chernigovsky duly reported to Pashkov who graciously pardoned him for his former acts.[13]

[11] Baddeley, op. cit., Vol. II, p. 195.
[12] Ho Chiu-tao, *The Strategy of Conquering the Russians* (in Chinese).
[13] Chen Pao-wen, *Sino-Russian Diplomacy* (in Chinese), Shanghai, 1928, p. 8.

One of the old forts was rebuilt and made habitable and ready for defence against any natives or Manchu troops who might dare to challenge the invaders' right to commandeer what they wanted. Later events were to prove that Chernigovsky's actions were not only approved but even abetted by the Russian authorities.

The resettlement of Albazin was the first reappearance of the Russians on the Amur after the destruction of Stepanov's forces. All the old fears were immediately aroused. Alarmed, a general was sent from Peking to examine the situation in Albazin. In 1670 a letter was brought to Nerchinsk, the Russian seat of government controlling much of south Siberia, demanding the vacation of Albazin.

In order to play for time, a Russian Envoy was ordered to Peking to negotiate with the Chinese Government concerning the frontier.[14] He was graciously received by Kang Hsi, but no solution of Sino-Russian problems, year by year becoming increasingly acute, could be reached.

In the following year, the Governor of Nerchinsk recognized Albazin as a part of the Russian State by sending to it an official, Okholkov. This official recognition of an outpost created by men who were virtually outlaws, gave the needed impetus for the mushroom growth of the settlement. Fugitives and adventurers flocked thither. All came under the protection of the Tsar. To give it the appearance of a law-abiding place, a cathedral and a monastery were built.

With Albazin as headquarters, exploration parties radiated from it like so many tentacles of an octopus anxious to clutch at whatever was within its reach. Kang Hsi, engrossed by a thousand and one details in the great empire he was ruling, neither had the time nor probably saw the need to take punitive measures against the Russians. He evidently did not consider them a real threat. If these Siberian tribes along the Amur and elsewhere, whose allegiance to him was of little material value, were helpless against the invaders, it was their misfortune. It was not opportune for him to render assistance to them, however pitiable their plight.

By the end of 1682, the inactivity of the rulers of the Chinese Empire resulted in the Russians occupying practically the whole of the northern tributaries of the Amur. The natives became a subject population with all the burdens of a ruthless subjection.

The Chinese Emperor could no longer disregard the threat that

14 Ravenstein, op. cit., pp. 45-53.

was growing so rapidly on the northern borders of his domain. Military measures on a grand scale were initiated. Fortresses were built in Tsitsihar and other cities. A large number of troops, well equipped and well led, totally unlike the mixed forces of regular troops and natives which had on many previous occasions fought the Russians, made its base at Aigun. For the first time in the Amur region, imperial Chinese troops fought against imperial Russian troops.

The Chinese forces made systematic attacks against the foreign settlements and fortifications, and by the end of 1683 every vestige of Russian occupation on the lower Amur and its tributaries disappeared. Only Albazin, magnificently fortified and well stocked with munitions and provisions, remained to be taken.

In 1684, the Chinese, through the medium of two Russian prisoners who had been specially sent from Peking, despatched to the Governor of Albazin a letter giving the terms for its surrender. They were rejected.

Early the next year, Manchu troops were despatched to Albazin by land and water to besiege the fort with the intention of starving the Cossacks. The besieged hurriedly destroyed all outbuildings and repaired within. The garrison consisted of about three hundred and fifty Cossacks and able-bodied men. The Chinese army that was approaching was much more numerous. A hundred boats and some eighteen thousand men, including land forces, with fifteen cannon and other weapons such as matchlocks and bows and arrows, confronted them. As they were anticipating early and large reinforcements, the Russians made preparations to resist the attack.[15]

The Manchu general made a demand for the immediate surrender of the fort and promised to be generous if his wishes were complied with. This was ignored. The Chinese onslaught began in earnest, and within a few days nearly a third of the Russian forces was killed. The havoc the Chinese fire was causing and the impossibility of further resistance, compelled the Russians to sue for mercy.

It would have been no cause for surprise if the Chinese troops had not heeded this plea. They had already promised to treat the Russians leniently if they had surrendered Albazin without fighting. What was of even more relevance was the fact that, for a great number of years, the Russians had sorely maltreated the natives and killed all who resisted them. The Chinese forces, however, treated them with astonishing magnanimity. They

---

[15] Yakhontoff, op. cit., p. 11.

allowed them to depart, not only with their goods, but with their arms as well.

The Chinese, believing that the Russians had had a sufficient setback after this defeat, ordered their troops to return to their base at Aigun. Soon afterwards a new Aigun on the left bank of the river was established, and the old Aigun lost its significance. As they were still chary of Russian aggression, a force of two thousand men was left here, while the main part of the army set off for other garrisons.

The Russians from Albazin made their way to Nerchinsk unmolested. After a brief rest, they were ready to break their word not to return to Albazin. Scouting parties brought back the news that the Chinese army had completely vacated it. In August 1685 new troops, this time under Beiton, marched to Albazin. New Albazin was still more strongly fortified by the following spring. The Chinese were slow to act at this flagrant example of treachery. But on July 7, 1686, they began a determined effort to take the fort. With a force smaller than that which had previously compelled the Russians to forsake the place, they vigorously attacked it. There were heavy casualties on both sides.

This vigilant investment and the constant attacks, coupled with the diminishing food supplies, began to tell seriously upon the fighting strength and morale of the besieged. Buoyed up by the hope that reinforcements would be sent from Nerchinsk, they continued their stubborn resistance for over three months. When the town was on the verge of falling into the hands of the Chinese, a decree suddenly came from the Chinese Emperor stating that the two Powers were going to negotiate peace, and that the siege of Albazin should be promptly raised. Had diplomacy not intervened, the destruction of the Russians would have been inevitable.[16]

7. Treaty of Nerchinsk

The Russian Government in the latter part of the seventeenth century was eager for a peaceful solution of the Amur question. This would have meant the expansion of commerce, which was of considerable importance to the government since it held high hopes of a government monopoly as we have seen. And it became an increasingly pressing matter with the depletion of the Moscow exchequer by military needs in Russia proper and internal economic depression.

[16] Ho Chiu-tao, op. cit., Vol. III.

Kang Hsi was also of the opinion that amicable relations with the Russians would be useful. So the conference was commenced at Nerchinsk. The Chinese delegation arrived at the scene with a large assemblage of officers, soldiers and servants, about ten thousand men, which led the Russians to complain that the Chinese had come to make war instead of effecting peaceful negotiations.

At Nerchinsk, the Chinese military were under the command of Son Go-to, while those who had come by water were under Lantan. When the conference began, the Manchus proposed the Lena as the boundary, but the Russian delegates refused to accept. After a fruitless discussion, which lasted almost till midnight, Lantan resolved to use force by deploying his troops. The Russians lost their nerve and peace was signed, the front being fixed from the Aigun to the Amur, and from the Gorbitsa to the sea along the crest of the Hsing-an Mountains.[17]

On September 7, 1689, the Treaty of Nerchinsk was signed. The Chinese wrote out one copy of it in Manchu and one in Latin. The Russians in their turn wrote out one in Russian and the other in Latin. The Latin text was duly signed and sealed and agreed upon as the official version.

This treaty consisted of six articles. The salient features of it appear to be these: The Western boundary was to be the River Aigun; the northern boundary to commence at the River Gorbitsa and to extend to the sea of Okhotsk, so that all the southern slopes of the Stanovoi Mountains with the rivers flowing from them towards the Amur were to belong to the Chinese, and all the northern slopes with the rivers flowing north to belong to the Russians. Furthermore, all Russian towns on the south of the River Aigun were to be removed to the north bank. The Russians were not permitted to navigate the Amur, and Albazin was to be destroyed. Finally, commercial relations were to be restored and receive official protection from both countries.

It might be deduced from the above that China, by a formidable military display, won all the points that were to her advantage territorially. Russia would not have been averse to extending her territory as well as putting on a proper footing her trade with China, which she considered of no little importance, but as she had not the means to obtain the former, she was content with the latter.

The Treaty of Nerchinsk, the first that any Chinese emperor had

[17] Chen Fu-kwang, *Sino-Russian Relations During Ching Dynasty* (in Chinese), p. 28.

signed with a foreign power, was destined to hold good till 1858. It served to settle China's continual squabbles with Russia and simultaneously permitted her to devote her undivided attention to eliminating the Eleuths as a menace to her northern territories.

The Russians, shortly after the Treaty of Nerchinsk, owing to their lack of success over the Buriats and Onkotes, vented their rage on these tribes, who dwelt within the territory that the Russians had previously annexed from the natives. Having manifested preference for Chinese rule, many of their villages were plundered and destroyed, and large numbers of the inhabitants were put to the sword. Galdan, the Eleuth prince, made overtures to the Russians to enlist their support against the Mongols and Chinese, but they were not hopeful of success and therefore rejected the temptation to side openly with them. Events justified their attitude, for the Eleuths, as we have stated before, were subdued by Kang Hsi who himself played an important military role for six successive years in exterminating the Eleuths.

8. Great Career of Muraviev

For more than one hundred and fifty years the frontier between China and Russia was peaceful and uneventful. Russia was content to colonize the lands strictly lying west of the Amur, while China made no further demands on the natives of the Amur except the customary tribute to be exacted every year. In 1846, however, the Tsar, Nicholas I, plunged himself again into the Amur question, ordering an investigation of the whole Amur as well as its adjacent territory to be made.

In the following year, September 6, 1847, the Tsar appointed Nicholas Muraviev Governor-General of eastern Siberia. This young, aggressive and far-sighted Russian, understanding that the Tsar had some plans about the Amur, was not slow to take advantage of China's terrible plight in face of increasing foreign encroachments from the west by sea.[18] Holding a high opinion of Russia's future in the Amur regions, since China had no longer the might wherewith to uphold the Treaty of Kiakhta, he considered that there was nothing to prevent Russia from extending her territory. Muraviev sent emissaries to St. Petersburg to persuade his government to give him a free hand in Far Eastern affairs, and, simultaneously, he enlisted Russian naval and military authorities on his side for a

[18] Yakhontoff, op. cit., p. 21.

forcible extension of Russian territory at the expense of the Chinese Empire.

In the next few years, he sent many expeditions to what are now called the Maritime Provinces, as well as armed fleets up and down the Amur. This was contrary to treaty rights, but the Chinese had no power to enforce them.

During that time, the Russian naval ministry was looking for a new port on the sea of Okhotsk. Muraviev thought this an undesirable situation, being too far north, and asked Captain Nevelskoy to explore the Amur with the object of searching for a suitable port. In 1849 Nevelskoy proceeded up the Amur River and discovered a port twenty-five versts from its mouth, which was named by him Nikolaevsk in honour of the Tsar. The Russian flag was hoisted on the spot. Nevelskoy also discovered that steamers going to sea could penetrate to the mouth of the river without rounding Sakhalin; such a discovery, of course, had great significance for Russia.[19] Nevelskoy instantly reported his new discovery to Muraviev. Naturally Muraviev was very pleased, and he went to St. Petersburg in person to report to the government. The Committee on Far Eastern Affairs discussed the matter and opposed the approval of this unauthorized step on the ground that such action would bring conflict with the Chinese Government. The Committee asked for immediate withdrawal, and insisted that Nevelskoy should be severely punished. The matter was brought before the Tsar for confirmation. The Tsar turned down the decision, saying, 'When the Russian flag has once been hoisted, it must not be lowered.'[20] He then ordered that the settlement should be maintained. This was a great relief to Muraviev, who was very much opposed to the decision of the Committee.

Muraviev pushed his scheme even further. He realized that he needed a stronger force to accomplish his tremendous task, and he succeeded in converting the natives at Nerchinsk into Cossack troops without further bothering St. Petersburg, since the Ministers were strongly opposed to sending any large forces to the Far East. He constantly received warning not to use arms against China. No money was appropriated by St. Petersburg. The Minister of Finance was strongly against adventures in the Far East, and tried to prevent them. Then came the Crimean War of 1854 which crushed Russia's

[19] Clyde, P. H., *International Rivalries in Manchuria*, Ohio, 1928, p. 16.
[20] Vladimir (pseudonym), *Russia, on the Pacific and the Siberian Railway*, London, 1899, p. 185.

power in Europe, giving Muraviev a good opportunity to win a lasting triumph on the Pacific coast. He was so ambitious that he said at the time: 'If Russia became stronger in the East, she might even act as the Protector of China.'[21]

Muraviev showed great solicitude for the precarious position of eastern Siberia, fearing a combined attack by the Franco-British naval forces. He therefore set forth a scheme of defence, necessary to provide for the military requirements of the situation. His statement impressed the Tsar so much that he was authorized to transact all diplomatic affairs direct with Peking without reference to St. Petersburg.

He returned to the Far East and, before sailing down the river, he despatched a note to the Chinese Government in Peking, informing the latter of the coming expedition and explaining that the war in Europe had compelled him to use the river for protection. Muraviev started his famous expedition down the River Amur with an adequate force and met with no resistance, though he had received warning previously not to use arms against China; but at the time, no Chinese authority existed along the left bank of the Amur. A series of towns were founded along the Amur, such as Blagoveshchensk, Khabarovsk and Nikolaevsk, where Cossacks, miners and farmers were transferred from Trans-Baikalia as new settlers. Muraviev reached the Chinese fortified town of Aigun on May 28 and sent delegates to the Chinese authorities to ask whether they had received any instructions from Peking. The governor of the town was quite embarrassed by this situation which had come about completely without his knowledge, and he let the unwelcome guests pass through in order to get rid of them. So Muraviev proceeded without any further hindrance. When he arrived at Petropavlovsk, he started to fortify the place in readiness to meet the attack of the Franco-British fleet. The allied forces finally gave up their attempt to attack the fort as the defence was too much for them.

We have the following brief translation of a petition sent by the Military Governor of Kirin to the Chinese Government:

'Despatch received from the Vice-Commander Hu Sun-pu of Hei-lung-kiang province stating that the Russian boats were going to the Eastern Sea by way of the rivers Amur and Sungari owing to recent events whereby various islands lying on the east have been occupied by England. News of such a necessary measure has

[21] W. C. Costin, *Great Britain and China, 1833-1860*, London, 1937, p. 247.

been communicated to the Lifan Yuan of Peking and free passage asked for. Hu Sun-pu, lacking instructions, naturally stopped them and was informed that their chief would come soon. Later in the afternoon, a large steamer with a bronze funnel anchored at the north bank of the city surrounded by several boats. Hu Sun-pu went on board, together with one of his associates, and saw the Russian Commander by the name of Muraviev who told them that he was ordered to come to rescue the eastern islands invaded by England. He was making a short cut through the Amur and Sungari, and he would not cause any disturbance to the locality to be passed through. Hu Sun-pu asked why there was no previous information, and then made further enquiries if any more men were coming. The reply was that there were only a thousand this time and no more to come. At this juncture, a special delegation was sent to investigate the situation on the Russian bank of the river. It was afterwards reported that there were altogether eighty-three boats with more than two thousand men. There was plenty of provisions but not much ammunition. Besides this, there were four rafts with about one hundred horses and eighty oxen together with two boats loaded with women. Since entering Chinese territory, they had not molested any one. Hu Sun-pu insisted that they should stop and sail no farther, but knowing the Chinese were not well prepared, he afterwards let them pass through in order to avoid any possible conflict. Some delegations were sent to pursue them to make investigations. The foregoing important report is hereby sent together with a copy of a despatch given by the Russian Commander to the Lifan Yuan for your consideration.'[22]

At the same time, other negotiations were carried on at Tientsin by Admiral Count Putiatin, Russian Minister to China. Putiatin informed the Lifan Yuan that on July 5, 1854, he had received a despatch from the Governor of Sibir (Muraviev) stating that of necessity he had had to pass through the Chinese Amur in order to reach the Eastern Sea, and that the military requirements of this operation had been carried out without the slightest detriment to China. Furthermore, he had no inclination to extend his power, which might cause sudden suspicion. The state of agreement between the two countries had lasted so long that they could easily understand

[22] Chiang Ting-fu, *A Collection of Chinese Diplomatic Documents* (in Chinese), Shanghai, 1931, Vol. I, p. 279.

each other. Besides, the coast of the Eastern Sea, though in Russian territory, was of great concern to China as well. Therefore it was to be understood that the necessary military precautions taken by the Russians had also materially benefited China. Hence China should co-operate with Russia without any prejudice or suspicion in spite of the movement of Russian troops. Russia would be glad to reciprocate some day if China were to find herself in difficulty. All he had to say merely carried out the instructions of the Tsar and, as soon as his delegate arrived at Peking, a more detailed report would be given the Lifan Yuan.

In August 1856, Muraviev went down the Amur with a second expedition on a much larger scale. The Chinese authorities, knowing that the Russians had the intention of settling down permanently in the lower Amur region, protested and demanded an explanation after the expedition had arrived at the city of Aigun. Delegations were sent on board to see the Russian Commander. On their arrival a large crowd of Russians, not less than eight thousand of both sexes, were found busy building their own houses on the river bank, and they even fired at the delegates as a demonstration when they came in sight. The delegates were then told by a certain Russian, who could speak a little Chinese, that Commander Muraviev was indisposed and unable to receive them, but promised to hold a conference on the morrow. On the following day, the delegates went on board again and saw Muraviev avoiding them by going to the stern. They were guided to a building under construction. After a long wait, they were received by Admiral Zavoiko, who told them of the absolute necessity of protecting the mouth of the Amur against the aggression of foreign powers. He and the other officials, each with a document in Russian and in Chinese, read out to them that all land on the left bank of the Amur and Sungari should be granted to and occupied by the Russians, and necessary fortifications would be made for their protection. The Russians would not fail to keep connections between the coast and the islands by boat in summer and horseback over the ice in winter. With such incessant communications, possession of the Russian islands might be secured. When the delegates stated that both the Amur and Sungari were territories of the Celestial Empire, the Russian officials had nothing to say, but added that the matter would be referred to Muraviev. Next day (September 22), a copy of the document in Russian and Chinese was sent to the delegation. Its contents were exactly the same as had been read the day before. On September 23, the delegates were received by Muraviev who put a map before him and stated that, to reach an amicable settlement, the left bank of the Amur and its mouth to the sea should be given to Russia for protection. Whether the local inhabitants would remain or evacuate was for the Chinese Government to decide. He urged the delegates to accept the document and to communicate to Peking his intention of starting a third expedition in the not-too-distant future. The Chinese delegates made it clear to Muraviev that though they received the document, it would have to be submitted to higher authorities and they could not foretell when a reply would be forthcoming. Muraviev then immediately went back to St. Petersburg to obtain the appointment of plenipotentiary of Russia in China in readiness for the conclusion of a new treaty with the Chinese Government.[23]

Muraviev returned to the Far East in 1857, and brought with him a thousand hard-labour convicts to be set free to cultivate the land and to colonize the country. He even released about one hundred hard-labour convict women to choose their husbands from among the men. As the river was fast getting near low water, there was no time to be lost. Muraviev asked all these men and women to stand together in pairs on the river bank. Then he blessed them, saying: 'I marry you, children. Be kind to each other; you men, don't ill-treat your wives—and be happy!' Such are the words written by Kropotkin who witnessed the strange scene.[24]

9. Treaty of Aigun

On May 16, 1858, Muraviev, taking swift advantage of the chaos in China as a result of the wars with Great Britain and France and the devastating effects of the Taiping Rebellion, compelled Prince Yishan, Commander-in-Chief of the Chinese forces of the Amur, to sign what is known as the Treaty of Aigun. Its terms were devastating. It set down in black and white what China had been obliged to permit in fact, the surrender to Russia of all the territory on the left bank of the Amur, while the territory on the right bank as far downstream as the Ussuri was to be recognized as Chinese, and the territory between the Ussuri and the sea was to be left undecided until a future date. Furthermore, it acknowledged, as a matter of course, the liberty of Russians to sail along the Amur and trade on

[23] Ravenstein, op. cit., pp. 117-25.
[24] Kropotkin, *Memoirs of a Revolutionist*, Vol. I, p. 216.

both banks. This was the beginning of a new stage in Russian penetration in Manchuria.

Prince Yishan first had no intention of accepting the humiliating demands, but owing to the furious attitude of Muraviev during the conference, he finally acceded to avoid any immediate conflict at the border. By this single stroke of diplomacy, Muraviev secured for the Tsar a territory almost as large as France without any bloodshed. He was later granted the title of Count Amursky by the Tsar for his brilliant service.

But when Prince Yishan reported to Peking the signing of the Treaty of Aigun, the Chinese Government was greatly alarmed and was disinclined to ratify it. Yishan was dismissed for his stupidity and for overstepping his authority. The petition sent by Prince Yishan to the Throne in Peking, June 14, 1858, which came to light only recently at the former Imperial House, Peking, was considered as one of the most humiliating documents in Chinese history. Prince Yishan, who signed the Treaty of Aigun, was the general responsible for the conducting of the Opium War. He commanded a large body of troops at Canton in the fight against the British. After he was completely defeated, he tried to deceive the Emperor by stating that the British were begging for peace. Certainly, Muraviev knew how to deal with him, forcing him to surrender by constant bluffing. By this method of dealing he got all he wanted, and the negotiations lasted only six days before the treaty was mutually agreed to and signed.

Russia's aggressive attitude was made so manifest that Sir J. Bowring, then British Minister to China, had become convinced of the desirability of establishing British influence in Peking, in order to strengthen the Chinese Government in a policy of resistance to the steady advance of Russia from the north. On November 27, 1855, Bowring wrote to the Earl of Clarendon, the Foreign Secretary, these words: 'Only a joint advance on Peking could prevent the Russians, with the Amur River as a base, from establishing settlements on territories inhabited by Tatars, Japanese or Koreans which they might wish to conquer or to claim.'[25] Again, he wrote to Clarendon on March 13, 1856: 'There was, too, a possibility that the Chinese authorities might make use of Russia to drive the Western Powers out of the five ports.'[26]

[25] Costin, op. cit., p. 195.
[26] ibid.

10. Treaties of Tientsin and Peking

About the same time, Admiral Putiatin had been carrying on some negotiations with the other Great Powers. The opening of five ports as the result of the Opium War by the Treaty of Nanking, signed in 1842, omitting Russia, who only had the privilege of trading with China in Kiakhta, naturally alarmed St. Petersburg. Putiatin had joined Muraviev down the Amur River, and proposed to his government the forcible occupation of Aigun. Failing to get permission to proceed to Peking by way of Mongolia, he took the sea route by sailing down the Amur and up to the mouth of the Pei-ho in Tientsin. He made the suggestion to the British and French naval forces in Shanghai that the mouth of the Pei-ho should be blockaded in order to make the drive effective. During such a critical time, China was anxious to preserve normal relations with Russia, and finally decided to negotiate with the Russian Minister, whereupon the Treaty of Tientsin was duly signed on June 14, 1858. The five ports were now open to Russian trade as well. The treaty, howeyer, gave Russia privileges which made Sino-Russian relations no longer those existing between two equal powers, as it was largely a one-sided affair. This treaty was basically the same as the unequal treaties signed with Britain, France and the other Western Powers. Putiatin also asked for the settling of the frontier question, because at that time he was completely ignorant that the Treaty of Aigun had already been signed by Muraviev.[27]

Less than two years later, China was once more at war with Britain and France. General Ignatieff, who had succeeded Admiral Putiatin as Minister in Peking, was no less adroit than his predecessor in utilizing the moment to further the aims of his own government. On the one hand, he promised to provide the Chinese Imperial Government with arms and cannon for the suppression of the Taipings, and also to mediate between the Chinese and the British and French allies; and, on the other, he threatened to send the Russian fleet to Peitang if they refused to ratify the Treaty of Aigun, and also to cede the Trans-Ussuri, the Maritime Province of Primorsk.

His cajolery and importunities succeeded. China had no alternative but to accede to the Russian demands. Refusal would have been utterly futile as she did not have the forces available to stem Russian aggression. She had already dangerously taxed all her

[27] Yakhontoff, op. cit., p. 23.

resources in challenging the two great western European Powers, and her hands were full trying to put down the Taipings. On November 14, 1860, the Treaty of Peking was signed in confirmation and elaboration of the Treaty of Aigun and the Treaty of Tientsin, reaffirming that the Amur should remain the frontier between China and Russia. Russia now had Vladivostok which had been already occupied by Muraviev on July 20, 1860,[28] as a seaport on the Pacific, since the territory to the east of the Ussuri River was recognized as belonging to Russia.

This closed one chapter in Russia's aggressive plans in the Far East. The further worsening of affairs in the Chinese Empire served to whet her appetite. From this time on the Russians were undisputed masters of all Siberia, a territory twice as large as the European part of Russia. Colonization went on more rapidly. The Amur, a highly important waterway, assumed its due importance. Steamboats gradually began to replace the old-fashioned barges.

But while this was going on, hundreds of thousands of Chinese, because of famine and civil war, began the long trek to Manchuria where there was much virgin soil waiting for the patient husbandman to reap rich return for hard work. The toiling Chinese poured into Manchuria in such vast numbers that they began to be dreaded by the yet sparse populations on the other side of the Amur.

11. Russia's Occupation of Manchuria

Following Russia's occupation of Port Arthur and Dairen-Wen in 1898, which will be dealt with in the next chapter, there were troublesome years in Manchuria. At the time of the Boxer Uprising in 1900, the anti-foreign movement began to spread into Manchuria. This was aggravated by the fact that the Russians had begun to build roads and harbours, causing the local population to feel an increased hatred against Russia. The Chinese Eastern and the South Manchurian Railways were seriously damaged by the Chinese rioters. Government troops joined hands with the Boxers while Russian troops could only patrol the neutral areas in the Liaotung Peninsula. Meanwhile, Russian ships on the Amur River were shelled and the city of Blagoveshchensk was heavily bombarded by the Chinese garrisons on the other side of the river. The Russian Government immediately despatched a great number of troops into north Manchuria. Fearing that the Chinese merchants in Blagoveshchensk

---

[28] Clyde, op. cit., p. 20.

might pass information to the Chinese garrison in Aigun, the Governor of Blagoveshchensk forced the Chinese merchants in the city to cross the Amur River; those who resisted were killed on the spot. The merchants proceeded to the river *en masse*, but there were no ferries to carry them across, while behind them were Russian Cossacks with fixed bayonets who forced these three thousand men and women, old and young, to plunge into the river where they were all drowned. This was regarded as the first massacre of Chinese by the Russians since the beginning of Sino-Russian relations, though this act was disowned by the Russian Government.[29] The Russians then proceeded to occupy Tsitsihar, the capital of Heilungkiang Province, and soon entered Harbin.

By that time the Boxers in Mukden had begun plundering and setting fire to houses, creating great disturbance in the city, while the Russians also took advantage of the situation to occupy that city. The Russian troops from the north and those from Port Arthur in the south were then able to meet and to occupy the whole of Manchuria.

When the Boxer Protocol was signed in September 1901 by the Powers, the Russian Government decided to withdraw troops at once from Peking and Tientsin, as it wanted to get on good terms with the Manchu Government while preparing future plans of aggression. But some of the Russian military officers opposed immediate evacuation, and Russia's change of attitude aroused suspicion and fear among the other countries, leading to the decision of Great Britain to make a treaty of alliance with Japan in 1902.

During the occupation of Fengtien Province by Russian troops, the Russian Commander, Alexieff, wishing to legalize the position, concluded the Provisional Treaty of Fengtien, known as the Alexieff-Tseng Agreement, with the Chinese Governor Tseng Chi. It consisted of nine articles which practically ceded the whole of Manchuria to Russia.

Peking did not hear of the treaty till after its signature, and the news surprised both Chinese and foreign circles. As Russia was contemplating a formal treaty with China, the Manchu Government instructed Yang Yu, the Chinese Minister in St. Petersburg, to carry on negotiations. Through the efforts of Count Witte, Russian Finance Minister, a proposed agreement of thirteen articles was drawn up which was even harsher than that previously concluded.

---

[29] Fraser, John Foster, *The Real Siberia*, London, 1902, pp. 177-80. See also Morse and MacNair, *Far Eastern International Relations*, New York, 1931, p. 474.

The revelation of the news of Sino-Russian negotiations in St. Petersburg inspired great uneasiness among the various Powers, particularly Japan, who formally obstructed the conclusion of such a treaty, warning China that Russia must not be permitted to occupy Manchuria for fear of international controversies. The Japanese Government then discussed the Manchurian question with Britain, stating that a special convention such as was being negotiated separately by Russia was contrary to the principle of solidarity and would materially lessen China's capacity to meet her obligations to the Powers.[30]

The British and American Governments warned Peking of the danger of signing the proposed convention. Some high Chinese officials including the Viceroy of the Yangtze memorialized the Throne that to reject the proposal from Russia was of the utmost urgency.

Russia, however, announced that her occupation of Manchuria was merely temporary, and that she would not insist on the signature of the convention. But in reality she was resuming her negotiations with China to bring about the conclusion of the agreement.

Negotiations, however, still continued. The crux of the problem was to cancel the provisional treaty, to which the Russian Government agreed. But later a draft of twelve articles was concluded by Lamsdorff, the Russian Minister, known as the Lamsdorff-Yang Yu Convention, which was worse still. It restricted the sovereign rights of China in Manchuria and north China and demanded the concession of the monopoly of the economic development in Manchuria to the Russo-Asiatic Bank.

The proposed draft, though secretly submitted by the Russian Government, quickly reached the ears of other countries. The United States Government then protested that the special privileges given to the Russo-Asiatic Bank would be a direct breach of the treaties made between China and America.

The Chinese people were indignant about it, and asked the government to refuse to sign such a treaty. The Chinese Government had thought that refusal would anger Russia, but it proved later that Russia had been making only empty threats. On February 28, 1901, the Russian Government declared its good intentions towards China and showed dissatisfaction over the attitude of the Powers since the Boxer trouble. Lastly, it declared that the proposal for a treaty should be set aside for the time being, and stated that the whole of

[30] Clyde, op. cit., p. 92.

Manchuria would be returned to China as soon as a strong Chinese Government came into being.

The Anglo-Japanese Alliance had accelerated Russian plans of permanently occupying Manchuria. Fearing that the Anglo-Japanese' Alliance would affect her control of the balance of power in the Far East, Russia extended the Russo-French Alliance to the latter area, merely to counteract the Anglo-Japanese Alliance. On March 26, 1902, Lassal, the Russian Minister in Peking, concluded an agreement with the Chinese Government for the return of Manchuria, in three successive periods of six months each. When the second period for the withdrawal of troops had expired in March 1903, Russia still refused to act according to the treaty stipulations but, instead, presented new demands, including the closing of Manchuria against the economic enterprises of any other nation but Russia. She even concentrated her troops at various strategic parts of Manchuria, and sent troops across the Yalu River, threatening the safety of Korea. Thus, the Russo-Japanese War, which had long been brewing, broke out. It resulted in the defeat of Russia and the conclusion of the Treaty of Portsmouth, whereby Russia entirely lost her predominant position in Manchuria, and after which her penetration into the Far East was terminated with the exception of her interest in the Chinese Eastern Railway, which will be dealt with in the next chapter.

Chapter V

CONSTRUCTION OF CHINESE EASTERN RAILWAY

IN the world history of railway building, no line of communication by rail has involved more international controversies, caused more intense international rivalry and proved more tragic in its results than the Chinese Eastern Railway. It is no exaggeration to say that the railway was 'born in sin'. Only 1,067 miles of single track in length,[1] the Chinese Eastern Railway not only led to the Russo-Japanese War of 1904, but also hastened the collapse of the two greatest empires—the Tsarist and the Manchu. The former played the role of a bully; the latter found itself in the position of a victim. Moreover, the Chinese Eastern Railway whetted the appetite of other Imperialist Powers for the spoils of the Far East, changing the whole map of power politics.

1. Conception of C.E.R.

The modern history of Manchuria started with the construction of the Chinese Eastern Railway, although it is true that the laying of the Peking-Mukden Line has also contributed to the opening up of the country. The stimuli to Russian expansion to the Far East were, on one hand, China's weakness and, on the other, Bismarck's policy. After the Berlin Conference of 1878, Bismarck constantly persuaded Russia to divert her forces to the East so as to leave the Germans a free hand in Europe.

Russia, lacking sea outlets, was trying by all possible means to improve her geographical situation. It was Peter the Great who built St. Petersburg as a new capital, and opened 'the window into Europe'. He also clearly understood the importance of Russian expansion to the East, and therefore paid considerable attention to oriental politics. It was said that Peter was influenced by Witsen, Mayor of Amsterdam, who was a prominent student of the

[1] Wang, C. C., *The Sale of the C.E.R.*, Foreign Affairs, October 1933, p. 65.

Orient.[2] The disagreeable climate of St. Petersburg induced him to look for other seaports. He succeeded in annexing a part of the Baltic coast and, although his attempt on the Black Sea was a failure, he was fairly successful with regard to the Caspian Sea. It is known that Peter left a will of thirteen points of which the third and the seventh were projects aiming at finding an outlet to the sea. However, it was Muraviev who went even further than the will of Peter the Great and opened 'the window into the Pacific'.[3]

The slow development of colonization in the Far East was due to the lack of communication in Russian Asia before the construction of the Trans-Siberian Railway. It was again Muraviev who originated the idea of building a gigantic road from the Baltic to the Pacific which would not only serve economic purposes, but also help in keeping an eye on the growing menace in Asia, caused by the activities of other Powers, especially Great Britain. Count Alexis Ignatieff also submitted a report to Tsar Alexander III in 1887, urging him to build a railroad connecting eastern Siberia with European Russia. A commission was formed to take preliminary measures after the scheme had been accepted by the Tsar.[4] The construction work was started in 1891 at both ends. The Ussuri Railway between Khabarovsk and Vladivostok was begun by Tsar Nicholas II who, before succeeding to the throne, had been sent by his father to make a round-the-world trip, including a visit to the Russian Far East. In 1901 the Trans-Baikalian Railway was completed as far as Chita, almost connecting Moscow with the very border of Manchuria. It was indeed a grand conception, magnificently executed. Concerning the importance of this line, the Russian authorities had announced frankly that it should be looked upon as a 'World Affair'.[5]

2. Russian Eastern Expansion after Sino-Japanese War

The Sino-Japanese War of 1895 ended in China's ignominious defeat. A treaty, signed at Shimonoseki, stipulated the cession of the Liaotung Peninsula to Japan. Tsarist Russia at once realized that her position in Asia would be jeopardized or, at least, pre-

---

[2] Vernadsky, George V., *Political and Diplomatic History of Russia*, 1937, Chapter XIX, p. 227.

[3] Sun Ch'i Ye, *The Sino-Russian Controversies* (in Chinese), 1929-30, Shanghai, 1931, p. 40.

[4] Yakhontoff, op. cit., p. 27.

[5] Romanov, B. A., *Rossia v Manchzhurii* (1892-1906), Leningrad, 1928, p. 4 (in Russian).

judiced, should Liaotung be turned over to the Japanese. For by that time Russia had become accustomed to look upon the Pacific as her future arena of expansion.

Tsar Nicholas II was egged on to this venture by his magnanimous cousin, Kaiser Wilhelm II, who once provokingly saluted Nicholas from a pleasure yacht after the manœuvres at Revel as 'the Admiral of the Pacific', himself adopting the title of 'the Admiral of the Atlantic'. 'I shall certainly do all in my power to keep Europe quiet and also guard the rear of Russia, so that nobody shall hamper your action towards the Far East.' These were the Kaiser's own words addressed to his cousin early in 1895.[6] The Kaiser even complimented his cousin by calling him 'the Master of Peking', when he was congratulating him on the occasion of the successful action at Port Arthur.[7] Thus, having secured promises of backing from Germany, Russia made a strong representation to Japan on April 23, 1895, advising her to return Liaotung to China and accept a large sum as indemnity instead. Owing to the joint intervention of the three Powers, Japan was compelled to accept the offer. A further pretence of friendship was made by Russia in the form of a loan of 400,000,000 francs, negotiated through French bankers at four per cent interest, to enable China to pay the indemnity exacted by Japan. The loan was absorbed by a Franco-Russian syndicate, and the security was the revenue receipts of the Chinese Maritime Customs, which were in turn guaranteed by the Russian Government.

3. Li Hung-chang's Mission

Then came into existence the Sino-Russian Treaty of 1896. At the time of the coronation of Nicholas II, the Manchu Government selected Wang Chih-chung as their representative. Count Cassini, the Russian Minister to China, at once informed the Tsung-li Yamen (Chinese Foreign Office) that the coronation just after the tripartite intervention for the return of the Liaotung Peninsula to China had its significance and should not be taken as merely a formal ceremony in view of the close relationship between the two countries. Cassini then hinted that none would be more acceptable at St. Petersburg than Li Hung-chang.[8] Meanwhile, to ensure the appointment of Li,

[6] Levine, I. D., Letters from the Kaiser to the Tsar, p. 10.
[7] ibid., p. 46.
[8] Gérard, A., Ma Mission en Chine (1893-1897), p. 124.

the Tsar sent a personal message to the Dowager Empress Tsu Hsi that it would please him greatly to see Li at his Court.

Later on, Li Hung-chang watched the development of events with interest and concern. He had his own scheme worked out, which, in short, was to play Russia against Japan. The Russian Government also regarded him as the most promising individual to deal with. Hence their eager desire to have Li participate in Nicholas's coronation. Complying with the wish of the Tsar, the Empress Dowager appointed Li to attend the ceremonies at St. Petersburg on behalf of China.

There was also an important figure in Russia who played a role similar to Li Hung-chang's in China. The name of Count Sergei Yulievitch Witte, then Minister of Finance of the Russian Government, will be always remembered in connection with the construction of the Chinese Eastern Railway. It is no exaggeration to say that he was the chief creator of the Chinese Eastern Railway. He must be given credit as one of the most able statesmen and practical economists of his time. We find him in the railroad service, in which he was later to play so distinctive a part, as early as 1877, when Russia was at war with Turkey. Later, he showed great efficiency in this capacity, and his promotions were so rapid that before 1892 he was made Minister of Communications and soon afterwards Minister of Finance. It is principally in the last capacity that we are concerned with him here.

Witte early showed interest in the Far East, which afforded the best available outlet for Russian expansion. He was specially versed in the state of affairs in Manchuria, and the building of the Trans-Siberian Railway was largely due to his efforts. Witte was one of the special commissioners appointed by the Tsar to discuss the question of intervention in the peace terms imposed by Japan on China, and he was mainly responsible for effecting Russian intervention. He advocated at a conference that:

' Russia's best interests demanded that China remain unchanged and that no Power be allowed to increase its territorial possessions at China's expense, that the integrity of the Chinese Empire be upheld, that Japan, as a victorious nation, be permitted to recover her war expenditure by imposing a more or less considerable indemnity upon China, and that, failing to obtain these results, there was no other course left to us than to open active operations.'[9]

[9] Witte, *The Memoirs of Count Witte*, 1921, p. 83.

Witte's ambitions in Manchuria were mainly concerned with colonization. He firmly believed that, firstly, Manchuria itself would repay all the expenditure incurred by Russia, a portion of which came from the French loan, in connection with the construction and future operation of the railway. Secondly, Manchuria would no doubt directly satisfy French capitalists with regard to the future tendency of exports. The splendid efficiency shown in the construction of the Trans-Siberian Railway was largely due to the financial support of French bankers. More than half of the capital of the newly established Russo-Chinese Bank came from France, where money was plentiful, and the Russian project was thought to be a good investment.

The building of the Trans-Siberian Railway to Vladivostok terminus struck some serious difficulties. From Chita to Vladivostok the road bed had to be built along the banks of the Amur and the Ussuri Rivers, which meant not only a detour in a great semi-circle, entailing an extra actual length of some 500 miles, but that this section of the railroad would have to pass through practically waste land with hardly any human habitation. This was unsatisfactory, both from the political and economic viewpoints, to say nothing of the enormously increased construction expenditure. It was Witte who originated the plan to build the railroad from China to Vladivostok directly through Manchuria, thus saving the expenditure of some 35,000,000 roubles. Notwithstanding the existing Russian influence over China, it was felt that this big project should receive the official sanction of the Manchu Government. As Russia had just retrieved for China the Liaotung Peninsula, it was only natural that China would be grateful and show her gratitude in a tangible manner. The only concern was how to make the most effective approach, so as to ensure maximum benefit. Consequently, Witte looked upon the coronation of Nicholas II as a God-sent opportunity to bring China's Grand Old Man to St. Petersburg to discuss with him the issue tête-à-tête and in a most confidential way.

Before describing the arrival of Li Hung-chang at St. Petersburg, it seems necessary to devote some space here to the activities of Count Cassini, then Russian Minister to Peking. Russia's request to build a railway through Manchuria, which had been made as early as April 1896, aroused suspicions in Peking at the very outset. In the report sent by Count Cassini, it was alleged that China, instead of paying respect to Russia, became suspicious and lost confidence in her, as it was always being predicted that Russia would soon present some special demand, which could not be complied with by the high Chinese officials. Other foreign advisers to the Chinese Government were trying to do all they could to embarrass negotiations.[10] The Chinese Government's plan to prolong the Shanhaikwan Railway to Chinchow was further evidence that China wanted to reject the Russian demand. According to Cassini, it was a proof that China would have nothing to do with Russia.[11] Practically speaking, such a project could in no way compete with the gigantic Russian scheme, and moreover, Chinese construction was so slow that they constructed only 115 miles in three years.

Count Cassini again received instructions to conclude negotiations at Peking, but the time was very unfavourable to Russia. The original scheme for constructing a branch line direct to Peking was not deemed fit for negotiation as it had already met with many obstacles. The British worked in secret for the concession of the Shanhaikwan railway project, which consequently fell into their hands. France, instead of helping Russia as predicted by Cassini, became her keen competitor. The French Minister, Gerard, had used his best efforts to obtain special rights for France, and had expressed to Chinese officials his opinion that the Manchurian Railway would be a tricky business. The Americans also took keen interest in this subject, and once made a proposal through Bush to the Russian Minister to organize a syndicate with a capital of $250,000,000 gold to build all the necessary railways in China, including the Manchurian Railway, with the approval of the Russian Government.[12] But, according to instructions received by Cassini, the right of building the Manchurian Railway and its branches could only be given to a Russian company, without any foreign participants.

Neither Bush nor Cassini felt optimistic with regard to this matter. Count Cassini visited the Tsungli Yamen twice—on April 6 and 18, 1896—and persuaded the Chinese high officials to agree to the lease of the territory to Russians for the purpose of building the Manchurian Railway. He even mentioned that this was the only way to make Russia help China against further Japanese aggression. In spite of his endeavours, the result was a complete failure. The Chinese Government, after serious consideration lasting twelve days, determined that they would never consent to the building of the Manchurian Railway by any foreign Power or any foreign con-

[10] Count Cassini's letter to Lobanoff, January 30, 1896.
[11] Romanov, op. cit., p. 101.
[12] ibid., p. 102.

cern. They could only agree to the employment of Russian engineers and the use of Russian materials in the building of the railway. This magnanimous offer was considered by Cassini as ridiculous, because China had no funds to meet the necessary expenditure. Eventually he informed St. Petersburg that if Russia insisted upon building the railway through Chinese territory, there remained only one thing to do, namely, to warn the Chinese Government that a flat refusal on their part would cause serious concern.[13] Thus, without previous preparations and appropriate funds, Count Cassini's efforts in Peking met with no success. There was much talk about the existence of the famous 'Cassini Convention', signed in Peking before Li went to St. Petersburg, but afterwards it was revealed that no agreement had been reached before the Li-Lobanoff Secret Treaty, signed on June 4, 1896, in St. Petersburg.

Scarcely had Li Hung-chang arrived at Port Said, the mouth of the Suez Canal, than an agent of the Russian Government, Prince Ukhtomsky, President of the Russo-Chinese Bank, took charge of him under the pretence of offering him a courteous escort to St. Petersburg, but actually to make sure that he was not first met by the representatives of any other Power and enticed to another European capital. As it was agreed by the two countries to transfer the outstanding problem to St. Petersburg for an amicable settlement, it was only natural that the whole enterprise fell into the hands of Count Witte, who lost no time in approaching Li. Concerning the preliminary talk, the Count made the following record in his diary:

'In my conferences with Li Hung-chang I dwelt on the services which we had recently done to his country. I assured him that, having proclaimed the principle of China's territorial integrity, we intended to adhere to it in the future; but, to be able to uphold this principle, I argued, we must be in a position, in case of emergency, to render China armed assistance. Such aid we would not be able to render her until both European Russia and Vladivostok were connected with China by rail, our armed forces being concentrated in European Russia. I called his attention to the fact that, although during China's war with Japan we did despatch some detachments from Vladivostok, they moved so slowly, because of the absence of railroad communications, that when they reached Kirin the war was over. Thus, I argued, to uphold the territorial integrity of the Chinese Empire, it was

[13] Count Cassini's letter to Lobanoff, May 1, 1896.

necessary for us to have a railroad running along the shortest possible route to Vladivostok, across the northern part of Mongolia and Manchuria. I also pointed out to Li Hung-chang that the projected railway would raise the productivity of our possessions and the Chinese territories it would cross.'[14]

Li Hung-chang at first objected, but, after a private audience with the Tsar, he agreed to the proposal. He telegraphed back to Peking that he was in favour of the scheme and stated that the building of the railway was beyond China's financial capacity, but if the concession were given to the Russo-Chinese Bank at Shanghai, China could secure the right of control, and no difficulties would arise. He emphasized the fact that Russia had no idea of encroaching upon Chinese territory, and that the sole aim of the building of this railroad was to facilitate the prompt conveyance of troops to China's rescue in case of need. It was also the idea of Li Hung-chang to form an alliance with Russia in order to take revenge for the humiliating defeat by Japan, and his proposal to the Throne was duly endorsed by the Empress Dowager. Such remarkable progress in the negotiations was a great surprise to Count Witte, who could hardly have expected the same terms from Cassini in Peking. This most complicated diplomatic question was made easier by the presence of Li Hung-chang at the Russian capital.

4. Li-Lobanoff Negotiations

The negotiations for a treaty were carried on between Li on the one hand and Prince Lobanoff-Rostovsky, Russian Minister of Foreign Affairs, and Count Witte, Minister of Finance, on the other. The text of this document was never made public until the Washington Conference, when the presentation of all existing treaties, secret or otherwise, was made necessary, and a telegraphic summary was given by the Chinese delegation. Only after the Russian Revolution was the original treaty found among the archives of the Foreign Ministry in Moscow.

This ' Secret Sino-Russian Treaty of Alliance ' provided for military co-operation, directed against Japanese aggression in Russian eastern Asia, China and Korea. In order to facilitate the transportation of Russian troops to China's aid in time of emergency, a direct railroad from Russia to China was an absolute necessity. After long dis-

[14] Witte, op. cit., p. 89.

cussions, Li Hung-chang agreed to give permission for building a railroad through Manchuria along a straight line between China and Vladivostok, but insisted that the railroad must be built by a private corporation and not constructed or owned by the Russian Treasury. Li also agreed to cede a strip of land sufficient for the construction and operation of the railway. Within that territory the corporation was permitted to have its own police and to exercise full control.

After lengthy discussion, Witte agreed to form a private corporation, to be called the Chinese Eastern Railway Corporation, which was to be, of course, completely in the hands of the Russian Government. Since nominally it was a private corporation, it would be within the jurisdiction of the Ministry of Finance. Perhaps Witte's only failure was that he was unable to persuade Li Hung-chang to grant the right of constructing this railroad to the Russian Government. Witte himself denied that this was a failure, and said that it was merely an illusion. He also insisted upon building a branch line to a seaport in south Manchuria. Li agreed to this, provided that the branch line should be of standard gauge, not the Russian wide gauge. Witte strongly opposed this, insisting that the branch line in south Manchuria should be of the same gauge as that in north Manchuria, but without avail.

From this it may be inferred that Witte had the ambition firstly to establish Russia's influence in south Manchuria in order to stop any Japanese military encroachments from the Korean border, and secondly to connect the ice-free port of Dairen with Russia by a railway of Russian gauge, so that the Russians could easily be made masters of the port. In this way, all strategic and political questions would be simultaneously solved.[15] Li Hung-chang had already made concessions, but would yield no further on the following two points: (1) The contract must be with a private corporation; (2) The branch railway in south Manchuria must be of standard gauge. These stipulations, made by China's Grand Old Man, were no doubt meant to restrain Russia's further political ambitions which might directly threaten the Chinese capital.

After the signing of the Secret Treaty, Count Witte wrote as follows:

'The Russo-Chinese Alliance meant two things: first, a great railroad, tending as far as Vladivostok on a straight line, without

[15] Romanov, op. cit., p. 115.

coming northward along the Amur River, and second, firmly established peaceful relations with our neighbour, the Chinese Empire.'

During that time there was another project for building a railway from Kiakhta to Peking, but it met with opposition on the part of Witte, who considered Vladivostok, as a seaport, to be the most desirable terminus for the Trans-Siberian Railway. He also predicted that such a line from Kiakhta to Peking would have brought an alliance of other Powers against Russia.[16]

Although the Secret Treaty of Alliance was signed by Li, Witte and Lobanoff, the final text was not agreed upon until June 1896, when Li had left St. Petersburg. The details were worked out by P. K. Romanov, the Russian Assistant Minister of Finance and Shu Ching-t'eng, the Chinese Minister at St. Petersburg. On August 26, 1896, the treaty was formally ratified by the Manchu Government, and on September 8, the agreement concerning the construction of the Chinese Eastern Railway was signed by Shu, representing China, and Prince Ukhtomsky and Rothstern representing the Russo-Chinese Bank.[17]

In spite of the stipulation in the treaty that China had the right to redeem the railway after a period of thirty-six years, or the whole line had to pass free of charge to the Chinese Government after eighty years, the Russian Government view it with little concern, for St. Petersburg thought at that time that, before the expiration of either period, Russia would have been able to put Manchuria under her control if not under her occupation.[18]

5. Organization of C.E.R. Company

Regarding the relationship between the Russo-Chinese Bank, the Chinese Eastern Railway Company and the Russian Treasury, it was evident that from the very outset the Russian Government had already obtained preferential rights as, practically speaking, the whole enterprise was turned over to them. The understanding was as follows:

The Russo-Chinese Bank was to secure all the shares in the Chinese Eastern Railway Company. The capital was divided into

---

[16] Witte, op. cit., p. 86.
[17] See also Gerard, op. cit., p. 147.
[18] Clyde, op. cit., p. 60.

1,000 shares, each share of 5,000 roubles. Out of the 1,000 shares, 700 were to be subscribed for by the Russian Government. Upon the issue of the shares the Russo-Chinese Bank was to hand over these 700 shares to the Russian Government, while the remaining 300 shares were to be subscribed for by individuals, either at the time of the signing of the agreement, or within six months after the agreement was signed. The Russian Government Bank would lend money to the Russo-Chinese Bank without interest, while the Russo-Chinese Bank could use the 700 shares already handed over to the Government Bank, together with any remaining shares which had not been sold to individuals, as security. The amount of money to be borrowed from the Government Bank should be equivalent to the face value of all the shares. Therefore, the dividend, if any, of the total shares, would become the profit of the Russian Government. In other words, the Russian Government had fully paid up the value of the shares and could take over all the shares whenever they thought fit. When the Russo-Chinese Bank turned over the 700 shares to the Russian Treasury, the Government, if requested by the Bank, could take up the remaining 300 shares not subscribed for by individuals.[19]

We see from the above that all that remained to the Russo-Chinese Bank were 300 shares, which were to be subscribed for by private individuals. The reason for this arrangement was the fear of the participation of French Bankers. Should they raise any objection against the Russo-Chinese Agreement, the Russian Government would be ready to turn over to them the remaining 300 shares. Since there was no disapproval from the French Bankers, the Russo-Chinese Bank, on sending the regulations of the Chinese Eastern Railway Company to the Ministry of Finance for sanction, announced that it was not necessary for the shares of the Chinese Eastern Railway Company to be sold to any third party. Hence, the Bank could, in accordance with the previous understanding, turn over the total amount of shares to the Russian Government.[20]

The regulations of the Chinese Eastern Railway Company were sanctioned on December 4, 1896. The issue of shares was started on December 17 and was advertised in the *Government Gazette* of the same date. The official time for the issuing of shares was fixed for

[19] Witte's petition to the Tsar, together with the draft of the Agreement May 18, 1896. The petition was written by Witte personally.
[20] Application from the Russo-Chinese Bank to the Russian Minister of Finance, November 4, 1896.

9 a.m., and, naturally, nobody was able to make any subscription. Only a few minutes later the office was closed. Thereupon the entire interest in the Chinese Eastern Railway Company became the property of the Russian Treasury.[21]

In the organization of the Chinese Eastern Railway Company, China appeared merely as a nominal participant. She had contributed only 5,000,000 kuping taels towards the cost of construction, while the total cost amounted to 400,000,000 to 600,000,000 roubles. It was understood that all profits and losses were to be borne in proportion to the number of shares.[22] Count Witte once wrote: 'At first, the Chinese Government and also our Treasury invested heavily in the institution! '[23]

Witte immediately requested the Chinese Eastern Railway Company to compensate the Russian Government for 'investigation expenses in Manchuria', naming a sum of 4,000,000 roubles. In this way, only 1,000,000 roubles capital was left to the Chinese Eastern Railway Company.[24] Since the shares, whose face value was 5,000,000 roubles, were all subscribed by the Treasury, why was it necessary to expend four-fifths of the subscribed capital in compensating the Treasury?

In order to understand this, we have to refer back to the original agreement between China and Russia. It was clearly stated in the agreement that, after eighty years, Russia should retrocede the whole line to China free of charge, and also that after thirty-six years (i.e. 1938), the Chinese Government would have the right to redeem the railway. Witte finally agreed to this, but he was determined that the fundamental condition for the redemption of the railway must be the guarantee of a huge profit to Russia over and above the return of what had been spent. Of course, it was only natural that Witte should try to make redemption difficult or even practically impossible. According to Article 12 of the Agreement, the Chinese Government was to reimburse the whole of the capital, as well as all outstanding loans and interest at the time of redemption. That is to say, after thirty-six years the Chinese Government would have to pay about 700,000,000 roubles for redemption. But even that China might by then be able to do. Therefore, Witte

[21] Letter from Rothstern to Witte (in French), December 17, 1896.
[22] See MacMurray, *Treaties and Agreements with and concerning China*, Vol. I, p. 78.
[23] Witte, op. cit., p. 85.
[24] Report by the Financial Committee of the C.E.R. Company on January 31 and March 15, 1897.

asked the Company to pay back four-fifths of the subscribed capital as compensation for the Russian Government's so-called 'investigation expenses in Manchuria'. Consequently, the Russo-Chinese Bank, under the direct control of the Ministry of Finance, had nothing to lose but was bound to gain.

In spite of the fact that the President of the Company was to be Chinese, in practice he had very little power. Matters were so manipulated that the Chinese were prevented from exercising their rights. The Russian Government having become the sole shareholder and creditor of the Company, it goes without saying that they secured entire control of ownership. It was further stipulated that the statutes of the Chinese Eastern Railway Company should follow those of the Russian railways. The result was that all important affairs, such as the employment of high officials, engineering and technical decisions, etc., had first to be approved by the Minister of Finance. In other words, the genius of Count Witte secured for Russia control of the railway in Manchuria for a period of eighty years.

There were many other points of advantage to the Russians, namely: (1) The adoption of the Russian wide gauge of five feet. (2) The stipulation that all merchandise proceeding in either direction need pay only one-third the usual Chinese Maritime Customs' charges. (3) The right of the Company to fix rates for the transportation of passengers and merchandise at its discretion. (4) The exemption of the Company from all taxes on materials and land used for the construction. (5) The right of the Company to acquire the ground space necessary for the construction of the line, and also lands in the vicinity of the railway necessary for procuring sand, stone, lime, etc., free in the case of state property or at current market value in the case of privately owned property. (6) The absolute and exclusive right of the Company to administer its lands and erect any kind of construction thereon. The last point was extremely vague, as the exact amount of land required was not mentioned, and it gave rise to the acquisition of extensive areas of Chinese territory by Russians, who claimed that jurisdiction in the growing cities and towns throughout the territory of the railway belonged to the railway company. The two last-mentioned items clearly expressed the idea of what later came to be called the 'railway zone', not only for the purpose of giving extraterritorial rights to the Russians, but also for the organization of a special court in the zone. This led to the establishment of a Municipal Council in

Harbin in 1907 which, together with its police forces, was entirely under the control of the Chinese Eastern Railway Company. Harbin, Russian official and commercial centre in Manchuria, became a centre of corruption and did not give a good reputation to the Russians in the Far East.

Such a policy not only interfered with Chinese politics and infringed upon Chinese sovereignty, but undoubtedly tended to lead to a gradual annexation of Chinese territories by Russia. The fact that the Company assumed authority to issue regulations and impose taxes on all merchants was also of the utmost importance. On February 10, 1908, an ordinance was issued to the effect that fines or imprisonment would be imposed upon those who failed to comply with Russian-made regulations, particularly those relating to police, building, sanitary and trade regulations, or who failed to pay all taxes and dues imposed by the administration of the municipalities. Thus the 'railway zone' was virtually turned into a concession. But worst of all was the fact that the control over this 'railway zone' was extended up to the railway terminus.

There is one more point worthy of notice. It was stipulated that the dividend surplus of the railway should be applied to the redemption fund on China's behalf, but what was to be the maximum dividend declared was not mentioned. The result was that there never was any surplus at all.[25] This omission was quite important, for the surplus dividend brought by a railroad of such magnitude might have been several times the original capital of five million gold roubles. This point was raised in 1920 by China, and a certain scale was agreed upon between the Chinese Government and the Russo-Chinese Bank, whereby a certain proportion of the surplus was set aside as dividends and another proportion as redemption fund.[26]

The Russo-Chinese Bank, acting as a vanguard of Russia's aggression against China, was reorganized and assumed the name of the Russo-Asiatic Bank. Survey work on the Chinese Eastern Railway was started in April 1897, and construction began the following August. In July 1903, the Chinese Eastern Railway started to operate.

[25] C. C. Wang, *The Sale of the Chinese Eastern Railway*, Foreign Affairs, October 1933, p. 68.
[26] Weigh, op. cit., p. 71.

6. *Lease of Port Arthur and Dairen-wan*

With the completion of the line, Vladivostok, Russia's naval base in the Far East, was rendered accessible by land. But Vladivostok was soon found to be no better than St. Petersburg, on account of the fact that the port was frozen during the winter months. Consequently, Russia kept on looking for an ice-free harbour. On the southern tip of the Liaotung Peninsula are twin harbours—Port Arthur and Dairen-wan—admirably suited to serve as naval and commercial ports respectively. These had long been looked upon with covetous eyes both by Japan and Russia. The latter requested a lease of the two harbours for a period of twenty-five years, with the privilege of building a branch railway from Harbin to Port Arthur. A Sino-Russian Convention was signed on March 27, 1898, and on March 29 the Russian flag was hoisted in Port Arthur. In 1899 the building of a 'free port' in Dairen-wan was begun.

It should be remembered that Port Arthur and Dairen-wan had both been ceded to Japan under the Shimonoseki Treaty of 1895, and returned to China only after the Tripartite Intervention, in which Russia took the most active part, forcing Japan to withdraw. Scarcely three years had elapsed, when Russia herself occupied Port Arthur following Germany's occupation of Kiaochow. Witte indignantly protested against the measure, stating:

'I remind my hearers that we had declared the principle of China's territorial integrity and that on the strength of that principle we forced Japan to withdraw from the Liaotung Peninsula, which comprises Port Arthur and Dairen-wan.'[27]

In spite of Witte's protest, Nicholas II carried out this project, the author of which was Muraviev, Minister of Foreign Affairs.

Germany's acquisition of Kiaochow was the result of a trick played by Kaiser Wilhelm II on his cousin, Nicholas II, when he visited him in Peterhof, and the occupation of Kiaochow and Port Arthur by Germany and Russia respectively was agreed upon by the two potentates without the knowledge of the Russian Ministers. Witte was not aware of the fact that the seizure of Port Arthur was a direct consequence of the acquisition of Kiaochow, and that it was entirely an imperial deal.[28] Witte wrote:

[27] Witte, op. cit., p. 99.
[28] Dillon, E. J., *The Eclipse of Russia*, New York, 1918, p. 251.

'The Chinese Eastern Railway was designed exclusively for cultural and peaceful purposes, but jingoist adventurers turned it into a means of political aggression involving the violation of treaties, the breaking of freely given promises and the disregard of the elementary interests of other nationalities.'[29]

The 'other nationalities' naturally became alarmed and acted accordingly. France seized Kwangchow-wan on May 27, and Britain secured the lease of Wei-hai-wei on July 1, to maintain the balance of power at the expense of China.[30] The lease of Dairen-wan and Port Arthur also led to the armed clash with Japan in 1904, about which Witte wrote frankly in his diary:

'The agreement was an act of the highest importance. Had we faithfully observed it, we should have been spared the disgrace of the Japanese War—I may say here that we ourselves broke the agreement and brought about the situation which we are now facing in the Far East.'

He considered himself an adherent of 'peaceful penetration', and he held Tsar Nicholas II responsible for the seizure of Port Arthur and the intrusion into south Manchuria, which made the Russo-Japanese War inevitable. Metaphorically speaking, the Chinese Eastern Railway was born as Count Witte's lawful child, while Port Arthur was the illegitimate offspring of Tsar Nicholas II, born as a result of his crooked and childish play of aggression, which contrasts unfavourably with Witte's 'peaceful penetration' in the spheres of commerce and culture. Witte once made an appropriate metaphor, stating that he could not be held responsible for his guests running wild and committing shame after he had taken them to the aquarium. He, however, omitted to say that even if his guests had all been on their best behaviour, the expense of the expedition would have been enormous.

The branch line of the Chinese Eastern Railway, known as the South Manchurian Railway, was completed in 1900, though a part of the main line was not finished until July 1903. Two years before, sectional operation had actually begun. The building cost of this railway was estimated at four hundred million gold roubles. Another branch line to Newchang was also constructed by the Company to

[29] Witte, op. cit., p. 102.
[30] Korff, S. A., Russia's Foreign Relations, 1922, p. 65.

facilitate the transportation of the necessary materials and provisions required in the construction of the South Manchurian Railway. During the Boxer uprising in 1900, the Chinese Eastern Railway was seriously damaged. Russia brought her troops to Manchuria and stayed there for almost two years. This action aroused suspicion and fears on the part of Great Britain, and made her sign the Treaty of Alliance with Japan, which contributed to the outbreak of the Russo-Japanese War.

The Japanese Government, having secured the support of England and the U.S.A., severed relations with Russia, and the Japanese opened hostilities by an attack upon the Russian squadron at Port Arthur without a formal declaration of war. The Russo-Japanese War was fought in Manchuria, on Chinese territory. China, though in a secret Treaty of Alliance with Russia, declared friendly neutrality in favour of Japan, and many local Chinese helped the Japanese army. The ignominious defeat of Russia, which was probably due to her unpreparedness,[31] resulted in the Treaty of Portsmouth, signed on September 5, 1905. By virtue of this treaty, Russia ceded to Japan, with China's consent, the southern branch of the Chinese Eastern Railway from Changchun to Dairen and Port Arthur, and also her other concessions in Korea and Manchuria.

7. America's Open Door Policy

Perhaps it will not be out of place to mention here America's 'Open Door' policy towards China and her role in Chinese Eastern Railway affairs. Although the United States was the only great power to keep hands off China at that time, she paid great attention to Manchurian railroad affairs as she had great commercial interests in China, which had to be safeguarded.

The continuous adventure in Korea and south Manchuria carried on by Nicholas II under the influence of an unscrupulous courtier named Bezobrazoff, compelled Witte to quit his office after warning had not been favourably accepted by the Tsar. The Minister of Foreign Affairs and the Minister of War also tendered their resignations. Baron Rosen, the Russian Minister in Tokyo, had warned his own government that inasmuch as Russia had already occupied an ice-free port in Manchuria, she should refrain from further encroachment upon Korea, because Japan could never allow others to lay

[31] See Kuropatkin, *The Russian Army and the Russo-Japanese War*, Chapters VIII and X.

hands on it. The Japanese Government even made hints to St. Petersburg through Baron Rosen that a reciprocal agreement could be made for preserving Japan's influence in Korea as Russia's in Manchuria without interference with each other. Russia, however, made no response. The result was, no further negotiation but an acceleration of the outbreak of the Russo-Japanese War.[32]

Shortly after the signature of the Portsmouth Protocol, Mr. E. H. Harriman, at the suggestion of the American Minister in Tokyo, journeyed to Japan with the idea of reaching an understanding with Tokyo regarding the sale of the South Manchurian Railway, which had just been ceded by Russia. Harriman had conceived a plan for a round-the-world transportation system under unified American control by way of Japan, Manchuria, Siberia, European Russia and the Atlantic Ocean. The Japanese section of the Chinese Eastern Railway—namely, the South Manchurian Railway—was then in a very unsatisfactory condition. Therefore he proposed to reconstruct and re-equip it with American capital, and make it the eastern part of his proposed Trans-Asiatic Line.[33] He supposed that the Russian Government, having lost Port Arthur, would gladly sell its section of this railway.

The Japanese Government was at first very favourable to the Harriman scheme, as Harriman had established close relations with the Japanese Government by virtue of American assistance in floating Japan's last war loan. In fact, the Japanese Government suggested Harriman's trip and encouraged his project.[34] Neither Prince Ito nor Premier Katsura had any objections to the sale, and Count Inouye was even of the opinion that it would be very foolish to let such a great chance slip.[35] On October 12, 1906, Harriman signed a 'Memorandum of Preliminary Understanding' with Count Katsura as follows:

'A syndicate to be formed to provide capital for the South Manchurian Railway, acquired by the Japanese Government, and its appurtenances: the rehabilitation, equipment, reconstruction, and extension of the same and the completion and improvement of the terminals at Dairen (Dalny); and it is understood that the two parties are to have joint and equal ownership in the properties

[32] See Baron Rosen, *Forty Years of Diplomacy*, Vol. I, pp. 156-7.
[33] Kennan, George, *E. H. Harriman: a Biography*, Vol. II, p. 3.
[34] Croly, Herbert, *Willard Straight*, p. 239.
[35] Kennan, George, op. cit., p. 13.

acquired. Permission to work coal mines (in connection with the railroad) to be given to a corporation by " special agreement in which there shall be joint interest and representation ".[36]

Harriman left for San Francisco in the hope that the agreement would be ratified even before he arrived there. Shortly afterwards he again set out for Tokyo, but this time Baron Komura strongly protested against the Harriman-Katsura understanding, stating that the Japanese people, disappointed with the peace settlement, would not allow the sale of ' nearly all that they had gained in two years of successful war '.[37] Harriman was therefore asked to hold the memorandum in abeyance. After Baron Komura had concluded the Peking Agreement with China, Harriman was notified by a telegram from Komura at Peking that it was the Chinese Government who refused to admit American capital for rehabilitating the railway, and in due course China would herself like to engage together with Japan in the work of rehabilitation. But China had never been consulted about the Harriman scheme, and, naturally, had never expressed any opposition. This statement was made by Tang Shao-yi, the Chinese Envoy, in Washington D.C. in 1909,[38] where he was sent to express China's gratitude for American retrocession of a part of the Boxer indemnity to China. Meanwhile, Japan found no difficulty in floating a loan in London sufficient to restore the South Manchurian Railway to running condition.

After the failure of Harriman's plan to purchase the South Manchurian Railway and the Chinese Eastern Railway, American efforts at securing an economic foothold in Manchuria still continued. Next came the Knox Neutralization Plan for securing all Manchurian railways under foreign control. Willard Straight, American Consul-General in Mukden, an energetic young man, was closely associated with Harriman. He succeeded in reaching an understanding with Governor Tang Shao-yi in the summer of 1907 for a loan of $20,000,000 for the purpose of establishing a Manchurian Bank, which would act as a financial agent for constructing the Hsinmintun-Aigun Railway and for the development of Manchurian commerce and industry. Both Russia and Japan promised not to interfere. Straight submitted the memorandum to Harriman, when he was recalled by the State Department. The Department was informed by Harriman that his banks were ready to finance the

[36] Kennan, George, ibid., p. 14.
[37] ibid., p. 16.
[38] Bland, *Recent Events and Present Politics in China*, p. 310.

Manchurian Bank, and notes were accordingly exchanged.[39] Harriman then went to Europe, and in June 1909 he entered into negotiations with M. Kokovtsoff, the Russian Minister of Finance, who was willing to sell the Chinese Eastern Railway to an international syndicate. Harriman despatched Straight as representative of the American group to China to induce her to grant the American syndicate a concession for the Chinchow-Aigun Railway. In spite of Harriman's death on September 9, 1909, Straight went ahead and signed a preliminary agreement with Hsi Liang, the Viceroy of Manchuria, for the construction of the railway.

The famous Knox Neutralization Plan came after the signing of the Chinchow-Aigun Railway Agreement, believed to be first originated by Straight. The memorandum was despatched separately to five Powers, namely Great Britain, France, Germany, Russia and Japan, after Great Britain had signified her approval in principle.[40]

It is interesting to note that, when Reynolds Hitt, German Charge d'Affaires in Washington, telegraphed back to Berlin the whole text of the Knox memorandum delivered on December 17, 1909, Kaiser Wilhelm II immediately predicted that the U.S. Government was too optimistic about the Russian and Japanese Governments agreeing to such terms. The Kaiser wrote in German: 'Certainly not by their own will' on the document, sent by von Bethmann-Hollweg, the German Premier, concerning Russia and Japan in the Knox Memorandum. The Kaiser agreed to the proposal made by his Premier that Germany should follow the lead of America, but he added in his commentary: 'Agree, let America go ahead, and any conflict or hatred which might occur is to be shouldered by the U.S. Government.'[41]

The Knox proposal, theoretically speaking, was not assailable, for he was following Hay's policy of the 'Open Door' in China, but diplomatically he made a serious blunder when he first approached Great Britain instead of Russia and Japan, which were the interested Powers and those most likely to oppose the plan. Of course, he trusted too much that Russia would be willing to sell her interests in the Chinese Eastern Railway. According to Harriman, Russian consent should be secured first, thus dividing Russia from Japan, with the result that Japan might be obliged to acquiesce in a *fait accompli*.[42] Russia was dissatisfied with the American proposal,

---

[39] Croly, op. cit., p. 272.
[40] See *Foreign Relations of the United States*, 1910, pp. 234-35.
[41] *Die Diplomatischen Akten des Answartigen Amtes 1871-1914.*
[42] Croly, op. cit., p. 297.

because she was not given due consideration at the outset of the negotiations. Isvolsky, the Russian Foreign Minister, vigorously opposed the proposal, though it had previously been endorsed by the Finance Minister.[43] America was conscious of having made a mistake and therefore stopped the loan negotiations. It was the opinion of Russia that nothing could be settled without her consent being first obtained. Had Knox taken the proper step as suggested by Straight, the whole affair might have been brought to an entirely different conclusion.

8. Japan's Objection

With regard to Japan, the American Ambassador at Tokyo was instructed to deliver only the substance of the memorandum sent to England, adding that this proposal had already been approved by Great Britain. Japan's suspicion with regard to American motives was increased. Tokyo was notified that Japanese participation in the Chinchow-Aigun Railway would be welcome, while the memorandum sent to the Russian Foreign Office did not mention the Chinchow-Aigun project. This raised the doubt in Russian circles that Russia might be deprived of the right of equal participation. These suspicions drew Japan and Russia together to defend their interests in opposition to the Knox Neutralization Scheme. On January 21, 1910, both Japan and Russia sent their formal replies, expressing their flat opposition almost in the same language, evidently after much consultation between themselves. The Russian note stated that Russia's 'interests involved in the Chinese Eastern Railway are notorious'. Therefore, to urge her to relinquish her rights and privileges would be 'to inflict on these interests an injury which nothing would warrant'.[44] The Japanese reply, with regard to the Chinchow-Aigun Railway, stated that the Japanese Government would agree to the principle of participation, but not until 'the necessary details regarding the matter are known'.[45] The Japanese Government then sent a note to China, stating their conditions for participating in the Chinchow-Aigun project. They concerned the furnishing of engineers and railway materials, and contained a stipulation that such a branch line should be built in such a way as to connect it with the South Manchurian Railway.

China could hardly acquiesce in such exorbitant demands. Her

[43] Croly, op. cit., p. 310.
[44] Full text given in Foreign Relations of the United States, 1910, pp. 249-52.
[45] ibid., p. 252.

refusal was considered tantamount to a flat objection to this project, though she had approved and consented to the neutralization plan. Moreover, the Russian and Japanese Governments had gone one step further through their representatives in Peking. The Japanese warning to the Chinese Government was this: 'Before the Chinese Government determines anything, the consent of my government must be obtained. Otherwise it will be hard to estimate the seriousness of the trouble that may be caused in the relations of the two countries.'[46] The Russian Minister in Peking also pressed China not to sign the final contract for the construction of the Chinchow Aigun Railway, which would actually reach Russian territory, alleging that this road would seriously affect the interests of Russia, both militarily and politically. He also revealed Russia's intention to exclude America from the development of Manchuria.[47]

The failure of the Knox Neutralization Plan was, on the one hand, due to the initial error of the State Department, which acted without sufficient diplomatic preparation and, on the other, to the selfish aims of Russia and Japan in the Chinese Eastern and South Manchurian Railways, which went contrary to the so-called 'Open Door' policy. The Knox neutralization proposal was actually detrimental to China in its results instead of bringing her any benefit, for from then on, whenever China wished to build any railway in her own territory, her neighbours, Russia and Japan, had first to be consulted. Furthermore, the Russo-Japanese Open Convention and the second secret treaty concluded on July 4, 1910, were also consequences of the failure of the Knox proposal, which brought these two countries into close co-operation. (The first secret Russo-Japanese Convention was signed on July 30, 1907.)

After the failure of the Knox proposal, American banking interests sought to enhance their prestige in China by organizing the so-called Quadruple Group (the Four-Power Consortium), with Great Britain, France, Germany and the United States as the principals, to handle Chinese loans, particularly for the development of Manchuria, and an agreement with the Chinese Government was reached on April 15, 1911. But shortly after the agreement had been made public, Russia and Japan strongly protested and were then invited to join the quadruple combination to form a Consortium to finance China on the basis of equality.

The third secret treaty signed on July 8, 1912, between Russia and

[46] Lawton, *Empires of the Far East*, Vol. II, p. 1352.
[47] ibid., p. 1354.

Japan, was prompted by the Chinese Revolution of 1911. It confirmed the existence of two previous secret conventions, dealing with Japanese and Russian special interests in Manchuria. The World War of 1914 compelled Russia and Japan to conclude another Secret Treaty of Alliance, signed on July 3, 1916, to the effect that in the event of any third Power interfering with the vital interests of both countries, or having hostile designs against Russia and Japan, they should confer with each other in order to safeguard and defend these rights and interests.

It was quite obvious that the third Power was meant to be the United States of America, which was then not only a neutral Power, but the one which took keen interest in the application of the 'Open Door' and equal opportunity towards China. It was only two years after the signing of the famous Portsmouth Treaty that Russia and Japan became fast friends on the strength of their common interests, forgetting all about their former enmity. The Russian Revolution of 1917 tore the secret treaties to pieces and further stirred up Japanese ambition to encroach upon the Chinese Eastern Railway. The events leading up to the sale of the Chinese Eastern Railway will be dealt with later.

Chapter VI

RUSSIA'S RELATIONS WITH CHINESE TURKISTAN (SINKIANG)

R ussia's advance in the Far East was not confined to Siberia,
Mongolia and the Amur, but was extended to Central Asia,
and eventually menaced Chinese Turkistan. Historically,
Central Asia and Chinese Turkistan were included as one territory
called *Hsi-Yu* or 'Western Regions' after the conquest of the whole
land by Gengis Khan as early as 1218. With the collapse of the
Yuan Dynasty, the various tribes there declared their independence
and broke up into separate states. At the beginning of the Ching
Dynasty, Chinese Turkistan was renamed 'Sinkiang' or the 'New
Dominion' after the subjugation of the Jungarian tribes. Various
tribes in Russian Central Asia also offered allegience to the
Manchu Emperor, but, owing to lack of communications, they were
not actually brought under control. Russia, in the midst of her
eastern expansion, therefore took advantage of this and advanced
to the heart of Central Asia in the early part of the eighteenth
century. By the middle of the nineteenth century, Russia had
absorbed Central Asia completely, and organized it administra-
tively as Russian Turkistan. Russia also made encroachments on
Chinese Turkistan, which became the target for further Russian
expansion.

1. Border Trade Relations

The initial step of Russian expansion in Central Asia was the
colonization of the country through immigration. Russian merchants also became active, and made their first contacts with
Sinkiang at Ili or Kuldja. In 1850 the Russian Government requested
China to open Kashgar for trade. This request was rejected, but
as conditions necessitated the regulation of trading arrangements,
a commercial treaty was signed at Ili in 1851, opening Ili and

Tarbagatai for trade. The Russians thus obtained a foothold in the westernmost frontier of China.

Kashgar was also opened for trade as an experiment on the same basis as Ili and Tarbagatai under the stipulations of the Treaty of Peking, 1860. Under this treaty, a barter trade free of customs duty was permitted, and the Russians could freely carry on their business and visit the bazaars, shops or houses of the local merchants, buying or selling various goods for cash or by barter and borrowing or lending money, without interference from the local authorities. The period of sojourn for merchants in places where trade was carried on was not limited by the treaty.

After the conclusion of the Treaty of Peking, the Russians demanded the right to come to Peking and to trade. This request was rejected by the Chinese, because the exemption from Customs duties was already an immense advantage to the Russians. However, after repeated negotiations, the Russians were finally permitted to carry on trade via Tientsin. But most of the Russians who came for purposes of trade travelled by the overland route and, therefore, some regulations were necessary for their passage through different territories. In 1862, the Sino-Russian Overland Trade Regulations, consisting of twenty-one articles, were signed in Peking and Customs duties were levied for the first time, though they were reduced to one-third of the duties imposed on the imports of other countries. Nevertheless, trade along the entire boundary line within a hundred *li* (about thirty miles) was still exempted from duty.

Russian trade with China had always occupied a favoured position. The Treaty of Nerchinsk and the Treaty of Kiakhta had both stipulated that Russian trade was to be exempted from taxation. While Russia, as far as the payment of duties on trade at the seven seaports was concerned, enjoyed the privileges of 'the most favoured nation' clause on signing the Treaty of Tientsin, the overland trade at that time continued to be duty-free, though as we have seen with the conclusion of the Overland Trade Regulations, trade was subject to taxation except within a hundred *li* of the land frontier. Even the revised Treaty of St. Petersburg, concluded in 1881, clearly stipulated that Russians were permitted to trade in Ili, Tarbagatai, Kashgar, Urumchi and other cities south and north of the Teinshan without paying any tax, though a clause was added that this exemption would be abolished and new taxes imposed when trade became prosperous. Thus the entire provinces of Sinkiang and Mongolia were exempted from taxation, giving Russia a degree of privilege rare in international relations.

2. *The Boundary Question*

The frontier line in the northern part of Sinkiang in the Kang Hsi period of the Ching Dynasty extended north of Zaisan Nor, covering the lower course of the Irtysh River for about a hundred miles. This was the original north-western boundary between China and Russia. After the submission of the Jungarians in Sinkiang, many tribes like the Kazaks, Kokandians and Kirghiz offered allegiance and paid tribute to China. The territory of Sinkiang at that time embraced almost the whole of the present Russian Kazakistan, Kirghizistan, Tajikistan, Uzbekistan and Turkmenistan. Such an immense tract of land had never been subjugated by China before. The boundaries of these dependencies were, therefore, the national boundary of China.

Not all of this immense area was directly administered by the Chinese authorities. Military Commanders were appointed to stations at Ili and Tarbagatai. Chinese pickets were placed near these points to limit the use of pastures by the Russian Kazaks. These Kazaks were accustomed to steal and plunder, and were a great grievance to the local population. Later on, permission was granted to the Russian Kazaks to spend their winters within the picketed area, but in the summer they were again driven back beyond the pickets. These pickets, therefore, were merely maintained to prohibit illegal pasturing and had nothing to do with the national boundary which, though not directly administered or patrolled, extended far beyond them. Because the pickets were mostly situated in desolate places, making it inconvenient for the transportation of provisions, many officials on duty at the pickets would stealthily move them nearer to the Chinese towns to make things easier for themselves. Thus, the territory bounded by the pickets gradually diminished in area, the picket line being moved time after time back towards the central localities.

At that time, Sinkiang was far from Russian territory. Being far out on the frontier it was desolate and undeveloped. However, as early as 1840, the Russians began to penetrate south to control the Kazaks, without objection from the Manchu Government. The Commander of Ili sent officers to investigate an area outside the picket line, but received a reprimand from Peking for creating trouble beyond the boundary. From that time on, all affairs beyond the picket line were neglected. What the Chinese did not value much, the Russians covetously made their own. About 1850, the Russians established a commercial mart at Alma Ata, beyond the Chinese pickets outside of Ili. Troops were also sent to the west of Alma Ata to build fortresses. Next, the town of Semipalatinsk was established to the north-west of Tarbagatai. Before long, Tashkent and Alma Ata were occupied by the Russians.

In 1860 Russia took advantage of the unrest in China occasioned by the Taiping rebellion to make China sign the Treaty of Peking, which specified that the boundary between Russian and Chinese territory in Central Asia should be based upon the existing line of the pasture-pickets. Both China and Russia were to appoint special commissioners to demarcate the boundary. Appointments were duly made by the two governments, and the two commissioners met in Tarbagatai for preliminary discussions. Owing to the outbreak of the Islamic revolt in north-west China and Chinese Turkistan, the Chinese Commissioner wanted to hurry back to Ili, and the conference was concluded with a temporary agreement known as the Boundary Treaty of Tarbagatai of 1864.

This opened the way for numerous future disputes, for it was arranged that all undetermined boundaries should follow the permanent Chinese pickets, as stipulated by the Treaty of Peking. The Chinese Commissioner, however, contended that the pickets were of two different kinds—permanent and movable. The movable pickets were situated on the extreme frontier for the purpose of preventing the barbarous tribes from pasturing there, while the permanent pickets were very close to cities and towns, as near as only ten or twenty miles. China's contention that the national boundary should be marked along the outermost pickets was of no avail. Vast tracts of land to the west of Uliassutai as well as on the eastern bank of Zaisan Nor as far as the River Ayagus were thus lost to China.

In 1870, when the boundary was staked at Tarbagatai, the Russians planted some stakes in Chinese territory, intruding for another score of miles and cutting the main thoroughfare between Tarbagatai and Altai. In 1880, the Sino-Russian Treaty was revised, but the Russians alleged that the boundary arrangements for the eastern part of Zaisan Nor made in 1864 were not completed, and requested the appointment of commissioners on both sides for re-demarcation. In this way, the whole of Zaisan Nor and the rich pasture lands farther west fell into Russian hands.[1]

3. Russian Occupation of Ili During the Islamiç Revolt

No sooner had the Manchu Government subdued the Taiping rebellion in 1864 than the Islamic revolt arose in the western part of China. The revolt first broke out at Kuchar in 1864, and four cities in the east of south Sinkiang fell into the hands of the rebels. Urumchi, the capital, was later attacked by the Mohammedans, led by an Assistant Garrison Commander who himself was of Turkish origin. At this stage the rebels elected as their leader Tuo-ming, a Tungan from Kansu, who proceeded to Urumchi and occupied the city. The power of the rebels was so augmented that they successively occupied many other cities, including Ili.

Meanwhile, a notorious chieftain, Chin Shan-ying, from south Sinkiang, intrigued with another Islamic leader in Andijan, the famous Yakub Beg, who came from Central Asia, and raised the standard of rebellion throughout the province. He conquered one important city after another until he reached Urumchi, where Tuo-ming was defeated, and the inhabitants suffered terribly under Yakub Beg's yoke. Yakub Beg conceived the plan of setting up a Mohammedan state in the territory adjoining Chinese, Russian and British possessions.

Of the three countries concerned, China was unable to send a military expedition against the rebels, owing to the depletion of the national treasury by the Taiping rebellion; Britain was bent on exploiting the situation, but Russia, who had only recently acquired new lands near by, was intensely opposed to letting the trouble spread, since she really desired a period of peace in which to consolidate herself in her newly acquired territories.

For that reason, while the Mohammedans were attacking Ili, the Russians despatched a division of troops to occupy the upper valley of the Tekes, commanding the pass to the main route south of the Tienshan. As Ili was in a state of disorder after falling into the hands of the rebels, the Russians in 1871 further took advantage of the situation by sending other troops under the command of the Governor of Turkistan to occupy the city under the pretext of maintaining peace and order.

[1] For details, see *The Illustrated Encyclopædia of Sinkiang* (116 volumes in Chinese).

Meanwhile the Russian Minister in Peking notified the Tsung Li Yamen of the Russian occupation of Ili. The Manchu Government, upon receiving this notification, demanded of the Russian Minister the reason for such occupation. The answer was that Russia was only occupying the area temporarily for the sake of peace and order, and that as soon as the Chinese Government was strong enough to extend its authority to that part of the land, the Russians would withdraw.[2]

Negotiations followed next year between the Chinese and Russian officials. The Russians at first declined even to discuss the question of Ili, and later stated that should Ili be returned to China, the revolt would break out once more. They contended that Ili could only be returned after China had recovered the whole of Sinkiang. In addition, the Russians demanded the opening of Kobdo and other towns to Russian trade in order to compensate them for their losses. They took a step further by informing the Chinese Garrison Commander that no administration should be extended to the inhabitants of Ili and no taxes imposed. Repeated negotiations were of no avail. Hence, in order to recover Ili, the Manchu Government had to send troops to quell the rebellion and retake Sinkiang.

4. Tso Tsung-tang's Historic Campaign

Meanwhile, General Tso Tsung-tang, Viceroy of Shensi and Kansu, one of the ablest statesmen in China's history, was charged with the arduous task of putting down the Islamic revolt in Sinkiang. He realized at once that only a carefully planned campaign would have a chance of success, and therefore he planted trees serving as landmarks for his return, and sent an advance guard to cultivate thousands of acres of waste land to increase his food supplies.[3]

By this time, Yakub Beg had already established a kingdom and proclaimed himself king. Russia, England and Turkey gave their qualified recognition. The British representative had been instructed to proceed to Kashgar to negotiate commercial treaties, as the southern part of Yakub Beg's domain, situated between Russian Central Asia and British India, would act a buffer state: the continuous advance of Russian forces would be a serious menace to India.[4]

[2] Cordier, Henri, *Histoire des Relatoins de la Chine avec les Puissances Occidentales*, 1860-1900, Vol. II, p. 173.
[3] Wu, Aitchen K., *Turkistan Tumult*, 1940.
[4] Curzon, G. N., *Russia in Central Asia in 1889*, p. 319.

The Court at Peking had by this time grown weary of the whole affair, and decided to recognize Yakub Beg as the head of an independent state under allegiance to the Throne, so that China could divert her full energy to action against the Japanese, who had invaded Formosa. The British Minister in Peking, Sir Thomas Wade, received instructions from his government and heartily supported this policy, and even Kuo Sung-tao, Chinese Minister in London, was of the same opinion.[5] Thereupon, Tso Tsung-tang memorialized the Throne, pointing out that unless and until Urumchi was recaptured, the Chinese Government would never regain control of Sinkiang: furthermore, that when the government troops came to check the rebellion, they should take back all the cities occupied by Yakub Beg, so that in the final result Russia's conditions for the return of Ili would be met. His strong wording is quoted below:

'Since very ancient times, China's frontier troubles have been graver on the north-west than on the south-west. . . . That is why to prize Sinkiang is to protect Mongolia; to protect Mongolia is to guard the capital (Peking). If Sinkiang is not fortified, there is no peace in Mongolia; then not only the borders of Shansi and Shensi are in danger of invasion, but there will be no assurance of peace in Chihli itself. Moreover, times have changed; the Russians are extending their territories to wider and wider areas. Over ten thousand *li* of our own frontier are contiguous with Russian territory. It is my humble opinion that the land (Sinkiang) should not be given up, and war operations should not be suspended. I am ready to lead the troops which were placed under my command back to resume garrison duty in order that foreign aggression be discouraged and our boundaries protected.'[6]

Tso Tsung-tang then instructed Liu Ching-tang to lead his troops towards Urumchi, and recaptured the city. Yakub Beg, in despair, died of fever in May 1877, in Korla. His eldest son, Beg Kuli Beg, succeeded to the throne after killing his brother, and before long he was defeated and fled to Russian territory before the fall of Kashgar.[7]

The British Minister in Peking insisted upon the cession of Kashgar, ostensibly for the purpose of enabling the Central Asian

[5] Tso Tsung-tang, *Compiled Letters and Documents* (in Chinese), Vol. XVII.
[6] Tso Tsung-tang, *Compiled Petitions to the Throne* (in Chinese).
[7] Boulger, D. C., *Life of Yakub Beg*, 1878, pp. 250-76.

state of Andijan, which eventually was annexed by the Russians, to set up a new kingdom. In this connection, Tso Tsung-tang memorialized the Throne to the effect that the British were helping Andijan with the intention of procuring an additional barrier on the border of India, thus robbing China of her possessions. This, he said, could by no means be tolerated.

Liu Ching-tang commanded his troops to advance to Kashgar, which was recaptured after fourteen years of occupation by the rebels. Thus the Islamic revolt in Sinkiang, lasting from 1864 to 1878, was brought to a close.[8]

It should be remembered that Tso Tsung-tang was held responsible by the Throne for the repression of the Sinkiang rebellion. He stationed himself at Suchow in Kansu for the purpose of giving instructions to different commanders fighting in Sinkiang, and in order to execute another duty of the utmost importance, namely, seeing that the army commissariat be properly supplied. After the rebels were all checked, the most serious problem confronting him was how to recover Ili from the Russians.

5. Treaty of Livadia

With this end in view, the Tsung-li Yamen at Peking made representations to Eugene Butzow, Russian Minister in China, demanding the withdrawal of Russian troops from the occupied territories. This demand was rejected by the Russian Minister, who suggested that the matter should be negotiated with the Tsar himself. Some time later, Butzow left for St. Petersburg, followed by the newly appointed Chinese Minister Plenipotentiary, Chung Hao. In 1879 the negotiations between Russia and China began, the Russian side being represented by Butzow. It must be mentioned here that Chung Hao, when travelling to Russia, took the sea route to St. Petersburg, instead of going through Sinkiang as previously arranged, and so was completely ignorant of the frontier situation or the military precautions taken there. Naturally he was trapped by the Russian diplomat and was made to sign the pact known as the Treaty of Livadia. It is interesting to note that the Russians did promise the return of Ili, but upon the condition that three main questions should be agreed upon, namely: (1) boundary demarcation, (2) a commercial agreement, and (3) an indemnity.

[8] For details, see *The Illustrated Encyclopædia of Sinkiang*, Vol. 54.

Chung Hao, ignorant as he was of international affairs, cared little for the contents of the eighteen articles of the treaty which he signed on behalf of the Chinese Government, so long as the Russians promised to return Ili to China. A perusal of some of the most important articles of the treaty at once reveals the preposterousness of the whole affair:

1. The western, the richer and larger part of Ili, with the Musart Pass commanding the Tienshan ranges and the route leading to Kashgar was to be ceded to Russia.

2. The Russians were to be exempted from all duties when importing and exporting goods from and to Mongolia and Sinkiang.

3. Russia was to be allowed to open consulates in five more cities in addition to those already established in Kashgar and Urga.

4. China was to pay an indemnity of five million roubles (2,800,000 taels) to defray the cost of the Russian military occupation of Ili.

When a copy of the signed treaty reached Peking, it naturally created a sensation. It was not only that a large stretch of land was to be ceded as a result of the new demarcation, but the whole treaty was worded as if a victorious nation were exacting demands from a defeated adversary. The Empress Dowager ordered Li Hung-chang and Tso Tsung-tang to study the matter and report to the Throne. Li Hung-chang memorialized the Throne on the outrageous demands of the treaty, voicing the opinion that measures should be taken forthwith to reverse this set-back, while Tso Tsung-tang advocated that China should prepare for war. In his memoir to the Throne, he stated:

'Ili was our territory, which, for a time, fell into the hands of Mohammedan rebels. Russia, under the pretext of helping us recover it, occupied this important area. As Russia no doubt realized it to be a hardly justifiable action, she promised to return Ili to us as soon as the Chinese Government recovered Urumchi and Manas. But these places have been recaptured, and Russia still occupies Ili. The mountain pass, Turfan and eight other cities have been recovered by China; Yakub Beg lost his life; Pei Yen-hu and several rebel leaders escaped into Russian territory. However, Russia not only refused extradition—she continues to occupy Ili. The rebel chiefs, who escaped into Russian territory, several times tried to attack the Chinese border under the disguise of merchants and were caught by the Chinese authorities. The Russian Government pretend not to know it. Chung Hao now agrees to the

Russian demand to establish more consulates—it is, really, more than the Russians could have expected. If we permit them to extend still farther and to reach Chiayukwan, it will affect the safety of the border and the livelihood of the people. The Chinese Envoy must be instructed to remain firm and resist Russia's importunate demands.'[9]

Among all the memorials submitted to the Throne, the one written by Chang Chih-tung, a scholar and later a statesman, became known far and wide. A part of his essay reads as follows:

'Russia, though a powerful nation, is at present deficient in military strength and resources as a result of her recent war with Turkey. The Russian people are greatly dissatisfied with the government to the extent that an attempt on the life of the Tsar is rumoured. If Russia should go to war with us, it would be tantamount to her committing suicide. The new treaty gives only the title of Ili to China; actually, China loses twenty thousand *li* of territory in addition to an annual expenditure of five million taels for military defence. Under these circumstances would it not be better for China to give up the province of Sinkiang entirely? . . . I humbly beg the Throne to command Li Hung-chang to conscript and train the necessary troops in readiness for war. If he brings victory to China he ought to be knighted; if, on the contrary, defeat should come, he ought to be severely punished. We can make good use of the very payment to Russia called for in the new treaty to employ a large number of foreign mercenaries who will be ready to fight for us. . . .'[10]

Though Chang's patriotism was indeed admirable, he was carried away a little by his enthusiasm. Butzow's thirty years of experience and observation in China made him confident that China would not be able to go to war with Russia even over an acute controversy. Influential ministers like Li Hung-chang, endowed with great insight and moderation, advised compromise, for the treaty was only a result of an inexcusable mistake on the part of the Court in empowering a man as incapable and cowardly as Chung Hao, as Minister Plenipotentiary to St. Petersburg.

Meanwhile, Chung Hao returned to Peking without having

[9] Tso Tsung-tang, *Compiled Petitions to the Throne*, Vol. 55.
[10] Chang Chih-tung, *Compiled Petitions to the Throne* (in Chinese), Vol. 2.

received the Imperial Edict authorizing his return. As a punishment, he was discharged from all public offices. After the Treaty of Livadia was thoroughly examined by the high officials, their unanimous opinion was that Chung Hao had disobeyed instructions given to him and exceeded his powers. By an Imperial Edict, issued on March 3, 1880, he was condemned to 'decapitation after incarceration'. The Diplomatic Corps were greatly shocked, especially the Russian Minister. The Russian Government lodged a protest with the Tsungli Yamen, requesting the release of Chung Hao according to the international practice that no government has the right to punish an Envoy for the failure of negotiations. It was unanimously thought that should Chung Hao be decapitated, war between China and Russia would be inevitable.[11] When the matter came to the knowledge of Queen Victoria of England, she sent a noble telegram in her own name to the Empress Dowager as from one woman to another, begging for the unfortunate Envoy's life. Queen Victoria's appeal proved successful, and thus Chung Hao's life was saved.[12] General Gordon, in whom China had great confidence because of his services during the Taiping Rebellion, was specially called to come to China to induce Chinese high officials not to provoke a war with Russia. Gordon offered two alternatives to Li Hung-chang, and later to the Chinese Ministers in Peking. 'If you will make war, burn the suburbs of Peking, remove the Emperor and archives from Peking, put them in the centre of the country, and fight a guerilla war for five years; Russia will not be able to hurt you. If you want peace, then give up Ili *in toto*, and escape the payment of five million taels. . . . Ili, if the passes are held by Russia, will never be really Chinese; it has always cost China more blood and money than it was worth.'[13] Li Hung-chang also disapproved of starting war with Russia. Kuo Sung-tao, the retired Chinese Minister to England, strongly emphasized the fact that the war atmosphere was entirely misleading. Both statesmen knew that a treaty signed by a plenipotentiary was not easily revoked. But General Tso Tsung-tang, a man on the spot, was impatient and would not compromise. He memorialized the Throne:

'Upon the occupation of Ili the Russians destroyed a large part of the city, using the material to build an extensive mart. It seems that Russia intends to make Ili a Russian colony. . . .

[11] Cordier, op. cit., pp. 192-4.
[12] Boulger, *The Life of Sir Halliday Macartney*, 1908, pp. 341-2.
[13] Boulger, op. cit., Letter to Sir H. Macartney, Nov. 2, 1880, p. 347.

According to Clause VII of the treaty negotiated by Chung Hao, territories extending as far as the banks of the Holkutz and Tekes Rivers to the south of Ili mountains should be given to Russia after Ili has been returned. These two areas though not marked on Chinese maps, are generally described as the south-western part of Ili which should be given to Russia. When a country is defeated in war it may be obliged to cede territories and sue for peace. But up to the present moment, not a single shot has been fired. Why should China sacrifice an important area to satisfy Russia's greed? It would be like throwing a bone to a dog to prevent it from biting. But when the bone has been eaten up, the dog would still want to bite. What a great pity! '[14]

Tso Tsung-tang obtained the Court's permission to negotiate for a foreign loan in order to meet his military expenses. Determined to retake Ili by force, he despatched his troops by three routes, helped by his famous commanders, while he started from Suchow for Sinkiang Province. To show his determination to die for the sake of the lost territory, and because he was about seventy years old by that time, he ordered his coffin to be carried behind him.[15] When he arrived at Hami, the Russians reinforced themselves in Ili and started active manœuvres along the Chinese coast, which brought considerable excitement to the inhabitants of the south-eastern provinces. Finally the Court decided to abandon the idea of war, and consequently Tso Tsung-tang was recalled to Peking for consultation. The project of despatching a properly qualified man to St. Petersburg to negotiate for modification of the Treaty of Livadia was put forward and supported.

6. Marquis Tseng's Brilliant Diplomacy

For this unenviable and almost hopeless task was chosen Marquis Tseng Chi-tse, son of China's great statesman, Tseng Kuo-fan, who was the prominent figure in putting down the Taiping Rebellion. At the same time, Chung Hao was reprieved, as a manifestation that China did not wish to hurt Russia's dignity, but, on the contrary, desired to continue friendly relations. This magnanimous action paved the way for negotiations—Russia's face was saved.

[14] Tso Tsung-tang, *Compiled Petitions to the Throne*, Vol. 55, pp. 33-40.
[15] *The Illustrated Encyclopædia of Sinkiang*, Vol. 5.

It is worthy of notice that Chung Hao held the rank of Minister Plenipotentiary, while Marquis Tseng was only Minister of the second rank. This considerably increased the difficulty of conducting negotiations, for it gave the Russian Foreign Office a pretext to refuse to hold discussions with Marquis Tseng, as a second-rank Minister could hardly change the treaty signed by a fully empowered envoy. Marquis Tseng wrote in a personal letter:

'A treaty entered into by the Minister Plenipotentiary of one country directly with the sovereign of another country is a solemn contract. Even a small and weak country will not submit to the complete revocation of such a treaty on the demand of another, to say nothing of a nation like Russia. . . . I have another apprehension that my official status may not command respect in St. Petersburg. Further, opinions are so diverse as to the parties concerned that even if I managed to work out some workable plan, I would have to meet all the obstacles with the result that I would follow the track of my predecessor.'[16]

Before he set out for St. Petersburg, Marquis Tseng memorialized the Throne with regard to his plan as follows:

'In relation to the question of Ili, there are three points of negotiation, namely: boundary demarcation, a commercial agreement and an indemnity. There seem to be also three ways of approach, namely: war, defence and compromise.'[17]

He discussed at full length China's new naval force, which was still in its infancy. Although the prospects seemed quite favourable, at that moment it was not a good policy to plunge into war. On the other hand, if the matter were allowed to stand as it was, it would mean the loss of Ili—which is not only a large and valuable piece of Chinese territory, but the key to the whole of Turkistan. He therefore suggested that the best way out would be a compromise.

In another of his memorials to the Throne, Marquis Tseng revealed his deep insight and determination:

'It seems to me that of all the three negotiable points the

[16] Marquis Tseng Chi-tse, *Compiled Letters and Essays* (in Chinese).
[17] Marquis Tseng Chi-tse, *Compiled Petitions to the Throne* (in Chinese), Vol. 2.

indemnity question is of the least importance. Then, comparing the demarcation issue with the commercial agreement, it is clear that the former is more important. . . . In spite of the fact that the treaty entered into by Chung Hao is greatly detrimental to China's interests, I greatly fear that it could not be revoked in full. It is my humble opinion that we should stand firm as to the question of demarcation, as it is of a permanent nature, while the commercial agreement should be only amended in its most detrimental articles, approval being given to the rest. . . . Negotiations will have to be carried step by step and in a compromising spirit, as one should not expect any concrete results in a short time.'[18]

It was Marquis Tseng's opinion that neither a demand nor a promise should be made light-mindedly: that is, when a demand was made, they should see to its satisfaction; likewise, when a promise was given, they should see to its fulfilment. Marquis Tseng continued:

'If we should gradually give way in what we now insist upon, merely because of arriving at a point when the Russians refuse to accommodate us . . . that would mean that what we now insist upon is but an attempt, based upon the urging of Chinese public opinion. If we give in when the attempt fails, it would remind one of the shopkeeper's art of bargaining and not of a government's attitude which should be directed to maintaining faith and righteousness as well as to pacifying distant neighbours. The Russians are known for their deceitfulness; if we should argue on every clause now and be forced to give in afterwards, it would only add to Russia's opportunities of practising their craft, in addition to arousing bad feelings on the part of other western countries. I believe that there is every sign of danger that, by signing this treaty, we shall recover very little, while endless troubles in diplomatic negotiations may follow. For this reason, I am of the opinion that we should persist unflinchingly upon the boundary question, whereas clauses relating to mutual trade should be accepted. Anyway, both the acceptance and refusal must be based on an unalterable plan, so as to avoid the need of giving way by force of circumstances on points upon which we at first insisted.'[19]

[18] Marquis Tseng Chi-tse, op. cit.
[19] ibid.

He continued:

> 'I have expressed my opinion that a certain amount of conces-
> sion should be made even before I set out for St. Petersburg. I
> might be called a coward and subjected to criticism. If I act only
> according to your instructions and make myself responsible for
> conveying the words of the two countries without thinking of
> either success or failure, my responsibilities would seem to be much
> lighter, which would be to my advantage. But, seeing that genera-
> tions of my ancestors received kindness from the Throne, I take
> the liberty of speaking out even though it is a matter that con-
> cerns me not. Since it is my responsibility, how can I remain
> silent merely to avoid criticism? . . .'

Marquis Tseng arrived at St. Petersburg in June of the sixth
year of Emperor Kwang Hsu (July 7, 1880), accompanied by Dr.
Macartney and M. Giquel together with one Chinese counsellor and
interpreter, paying his first call on the Foreign Minister on June 29.
The following is an extract from Marquis Tseng's diary:

> 'On the 29th, I, accompanied by my secretaries, called on
> Foreign Minister Giers, Russian Minister to China—Butzow and
> Manikoff, Director of the Foreign Ministry, were also present.
> Giers received me in a cool manner and stated in strong words at
> the outset that the treaty could not be altered. Then he dragged
> on, mentioning that there were cases when certain countries
> amended their agreements, even after they had been signed, but
> nobody had ever heard of a country, before an agreement had
> been effected, punishing the envoy who signed the treaty. The
> reinforcement of troops at the frontiers was another sign that it
> would be best to be ready for action. His reproving talk continued
> for some time, but, finally, he promised to memorialize the situa-
> tion to the Throne and to settle the date for the presentation of
> my credentials.'

It was only natural that Russia, knowing herself to be superior in
military strength, and relying upon the fact that the treaty had
already been signed and only awaited ratification, was not willing to
consent to the amendments desired by the Chinese Government. It
would be interesting to refer to some more details:

> 'On June 29, sixth year of Kwang Hsu, Marquis Tseng, accom-

panied by a counsellor and an interpreter, called on Foreign Minister Giers, Minister Butzow and Director Manikoff. After the exchange of complimentary words, His Excellency Giers said: "I have received a document from Your Excellency, and I wonder whether Your Excellency will stay here permanently or has come as a special Envoy." Marquis Tseng answered: "I have come here as Chinese Minister. I possess the authority to deal with any outstanding cases between our two countries." His Excellency: "While your country's Plenipotentiary Chung Hao was here, we settled all the necessary points. The treaty only awaits ratification. However, we have received no word from your government since then, and have heard that your government have imposed upon the Envoy Chung Hao a heavy punishment, and simultaneously strengthened the defence on the border. This brings anxiety to both countries, and a clash seems inevitable. How can you hope to renew negotiations under these circumstances? "

'Marquis: "His Imperial Majesty had ordered the punishment of Chung Hao on account of his disloyalty. But when His Majesty was informed that this act would embarrass your esteemed country, Chung Hao was reprieved from punishment in order to prove to your country China's intention to maintain friendly relations with your government."

'His Excellency: "The imposition of punishment on Envoy Chung Hao not only brought great embarrassment to my country —it made a bad impression upon all other countries. The agreement entered into between us was carefully weighed and considered for more than a year. Envoy Chung Hao tried his best in the interests of his country, arguing upon every point until he brought the agreement to a conclusion. I feel that it is the Envoy's mission to do his best for the sake of his nation, and therefore the agreement was made between us in a most amicable way. The treaty is awaiting ratification. I see no ground for a renewal of discussions."

'Marquis: "Does this mean that Your Excellency will refuse to hold conferences with me? "

'His Excellency: "I would not put it that way, but all the alterations made by my country have been clearly specified in the treaty and the letters exchanged with Envoy Chung Hao. What remains to be done is the ratification of the treaty." '[20]

[20] *Memorandum of Sino-Russian Conversations Relating to the Retrocession of Ili* (in Chinese).

From the foregoing we can see what a sharp attitude was assumed by the Russian Foreign Minister. It seemed that no further negotiations were possible. Nevertheless, Marquis Tseng, in his capacity of Chinese Minister, could not be prevented from further negotiations with the Russian Government, and it soon became clear that the extremely uncompromising attitude adopted by Russia right at the beginning of the negotiations was merely a gesture, intended to secure a better bargaining position for the future. Marquis Tseng, being a statesman and a diplomat, knew what it all meant, so he dealt with the matter in the friendliest and calmest way. He would not offend the Foreign Minister, but he pressed his view in the most carefully chosen words. After a lengthy argument, the Russian Foreign Minister agreed to report to the Throne, awaiting further instructions. It was even hinted that the Tsar might not receive Marquis Tseng because he was of lower rank than the previous Minister.

But the Tsar determined to receive Marquis Tseng, who presented his credentials and then started negotiations in the capacity of the Chinese Minister.

On the next day Marquis Tseng again called on the Foreign Minister, outlining those articles in the Treaty which China wanted to have modified, and how such modifications should be effected. Below is an extract from the conversation:

' My country's point of view may be summed up under three headings: First, China cannot agree to some points in the treaty which are detrimental to her interests. Secondly, there are points which are not explicit enough; they should be described in full detail in order to avoid any misunderstanding in carrying them out in the future. Thirdly, privileges which were stipulated in old treaties should not be included in the new agreement. The above three points may be further divided into six items:

' 1. China is unwilling to cede any of her territories to any country. Since your esteemed country expressed willingness to return Ili to China, it is hoped that the whole territory of Ili will be returned.

' 2. The boundary line of Tarbagatai and Kashgar should remain unchanged. Any minor adjustments which might seem necessary should be made by delegates of both countries on the spot.

' 3. With regard to special privileges desired by Russia, such as that Chiayukwan (in Kansu) be opened for trade, and the opening of two trade routes through Nerchinsk (on the Heilungkiang frontier) and Kobdo (in Outer Mongolia), China is willing to grant them, provided that Article I has been satisfactorily amended.

' 4. The places where Russia wants to open new consulates are too numerous. Though the establishment of consulates cannot prove detrimental to China in any way, it is to be feared that should the negotiator agree to this point, he would be blamed for yielding too much. Hence Russia may for the time being open a new consulate only at Chiayukwan; the establishment of consulates at other places should be postponed to the time when trade has actually developed.

' 5. Although Russian consulates may not be established in the cities of Hami, Kucheng, Barkul, etc., Russia may choose one place for storing Russian merchandise along the line allowed for in Kalgan.

' 6. Sinkiang is in many respects similar to a coastal province. If Customs duties were to be exempted along the border, the loss suffered by China would be tremendous. Further discussions concerning this point are therefore necessary.'[21]

These six items presented by Marquis Tseng did not include all that was wished for by the Peking Court, as his intention was to save some margin for compromise. But even what he did present irritated the Russians so much that the negotiations nearly broke off. Butzow was again sent to Peking to conduct negotiations with the Chinese Government, and it was only after a vigorous protest, filed by Marquis Tseng, that Butzow was recalled. However, Russia still flatly refused to make concessions. There proved to be many knotty points, which more than once nearly caused the suspension of the conference. Marquis Tseng nevertheless had no intention of yielding. He wired to Peking suggesting that since it was China that was asking for the retrocession of Ili and inasmuch as Russia did not seem to be willing to meet her request, perhaps it would be better to reserve the demand until a more opportune time. Peking endorsed this suggestion, whereupon Russia requested that the Marquis sign a paper, confirming that Russia would not be asked to return Ili. Marquis Tseng replied that he was only suggesting time for further consideration on the part of the Russian Government. If he signed the confirmation requested by Russia it would be tantamount to ceding the territory, and there would be no need for Peking to send envoys to carry out further discussions. Later on, Russia offered to return Ili to China upon exorbitant terms, which were turned down by Marquis Tseng.

[21] *Memorandum of Sino-Russian Conversations Relating to the Retrocession of Ili* (in Chinese).

7. Treaty of St. Petersburg

The negotiations dragged on for many months, the most vital questions being the cession of the territory, and the commercial rights in the interior. Butzow's behaviour throughout the conference added to the difficulty of arriving at any agreement. Fortunately, the Tsar himself interfered and decided that it was meaningless to carry on such a long controversy. He instructed the Foreign Minister to make concessions, and the situation took a more favourable turn for China.

A revised treaty was concluded consisting of twenty articles, of which the most important were the following:

1. China agreed to pay an indemnity of nine million roubles to Russia, to cover the losses suffered as the result of defending Ili on behalf of China.

2. Lands to the west of Ili were to be handed over to Russia for the purpose of accommodating the inhabitants who were forced to give up their lands in order to get Russian citizenship. Detailed boundary specifications were attached to the treaty.

3. Commercial and other privileges were granted in Sinkiang and Mongolia, such as the establishment of Russian consulates in Chiayukwan and Turfan, not hitherto open for trade. Permission for the establishment of consulates in other cities was to be given after the trade had prospered.

4. A free trade zone, extending for fifty versts on either side of the Russo-Chinese frontier was created.

5. The commercial stipulations of the treaty, as well as the regulations serving as its complement, were to be subject to revision after ten years. If, however, within six months prior to the expiration of the agreement, neither of the Contracting Parties should manifest the desire to proceed to its revision, the commercial stipulations, as well as other regulations, were to remain in force for a further term of ten years.

Another point insisted upon by Marquis Tseng was that Russian trade on which duties were not to be imposed, should be limited to certain routes and places. All the previous treaties exempting foreign trade from duties never specified where the line was to be drawn. This may appear to be an insignificant point, but Marquis Tseng foresaw its weighty effects and insisted upon the specification even at the risk of another deadlock, threatened by the Russian Foreign Minister.

The difference between the terms of this new treaty and that concluded by Chung Hao lies in the retrocession of the broad valley of the Tekes River to China, ceding only a small territory to the west of Holkutz to Russia. Also, in the original treaty concluded by Chung Hao, Russia had been permitted to establish consulates in the seven cities of Chiayukwan, Turfan, Kobdo, Uliassutai, Hami, Urumchi and Kucheng. The revised treaty granted Russian consulates only in Chiayukwan and Turfan. The Russians also wanted to enter China proper via Kiayukwan, passing Sian and Hanchung and reaching as far as Hankow. Marquis Tseng argued strongly for the cancellation of this plan.

The whole incident was really an unprecedented affair in the diplomatic history of China. In the capacity of plenipotentiary, Chung Hao's actions were those of the Chinese Government. Theoretically speaking, the treaty concluded by him could not be said to be without effect. But the cession of territories was going beyond any power entrusted to him by the Throne. Notwithstanding that the Chinese Government's refusal to approve the treaty was based on international law, the government could hardly deny responsibility in appointing a minister who dared to act beyond his power. Fortunately Marquis Tseng was able to manage the affair smoothly just when the two countries were on the point of breaking relations, taking back for China important territories already ceded.

The revised treaty was signed at St. Petersburg on February 24, 1881. Thus through the efforts of Marquis Tseng, one of China's ablest statesmen and diplomats, the most acute and outstanding problem between Russia and China was brought to a close. China had won military victories in her history of many centuries; but a bloodless diplomatic triumph such as achieved by Marquis Tseng was new in her experience.

8. The Question of Pamirs

There remains one more thing to be said about the relations between China and Russia, which concerns the Pamir. The Pamir Plateau lies on the ridge of the Karakoram Range, known as 'The Roof of the World', where the boundaries of China, India and Russia meet. Though described as a plateau or tableland, it has numerous peaks rising from its roof, which divide it into several sections. Each section has its own name, while the whole area is known under the name of Pamir, which 'is nearly surrounded by a horseshoe of mountain ranges bounded north and south respectively by the Tienshan and Hindu Kush Mountains, and on the west and east by Afghanistan and Chinese Turkistan '.[22] Captain Younghusband wrote: 'The Pamirs form a sort of no-man's-land between the British dependencies on the south, the Russian on the north, the Chinese on the east, and the Afghan on the west.'[23] The whole plateau, estimated at 30,000 square miles in area and from 12,000 to 14,000 feet above sea-level in height, is divided into eight Pamirs, big and small. On one of these peaks is a stone tablet, inscribed by Emperor Chien Lung, which is proof that it is Chinese territory.[24]

In 1878, when the Islamic Revolt in Sinkiang was suppressed, Governor Liu Ching-tang established frontier posts along the border in order to prevent Russia, Afghanistan and Hunza from entering into Pamir. In 1891, Russia despatched a number of troops together with scientific expeditions into Pamir, claiming it to be Russian territory, whereupon Britain hastily invaded Hunza to strengthen the Indian border. This was the era of Anglo-Russian rivalry in Chinese Central Asia. Tao Mu, the Governor of Sinkiang, then demanded an explanation of their respective unjustifiable actions from the Russian Governor of Tashkent and the British authorities in India. At the same time he reported to the Tsungli Yamen, requesting that a protest be lodged with the Russian and British Ministers in Peking, and that Chinese Ministers to Russia and Britain be instructed to make the same protests. Great Britain stated that her action was a precaution against Russia; the Russian excuse was that it was a precaution against England. Seeing that his efforts were fruitless, Governor Tao sent troops to garrison various strategic points. In the following year, the Tsungli Yamen disgracefully yielded to Britain and Russia, and instructions were sent to Governor Tao to withdraw his garrison troops.

When Britain invaded Hunza, a proposal was made to China to divide the Pamir Plateau, which China refused to do. Then Afghanistan was asked to occupy the central part of Pamir. When China agreed to divide the area, it was already occupied by Afghanistan. Soon afterwards, Britain and Russia drew a boundary line on the Pamir, demarcating their respective borders, and entered upon what is known as the Pamir Treaty. China was not even notified of this act, though there was an understanding between the countries concerned that China should be consulted with regard to the Chinese

[22] Lansdell, Harry, Chinese Central Asia, 1893, p. 9.
[23] Younghusband, F. E., The Heart of a Continent, 1884-1894, p. 291.
[24] The Illustrated Encyclopædia of Sinkiang.

Pamirs. Of the eight Pamirs divided by natural barriers, only one, lying in Sariquol, is still in Chinese hands. The other seven are distributed between Britain and Russia.[25]

It may be added that, after Russia had despatched troops into the Pamirs, Britain, out of fear of Russian invasion of India, began to interfere in the internal politics of Hunza. It was once announced by the British Foreign Ministry that 'Britain never harboured any intention to prevent Hunza from continuing to send tribute to China; nor would Britain interfere with any of China's rights and privileges in Hunza. Britain only plans to protect the border against a possible Russian invasion. If no actual invasion is attempted by Russia, Britain would not contemplate any action beyond the boundary line of the Hindu Kush Mountains. But in case Russia should send troops, the Chinese territory to the east of this boundary line would no doubt be invaded, and this would menace India.'

It is interesting to note that, after the Russian invasion of the Pamirs, Hunza continued to send tribute to China up to recent years. The tribute was delivered to the Chinese authorities at Kashgar,[26] making Hunza the last remaining of China's tributary states.

[25] *The Illustrated Encyclopædia of Sinkiang.* See also Curzon, G., *Russia in Central Asia*, 1899, pp. 343-70.
[26] See also Teichman, Sir Eric, *Affairs of China*, London, 1938, p. 215.

PART II

CHINA AND THE SOVIET UNION
1918-1930

Chapter VII

SINO-SOVIET RELATIONS DURING THE RUSSIAN
REVOLUTION

THE Russian Revolution, which put an end to Tsarism, was born in the events of February 1917. The so-called October Revolution of the same year brought into existence the Soviet régime, which declared null and void all treaties of an aggressive nature entered into by the Tsarist Government with other governments, thus changing the whole aspect of Sino-Russian relations in the Far East.

When the Soviet Government came to power, the Western Powers were still engaged in the Great War, and had no time to pay attention to the Russian Revolution. After the Great War was over, the Powers not only refused to recognize the Soviet Government, but engaged themselves in armed interference and economic blockade against Soviet Russia. China, being on the side of the Allies in the Great War, had to follow suit, and in concert with the others sent troops to Siberia through Mongolia for an attack against the Soviet Government. As a result, China was precluded from recognizing the Soviet Government. But, since Russia and China had many interests in common, unofficial relations between the two countries continued to exist, although diplomatic relations between them were interrupted between 1917 and 1924. It was only reasonable for China to seize the opportunity to recover what she had been compelled to give away and to reassert her sovereign rights in her own territories. Before the signing of the Sino-Soviet Agreement of 1924, all cases brought about by the changed circumstances were negotiated in an informal way. The most important negotiations between the two countries during this period are described in this chapter, except the negotiations over Outer Mongolia, which deserve a chapter to themselves.

1. Controversies over the Chinese Eastern Railway

Before the outbreak of the World War, Russia had stationed about 30,000 troops in Harbin. Another 60,000 troops were kept to protect the Chinese Eastern Railway between Harbin and Chang-chun. When Russia was at war with Germany and Austria, most of these troops were removed to the battlefields in Europe, and those left for the protection of the railway were divided into old and new factions, which could not get along together, and even fought with each other. Naturally these conditions were not favourable for the maintaining of peace and order in the railway zone. Things were further aggravated by the fact that the manager of the railway, General Horvath, belonged to the Russian Royal Family and, consequently, was strongly opposed to the Revolution. He consolidated his position in the railway zone and declared independence from the Soviets. As there was nobody to question his authority, he made himself virtual dictator, and for a time ruled the railway zone almost as if it were his own domain.

He was approached by a Japanese military general in Harbin who promised him assistance from Tokyo. It would be given only in return for the demolition of Vladivostok's fortifications to enable Japan to obtain freedom of navigation in the Amur and some exclusive rights such as mining, timber, fishing and land concessions for Japan in Siberia. This offer, however, did not materialize, and the Japanese entered into negotiations with a Cossack leader, Ataman Semenov, a military commander of the Imperial Russian Army, who for a time bestrode the railroad near Chita, cutting off the connections between eastern and western Bolshevists.[1]

Shortly after the Russian Revolution in February 1917, a Council of the Soldiers' and Workmen's Delegates was organized in Harbin and assumed control of the Harbin Municipality. From then on, the struggle between the Whites and the Reds began in earnest. The administration of the railway was interfered with, and confusion

[1] Morse and MacNair, *Far Eastern International Relations*, Shanghai, 1928, p. 929

reigned among the workers. The workmen's delegates declared themselves the official representatives of the Petrograd Government, and their stand was supported by a personal telegram from Lenin, who instructed them to take over the control of the railway from General Horvath. The workers, being all in favour of the Soviet régime, called a strike, announcing that the railway would stop operating as long as Horvath remained at his post.[2]

In view of the situation prevailing, the Chinese Government, fearing that the Bolshevik blaze might spread all over Manchuria, sent a regiment into the railway zone to intervene whenever conditions warranted. Horvath was asked to hand over the authority, which, in fact, he no longer possessed, as the workmen's delegates had assumed *de facto* control of the railway.

In January 1918 the Chinese Government itself took over control of the southern section of the railway from Harbin to Changchun, while the Russian soldiers in that area were disarmed and sent back to the Siberian frontier. Kuo Tsung-hsi, Civil Governor of Kirin, was appointed President of the Chinese Eastern Railway. The right to make such an appointment, though stipulated in the contract of September 8, 1896, had not been exercised by China for a period of seventeen years. Chinese soldiers were posted at different stations along the line to maintain peace and order. It was thus that China finally regained her right of control over the Chinese Eastern Railway.

About this time, the Board of Directors of the Chinese Eastern Railway Company was short of a quorum, and the Russian Delegation at Peking called a meeting of shareholders under the authority of the Russo-Asiatic Bank, which had been reorganized in Paris. China was represented by the new President of the railway. A new Board of Directors was elected, and General Horvath remained the Managing Director.

It should be noted that the Russian Revolution stirred up Japan's ambition to extend her influence to the Chinese Eastern Railway. The suggestion made by the Allied Powers in Peking that the Chinese Government should take control of the entire railway administration was opposed by Japan. She sent more troops into Manchuria as a measure against the actions of the Chinese Government, and even despatched forces into north Manchuria with the ostensible mission of protecting the Chinese Eastern Railway. In this way, the Japanese were able to prevent China from taking complete control of the Chinese Eastern Railway, and, by intriguing for

[2] Ho Han-wen, *History of Sino-Russian Relations* (in Chinese), p. 304.

the retention of Horvath, they did their best to secure a tool for further Japanese expansion. They tried to negotiate a loan to the Chinese Eastern Railway as a good excuse for intervention, but were unsuccessful. Then they pressed China to conclude the 'Sino-Japanese Military Pact' of May 16, 1918, by which the two contracting parties 'agreed that they would promptly consider in common the measures to be taken in order to meet the exigencies of the situation and to do their share in the Allied cause for the prosecution of the present war '.[3]

The other stipulations were that the two countries, being considered on an equal footing, should despatch troops jointly to places outside Chinese territory whenever necessary, and that the Japanese troops in Chinese territory 'shall be withdrawn as soon as military operations cease'. The use of the Chinese Eastern Railway was stipulated whenever military transportation should become necessary. The methods of transportation were specified in a supplementary agreement of September 6, 1918. A Sino-Japanese joint bureau was to be established to arrange troop movements with the railway authorities. The Chinese military forces in the Siberian provinces of Transbaikalia and Amur were to be directed by Japanese commanders in order to obtain military unification and harmony.[4] China's forces operating from Urga towards Transbaikalia were to command Japanese forces sent to aid in this area. The details of the pact were kept secret at first, but later were published in order to appease the public who were suspicious of the existence of such a pact.

Japan took advantage of this pact and began to move about 60,000 troops north of Changchun without previous consultation with China. Later, Japanese troops assumed police authority within the railway zone, although China had conceded to Japan only the right to transport her troops by the Chinese Eastern Railway into the two Siberian provinces of Transbaikalia and Amur.[5]

Meanwhile the situation in Siberia grew worse. Some 50,000 Czechoslovak troops who had surrendered to the Russians in Europe refused to accept the humiliating terms of the Brest-Litovsk peace treaty which Germany forced upon the Russian Revolutionary Government. They fought their way out of Siberia past the Bolshevik Red Guards, who attacked them at every opportunity.

[3] MacMurray, *Treaties and Agreements with and concerning China*, Vol. 11, p. 1408.
[4] ibid., pp. 1411-13.
[5] Morse and MacNair, op. cit., p. 930.

Fifteen thousand Czechoslovaks marched into Vladivostok and captured the city. Warships of Allied forces in the harbour landed small forces to protect their own nationals. Other Czechoslovak forces were struggling at various points along the Trans-Siberian Railway. The whole of Siberia was therefore in a chaotic condition.

The Allies then decided on intervention in August 1918. The idea proposed by the United States was that the four leading Powers, namely Great Britain, France, Japan and America, should each send seven thousand troops into Siberia for the sole purpose of aiding the Czechoslovak forces from attacks by armed Austrian and German prisoners. The United States announced to the world that such action 'contemplates no interference with the political sovereignty of Russia, no intervention in her internal affairs'.[6]

The opposition to foreign intervention was strengthened by the declaration of Chicherin, the Soviet Commissar for Foreign Affairs, that, far from being attacked by war prisoners, the Czechoslovaks were being used by counter-revolutionists against the Soviet masses. No attention, however, was paid to this assertion. China was also asked to participate because the Chinese Eastern Railway ran through Chinese territory. But Japan, using the military pact with China as a pretext, undertook to decide whether China should participate in the intervention. Notwithstanding Japan's pressure, unprecedented in history, Chinese influence had spread to the Siberian provinces. Chinese troops were heavily stationed along the frontiers, and Chinese cruisers were anchored at the port of Vladivostok. The Chinese Consul-General in Vladivostok was made dean of the consular corps representing many other countries.

The military situation in the Chinese Eastern Railway zone changed in character after the signing of the Armistice in Europe. The Armistice also synchronized with the rise of Admiral Kolchak, who set up a strong government at Omsk in western Siberia. With the military aid of foreign troops in Siberia, numbering nearly 200,000, it appeared possible that Admiral Kolchak might overturn the Bolshevik Government. His government was accorded conditional recognition by the Council of Four at Paris and also by Japan.[7]

The writer was sent by the Amur Provisional Government to Vladivostok from Harbin in the autumn of 1919 on a mission when the city was under the rule of Admiral Kolchak. However, the

---

[6] Foreign Relations of the United States, 1918, *Russia*, Vol. II, p. 398.
[7] Morse and MacNair, op. cit., p. 935.

tide turneed rapidly against Kolchak, and his government completely collapsed after the evacuation of Omsk in January 1920.

The American Government, in view of the disorganization of the transport system, suggested the creation of a special Inter-Allied Committee composed of representatives of all the Allied Powers having military forces in Siberia, including Russia. The suggestion met with approval from the Japanese Government whose co-operation with the Allies in Siberia was promised on the eve of the Armistice. Two Boards—a Technical Board and an Allied Military Transportation Board—were to be formed under an Inter-Allied Committee. The Russian manager was to continue the general management of both the Siberian Railway and the Chinese Eastern Railway, while the Technical Board, composed of railway experts of the nations having military forces in Siberia, was to be competent to deal with the technical operations of the railways. An agreement to this effect was at first not willing to endorse it, on the ground that the Chinese United States Government, Colonel John F. Stevens, an American engineer, was appointed President of the Technical Board.[8]

The Chinese Government, when informed of the above agreement, was at first not willing to endorse it on the ground that the Chinese Eastern Railway was within Chinese territory and entirely different from the Siberian system. However, a compromise was reached on March 10, 1919, to the effect that the Chinese Eastern Railway was to come under the protection of the Chinese military forces, and the only foreign troops permitted to stay within Manchuria were to be one thousand Americans, garrisoned at Harbin, and the Japanese forces at Manchuli. The Japanese troops, in spite of the agreement, continued to occupy the Chinese Eastern Railway zone. On the other hand, Semenov at Chita was nullifying the agreements relating to the railways. He was entirely under the control of the Japanese who gave him money and munitions for the control of the railway area where the Chinese Eastern Railway meets the Trans-Siberian. He later announced his pretentions as temporary ruler of Siberia.[9]

The Technical Board succeeded in securing a loan of five million gold dollars for the rehabilitation of the railway and for meeting the heavy expenses of the Allied expedition and the repatriation of the Czechoslovak forces. The Technical Board repeatedly protested against Japanese encroachments in the Chinese Eastern Railway

[8] Morse and MacNair, op. cit., p. 936.
[9] ibid, p. 936.

zone. Japan's intention was to expel the representatives of other nations from Manchuria, so that only Russia, Japan and China should be represented there.

Japan, instead of sending 7,000 men, as originally agreed, despatched 72,000, and instead of sending them to Vladivostok, as was expected, she sent them by three routes with one route to Nikolaevsk, at the mouth of the Amur River, where they met a humiliating defeat, and no fewer than 700 Japanese were massacred by the partisan bands in March 1920—the Nikolaevsk Affair.[10]

The writer was then in Mukden, and was an eyewitness at the station when hundreds of small boxes arrived containing the remains of the victims after cremation. Each box bore the name of the dead soldier, and they were to be shipped to Japan and delivered to the relatives of the victims at Nikolaevsk. The Japanese had spent about 700,000,000 yen and incurred heavy casualties in four years of intervention. They met with little success, excepting the seizure of northern Sakhalin, opposite Nikolaevsk, which had been in the possession of Russia since 1857. In spite of American protest as direct violation of the agreements reached between Japan and the United States, the Japanese position in Siberia was not affected.[11]

In April 1920 the American forces, as well as the French, British, Italian and Chinese forces, but not the Japanese troops, were completely withdrawn from Siberia. The Japanese, in these circumstances, announced their inability to immediately withdraw, promising to do so as soon as the political situation in Siberia had become normal, and after the evacuation of the Czechoslovak forces had been completed. But in the Inter-Allied Agreement, it was clearly stated that the Technical Board was to function until all foreign troops were withdrawn from Manchuria. The Japanese were therefore notified that the Board would continue to operate until the Japanese forces were also withdrawn. It was only after the Washington Conference that Japan finally withdrew her troops and the Board was dissolved.

But the Chinese Eastern Railway remained in a chaotic condition so long as General Horvath remained in office. Being a confirmed anti-Bolshevik, he was connected with Semenov, a reactionary 'white' general. General Horvath once even went so far as to issue a proclamation that owing to the circumstances prevailing, he considered himself authorized to assume full governmental power over the Rusian population in the Chinese Eastern Railway zone. The

---

[10] Morse and MacNair, op. cit., p. 939.
[11] ibid., pp. 940, 949.

Chinese authorities declared, however, that General Horvath had exceeded his powers in attempting to conduct a political movement within the railway zone, and had violated international law in his method of carrying out administrative measures in the territory of another country. He was advised to confine himself to matters relating to the railway, but Horvath would not listen to this admonition. On the contrary, he even disbursed the railway funds to push through his own political aims. The result was that the pay of the railway employees fell two months in arrears. This caused a general strike of the railway employees, who requested the immediate dismissal of Horvath before they would return to work.

General Horvath was at last compelled to resign from his post, and the Chinese authorities then made it known that in future no Russian party or individual would be allowed to make use of the railway for pushing forward political aims. The strike was thus ended.

However, the controversies over the Chinese Eastern Railway showed no sign of abatement after the assumption of full control by the Chinese Government. It was only natural that China should seize the opportunity to recover her sovereign rights and to eliminate any third Power from participation in the railway. She was even preparing a revision of the original contract relating to the Chinese Eastern Railway, pending the establishment of a stable Russian Government. This action met with vehement protests on the part of the Russo-Asiatic Bank, supported by the French Government. During the negotiations between the Bank and the Chinese Government, the main controversy centred upon the number of Directors to be appointed. The Chinese Government asked for four Chinese Directors, while the Bank would only agree to three, evidently under instructions from Paris. At last the Chinese claim was met, and the so-called supplement to the Agreement for the construction and exploitation of the Chinese Eastern Railway was signed between the Chinese Minister of Communications and the representatives of the Russo-Asiatic Bank on October 2, 1920. Its important items are summarized as follows:

1. The rights and the obligations of the Company were henceforth to be only of a commercial character; the Chinese Government reserved the right to restrict at any moment any political activity.

2. The administration and the police of the railway were to be under the control of the local Chinese authorities.

3. The Chinese Government was to have the right to appoint to

the Board of Directors, in addition to the President, four members
of Chinese nationality, and likewise to appoint two Chinese on the
Committee of Auditors.

4. In accordance with the original contract of 1896, a sum of
5,000,000 Kuping taels was to be paid by the Company to the Chinese
Government at six per cent compound interest from the date of the
opening of traffic up to the year 1920.

5. Employment in the service of the railway was to be equitably
distributed between Chinese and Russians.

2. Police, Judicial and Municipal Problems in the C.E.R. Zone

A. Police Problem

The contract for the construction of the C.E.R. had stipulated that
police authority in the railway zone belonged to China; but the
railway regulations stated that, for the sake of maintaining order
in the railway zone, the Railway Company should appoint certain
police, and that Police Regulations were to be worked out. In 1909
it was agreed by China and Russia that detailed regulations for the
railway police should be redrafted within one month. The Manchu
Government procrastinated, and the regulations were never drawn
up. In 1911 the Tsarist Government took advantage of the Chinese
Revolution to grant authority to apply the Russian criminal code
in the C.E.R. zone.

During the Russian Revolution, the Russian officials of the C.E.R.
naturally lost their home support. In February 1918, China first
organized a police bureau to co-operate with the Russian police for
maintaining order in the railway zone. When General Horvath
resigned from the railway in 1920, the Chinese Government proclaimed that the area along the line of the C.E.R. was to be made
a special district, with police headquarters at Harbin and sub-
stations in various populous sections. Thus, the policing of the
railway was completely turned over to the Chinese military
authorities. At last China began to feel herself master in her own
territory. A Presidential mandate was then issued in which it was
stipulated that 'in order to ensure the safety of the railway, the
Chinese Government will temporarily assume responsibility and
exercise the right of control regarding the administration of the
railway, which formerly belonged to the Russian Government as
provided in the original agreement made between the Chinese
Government and the Russo-Asiatic Bank '.

B. *Judicial Problem*

According to the contract for the construction of the C.E.R., no provision had been made as to the judicial authority in the railway zone. Later on, the Russians made regulations providing that cases should be tried jointly by the Chinese and Russian authorities. But in fact the Russian Government marked out zones along the railway which were placed under the jurisdiction of the local law courts of Chita, Vladivostok and Port Arthur; the last was later moved to Harbin. In 1913 Russia unilaterally established a civil court, thus completing the legal system. Along the whole line there were no fewer than eleven Russian preliminary courts, while those in Harbin were more elaborate in organization. The circuit system was also adopted, under which judges were sent to the various stations to hear cases.

China, however, did not forget this humiliation. On September 23, 1920, after withdrawal of recognition of the Tsarist diplomatic representatives in China, the Chinese Government announced its assumption of control over the Russian law courts and promulgated certain regulations for the organization of law courts in the Special Area. The Russian ex-chief judge and procurator were engaged as advisers, and some Russian clerks were employed and paid by the Chinese Government. The Russian law courts were thus brought under Chinese authority in November 1920. In March 1921, regulations for clearing up outstanding Russian cases were promulgated, in which it was provided that the existing procedure in accordance with Russian laws should thenceforth be abandoned. It was only then that the Chinese again exercised full jurisdiction in the C.E.R., which, it must be remembered, was Chinese territory.

C. *Municipal Problem*

The Russians were not much concerned over municipal affairs in the C.E.R. zone. In 1908 the Chinese Government with the Russians made a set of regulations consisting of eighteen articles for joint management of the railway zone. These regulations were incomplete to start with, and were never enforced. The Russians then took another step forward in 1911, by proclaiming self-government for the railway zone. Meanwhile Russia concluded a pact with England, granting British·subjects equal rights with Russians, thus appeasing England and winning international recognition for the self-government of the railway zone. This, to say the least, was unfair and incomplete.

It was not until the Russian Revolution that a supplementary agreement was made with the Russo-Asiatic Bank on October 2, 1920, for the joint management of the C.E.R., limiting the activities of the railway to commercial matters. All political activities were prohibited, and could be vetoed by the Chinese Government at any time. China later promulgated a few municipal regulations converting the self-governing council of the municipality into a subsidiary organization of the railway. Although the administration of the municipality had not been completely recovered by China, the conditions along the railway zone as a whole were much better than before.

3. Retrocession of Navigation on the Sungari and Amur Rivers

During the Tsarist régime, Russia, in her attempt to exploit northeastern China, actively engaged in developing the navigation system on the Sungari and Amur Rivers. After the Revolution, most Russian private steamship companies wound up their businesses because they were afraid of the confiscation of their vessels by the Soviet authorities. A Chinese steamship company, the Wutung S.S. Company, was then organized with a capital of $2,000,000, a part of which was subscribed by the Chinese Government. Twenty-nine vessels were bought, and operations began in July 1920.

After the inauguration of the Wutung S.S. Company, those of their ships which happened to be on the Russian bank of the Amur were interned by the Soviet Government and released only after repeated protests from the Chinese Government. China then obtained the right of navigation from the lower course of the Amur up to Khabarovsk, which was Russian territory; China's navigation area was thus considerably enlarged. The Russian Government, having spent a large amount of money on navigation, demanded that the Chinese Government should reimburse half of this amount. After detailed investigations, the Chinese Ministry of Communications suggested the following points for the consideration of the Russian Government:

1. As specified in the Aigun Treaty, only China and Russia were to have the right to navigate on the River Amur.

2. Russian vessels might use the Chinese side of the river, and Chinese vessels might use the Russian side, but all vessels were to observe the regulations in force at the various ports of call.

3. Commercial facilities and protection were to be accorded to all vessels on a reciprocal basis.

4. The establishment of all navigational aids and their management were to be governed by separate regulations.

At the time when China was ready to open negotiations with the Russian Consul at Harbin regarding these four points, the Russian Revolution had reached its height, and there was no responsible person with whom to deal, so no negotiations could be conducted.

Meanwhile the ships of the Wutung S.S. Company were navigating all the routes planned beforehand on the Amur and the Ussuri Rivers. The farthest port of call was Nikolaevsk, at the mouth of the Amur, 1,000 miles from Chinese territory. At the same time, the vessels belonging to the C.E.R. were still running; certain agreements were also made regarding the joint operation of Soviet vessels. In March 1924, the Chinese Government forbade the C.E.R. vessels to ply on the Sungari, and vessels under the Tsarist flag were entirely prohibited. The Japanese Consul at Harbin, supported by representatives of other nations, lodged a protest; the Japanese Minister in Peking also declared to the Chinese Central Government that a large part of the capital of the Russian steamship companies was Japanese. However, Japan found no treaty right to support her claim, and finally all Russian vessels were sold to Chinese merchants.

In the autumn of 1926 the Government of the Three Eastern Provinces, acting on the strength of the precedent established by the Soviet Government in taking over the Golden Horn Wharf in Vladivostok, together with eleven tug boats belonging to the C.E.R., took over eleven steamships, thirty tug boats and other properties of the Steam Navigation Department of the C.E.R. From then on, no foreign vessels appeared on the Sungari, and the privileges enjoyed by the C.E.R. of sailing on the China Sea and on rivers in Chinese territory were cancelled by China.

4. Retrocessions of Russian Concessions and Abolition of Extraterritoriality

In the time of Tsarist Russia, all Russian citizens, by force of treaty stipulations concluded with China, enjoyed the privileges of extraterritoriality similar to those enjoyed by the nationals of other treaty powers in China. After the Russian Revolution of 1917, Ministers of the Tsarist Government resident in foreign countries naturally could not represent the Soviet Government. According to international practice, such ministers might either be refused recognition or still continue to be recognized by the governments of the countries to which they were accredited. This right was given at the discretion of each particular government. For instance, Japan, having concluded secret treaties of mutual assistance with the Tsarist Government in respect of their aggressive policies in China, which were subsequently completely denounced by the Soviet Government, continued to recognize the Tsarist diplomatic and consular representatives in order to resist the newly established Soviet régime. China, however, took a different point of view, and the question of whether to continue giving recognition to the Tsarist Minister was subject to a consideration of the advantage to the Chinese Government, in deciding one way or the other.

Prior to the conclusion of the Sino-Soviet Agreement in 1924, China recognized no legally constituted government in Russia, and therefore adopted a new scheme of administration of the affairs of Russians in China, particularly in the C.E.R. zone. The Chinese Government, however, continued to recognize the Tsarist representative at Peking for some time after the Bolshevik Revolution started. Prince Koudachev was, therefore, able to continue taking care of Russian interests in China, and was even asked by the Chinese Government to suppress Bolshevik activities in Chinese territory.

In August 1917 China, in compliance with the wishes of the Allied Powers, declared war on Germany, and consequently the Allies suggested the postponement of the Boxer Indemnity instalments for a period of five years. The Russian Minister alone offered a postponement of payment of only one-third of the instalments, with the other two-thirds to be paid on time. It is to be remembered that the total amount of the Boxer Indemnity was 450,000,000 taels, of which Russia received the largest share, amounting to 132,371,120 taels. China could have refused to pay on the good ground that the Tsarist Government was no more in existence, and that the *de facto* Soviet Government had already made overtures to China promising to abrogate all unequal treaties and extraterritorial privileges contracted by the Tsarist régime. But the Chinese Government continued to pay two-thirds of the Boxer Indemnity Fund, for reasons unknown.

In November 1919 the Far Eastern Republic was established with Chita as its capital. M. Yourin was appointed in July 1920 with plenipotentiary powers, representative of that government in Peking. He made it known to the public that all unequal treaties contracted by China with the Tsarist Government were to be nullified, and that the Tsarist Minister and consuls had no right to represent the Russian Government. He proposed to China that new commercial treaties based on an equality of rights should be negotiated between the two countries. By that time, the Tsarist representatives had been refused recognition by many other countries, and China followed suit by withdrawing recognition of the Tsarist Minister and forbidding him to use secret telegraph codes. The payment of the Boxer Indemnity instalments to the Russo-Asiatic Bank was also suspended. Prince Koudachev protested to Dr. W. W. Yen, Chinese Minister of Foreign Affairs, against the prohibition on sending telegrams by private code. Dr. Yen explained that the use of code telegrams, which might be of political significance, would cause further difficulties to the Chinese Government. He suggested that the Minister should retire voluntarily to simplify the matter. In a letter to the Foreign Minister, Prince Koudachev expressed his willingness to retire, but said that since he had no instructions from his government he would not give up his office voluntarily. A Chinese Presidential mandate was then issued on September 23, 1920, stating that because Russia had been in the clutches of civil war for some years without a legal government having been instituted, the diplomatic and consular corps in China instituted by the Tsarist Government had lost their representative power, and therefore had no right to claim recognition from the Chinese Government. The recognition of the Russian Minister and consuls was therefore suspended.

The mandate continued to the effect that China would adopt an attitude of neutrality with regard to the Russian civil war and, taking into consideration the everlasting friendship between the two countries and their adjacency to each other, all Russian citizens residing in China were to be given protection with regard to person and property, whereas Russian concessions and the territory of the Chinese Eastern Railway should be dealt with by special departments and provincial authorities. Prince Koudachev was duly informed of this action, but he continued to protest and even attempted to enlist the support of the Diplomatic Corps.

As to the Russian properties in China, various Powers tried to interfere. However, in view of the fact that the Chinese Government did not sever relations with Russia, it was logical that it should assume protection over all Russian properties with the exception of the Russian Legation in Peking, which had been turned over to the joint control of the diplomatic representatives specified in the 1901 Protocol. All Russian consulates were taken over by the Chinese local authorities. Russian concessions both in Hankow and Tientsin were taken over by the local Chinese Commissioner for Foreign Affairs.

Incidentally, it may be added here that at that time the writer was the Commissioner for Foreign Affairs in Hankow, whose task was to take charge of the Russian Consulate there. The former Russian Consul General acted as his adviser. In March 1924 he took over the Russian concession on behalf of the Chinese Government. It was renamed a Special District Administration, and the writer was appointed its first Director. New by-laws were duly drawn up with the approval of the ratepayers and the Chinese Government. The Municipal Council consisted of seven members with the Director of the Special District as Chairman, *ex officio*, while the other six members were elected equally by the Chinese and foreign ratepayers in the Special District. One significant point in the by-laws was inserted in order to gain the confidence of the ratepayers, that all cheques should first be made out by the secretary and then signed by the Director and countersigned by the Finance Council member. The new organization ran so smoothly that it was later made the basis not only for Chinese administration of the former German concession, but also for the administration of the British concession in Hankow which under the famous Chen-O'Malley Agreement was retroceded to China on March 15, 1927, after the Hankow incident which lasted for months.

5. Problem of Commercial Relations

China's overland trade with Russia was very extensive. By virtue of the Aigun and Ili Treaties, Russia was in an advantageous position compared with other Powers as far as trade with China was concerned. After the Russian Revolution, when internal strife between White and Red parties became intense, Russia's trade with China fell into a state of chaos. Upon the arrival at Peking of Yourin, the Soviet Plenipotentiary, and his request for the negotiation of commercial treaties, the Chinese Foreign Ministry on January 27, 1921, proposed five points for preliminary discussions, as follows:

1. All special privileges in force during the Tsarist régime to be nullified.

2. The Overland Commercial Treaty of 1881 to be abrogated.
3. A provisional Commercial Treaty to be made, pending the complete establishment of a stable government in Soviet Russia.
4. Pending the conclusion of a formal treaty, the consuls of both countries to act only in the capacity of Trade Commissioners.
5. The draft version of the Commercial Treaty to be modified after a local treaty had been signed with the government of Sinkiang.

However, no definite result came of these proposals. By the spring of 1922, forty years had expired since the conclusion of the last Sino-Russian treaties and the Overland Commercial Treaty. In the absence of a recognized Russian Government to negotiate the revision of these treaties at that time, another Chinese Presidential mandate, declaring all previous treaties to be null and void, was published, and read as follows:

'The Sino-Russian Commercial Treaty and the Overland Route Commercial Agreement have come to an end. The trade passing through the Sino-Russian border is growing with every day, and conditions rapidly change. The original treaty is therefore out of date and should be immediately revised, which has been repeatedly proposed by the Chinese Government.

'In view of the fact that up to the present the government in Russia has not been stabilized, the revision of these treaties cannot be effected. However, for the sake of facilitating the trade between the two countries, the Chinese Government offers that all provisions for the reduction of duties by one-third, duty-exempted areas, duty-exempted commodities, etc., as specified by the Sino-Russian Treaty and the Overland Route Commercial Agreement, be abrogated and the procedure relative to the above be discontinued as from April 1 of the present year. All merchandise seeking entry into China and all Chinese and foreign goods sent to Russia should be subject to the imposition of import and export duties, according to the scale of rates of the Maritime Customs.'[12]

Thus, the Sino-Russian Commercial Treaty which had been in force for over sixty years was abolished, pending the conclusion of a new commercial treaty.

[12] Ho Han-wen, op. cit., p. 314.

Chapter VIII

PRELUDE TO THE RESUMPTION OF SINO-SOVIET
RELATIONS (1918-1924)

THE rule of the proletariat in Soviet Russia met with bitter opposition on the part of all capitalist countries. After the conclusion of the World War, the Imperialist Powers engaged in armed intervention in Soviet Russia, using the Chinese Eastern Railway, which had been constructed by the Tsarist Government, and was intended for an aggressive weapon against China, as one of their bases of attack. The Soviet State, with Russia completely isolated from the whole world, was at bay by that time. She had entered into treaty relations with Germany. But the latter, being also in a state of chaos after defeat in the World War, could not give any assistance to Russia. For this reason, Soviet Russia turned her face to the Far East, and started her friendly overtures to China in order to re-establish peaceful relations between the two countries.

1. First Soviet Declaration of 1919

As far back as July 1918, Chicherin, Soviet Commissar for Foreign Affairs, made the following announcement:

'We have notified China that we relinquish the conquests of the Tsarist Government in Manchuria, and that we recognize Chinese rights in this territory, where the principal trade route runs, namely the Eastern Siberian Railroad. This railroad, which is the property of the Chinese and Russian people, has already devoured millions of the money of these peoples, and therefore of right belongs to these peoples and to nobody else. More than this, we are of the opinion that as the Russian people advanced funds to defray part of the expenses of this railroad, these should be repaid and China buy the railroad outright, without waiting for the terms embodied in this particular treaty violently imposed upon China.'[1]

During the most critical time for Soviet Russia, when the Allied Forces made their attack along the Siberian railway and the White Russians were very active in eastern Siberia and Manchuria, Karakhan, Soviet Acting Commissar for Foreign Affairs, made the famous First Declaration on July 25, 1919, which sounded to Chinese ears as a new diplomatic Magna Charta.[2] It was the intention of the Soviet Government to win over the Chinese people and gain Chinese recognition. The first declaration reads as follows:

'All people, whether they are great or small, whether they have lived until now a free life, or whether they form against their own will a part of another country, shall be free in their inner life, and no power shall interfere with them within this limit. The Government of Workers and Peasants has then declared null and void all the secret treaties concluded with Japan, China and the ex-Allies, the treaties which were to enable the Russian Government of the Tsar and his Allies to enslave the people of the East, and principally the people of China by intimidating or buying them for the sole interests of the capitalists, financiers, and the Russian generals.

'The Soviet Government invites, henceforth, the Chinese Government to enter into negotiations with the object of cancelling the treaty of 1896, the protocol of Peking of 1901, and all the agreements concluded with Japan from 1907 to 1916. That is to say, to give back to the Chinese people all the power and authority which were obtained by the Government of the Tsar by tricks or by entering into understandings with Japan and the Allies. . . .

'We herewith address the Chinese people with the object of making them thoroughly understand that the Soviet Government has given up all the conquests made by the Government of the Tsar, which took away from China, Manchuria and other territories. . . .

'The Soviet Government returns to the Chinese people, without demanding any kind of compensation, the Chinese Eastern Railway, as well as all the mining concessions, forestry, gold mines, and all other things which were seized from them by the Govern-

---

[1] Reinsch, Bolshevism in Asia, April 1920.
[2] Dennis, A. L. P., Foreign Policies of Soviet Russia, p. 316.

ment of the Tsar, that of Kerensky and the brigands, Horvath, Semenov, Kolchak, the Russian ex-generals, merchants and capitalists.

'The Soviet Government gives up the indemnities, payable by China for the insurrection of the Boxers in 1900. . . .

'The Soviet Government has abolished all the special privileges and all the factories owned by the Russian merchants in Chinese territory; no Russian official, priest or missionary should be allowed to interfere with Chinese affairs; and if they should commit any crime, they must be judged according to the local laws in local law courts. No authority or law court should be allowed to exist in China except the authority of the Chinese people.

'Besides these principal points, the Soviet Government, represented by its Plenipotentiaries, is ready to negotiate with the Chinese people all the other questions and to settle once for all the cases of acts of violence and injustice of Russia, acting together with Japan and the Allies.'[3]

The object of this declaration, apart from an expression of willingness to abolish all unequal treaties and conquests made by the Government of the Tsar, was to pave the way for concluding a new treaty on an equal footing with China which, it was thought, would please the Chinese and gain their co-operation in wiping out the White Russian forces in the Far East. The White Russians were very active in Manchuria, the Chinese Eastern Railway being the centre of their activities. They had even seized the revenues of the railway to meet the expenses of their anti-Bolshevik campaign. The Soviet Government which was busy contending with chaos in European Russia, had no time to look after the Far East, particularly the Chinese Eastern Railway zone. It was generally recognized that the issue of the first declaration was a clever policy, as it not only gained the sympathy of the Chinese public, but also was the first step towards the destruction of the foothold established by the White Russians in the Chinese Eastern Railway zone.

The Chinese public rejoiced upon learning of the contents of the first declaration, and expressed their feelings to the Soviet Government. Especially significant was the response of the Chinese students. It was not, however, until March 26, 1920, that the official French text of this declaration was cabled to Peking from Irkutsk by a representative of the Foreign Office of the Far Eastern Republic,

[3] *China Year Book*, 1924, p. 868.

so the Chinese Government was, for a time, very much in doubt as to its authenticity. Chinese official circles even suspected the communication to be a forgery.[4] China at that time was still bound to the Allies, and was not bold enough to accept the manifesto at her own discretion. Moreover, China underestimated Soviet Russia, thinking that the new government would only be temporary, and paid no attention to the seductive declaration.

It was later generally believed that the Chinese Government had made a great blunder, that China should have recognized the Soviet declaration as sincere and taken over the whole of the Chinese Eastern Railway and its attached concessions. Instead, she allowed the enterprise to fall into the hands of an international body, though she alone had paramount interest in it. The situation became even more ridiculous when she entered into an agreement with a third party, the Russo-Asiatic Bank.

2. Second Soviet Declaration of 1920

On September 27, 1920, General Chang Shih-lin, at the head of a Chinese Mission, visited Moscow, where he was honoured by Karakhan, who delivered a second declaration to him for transmission to the Chinese Government. In the first place, the declaration expressed the Soviet Government's regret that an early *rapprochement* between China and Soviet Russia had been delayed. In this declaration, the Soviet Government declared more specifically in an eight-article agreement the principles laid down in the first declaration of July 25, 1919, the intention of which was to establish friendship and good will between the two nations:

Article 1

The Government of the Russian Socialist Federated Soviet Republic declares null and void all the treaties concluded with China by the former governments of Russia, renounces all seizures of Chinese territory and all Russian concessions in China, and restores to China, without any compensation and for ever, all that had been predatorily seized from her by the Tsar's Government and the Russian *bourgeoisie*.

Article 2

The Governments of both Republics shall take necessary

---

[4] See *Millard's Review*, June 5, 1920, p. 24.

measures for immediately establishing regular trade and economic relations. A special treaty to this effect shall be subsequently concluded on the principle of the clause of the most-favoured nation, applying to both contracting parties.

Article 3

The Chinese Government pledges itself: (1) not to proffer any aid to Russian counter-revolutionary individuals, groups or organizations, and not to allow their activities in Chinese territory; (2) to disarm, intern and hand over to the Government of the Russian Socialist Federated Soviet Republic all the detachments and organizations to be found in Chinese territory at the time of the signing of this treaty, which are fighting against the R.S.F.S.R., all their arms, ammunitions and property; (3) the Soviet Government shall bear the same responsibility towards Chinese counter-revolutionary individuals or organizations.

Article 4

All Russian citizens residing in China shall be subject to all the laws and regulations acting in the territory of the Chinese Republic, and shall not enjoy any rights of extraterritoriality. Chinese citizens residing in Russia shall be subject to all the laws and regulations acting in the territory of the Russian Socialist Federated Soviet Republic.

Article 5

The Government of the Chinese Republic pledges itself: (1) immediately after the signing of the present treaty to sever connections with persons styling themselves as diplomatic and consular representatives of the R.S.F.S.R., and to deport such persons from China; (2) to hand over to the Russian State in the person of the R.S.F.S.R. the buildings of the Embassy and consulates and other property and archives of the same situated in Chinese territory and belonging to Russia.

Article 6

The Government of the R.S.F.S.R. renounces any compensation paid out by China as indemnity for the Boxer rising, provided that under no circumstances shall the Government of the Chinese Republic pay any money to the former Russian consuls or to any other persons or Russian organizations putting up illegal claims thereto.

Article 7

Following immediately upon the signing of the present treaty, there shall be mutually established diplomatic and consular representatives of the Republic of China and the R.S.F.S.R.

Article 8

The Russian and the Chinese Governments agree to sign a special treaty on the way of working of the Chinese Eastern Railway with due regard to the needs of the R.S.F.S.R., and, in the conclusion of the treaty there shall take part, besides China and Russia, also the Far Eastern Republic.[5]

Let us now compare the second declaration with the first one. Although the Soviet still offered the abolition of the existing unequal treaties and the conclusion of a new treaty with China as a bait for wiping out the remaining White Russian forces in the Far East, the way of treating the subject of the Chinese Eastern Railway was quite different in tone. Instead of saying the Soviet Government returns to the Chinese people the Chinese Eastern Railway 'without demanding any kind of compensation' as in the first declaration, it was now stipulated in Article 8 'that the Russian and Chinese Governments agree to sign a special treaty as to the way of working of the Chinese Eastern Railway'. In other words, the Chinese Eastern Railway was only to be put under joint control—not to be returned to China without compensation as under the earlier offer. Even with regard to the Boxer Indemnity Fund there was a typical clause: 'Provided that under no circumstances shall the Government of the Chinese Republic pay any money to the former Russian consuls or to any other persons, or Russian organizations putting up illegal claims thereto.'

It seemed that in the second declaration the Soviet Government was not magnanimously returning what was acquired by the Tsarist Government by armed aggression, as had been stated in the first declaration. The reason why the Soviet attitude was now not so generous as before was that the remnant of White Russian forces were gradually becoming eliminated from Manchuria, and the Soviet Government was becoming stabilized.

The Chinese Government, although having missed the first opportunity, paid no proper attention to this second declaration. The situation was quite difficult, for there was still a Tsarist Minister in Peking claiming *de jure* recognition with the support of the Dip-

[5] See text in *China Year Book*, 1924, pp. 870-972.

lomatic Corps, while the new Soviet Government were demanding recognition *de facto*, in exchange for terms more generous than had ever before been offered to China. The problem was whether to recognize the new order in Russia, at the risk of displeasing the other Powers, by withdrawing recognition from the old Tsarist Russian representatives. China still thought the future of the new government uncertain, and was afraid that the old régime, which was not entirely out of existence, might regain its power. Consequently, after lengthy Cabinet discussions, China decided to take a middle course. She suspended recognition of the old Russian representatives in China, and took all Russian interests under her own control, until such time as she should recognize the new Soviet Government.

When the Soviets realized the failure of Bolshevik activities in Europe, they wanted to be still more friendly with China. After having published the second declaration to the Chinese people, the Far Eastern Republic sent a plenipotentiary in the person of Yourin from Mongolia to Peking to discuss with the Chinese Government ways and means of concluding new treaties between China and Soviet Russia. The Chinese Government, at that juncture, was still in fear of foreign intervention, particularly by Japan and France, whose representatives in Peking were using pressure to prevent China from resuming friendly relations with Soviet Russia. China, therefore, dared not start any negotiations.

3. Activities of Yourin and Paikes

After the arrival of the Yourin Mission at Peking, the Chinese Government proposed four main points of discussion: (1) The mission was not to be allowed to undertake any Bolshevik propaganda; (2) An indemnity was to be paid to Chinese merchants in Siberia to cover their losses and damages; (3) The protection of Chinese in Siberia was to be guaranteed; (4) Measures were to be taken to prevent any recurrence of certain specified incidents. In spite of Yourin's willingness to negotiate along these lines, the Chinese Government further asked for some written confirmation from the Soviet Government. As Yourin was hardly in a position to produce this, matters remained at a standstill.

Consequently, Yourin had no choice but to turn his attention to the Chinese people in the hope of winning from among them friends to Russia and converts to Sovietism. With this end in view, he tried hard to get in touch with parliamentary members and prominent educators. He publicly declared the intention of the Soviet Government to remit the Russian share of the Boxer Indemnity Fund for educational purposes. His idea was to use this as a bait for winning the sympathy of Chinese educational circles. On the strength of introductions obtained from several college professors, he cultivated close relations with Chinese students. However, Yourin's stay in China brought no more fruitful results, and in the summer of 1921 he returned to Russia.

After Yourin, another Soviet representative, Paikes, came to Peking. His activities were also limited to work among the Chinese people, and he was unable to open negotiations with the Chinese Government. The failure of both missions may be ascribed to the fact that these two men were not of sufficient distinction. Besides, the international situation was not favourable to them.

After these two representatives failed to conclude negotiations with the Chinese Government, the Soviet representative, Krassine, in London approached Dr. Wellington Koo, Chinese Minister to Britain, requesting that friendly relations between Soviet Russia and China be resumed, and stating that he was empowered by the Soviet Government to conclude new treaties with China on the basis of recent treaties with Britain, Germany, Italy, Switzerland, etc. Dr. Wellington Koo communicated with the Chinese Foreign Minister, who admitted that negotiations could be undertaken. Meanwhile, the Ministry telegraphed the Moscow Government that China was ready to enter into negotiations on the condition that Soviet Russia accepted the declarations of 1919 and 1920 as a basis. To this proposal, the Soviet Government agreed without demur.

4. Arrival of Joffe

In the summer of 1922 the Soviet Government sent a first-rate diplomat, Joffe, to China. He arrived at Peking on August 12. Joffe had been a professor of International Law in Russia, and had won fame by successfully negotiating a trade agreement with Germany after the Revolution. His series of speeches, denouncing western imperialism and declaring the liberation of mankind through Soviet policy, made shortly before his arrival in Peking, unquestionably received hearty welcome among the Chinese intellectuals. He was a diplomat of rare distinction, vested with great power, and he aroused general attention and understanding. He immediately set to work to disseminate Soviet propaganda on the one hand, while on the other he plunged into diplomatic activities. On September 2 he made a proposal to the Chinese Foreign Ministry to open a Sino-Soviet Conference prior to the date set for the Soviet Japanese Conference at Changchun. Dr. Koo, formerly Chinese Minister to Britain and at this time Chinese Foreign Minister, immediately raised the question of the Bolshevik occupation of Outer Mongolia, and demanded the withdrawal of Soviet forces as a guarantee of 'good faith' before opening negotiations. Joffe claimed that 'it was inadmissible that any separate question should be picked out of the whole complex of questions to be discussed at the conference'.[6] He also pointed out to the Chinese Government 'the stationing of Soviet troops in Mongolia concerns Chinese interests no less than the Soviet interests, and while in the name of my Government I reject energetically the demand of their withdrawal from Urga, the only reason is that I am totally convinced that not only would this be impossible at the present moment from the viewpoint of Soviet interests, but that it would be impossible also from the viewpoint of real Chinese national interests rightly understood, let alone the interests of the people of Mongolia who still energetically demand that Soviet forces be left in Outer Mongolia'.

In the same communication, he blamed the Chinese Government for shielding the 'Whites', who used Chinese soil to attack Soviet territory. The Chinese Government then ordered local authorities to disarm any 'Whites' who might seek shelter in Chinese territory, but insisted that the 'Reds' should evacuate Mongolia before the conference could begin.

In another note to the Chinese Government, Joffe accused Ostroumoff, the Engineer-in-Chief of the Chinese Eastern Railway, of being 'guilty of most corrupt practices'. He urged that a new management be provisionally established pending the settlement of this question at the coming conference. His sharp attack upon Ostroumoff was dismissed entirely after an impartial investigation by J. F. Stevens, who proved that the railway was as efficiently run as ever.[7]

Then came, for the first time, the controversy over the Karakhan declarations. The Chinese Government, in reply to Joffe's note, stated that the alleged corruption of the administration would be investigated, but, in concluding their memorandum, the Chinese Government asked Joffe to declare that the Soviet Government would return

[6] *China Year Book*, 1924, p. 859.
[7] ibid.

the railway without compensation, as promised in the 1919 and 1920 Declarations made by Karakhan, as the only solution of the railway problem.

In his reply of November 6 to the Foreign Ministry, Joffe repudiated any inference that Russian interests in China had been renounced by the Declarations of 1919 and 1920. He wrote as follows:

> 'Russia has denounced the predatory and violent policy of the Tsar's Government and promised to renounce those rights which had accrued to Russia from this policy. But, first, until all these questions shall have been settled by a free accord between Russia and China, Russia's rights in China will not have lost their force; and, secondly, these declarations do not annul Russia's legal and just rights in China. In particular, for instance, even if Russia vests in the Chinese people her title to the Chinese Eastern Railway, this will not annul Russia's interests in this line, which is a portion of the Great Siberian Railway and unites one part of Russian territory with another.'[8]

Joffe even categorically disavowed the most important clause of the first Declaration, stipulating the restoration of Chinese sovereignty over the Chinese Eastern Railway without compensation. He asserted that the 1919 Declaration was merely a fundamental programme of Russia's foreign policy towards China, but did not include any concrete propositions or detailed conditions. Dr. Koo pointed out that Article 1 of the 1920 Declaration read:

> 'The Government of the Russian Socialist Federated Soviet Republic declares null and void all the treaties concluded with China by the former governments of Russia, renounces all seizures of Chinese territory and all Russian concessions in China, and restores to China, without any compensation and for ever, all that had been predatorily seized from her by the Tsar's Government and the Russian *bourgeoisie*.'

Joffe retorted that the above was made conditional by Article 3 of the same Declaration, which proposed that China declare her intention to disarm, intern and hand over all the White Russian forces in China, whose activities were directed against Soviet Russia and its

---

[8] *North China Herald*, November 14, 1922.

allies. This, he alleged, had not been carried out by China. He also pointed out that Article 7 of the same Declaration provided for a special treaty concerning the Chinese Eastern Railway with due regard to the needs of the R.S.F.S.R. At the end of his memorandum to the Chinese Foreign Ministry, Joffe refuted the rumours that the Red Army had the intention of seizing the Chinese Eastern Railway by force.[9] However, it was a well-known fact that the Soviets had seized properties of the Chinese Eastern Railway along the Manchurian border, despite protests lodged by the Chinese Government. According to Joffe, on the other hand, China had been interfering with the administration of the Chinese Eastern Railway for the last five years.

On December 28 Joffe sent another note to the Foreign Ministry, stating that the Soviet manifesto of 1919, in which the Soviet Government engaged to give up its rights with regard to the Chinese Eastern Railway, could not be interpreted in such a way as to imply their unconditional return to China. Because of these controversies, the opening of the Sino-Soviet conference was postponed indefinitely. In the meantime, the Chinese public began to realize that the policy of the Soviet Government was following the usual traditional lines. Every word and move made by Joffe began to be regarded with suspicion.

Joffe's desire to create a new atmosphere in diplomatic relations and promote revolutionary work in China failed because of his poor health. He left Peking for Shanghai on January 16, 1923, and proceeded to Japan at the request of Baron Shimpei Goto,[10] who urged him to seek convalescence at the hot springs in Japan. During his stay in Shanghai, he had several conferences with Dr. Sun Yat-sen, and succeeded in announcing a joint declaration relating to the identity of their views with regard to Sino-Soviet relations. This joint declaration, which, in a way, foreshadowed the future destiny of China, will be dealt with in another chapter.

Joffe's visit to Japan, which was ostensibly made for the purpose of recuperating his poor health, actually aimed at reaching an understanding with Japan with regard to China. The Chinese public was rather nervous over this visit. Apprehension was expressed that he might conclude an agreement with Japan detrimental to the interests of China. Some members of the Chinese Parliament even warned Joffe that any agreement which he might reach with Japan

[9] *China Year Book*, 1924, p. 862.
[10] Baron Shimpei Goto was made a Count on account of his services in connection with the Soviet-Japanese *rapprochement*.

would not meet with recognition by China. However, Joffe announced that he would come back to Peking to resume negotiations as soon as he had recovered.

Upon his arrival at Tokyo, Joffe had several unofficial meetings with Baron Goto, who was strongly in favour of a *rapprochement* between Tokyo and Moscow. But the time was not opportune for concluding such an agreement. Moreover, Joffe was not very amicably received by the Japanese: Baron Goto's residence was stoned, and inscriptions appeared in the main streets, which bitterly attacked the newcoming envoy. This might have brought anxiety to Joffe, for, contrary to expectations, the hot springs worsened his state of health and he nearly lost his life. Realizing that it was impossible to continue with the Soviet Japanese Conference, he went back to Russia.

5. Wang-Karakhan Negotiations

The next Russian Envoy to China after Joffe was Karakhan, who immediately upon his arrival received a hearty welcome both from the Chinese Government and the Chinese people. The main reason for this was the fact that both the 1919 and 1920 Declarations had been signed by him, and, as we know, they had been received with warm and deep sympathy by the Chinese.

Prior to Karakhan's arrival, the Chinese Government had appointed Dr. C. T. Wang on March 18, 1923, as head of the Sino-Soviet Negotiations Commission, which action was meant as a hint of opposition to the Soviet opinion that the negotiations should be transferred to Moscow during the absence of Joffe. Karakhan arrived at Peking on September 2, but he broke his journey at Mukden to have an interview with Chang Tso-lin, the warlord of Manchuria. His intention was first to reach some understanding with the warlord concerning the Chinese Eastern Railway, and then to go on to Peking for the endorsement of such an agreement. However, he failed to convince Chang and hurried to Peking.

After his arrival in the Chinese capital, Karakhan made public speeches, mentioning the Chinese people as 'the best ally of the Russians in Asia'. At a luncheon given in his honour by Dr. C. T. Wang, he said that 'during his stay in Harbin nothing could please him more than to see there a Chinese administration, Chinese laws and the realization of Chinese sovereignty'.[11]

[11] *China Year Book*, 1924, p. 865.

On September 7, 1923, Karakhan made his first visit to the Foreign Ministry and told the Chinese Minister that his government insisted upon formal recognition being effected before negotiations. China flatly refused this request, for the conclusion of a trade agreement and the resumption of diplomatic relations were two different things. The Chinese Government was fully aware that if the Soviet Government were to be recognized, it would imply the recognition of the Soviets as the legal heir of Tsarist Russia, legally able to claim all the rights belonging to Russia of the old régime. While China requested that negotiations should be opened first, Karakhan insisted upon formal recognition, and, judging from the change of tone of the Soviet Envoy, it was apparent that the Soviet demands would be difficult to meet.

Meanwhile, Karakhan began to launch attacks upon the Chinese Government, accusing it of retaining certain vessels of the Russian Volunteer Fleet, permitting intolerable outrages against the Soviets on the Chinese border, and using the Boxer Indemnity Fund for the payment of Russian diplomatic agents belonging to the Tsarist régime. The Chinese Government gave appropriate explanations to meet these allegations. The matter was then further complicated by renewed controversies as to the authenticity of the text of the 1919 Declaration. The newly published authorized version of the 1919 and 1920 Declarations by the Soviet mission omitted the clause providing for the restoration without compensation of the Chinese Eastern Railway to China, and likewise the sub-paragraph of Article 3 of the 1920 Declaration was left out. Thus China felt herself to be in a dilemma at such a critical moment, especially when Karakhan requested *de jure* recognition before negotiation.

On November 30, Karakhan addressed a lengthy memorandum to Dr. Wang, in which he again insisted upon the establishment of normal relations before the conference could begin, as 'a preliminary evidence of sincerity and friendliness on the part of the Chinese Government'. With regard to the Chinese Eastern Railway, he stated:

'Never and nowhere could I have said that all the rights on the Chinese Eastern Railway belong to China. . . . But even now I can confirm what was said four years ago, namely, that the sovereignty of China in the territory of the railway is fully recognized by us and that we shall not insist on any one of those privileges which the Tsarist Government had, and which the other Foreign Powers still have to-day, in the railway zone.'[12]

The conference was again postponed, though Wang had constantly urged Karakhan to set a date for the formal opening of discussions on all outstanding questions. During this time, Britain and Italy had formally recognized the Soviet Government, and public opinion in China grew more in favour of obtaining strong and solid agreement with Soviet Russia.

Informal discussions, however, were conducted by Wang and Karakhan on the basis of the 1919 and 1920 Declarations. The result of these discussions was the completion on March 14, 1924, of the Outline Agreement for the Settlement of Pending Issues in Sino-Soviet Relations, in fifteen clauses, the Provisional Agreement for the Management of the Chinese Eastern Railway, in eleven clauses, and other documents. On the morning of March 16 an agreement was initialed by Wang and Karakhan. It was mutually agreed that diplomatic and consular relations between the two countries should be immediately restored, and a conference should be held one month after the signing of this agreement to discuss the following questions: (1) The nullification of all the agreements entered into between China and Tsarist Russia and their replacement by new agreements on the basis of equality, reciprocity and justice, and in the spirit of the 1919 and 1920 Declarations; (2) the withdrawal of the Soviet troops from Outer Mongolia; (3) the redemarcation of the national boundaries of the two countries; (4) the conclusion of a Commercial Treaty and a Customs Tariff Agreement between the two contracting parties.

The Soviet Government agreed to renounce the Russian portion of the Boxer Indemnity and to relinquish the rights of extraterritoriality and consular jurisdiction for Russian subjects in China. With regard to the Provisional Agreement for the management of the Chinese Eastern Railway, it resembled very much the Supplementary Agreement reached in 1920, with the Soviet Government taking the place of the Russo-Asiatic Bank, except that the time limit for the restoration of the railway to China without compensation was reduced from eighty to sixty years.

It was generally supposed that no further question would now stand in the way of the recognition of the Soviet Union by China. At this juncture another deadlock led to serious political controversy.

[12] *China Year Book*, 1924, pp. 873-6.

6. Breaking-off of Negotiations

When the conclusion of the Wang-Karakhan Agreement became known, Dr. Wellington Koo, Minister of Foreign Affairs, raised objections to the effect that Dr. Wang had been empowered by the Presidential mandate only to prepare for, and carry on, the Sino-Russian negotiations, but not to sign any agreement, and that the conclusion of the agreement which had been initialed by Dr. Wang was an unauthorized act which could in no way be considered as final. Dr. Koo reported to the Cabinet the necessity of three essential modifications, namely, the nullification of treaties made by Russia and Outer Mongolia, the immediate withdrawal of the Soviet troops from Mongolia and the transfer of churches and immovable properties to Soviet Russia. These points were afterwards announced by the Cabinet in a circular telegram sent to the local authorities.[13]

When it was known that the Chinese Government would not approve the Wang-Karakhan Agreement without modifications, Karakhan lost his temper and refused to make alterations on the ground that signatures had already been attached to this agreement. Subsequently, controversies arose. On March 16, the Soviet representative sent Dr. Wang a letter in the nature of an ultimatum. It read:

'On the morning of the 14th inst. Your Excellency, representing the Chinese Government, and myself, representing the Government of the Soviet Union, concluded and signed some draft agreements for the resumption of relations between China and the Soviet Union; it was also agreed that, as soon as the final copies of those agreements were made out, they should be formally signed. I understand that the Chinese Government refuses to approve these agreements and also forbids Your Excellency to sign them formally; to this I must draw Your Excellency's attention. I shall await the Chinese Government to recognize the agreements referred to within a period of three days from date, beyond which I shall not be bound by the conditions specified in those agreements. Again, I shall have to make it known to Your Excellency in the name of the Soviet Government, that for all incidents which shall arise out of the breaking-off of negotiations

[13] See the exact translation of the circular telegram below, also *China Year Book*, 1924, p. 883.

the Soviet Government deems that the Chinese Government should be held solely responsible. Kindly inform your government to this effect.'

Having received this three-day ultimatum, Dr. Wang made a suggestion to the Cabinet that the agreements should be signed accordingly, but the Cabinet refused to recognize that the negotiations had been concluded and was greatly surprised that the Soviet representative should set a period for the approval of the agreements, which Dr. Wang was not permitted by his government to sign. The Cabinet further instructed Dr. Wang to continue negotiations with the Soviet representative in accordance with decisions arrived at. Meanwhile, the Soviet representative sent a note to the Chinese Ministry of Foreign Affairs, which read:

'A note was received from you on March 28, 1923, to the effect that the Chinese Government had formally appointed Dr. C. T. Wang as its official representative. Discussions were completed by March 14, 1924, and various agreements were signed. Final copies of these agreements should have been made on the same day for signature. But the Chinese Government refused to recognize the signature of its formal representative, and those agreements were nullified. On account of the above-mentioned conditions the Soviet Government instructed me to inform you as to the following:

'1. The Soviet Government regards the discussions with the formal representative of the Chinese Government as concluded.

'2. The Soviet Government firmly refuses to discuss further the various agreements already signed.

'3. The Soviet Government warns the Chinese Government against making irreparable mistakes, which might affect the future relations between China and the Soviet Union.

'4. Upon expiration of the time limit given in my letter to the Chinese representative on March 16, the Soviet Government will not be bound by the conditions specified in the various agreements signed on March 14. The Soviet Government also reserves the full right to make its own conditions in its future agreements with the Chinese Government.

'5. Upon the expiration of the time limit above named, the Chinese Government shall not reopen discussions with the Soviet

Government before the Chinese Government shall have resumed normal relations with the Soviet Government unconditionally and without treaties.'

This note practically declared the breaking-off of the Sino-Soviet negotiations. Consequently, the Chinese Government wound up its office for Sino-Soviet negotiations, and its affairs were taken over by the Foreign Ministry. On March 22, Dr. Wellington Koo, Minister of Foreign Affairs, replied to the Soviet representative in the following terms:

'. . . It is not possible to accept the time limit set by Your Excellency in your letter to Dr. C. T. Wang. Before signing the draft agreements, Dr. Wang had not obtained permission from the government. Hence, the Chinese Government cannot admit that the discussions had been concluded. Moreover, the appointment given Dr. Wang by the Chinese Government on October 2, 1923, only commissioned him with the power to discuss and arrive at decisions; all such decisions, after having received approval from the government, would be put into practice. Your Excellency stated by word of mouth that you had not seen the credentials of appointment. If you had read them, you would not have acted thus. For this reason the Chinese Government cannot recognize these signatures. On the 20th inst. a mandate was received from the President of China, stating that: "The Sino-Russian negotiations are of great importance. Though we have been gradually getting closer with the Russian representative since Dr. C. T. Wang began preliminary discussions, the conditions have not yet been made definite. These affairs shall be taken over by the Ministry of Foreign Affairs." In obedience to the above, I am ready to continue negotiations with Your Excellency in order to arrive at the conclusion. Kindly communicate this to your government.'

At this time Dr. C. T. Wang sent a circular telegram to various provinces to plead his own case, as well as to point out that the blame lay with the government. The Cabinet also sent a circular telegram to report on the points of controversy in the negotiations and received another telegram from Dr. Wang. Many telegrams of enquiry were sent to the government from the provincial authorities. Non-official educational leaders issued a manifesto, advocating unconditional recognition of Soviet Russia. The Chinese intelligentsia were greatly concerned.

7. Signature of Sino-Soviet Agreement

By this time, the negotiations between China and Soviet Russia had come to an impasse, while negotiations between Russia and Japan were in full swing. It reached the ears of the Chinese people that Soviet Russia was prepared to concede the southern section of the Chinese Eastern Railway to Japan. The Peking Government also received information that both Mukden and Canton were negotiating with Soviet Russia, and felt rather uneasy. Chinese public opinion was, however, in favour of the endorsement of the Wang-Karakhan Agreement, and blamed the government for losing the opportunity, in spite of the excellent reasons for rejecting it raised by the Cabinet.

It may be added here that the French Minister at Peking warned the Chinese Foreign Minister on March 12, that the interests of the Russo-Asiatic Bank must be protected, and demanded that his Government be consulted on any settlement reached with regard to the Chinese Eastern Railway.[14] This protest, however, had no juridical basis, because the Russo-Asiatic Bank had no claim whatever to the Chinese Eastern Railway. It is an undeniable fact that France had lent an immense amount of money to Tsarist Russia, a part of which went to the Russo-Chinese Bank, which was afterwards reorganized in Paris as the Russo-Asiatic Bank. The loans, however, were made to the Russian Government, and it was unreasonable for the reorganized Russo-Asiatic Bank to claim any rights in the Chinese Eastern Railway. In a note from Karakhan, addressed to Dr. Koo on March 22, the following passage is worthy of notice:

'The French note of March 12 could not have been written in defence of non-existing French interests in the Chinese Eastern Railway, but it is an unusual attempt of French Imperialism to deal a blow directed against the U.S.S.R.'[15]

The Foreign Ministry, in answer to the French note, flatly denied the right of either the French Government or the Russo-Asiatic

[14] *China Weekly Review*, March 22, 1924.
[15] ibid.

Bank to interfere with the settlement of the Chinese Eastern Railway question.

The American Government also sent a note to China on May 3, reminding her of the existence of the Washington Conference resolution regarding the Powers' reserved right to insist on China's responsibility for the performance or non-performance of obligations towards foreign stockholders, bondholders and creditors of the Chinese Eastern Railway. An identical representation was received from the Japanese Government.

In answer to these protests, the Chinese Government replied that the reference to the history and agreement of the Chinese Eastern Railway concerned only Russia and China, and asserted that, in the future, they would settle all questions relative to the Chinese Eastern Railway at their own discretion. In view of the unexpected representations from different Powers, Karakhan proposed to resort to secret diplomacy. Knowing of the deadlock, which had lasted for about two months, the Chinese people were accordingly taken by surprise at the sudden issue of a communiqué by the Foreign Ministry on May 31, 1924, to the effect that a Sino-Soviet Agreement on General Principles, and an Agreement for the Provisional Management of the Chinese Eastern Railway, together with seven declarations and an exchange of notes had been signed at the Foreign Office at two a.m. by Dr. V. K. Wellington Koo, Chinese Foreign Minister, and M. L. M. Karakhan, the Soviet Extraordinary Plenipotentiary, representing the Republic of China and the Union of Soviet Socialist Republics respectively, and that normal relations between the two countries had thereby been restored.

In view of the popular rumour then current that there was rivalry between Dr. Wellington Koo and Dr. C. T. Wang for the honour of signing the Sino-Soviet Agreement, the writer specially interviewed Dr. Koo in the Chinese Embassy in Paris on April 15, 1939. Dr. Koo recollected past events and made the following remarks:

'During the period of the Sino-Soviet negotiations, Dr. C. T. Wang was appointed Tupan (Head of the Commission), and I acted in the capacity of Minister of Foreign Affairs. Though Dr. Wang was appointed as the Head of the Commission, he was authorized only to negotiate, but not to sign any agreement before it passed through the Cabinet meeting and was approved by the President. Such is the international practice.

'After Dr. Wang assumed his office, he held several meetings with M. Karakhan, the Soviet Plenipotentiary, but the Foreign Ministry received no reports about them. I gained some information about the progress of the conference through my subordinates and those who worked in the Sino-Soviet Negotiations Committee, and on several occasions when I happened to be dining together with Dr. Wang, I asked him personally what was going on.

'One day, I noticed with surprise that the *Tao Pao* (Peking vernacular paper) published very prominently news of the Sino-Soviet negotiations, and stated that a draft agreement had been signed between Wang and Karakhan, representing China and the Soviet Union respectively, in the Soviet Legation at 4 a.m. on March 16. It was reported that the conference lasted from 8 p.m. to 4 a.m.

'I wondered why the Foreign Ministry and the Cabinet were not kept informed. I instructed my secretary, Mr. Chao Chuan, to obtain the original copy of the signed document. I found in it three items which had not been negotiated satisfactorily. They were:

'1. Regarding the existing treaties between Soviet Russia and Outer Mongolia, China suggested that such treaties should be declared null and void in the agreement, while the Soviet representative agreed to nullify only those treaties which were made with a third party and were detrimental to Chinese interests.

'2. The clause regarding the transfer of churches and immovable properties to Soviet Russia was not in conformity with the 1919 and 1920 Declarations. It was feared that, after the return of these properties, Soviet Russia would use them to spread propaganda.

'3. Regarding the agreement to effect the retrocession of the Russian portion of the Boxer Indemnity Fund by organizing a Joint Committee of two members only, one from each side, to decide and endorse any expenditures to be made, this did not correspond with the former declarations. As a matter of fact, the Ministry of Finance, after having learnt of the declarations made by the Soviet Union had already suspended payment and was using that Fund as security for issuing National Bonds.

'Meanwhile, when the Ministry submitted the treaty to the

Cabinet meeting, the members of the Cabinet were not a little amazed. They unanimously agreed that the Sino-Soviet negotiations were not legally concluded, and that Dr. C. T. Wang was not authorized by his government to sign any agreements. A Presidential mandate was issued at midnight on March 21, which stated: "All the outstanding problems conducted by C. T. Wang in the Sino-Soviet negotiations are henceforth transferred to the Foreign Ministry for the continuation of negotiations." From then on, a violent political storm ensued. Marshal Wu Pei-fu and Marshal Chi Hsieh-yuan from Loyang and Nanking respectively, together with provincial governments, sent successive telegrams to Peking stating that the above complication came as a result of competition between Koo and Wang. They thought that if China did not conclude any agreement with Soviet Russia at this time, the opportunity might be lost for ever. One of the most violent messages even contained the phrase: "The Foreign Ministry should be held responsible."

'The Soviet representative, Karakhan, insisted that inasmuch as the agreement had already been signed, the negotiations must be considered as concluded, and no modification of them could be made. He sent a note to the Ministry, setting up a three-day time limit for a satisfactory reply, which was tantamount to an ultimatum.

'I still remember that on April 1 I had high fever, but was nevertheless obliged to draw up a reply myself, making clear the fact that Dr. Wang was instructed by Presidential mandate only to prepare for and carry on the Sino-Soviet negotiations, but not to sign any agreement, and calling M. Karakhan's attention to the fact that it was not known whether both parties had examined each other's credentials before they affixed their signatures. I further blamed M. Karakhan for setting a time limit for our reply, for it appeared to be an unprecedented procedure in international affairs for one party to set a time limit for the other in the nature of a threat when both were engaged in the common task of establishing friendly relations. It was again stressed that the Soviet Envoy had no right to impose a time limit for the Chinese Government's actions, and he was not asked to prolong it.

'At this juncture, there were wild rumours that the Cabinet would be reorganized, and Dr. C. T. Wang would be appointed as the Foreign Minister. Suddenly, an unexplained incident occurred in my residence at Te-shih-tze Hutung, Peking, where a bomb exploded. The bomb was introduced into my house by a messenger who came with a visiting card and a heavy box, on which was written: " Newly excavated white gold seal of Ching Dynasty from Chengchow, Honan, to be presented to Minister Koo as a gift." The sender was stated to be the Chinese Geographical Society.

'I immediately suspected that this very heavy and clumsy box might contain something else, and ordered one of the servants to take it away and throw it into the fish pond. I warned the servants to be careful, but they ignored my admonition and tried to open it with a knife. All of a sudden it exploded with a loud report, and three servants were seriously wounded, one of them even losing both arms.

'The members of the Diplomatic Corps sent their delegates to express their sympathy, including one from M. Karakhan, the Soviet Envoy. Later I instructed Mr. Chao Chuan to see M. Karakhan to return my thanks, and at this juncture it so happened that the Sino-Soviet negotiations were brought to light again, and both Chao and Karakhan were of the opinion that it would be a great pity to let the matter drop simply on account of incompleteness of procedure. M. Karakhan, however, promised to modify the text to a certain extent. Both sides agreed to carry out the negotiations in the most secret way in view of strong opposition, coming both from within and without. By so doing, the final agreement, as well as other documents, was finally signed by M. Karakhan and myself, representing our respective countries, on May 31, 1924.

'Prior to signing, I reported the matter to Mr. Sun Pao-chi, the Premier, and advised him as to the progress of the negotiations, mentioning that they had passed into my hands. I requested him to forward this statement to the President, Marshal Tsao Kun, to authorize Dr. C. T. Wang to sign the Pact in order to complete his honourable task. The Premier agreed and asked me to accompany him to the President. In the interview with the latter, we put forward our suggestion. President Tsao, without any hesitation, said that this matter was under the jurisdiction of the Foreign Ministry, and the Pact should be signed by Minister Koo. He then personally wrote the credentials and delivered them to the Premier. These credentials are still kept by me, because they are in the handwriting of President Tsao.'

It is no exaggeration to say that the public was totally taken by surprise when it was made known that the Sino-Soviet Agreement had been signed and published by the Ministry of Foreign Affairs. Even those who were in close association with the government had been kept in ignorance, and only a few days before, Karakhan had stated to the Press that the impasse remained unsolved. The public was greatly excited to hear of the conclusion of negotiations, because the people were in favour of the Wang-Karakhan Agreement and wanted to have it endorsed, although they did not deny that the opinions expressed by the Cabinet were also sound. Dr. Koo's brilliant stroke of diplomacy, intended to appease public sentiment at the right moment, ought to be appreciated.

Did Karakhan actually yield, and if so, to what extent, in modifying the already signed Wang-Karakhan Agreement? Both Agreements on General Principles and for the Provisional Management of the Chinese Eastern Railway remained practically unchanged. The first declaration slightly differed from the second in respect of the reciprocal transfer of real estate and immovable property, and did not include the Russian concessions at Hankow and Tientsin owned by the Tsarist régime. Another modification in the second declaration was with regard to the transfer of buildings and landed property of the Russian Orthodox Church in accordance with internal laws and regulations existing in China regarding property and holdings in the interior. This was intended to remove the fear of establishing a precedent, which might be followed by the nationals of other countries in China.

A slight modification had also been made with regard to the Russian share of the Boxer Indemnity Fund; by means of organizing a special Commission to administer and allocate the fund for the promotion of education among the Chinese people. The Commission was to consist of three persons, two of them Chinese, appointed by the Chinese Government, instead of the one-to-one ratio as stipulated in the Wang-Karakhan Agreement. Notwithstanding the fact that in the third declaration it was stipulated that the Chinese Government would not and did not recognize as valid any treaty, agreement, etc., concluded between Russia since the Tsarist régime and any third party or parties, affecting the sovereign rights and interests of China, there was nothing said about the withdrawal of Soviet troops from Mongolia, which was one of the three essential points presented for modification by the Cabinet.

Thus by mutual concessions the almost hopeless situation, which had dragged on for months, was saved. The Sino-Soviet Treaty opened a new epoch in the diplomatic history of China, as it was the first time that China was placed on an equal footing with a Western Power. Moreover, it established the precedent of voluntary relinquishment of extraterritoriality and consular jurisdiction. (See full texts in Appendix A.)

Chapter IX

WHITE-RED CONTESTS IN OUTER MONGOLIA

THE Tripartite Agreement entered into by China, Russia and Mongolia in 1915 was ended by the Russian Revolution of 1917. The Mongolian princes were then forced to renounce their autonomy, and sought to come back under Chinese administration.

If the Chinese Government had been in a position to do so, it could at that time have incorporated Outer Mongolia as an integral part of the Chinese Republic. But it had its hands more than full with the problem of dealing with the various warlords, who were virtually besieging Peking. Meanwhile, after the collapse of the Tsarist Government, Ataman Semenov started in Siberia a campaign against the Revolutionary Government. Later he moved to Outer Mongolia, where he and his followers tried desperately to gain a foothold against the Bolsheviks. His scheme was ambitious in the extreme—he aimed at nothing less than an empire, which was to include not only Outer and Inner Mongolia, but also Tibet and other areas, altogether a wide territory.

1. Semenov, Head of White Russian Activities

When Semenov considered matters ripe enough to start the venture, he called a conference at Verkhne-Udinsk, to which representatives of Outer and Inner Mongolia, Tibet and Buriat land were invited. The conference opened on March 2, 1919, and adopted the following resolutions:

1. A unified central government for the areas represented should be organized.

2. The seat of this central government should be at Hailar.

3. A provisional government should be immediately established, and a delegate should be sent to the Paris Peace Conference to seek formal recognition.

It was also decided that an expeditionary force, consisting of about four thousand troops then available, should be sent to Mongolia to make sure that the latter would sever her relations with China.[1]

It was not difficult to find out who was backing Semenov. Japan had always been at loggerheads with Russia over the spoils in Mongolia and Manchuria, and this dispute had become even more intensified after the Russo-Japanese War. For fear that the Russian Revolutionary Government would gradually extend its influence through Siberia and Outer Mongolia, which would bring Russia to the very door of what Japan regarded as her 'sphere of influence', the latter eagerly participated in the Siberian intervention movement organized by the Allies after the first World War, with the avowed intention of surrounding and circumscribing Bolshevism and preventing it from contaminating the rest of the world.

As the Siberian intervention movement failed both with regard to its declared purpose and Japan's private motive, Japan found her hopes dwindling. But at that time there came a God-sent opportunity in the person of Semenov. It was clear that Semenov would not have been able to bring his scheme to realization without substantial assistance from some major Power. Japan was extremely willing to supply such assistance. She was even willing to undertake the mission of trying to induce the Hutukhtu or Living Buddha of Outer Mongolia to agree to the terms of the Verkhne-Udinsk Conference.

The Hutukhtu at this time was favourably disposed towards China, particularly as the latter had recently accorded him autonomy in Outer Mongolia on extremely generous terms. Consequently he was not willing in any way to involve himself in an enterprise unfavourable to China. Thus, in spite of the opportunity offered by Semenov's campaign, the Japanese met with very little success. Semenov, however, turned his attention to brewing discontent among the various factions of the Government of Outer Mongolia. The Government of Outer Mongolia from time immemorial had consisted of: (1) the princes of the various tribes, representing the lay branch of power, and (2) the religious branch of power, headed by the Hutukhtu or Living Buddha. The Hutukhtu was of an advanced age and physically infirm, and was not expected to live very much longer.

[1] Chu, C. L., *The Last Ten Years of Russo-Chinese Relations* (in Chinese), 1926, p. 159.

The cunning Semenov lost no time in taking advantage of the situation, and hinted to the Hutukhtu that, if he persisted in his refusal, he might expect some serious political trouble, whilst if he showed himself agreeable and acquiescent to his (Semenov's) demands, things would go smoothly with him. The incapable Hutukhtu had no choice but to give in to this threat of force. But before long Semenov was pursued by the Red forces, which finally ousted him from Mongolia.

2. *Little Hsu's Appointment*

It may be recalled that when China was induced to join the Allies during the first World War, a 'War Participation Bureau' was created to look after affairs directly concerning China's participation in the war. This Bureau was headed by General Hsu Shu-tseng, papularly known as 'Little Hsu', who was renowned for his tactical skill. Upon the termination of the first World War, the Bureau changed its title and became known as the 'North-western Frontier Defence Force'. General Hsu was appointed its Commander-in-Chief. With the reins of the Defence Force securely in his hands, General Hsu bethought himself of doing something to remedy the situation in Outer Mongolia.

When Outer Mongolia first renounced its autonomy, the Chinese Government commissioned a resident officer in Urga to act in the capacity of adviser. Chen Lu was appointed to the post. He was succeeded by Chen Yi, who had been trying to persuade the Mongols to renounce their autonomy which had been engineered by Semenov and the Buriats, backed by Japan. Many Mongolian princes and lamas or religious rulers were favourably inclined towards reaccepting Chinese sovereignty, as they were rather disappointed with the new state of affairs.

On the side of China there had been, from the time the Russian Revolution broke out, suggestions in favour of the termination of Outer Mongolia's autonomy and the abrogation of the Russo-Chinese-Mongolian Pact. But the Peking Government at that time had not the courage to take such steps. In December 1918, Dr. Wellington Koo, then Chinese Minister to the United States, transmitted an enquiry from the American Government as to what was China's policy towards the question of Outer Mongolia. The Foreign Ministry replied: 'In regard to Outer Mongolian affairs the Chinese Government, for the sake of keeping the good will of the Mongol people, is in no haste to alter its autonomous state but only desires to cancel the Russo-Mongolian Agreement.' A telegram from the Foreign Ministry to Mr. Chen Yi, Resident Official at Urga, dated January 5, 1919, instructed him to enter into a new agreement with the Government of Outer Mongolia to take the place of the existing Russo-Chinese-Mongolian Pact, in order that the ground might be prepared for the time when China would discuss the recognition of the Soviet Government.

A tentative draft, consisting of sixty-three articles, most of which were favourable to the Mongols, was drawn up, and received the approval of the Hutukhtu himself. The document was forwarded to Peking for consideration.

It is necessary to point out that the appointment of 'Little Hsu' was made after Chen Yi had already settled with the Hutukhtu the question of the renunciation of autonomy. It seems that 'Little Hsu' was rather an egoist and wanted to claim for himself the sole and entire merit for bringing Outer Mongolia back under Chinese sovereignty. For this reason, he maintained no intercourse whatever with Chen Yi, the Chinese Resident in Outer Mongolia, although, under the circumstances, he should have consulted him constantly. However, Chen Yi later got his revenge.

General Hsu set out straight for Urga, letting it be known that his purpose was to inspect the Chinese garrisons stationed in that city. From Urga he telegraphed to Peking, expressing his opinion that the conditions upon which Outer Mongolia was to renounce its autonomy should be simple but effective and entirely free from international entanglements. The reply was that his opinion was sound in principle, but that he should act in consultation with Chen Yi. This procedure did not seem to suit General Hsu, so, instead, he requested an interview with the Hutukhtu without even informing Chen Yi of his intention.

Chen Yi, who had stayed in Outer Mongolia much longer than General Hsu and acted all the time in a sort of liaison capacity between the Hutukhtu and Peking, had won the confidence of the former. Furthermore, Chen was always sure of his own position, and he succeeded in persuading the Hutukhtu to postpone meeting General Hsu, for Chen, too, wanted to acquire the sole credit for bringing about the renunciation of Mongolian autonomy. At length the Hutukhtu gave an audience to General Hsu and Chen Yi at the same time, and informed them that the time was not yet ripe for discussing the renunciation of Outer Mongolia's autonomy. General

Hsu, using the strong-arm tactics of a military man, brought a number of troops with him and arrayed them before the palace of the Hutukhtu throughout the audience, to intimidate him if he should prove obstinate. The high-handed gesture, however, did not produce the desired effect upon the Hutukhtu. This was a loss of face for General Hsu, who therefore determined to use greater pressure to attain his end if it should appear necessary. The following morning he delivered to the Hutukhtu a revised version of the conditions upon which Outer Mongolia was to renounce its autonomy. The new version was in much stronger terms than the old one. He had altered to a great extent the original sixty-three articles drawn up by Chen Yi, which had actually been mutually agreed upon, omitting those which were favourable to the Mongols. Acceptance was demanded within forty-eight hours, failing which the Hutukhtu and his ministers were threatened with forcible arrest and removal from the capital.

3. Mongolia Cancels Her Independence

This uncalled-for and oppressive demand of 'Little Hsu' aroused the bitter anger of the Mongols, and there was talk of armed resistance. But, upon calmer deliberation, they realized that they were no match for the Chinese troops commanded by General Hsu. They were forced to accept General Hsu's terms. The Hutukhtu, however, uncompromisingly refused to sign that humiliating paper, and it was signed only by the State ministers.

This paper, in the form of a petition from the Government of Outer Mongolia to the Chinese Government, to permit the renunciation of its autonomous status, in view of the danger of a foreign invasion (White Russians), consequent upon the scheme for establishing a so-called Mongolian Empire, was handed to General Hsu to be delivered to the Chinese Government in Peking. The petition was approved by a Presidential mandate, which stated that 'the most sincerely expressed desires of the people of Outer Mongolia are thereby complied with, so that peace and good relations may for ever be maintained between the Central Government and Outer Mongolia'. The Mongolian forces were made to surrender their arms, and Chinese were appointed to all important posts in the Government of Outer Mongolia. General Hsu himself received the appointment of Pacification Commissioner of Outer Mongolia concurrently with his other posts.

The activities of the Chinese Government amounting as they did to a direct interference with the affairs of Outer Mongolia were, as might have been expected, not in harmony with the desires of Soviet Russia, who immediately lodged a protest with Peking, pointing out that the action of the Chinese Government was tantamount to a breach of international obligations. Peking's reply was that, as Soviet Russia could hardly maintain peace and order within her own country, and as she had not the power to curb the disturbances created by the Russian bandits in Outer Mongolia, it was only fit and proper for China to come to the help of the Mongol people. Moreover, as the renunciation of autonomy had been voluntary on the part of Outer Mongolia, what had happened was no concern of Soviet Russia.

Meanwhile, General Hsu negotiated a loan of $15,000,000 with a Japanese bank upon the security of the mining and agricultural resources of Outer Mongolia. A few months after the renunciation of Outer Mongolia's autonomy, the Peking Government fell, and General Hsu was replaced by Li Yuan and then by Chen Yi, who thus had his revenge.

'Little Hsu's' failure resulted in a second declaration of independence by Outer Mongolia engineered by Japan. Though Semenov was then without any foothold in Mongolia and Siberia, the Japanese still supplied him with arms, enabling the remnants of his forces to co-operate with the Mongolian outlaws in starting a fresh campaign in Outer Mongolia. Thus Semenov's follower, Baron Ungern Sternberg, known as the 'Mad Baron', succeeded in attacking Outer Mongolia and occupied Urga in February 1921, with the aid of the Mongolian bandit forces.

4. Baron Ungern's Tyranny

The White régime in Outer Mongolia was a real reign of terror.[2] Baron Ungern, a maniacal leader of anti-Revolutionary Russian forces, was responsible for wholesale executions, purging his troops of all suspicious elements.

The next move of Baron Ungern was to carry out the policy of Semenov in establishing a Pan-Mongolian state. The Peking Government asked Chang Tso-lin, the warlord of Manchuria, to suppress the White Russians in Outer Mongolia and bring the country back to China's control. Had Chang Tso-lin really taken up the matter

[2] See Ossendorski, *Beasts, Men and Gods*, 1922.

seriously by moving his troops without delay, Ungern's forces would have been checked. But he deliberately postponed his Mongolian expedition even after having received ten million dollars from Peking. He sent his troops only as far as Kalgan, and kept his main forces in Peking for other political reasons. It was afterwards learnt that the Semenov-Ungern schemes were carried out with the actual connivance of the Manchurian warlord. Chang Tso-lin secretly made close connections with Baron Ungern, who, in turn, expressed his zealous support of Chang Tso-lin's ambitions to restore the Manchu Dynasty.[3]

The Semenov-Ungern scheme, besides furthering the ambition of Chang Tso-lin, fitted in with the Japanese desire to create buffer states in Manchuria and Mongolia. According to an official Japanese statement, the Japanese themselves acknowledged that they supported Semenov and Ungern and supplied them with arms. A secret treaty was made between Semenov and the Japanese Siberian command, in which it was agreed that Semenov would attack Khabarovsk, the Cossacks would revolt in the Amur region, and Ungern would attack from his Mongolian base to cut communications between the Far Eastern Republic and the Soviets. The campaign was not successful, for it was only Ungern who actually fulfilled the agreement, while the other parties failed to participate.

5. Counter-move of the Reds

Meanwhile the Reds were slowly but surely gaining the upper hand in practically the whole of Siberia. The Soviet Government was therefore watching the change of events in Outer Mongolia with deep concern and not a little alarm. The Semenov-Ungern operations in Mongolia gave the Soviets a good excuse for intervention. It was hoped that China would suppress the Whites who were determined to undermine the Soviet Government. But China seemed in no haste to put down the various White uprisings in Outer Mongolia. On the contrary, a rumour was gradually obtaining credence that the Government of the Three Eastern Provinces was actually bargaining with the remnant White forces for terms, by which those forces were to enlist in the service of the government. The Soviet Government formally requested the Chinese authorities to despatch troops for a joint expedition to suppress White activities in Outer Mongolia, but the request was refused.

[3] Letters captured from Baron Ungern, published during the Washington Conference.

It should be recounted here that, upon the capture of Urga by Baron Ungern, many Mongols, whose sympathies were inclined towards the Reds, found it impossible to remain in Outer Mongolia. They smuggled themselves into Siberia, which was under Soviet rule, and were kindly received and well treated by the Soviet authorities. It was with Soviet assistance and direction that they joined with a number of Buriats and organized the Mongolian People's Revolutionary Party, afterwards known as the Mongolian Nationalist Party, which set up a provisional government in Kiakhta.

Finding the Chinese Government either unready or reluctant to make a move, the Soviet Government despatched troops into Outer Mongolia and, in conjunction with the Mongolian Provisional Government, attacked Urga, where the Government of Outer Mongolia had been organized and controlled by Baron Ungern for some time.

After the storming of Urga by Red troops and the Mongolian Nationalist Party, Baron Ungern retreated east of Urga where he was finally defeated and captured by Red pursuers. On September 10, 1921, Moscow announced his execution together with sixty-one of his officers,[4] and with his death ended all White Russian hopes of establishing a base in Outer Mongolia.

6. Mongolian Nationalist Party

The Red troops and the Mongolian Nationalist Party lost no time in establishing themselves in Urga, and set up a Nationalist Government of Outer Mongolia, still retaining, however, the Living Buddha as a figurehead with a view to better obtaining the allegiance of the Mongolian people. Needless to say, the Government of Soviet Russia was the first to recognize this Nationalist Government of Outer Mongolia, inviting it to send to Moscow a diplomatic representative with plenipotentiary powers to discuss and enter into friendly treaties. The Soviet Government's recognition of the Nationalist Government of Outer Mongolia as the one and only legally constituted government of Outer Mongolia had already been implemented by the despatch of a Soviet Ambassador who was on his way to Urga.

Paradoxically, the Mongolian People's Revolutionary Party drew its first members mainly from the aristocratic and the lama classes. The explanation appears to be that the Mongolian proletariat was

---

[4] Pasvolsky, Leo, *Russia in the Far East*, 1922, p. 119.

largely illiterate and therefore lacked the necessary qualifications. However, as soon as more of the rank and file were found to be qualified to take up membership and revolutionary work, a purge of the party was instituted. In the autumn of 1922 nearly all the aristocratic members, including Comrade Bodo, the Premier and Minister of Foreign Affairs, were accused of reactionary activities and ousted. The proletarian dictatorship within the Party was thus achieved.[5] All influential Mongols were excluded from the administration, and the vacancies filled by puppet Buriats, who were convinced Bolsheviks. The aim and purpose of the People's Revolutionary Party was the sovietization of Outer Mongolia.

Along the lines of the Young Communist League in the Soviet Union, there existed also a Mongolian Youth Revolutionary Corps. It consisted mainly of fugitives, who, during their stay in Soviet territory, had thoroughly absorbed Communistic ideas. It is to be noted that the Mongolian Youth Revolutionary Corps did not take its orders from the Mongolian People's Party, but direct from Moscow. Indeed, it served as a check on the other party, spying on its activities under instructions from Moscow. Later the deposition of the Living Buddha was also due to the Youth Corps.

The progress of the People's Revolutionary Government of Outer Mongolia towards complete sovietization was managed step by step parallel with the purging of undesirable elements from the Revolutionary Party. The primary objective was stated to be the ousting of White Russians. When this had been achieved, additional steps were taken to consolidate the administrative power. The opportune moment came when the Living Buddha died, three years after the establishment of the People's Government, and Outer Mongolia began its national life as a full-fledged Republic, constructed on the Soviet model though not included within the Soviet Union.

It should be pointed out that in the organization both of the Outer Mongolian Government and the Nationalist Party, the appointment of Soviet citizens as advisers in every office was the rule. These advisers acted more in the capacity of supervisors and were actually closely connected with their government.

One of the first acts of the Nationalist Government of Outer Mongolia was the drafting of a constitution, which provided for the abolition of the feudal system and the emancipation of slaves. It stipulated that the two primary obligations of citizenship were the

[5] Pan Su, *Soviet Russia's Far Eastern Policy*, in Japanese, translated into Chinese, p. 150.

payment of the legal taxes and military service. These provisions, liberal though they were, if the historical background of the Mongols be kept in mind, were not advanced enough to satisfy the Soviet Government. Especially since the appointments were announced, it was found that the former princes and lamas were still holding important positions in the government, and they, naturally, could not be expected to accept Bolshevism or Communism *in toto*. The Soviet Government had aimed at nothing less than the total and complete sovietization of Outer Mongolia. To achieve this purpose the Soviets had, as we have seen, already conceived the plan of training a large number of Mongol youths of the proletarian class and organizing them into a body, nominally as candidates for the Nationalist Party, but actually distinct from and under no obligations to this Party, and under direct Soviet influence. The numbers and influence of this new organization gradually grew, and all the members were loyal to left-wing leadership.

7. *Soviet Influence over Mongolia*

Some time in October 1921, when the Soviet Government was sure of the strength and dependability of these trained youths, it proffered to the Government of Outer Mongolia a demand, consisting of seven items, the sum and substance of which was neither more nor less than the complete sovietization of the political and social establishments of Outer Mongolia. With the threat of Soviet troops from the outside and that of the Mongolian youth organization from inside, the Government of Outer Mongolia was constrained to acquiesce.

A further development was made known at the end of July 1921 in the form of a request from the Mongolian Government to the Soviet Government not to withdraw its troops from Outer Mongolia before the complete removal of the common enemy, who was seeking reinforcement in the eastern steppes (meaning Semenov and his followers).[6] The Soviet Government's answer is reproduced below:

' Welcoming the first steps of the People's Revolutionary Government of Mongolia on the road towards creating a new order in its country, now freed from the enemy by a common effort, the Russian Government notes with great satisfaction the appeal

[6] See Morse and MacNair, *Far Eastern International Relations*, Shanghai, 1928, p. 955.

addressed to it by the People's Revolutionary Government of Mongolia, which appeal expresses the wish that the Soviet troops should not be removed from the territory of Mongolia until the complete destruction of the common enemy shall have been encompassed. Considering this proposal a manifestation of the steadfast, close and friendly bonds which united the liberated people of Mongolia with the workmen and peasants of Russia who have thrown off the yoke of the exploiters, the Russian Government declares that it recognizes fully the seriousness of the situation and the common interest of Russia and Mongolia in the destruction of the common enemy. Having firmly decided to withdraw its troops from autonomous Mongolia, which is bound to Soviet Russia only by the ties of mutual friendship and common interests, just as soon as the menace to the free development of the Mongolian people and to the security of the Russian Republic and the Far Eastern Republic shall have been removed, the Russian Government, in complete harmony with the People's Revolutionary Government of Mongolia, notes that this moment has not yet arrived. In response to the request addressed to it by the People's Revolutionary Government of Mongolia, the Russian Government announces its decision to give this request complete satisfaction.

'The Russian Government is convinced that, in the near future, by the united efforts of the two peoples who are struggling against the violence of the Tsarist generals and against foreign aggression and exploitation, the free development of the Mongolian people will be secured on the basis of its autonomy, and that, as a result of its organization of the apparatus of popular revolutionary authority in Mongolia, such authority will be definitely established and firmly secured there.'[7]

Thenceforward, the strength and influence of the conservative party declined rapidly, while the Soviet Government both openly and secretly supported the radical party in the struggle. Even members of the radical party who were found to be inclining towards a reactionary or politically unstable position were disgraced and ousted, until the Government of Outer Mongolia became completely sovietized.

For further security the Soviet Government concluded a secret treaty with the Government of Outer Mongolia in 1923, in which no

[7] *Living Age*, August 27, 1921.

reference was made to China. Some highlights of this secret treaty are given below:

1. Outer Mongolia should nationalize all lands, forests, and mineral resources within its territory by the promulgation of a decree.

2. Unclaimed lands in Outer Mongolia should be distributed to Soviet citizens and the Mongolian proletariat for cultivation.

3. The stationing of Soviet troops in Outer Mongolia should be permitted.

4. Gold mines in Outer Mongolia should be developed by Soviet labourers.[8]

8. Sovietization of Outer Mongolia

The last obstacle in the way of the sovietization of Outer Mongolia was removed by the death of the Living Buddha, and the People's Revolutionary Government of Outer Mongolia issued a manifesto, abolishing monarchy and adopting the Soviet form of government, with a constitution modelled after that of the Soviet Union. A new Mongolia was thus created, and the governmental machinery completely reorganized. Each post was occupied by three administrative officers, viz., a Mongol, a Buriat and a Communist Russian. The Mongol was to be the nominal chief, but all the actual power was in the hands of the Russian, while the Buriat acted as his adjutant. 'Soak the rich' taxes were imposed upon cattle and other forms of property. But as nine out of ten Mongols owned some livestock, it turned out that the taxation was actually soaking the entire people. Conscription was announced for all males from fourteen to forty. Foreign trade was discouraged, but exports to Soviet Russia were on the increase. A currency embargo was imposed which, nevertheless, did not apply to Soviet Russia. Many who found living conditions irksome migrated out of the land, until a law was passed forbidding emigration. People smuggled themselves out mostly to Inner Mongolia, for the simple reason of its geographical proximity. Some were intercepted and brought back. A large number of refugees from Outer Mongolia are still to be found in various parts of Inner Mongolia and Chinese Turkistan.

The sovietization of Outer Mongolia was not limited to the spheres

[8] Liu Kwei-han, *The Past and Future of Outer Mongolia, The Eastern Miscellany*, February 16, 1935.

of political and military affairs, but spread into economics and culture. Commerce in Outer Mongolia used to be largely in the hands of the Chinese, but after the introduction of Soviet influence pressure was brought upon Chinese merchants, who were obliged to pay a high business tax in addition to the usual taxes, and sometimes had their properties altogether confiscated. Thus China began to lose her economic hold over Outer Mongolia, and her place was taken by the Soviet Union on account of its political power and the convenience of communication. Soviet trade with Outer Mongolia reached tens of millions of dollars and was much more extensive than that with China or Japan. Communications in Outer Mongolia were also dominated by the Soviet Union—motor roads were opened. In 1925 the Soviet Union signed a contract with Outer Mongolia for building a Kiakhta-Urga-Pangkiang Railway with Soviet capital.

The educational system in Outer Mongolia was also sovietized. All teachers of the National University, normal colleges, middle schools and military academies were either Soviet citizens or Buriats.

In 1922 Urianghai was established as a republic independent of Outer Mongolia. It consists of a territory, partly Mongol in population, formerly constituting a special region in the extreme northwest of Outer Mongolia, and is very rich in natural resources. A Soviet note addressed to the 'people of the Urianghai territory' stated 'the sole object of the occupation of their land by the Red troops was to defend them from the reactionary Tsarist officers who had found refuge among them, and to protect the territory of Soviet Russia from these bands'.[9] It may be further added here that Urianghai was renamed as 'Tannu-Tuva'—and was organized as the Tannu-Tuva Republic, which signified its separation from Outer Mongolia but brought it into closer relations with the Soviets, especially Siberia.

In view of the general dissatisfaction with the sovietization of Outer Mongolia, the People's Revolutionary Government began to become aware that no good could be derived from such a fundamental separation from China, and that friendly relations with the latter should be resumed at the earliest possible date. Overtures were made with this end in view. The Chinese Central Government flatly refused to bargain except on the predetermined condition that Outer Mongolia be returned to China as a province. The People's Revolutionary Government in despair asked Soviet Russia to mediate,

[9] *China Year Book*, 1923, p. 677.

for she was then the only third party with whom it could get in touch.

China, like most other countries at that time, had not yet accorded official recognition to the Soviet Union. The latter was extremely anxious to obtain it and sent to Peking one envoy after another to negotiate. Here was an opportunity for Soviet Russia to ingratiate herself in China's eyes. Consequently, the Soviet People's Commissariat for Foreign Affairs assured the Mongolian Government in a reply note that the Soviet Government was ready and willing to take up this office on Mongolia's behalf. Yourin was sent to Peking to negotiate for the resumption of relations. He failed in his mission, and was succeeded by Paikes. Unfortunately, Paikes's arrival at Peking was ill-timed, because the secret treaty between Soviet Russia and Outer Mongolia, mentioned in the foregoing section, had just been made public. The Chinese Government virtually refused to admit him and lodged a strong protest to the effect that any treaty secretly concluded between the Soviet Government and Outer Mongolian would not be recognized by the Chinese Government.

It should be remembered that the Sino-Soviet Agreement, concluded in 1924, contained an article which read as follows:

'The Government of the U.S.S.R. recognizes Outer Mongolia as an integral part of the Chinese Republic and respects China's sovereignty therein. The Government of the U.S.S.R. declares that, as soon as the questions for the withdrawal of all the troops of the U.S.S.R. from Outer Mongolia, namely, as to the time limit of the withdrawal of such troops and the measures to be adopted in the interests of the safety of the frontiers—as agreed upon at the conference, as provided in Article 2 of the present Agreement—it will effect the complete withdrawal of all the troops of the U.S.S.R. from Outer Mongolia.'

Facts, however, did not conform with the Agreement. The conference for the discussion of the withdrawal of troops had never materialized. Soviet troops had never been withdrawn. A Soviet ambassador was then stationed in Urga, whose power was daily increasing. It looked as if Outer Mongolia would sooner or later fall under the influence of the Soviet Union.

M. Chicherin, the Soviet People's Commissar for Foreign Affairs, made the following statement in an address at Tiflis in March 1925:

'The Soviet Government recognizes Mongolia as a part of the

whole Republic of China, enjoying, however, autonomy so far-reaching as to preclude Chinese interference with the internal affairs, and to establish independent relations of Mongolia. It ought to be noted that, after several crises, the internal situation in Mongolia has settled down and been consolidated on a basis somewhat similar to the Soviet system.'[10]

It was quite apparent that Outer Mongolia was detached from China and became a part of the Soviet Union, though not officially admitted. In spite of numerous protests by the Chinese Government and of equally numerous promises of fair play on the part of the Soviet authorities, Outer Mongolia had practically been united to the Soviet Empire.

Since then it has been rather difficult to secure any unbiased information about Outer Mongolia. However, we may quote here the following passage from the *China Year Book*:

'Outer Mongolia is a People's Republic of a type regarded as pre-Communistic, i.e., permitting the subsequent development of Communism. Its capital, Urga, has been renamed Ulan Bator Khota (City of the Red Hero). The government is in practice affiliated to, but not formally recognized as part of, the Union of Soviet Socialistic Republics. Thus, for purposes of international negotiations, Outer Mongolia is not a member of the U.S.S.R.; nor does the U.S.S.R. claim sovereignty. Any nation wishing to negotiate with Outer Mongolia would therefore have to approach the Urga Government itself, or else the Government of China, which claims sovereignty. As, however, the Urga Government repudiates Chinese authority, and no government except that of the U.S.S.R. has recognized Urga, the only foreign relations of Outer Mongolia are, in practice, with Moscow.'[11]

It may be noted that the Red manœuvres in Outer Mongolia looked like producing a rich and abundant harvest. As far as material results are concerned, the Reds have succeeded a good deal better than the Whites, and perhaps even more so than Imperialist Russia, when she instigated Outer Mongolia to declare its independence from China for the first time in 1912.

[10] Morse and MacNair, op. cit., p. 956.
[11] *China Year Book*, 1938, p. 28.

Chapter X

CONTROVERSIES OVER THE SINO-SOVIET CONFERENCE

THE opening of the Sino-Soviet Conference for the settlement of outstanding questions between the two countries was postponed until August 27, 1924, three months after the signing of the Sino-Soviet Agreement. It seemed that Karakhan was delaying the opening date by signing a secret pact with Mukden on September 20, 1924. The situation was aggravated by disputes over the Chinese Eastern Railway, in the course of which Ivanoff, the Soviet assistant manager of the railway, was finally removed from office, and Karakhan, the Soviet Ambassador, recalled. Neither the Sino-Soviet nor the Soviet Mukden Conference accomplished anything. The working of the Sino-Soviet Agreement was further embarrassed by the Soviet-Japanese Treaty signed at Peking on January 20, 1925.

1. Soviet-Mukden Pact

We have already noted how the Sino-Soviet Agreement was signed in the year 1924, and approved by the Cabinet of the Peking Government, and that Sino-Soviet diplomatic relations were resumed on May 31 of the same year.

It has to be pointed out that the Peking Government at that time was extremely impotent, so much so that its orders and promulgations were not respected outside the city of Peking. An independent government had been in existence in the south for some time. As for Manchuria, it was also a separate political unit for all practical purposes. The Southern Government, being more radical, raised no objection whatever to the signing of the Sino-Soviet Agreement. It was not so in the case of the Manchurian Government under Marshal Chang Tso-lin, to whom the Peking Government sent a representative in the person of General Pao Kwei-ching to negotiate for acceptance of the agreement but in vain.

Karakhan was just as anxious as the Peking Government for the co-operation of the Three Eastern Provinces, for that was the part of China that counted most as far as the Sino-Soviet Agreement was concerned. To Marshal Chang Tso-lin, therefore, Karakhan also sent representatives of his own to open negotiations, informally and confidentially. Discussions were protracted over a period of three months, and finally resulted in a secret pact being signed on September 20, 1924, in Mukden, known as the famous Soviet-Mukden Pact.

In addition to the pact proper, there were also signed two supplementary documents. The first consisted of a declaration concerning the handing over of all Tsarist Russian consulates in the Three Eastern Provinces; the second stipulated that all Russian employees of the Tsarist régime still holding office in the Three Eastern Provinces were to be suspended.

Actually the Soviet-Mukden Pact followed textually many of the corresponding provisions of the Sino-Soviet Agreement signed at Peking. The salient points of variance may be cited: (1) The period for the retrocession of the Chinese Eastern Railway was reduced from eighty to sixty years; (2) A commission was to be appointed by the two governments to settle the question of the disposition of the railway profits; (3) Affairs concerning the Chinese Eastern Railway were to be settled by the Soviet-Mukden Conference. (See full text in Appendix A.)

Upon learning that a pact had been signed with Mukden by Soviet Russia, the Peking Government demanded an explanation from Karakhan, but received no definite or satisfactory reply. The Soviet-Mukden Pact was later, on March 12, 1925, reluctantly approved by the Peking Government as a supplement to the Sino-Soviet Agreement itself on the recommendation of the Foreign and the Communication Ministries. Notification to that effect was forwarded to Karakhan, to be transmitted to the Government of the Soviet Union. Thus the question was regarded as closed.

2. Opening of Sino-Soviet Conference

It was then necessary to consider the procedure for opening a Sino-Soviet Conference to settle all outstanding questions between the two countries, as provided for by the Sino-Soviet Agreement, the second clause of which specified that within one month after the signing of the present agreement, the two contracting parties should hold a conference, to discuss, in detail, the settlement of all outstanding questions, and such arrangements should be decided upon and put into execution not, in any case, later than six months from the time of the opening of the said conference. However, the conference was not opened till many months later. The delay can be traced to several causes:

1. Lack of sufficient political power on the part of the Peking Government.
2. The question of returning the Russian Legation cropped up at the beginning of the conference.
3. Obstruction arising from the Manchurian Government not recognizing the Sino-Soviet Agreement, which brought about the Soviet-Mukden Pact.
4. Karakhan was busily engaged in the negotiation of a Soviet-Japanese Pact.
5. The conference was purposely delayed by Soviet Russia to escape binding conditions.

It was not until the early part of March 1925 that Dr. C. T. Wang was appointed Director General of the Sino-Soviet Conference, and Tseng Chien, Mukden's henchman, Vice-Director. The Chinese office for participation in the conference was formally set up on April 9, 1925, and discussions were opened with Karakhan who, however, sidetracked the negotiations. In this way the conference was put off for the time being.

In accordance with the conditions provided in the agreement, Soviet troops stationed in Outer Mongolia should have been withdrawn immediately after the signing of the treaties. On March 6, Karakhan, Soviet Ambassador, delivered a note to the Chinese Foreign Ministry at Peking stating that, ' The Soviet Government, with the approval of Mongolia, began to withdraw its troops from the latter place. The troops have now been wholly withdrawn. The Soviet Government hopes that situations which necessitate the presence of Red troops in Mongolia will not arise, and that a peaceful understanding with Mongolia will be reached.' In point of fact, the Red troops in Mongolia had never been withdrawn. On the contrary, in the middle part of May, Outer Mongolian troops, under the command of Soviet officers, crossed into Altai in Sinkiang province.[1] Against this incident, the Chinese Foreign Ministry

[1] Chen Pao-wen, *Sino-Russian Relations* (in Chinese), p. 139.

protested to the Soviet Ambassador, but the protest was without avail.

The delay was also caused by Karakhan's protest against the alleged employment of 'White' guards in the military service of Marshal Chang Tso-lin,[2] and to an incident which occurred on the Chinese Eastern Railway on April 9, 1925. Meanwhile the Chinese Eastern Railway had already been reorganized according to the conditions of the agreement. The five Chinese Directors were headed by General Pao Kwei-ching, who was concurrently Chairman and Director General, while the same number of Soviet Directors were headed by Ivanoff, concurrently Vice-Chairman and co-Director General. Ivanoff was also appointed as the General Manager of the railway. Serious friction developed between the Chinese and the Soviet Directors. On April 9, 1925, Ivanoff issued an order that 'all employees other than registered citizens of the Chinese Republic and of the Soviet Union are to be dismissed by June 1, 1925'. The order led General Pao Kwei-ching to declare on May 9, 1925, that the General Manager, in issuing such an order without the approval of the Board of Directors, 'has exceeded the rights accorded to him and, therefore, the order is fundamentally irregular and cannot possess legal force'.[3] An open conflict was thus started. On May 23, Karakhan lodged a protest with the Foreign Ministry, alleging Pao Kwei-ching's order to have been in violation of the Sino-Soviet Agreement, demanding that he be replaced as Chairman of the Board of Directors of the Chinese Eastern Railway, that all non-Russian and non-Chinese employees be suspended, that Pao's order be rescinded and that Chinese employees be forbidden to befriend the imperialists.[4]

Another note was delivered to the Foreign Ministry at the same time, protesting against the actions of certain military authorities in assisting Nechaev, a White Russian, enlist Russian youths for training, alleging that the object of such enlistment for military training was to oppose the Soviet Union. The Chinese Government was requested to deal with the said military authorities in accordance with the law, to return the boys so enlisted to their parents and to stop further enlistment forthwith. The dispute was settled on June 6 through the mediation of the Soviet Consul, by cancelling Ivanoff's original order, for which another order was substituted providing for the dismissal of over two hundred employees of non-

[2] *North China Herald*, April 18, 1925.
[3] ibid., May 30, 1925.
[4] Ho Han-wen, op. cit., p. 350.

Chinese or non-Soviet citizenship. The matter was then considered settled.

During the dispute, Karakhan was delaying the Sino-Soviet Conference more obviously than before. On August 20, Dr. C. T. Wang started for Shanghai on business. The very next day Karakhan notified the Foreign Ministry by telephone that he was leaving for home at the end of the month and that he desired to have the Sino-Soviet 'Conference formally opened before he left. The Chinese Commission for the Conference immediately telegraphed Dr. C. T. Wang, from whom a reply was received, that Dr. Wang would return to Peking on the 25th, and that Karakhan be notified that the formal opening would be on the morning of the 26th. The notification was transmitted to the Soviet Embassy on the 24th, at 3 p.m. No statement was made by Karakhan. The next day Dr. Wang reached Peking at 2 p.m. and called on the Soviet Ambassador at 5 p.m., when he was told by Karakhan that he had not yet decided to proceed with the opening ceremonies on the 26th, his excuse being that he had first to ask permission from Moscow.[5]

On the 26th, Dr. C. T. Wang, acting on the instructions of Tuan Chi-jui, Chief Executive of the Peking Government, again called at the Soviet Embassy, drawing Karakhan's attention to the fact that unsettled questions between the Soviet Union and China had been allowed to remain outstanding too long and that, for the sake of friendly relations between the two countries, it was desirable that the Sino-Soviet Conference be formally opened before Karakhan left Peking. If this were not done, not only would the peaceful relations between China and the Soviet Union be endangered, but attacks from outside would also be courted. Karakhan then consented to proceed with the opening ceremonies at the Foreign Ministry at seven o'clock that same evening, after nearly half a year's delay. The ceremony, however, was merely a formal exchange of greetings by the delegates.[6]

Meanwhile Karakhan departed for Moscow on the very next day after the opening of the conference (August 27) and again delayed discussions. It was not until November 28 that informal meetings were held. By December 1 Karakhan returned to his post, and the discussions proceeded smoothly for some time. Shortly afterwards, however, problems again arose concerning the Chinese Eastern Railway, and negotiations were again postponed.

[5] Ho Han-wen, op. cit., p. 351.
[6] *Shun Pao*, August 29, 1925.

3. Disputes Regarding Chinese Eastern Railway

It should be observed that after the inauguration of the new administration of the joint management of the Chinese Eastern Railway, the control of the Board of Directors did not function effectively, largely because of the absence of the Chinese members. The Soviet Assistant Manager, Ivanoff, who enjoyed the support of the Soviet members of the Board, took advantage of this to grasp all the power, and within a year all actual authority fell into his hands.

On November 10, 1925, Ivanoff, acting on his own responsibility, issued an order that, as from December 1, 1925, Chinese troops would have to pay the regular fare when being transported by the railway. A meeting of Directors was held in Harbin on November 30 to discuss this question, but the Chinese Directors objected to the measure. The Soviet side insisted that Chinese troops, including railway guards, had to pay the regular fare in advance, while the Chinese side argued that Chinese troops of all descriptions enjoyed the privilege of being transported without first paying the necessary fare. It happened that General Kuo Sung-lin was at that time starting a revolt against Marshal Chang Tso-lin, and the problem was, therefore, looked upon as very serious.

On January 17, 1926, sixty railway guards were sent to put down some bandits. Ivanoff refused to allow them to board the train to be carried free of charge as had been the practice hitherto, and thereafter a conflict developed. Ivanoff ordered the suspension of all regular traffic on the Changchun-Harbin section. General Chang Hwan-hsiang, commander of the railway guards, ordered resumption of traffic, and threatened to operate trains by force. He instructed the railway employees to run trains as usual, but Ivanoff secretly counter-instructed them not to start the trains. Meantime, Karakhan lodged a protest with the Peking Government against the Chinese troops forcing the railway to run the trains. On the 22nd, the Chinese guards again forced the southern section to run the trains. Ivanoff then secretly instructed the employees to go on strike, whereupon the commander of the guards arrested Ivanoff. On the 23rd, Karakhan again protested to the Peking Government and to the Mukden warlord, demanding the release of Ivanoff and the cessation of military activities on the railway. In his strong protest, Karakhan declared: 'I reserve the right to return to the matter of this arrest, and to demand satisfaction for such an unheard of violation of the agreement of 1924.' By that time, the Soviet Red army was preparing for mobilization, and Chang Tso-lin also ordered the troops of Kirin and Hei-lungkiang to adopt active military measures. The situation was tense and considered to be very serious.[7]

The Chinese case for arresting Ivanoff was set forth in a letter stating: 'Railway guards accompanying passenger trains always have military tickets, and military detachments requiring transportation have proper vouchers. As this custom has been in force for many years on the railway, nobody could change it on his own initiative. The action of the Soviet Manager is, therefore, unlawful.'

The Foreign Ministry, on the basis of the report of the commander of the railway guards, telegraphed the Chinese *chargé d'affaires* at Moscow, Tseng Yen-hsi, to inform the Soviet Foreign Commissariat of the grounds on which Ivanoff had been arrested, and to state that his release could not be effected except on the definite guarantee of the Soviet Government. It was also demanded that Ivanoff be dismissed from his post. But Chicherin, the Soviet Foreign Commissar, had already instructed Karakhan to deliver a three-day ultimatum to the Chinese Foreign Ministry and Marshal Chang Tso-lin for the release of Ivanoff and the restoration of order on the Chinese Eastern Railway. This gave the Peking Government cause for concern, and a telegram was sent to Chang Tso-lin, requesting him to use utmost tact. A *modus operandi* was arrived at between the Marshal and the Soviet Consul-General at Mukden on the following terms:

1. Ivanoff and other railway employees to be released.
2. Running schedules to be resumed.
3. The transportation of Chinese troops to be paid for out of China's share of the profits from the railway.
4. Transportation of troops to be effected in accordance with the railway regulations.
5. Losses suffered by the railway and other demands to be discussed later.[8]

Ivanoff was released on January 25, 1926. The foreign Press in China attacked Ivanoff's order rather vigorously, stating that he had no right to do this, when managing a purely commercial enterprise

---

[7] Ho Han-wen, op. cit., p. 352.
[8] ibid., p. 353.

in Chinese territory, particularly during a revolt in Manchuria, when traffic should not be suspended. The Soviet Government was also dissatisfied with Ivanoff's action, considering the issue of the order as an abuse of his proper authority. Ivanoff was then dismissed by the Board of Directors on April 19, and was replaced by Emshanoff. General Chang Hwan-hsiang, the railway guard commander, was also dismissed by Chang Tso-lin. The dispute was again temporarily settled.

With the tension eased, the Sino-Soviet Conference held a compensation committee meeting on March 11. The Chinese put forward a demand for compensation to the amount of 3,400,000,000 roubles. The Russians rejected the demand entirely. The Chinese insisted on this compensation on the strength of the various Soviet declarations and the Sino-Soviet Agreement. The committee met a second time on April 27. Investigation of the loss of goods had largely been completed. Several more meetings were held, and the Soviets were requested to pay without delay such compensation for loss of goods as had been verified by investigation. However, the Soviets evaded the responsibility for payment.

There arose another dispute concerning the deposit of the profits of the railway. By that time the railway had earned enormous profits amounting to thirty million gold roubles, but no dividend had been paid. The money was deposited in a Soviet bank by the Soviet manager, and the Chinese authorities of the railway rightly argued that the profit should be deposited in both Soviet and Chinese banks. They further stated that the accounts of the Soviet Dalbank relative to the railway deposits did not indicate the exact amount of money deposited, nor the manner in which the money was to be protected. The dispute was very tense at one time, but finally the Soviet side yielded, and the question was settled amicably by acceptance of the Chinese proposal.

4. Soviet-Mukden Conference

Because of the Chinese Eastern Railway affair, Marshal Chang Tso-lin harboured very unfriendly feelings for Karakhan, and repeatedly instructed his staff to discuss, with the Soviet Consul-General at Mukden, the recall of Karakhan. The Soviet Government, in view of the tense feeling created by Ivanoff and Karakhan, had sent Shelebrokoff to China to remedy the situation. Shelebrokoff first interviewed Chang Tso-lin on April 21. Questions relating to the Chinese Eastern Railway were discussed. Chang suggested limiting the power of the railway manager, giving equal opportunity for Russians and Chinese to be employed as railway operatives, and assigning economic and financial power to the Board of Directors. In consequence of this, the Sino-Soviet Conference was unofficially shifted to Mukden. A representative of the Mukden Government met the Soviet representative, Shelebrokoff, on May 21 in an informal conference to discuss Chinese Eastern Railway affairs. Subsequent meetings were arranged, and the Soviets made the following proposals:

1. The Mukden Government should withdraw its demand for the recall of Karakhan.
2. All police, municipal and other administrative offices along the Chinese Eastern Railway should engage Soviet citizens as high advisers, and the Municipal Council should be made up of a fifty-per-cent Soviet membership.
3. The organization of the Railway Employees' Association in Manchuria should be recognized.
4. White Russians in the employ of government offices and in the army should be dismissed.
5. The supervisory office of the Chinese Eastern Railway should be abolished.
6. The paper currency issued by the Soviet Government should be allowed to circulate.
7. North Manchuria as far as the Sino-Soviet boundary should be protected by both Soviet and Chinese troops.
8. The properties of the Soviet Government as well as those of the Chinese Eastern Railway should be restored.[9]

It goes without saying that these harsh conditions were rejected by the Mukden Government, and the Soviet-Mukden Conference gradually slowed down to a stop. On June 7, General Yang Yu-ting, on behalf of the Mukden Government, adjourned the conference while the Soviet representatives were making ready to leave for Moscow. But the conference was reopened on July 22, and Shelebrokoff again returned to take part in it. Mukden immediately proposed that Karakhan be recalled, which once more ended the conference without result.

[9] Ho Han-wen, op. cit., pp. 354-5.

5. Sino-Soviet Committee

On July 31, 1926, the Chinese Foreign Ministry telegraphed its *chargé d'affaires* in Moscow, Tseng Yen-hsi, to make formal representations to the Soviet Government for the recall of Karakhan. On August 9, Tseng telegraphed back forwarding the Soviet reply that negotiations could not be carried on until a regular government was established in China. Three days later, the Foreign Ministry again telegraphed Tseng to urge the Soviet Government to recall Karakhan without further delay, and the Soviet Government finally complied with their request. Karakhan left China on September 10. To take his place, the Soviet Government sent Chernik.

By this time the Sino-Soviet Conference had come to a standstill, and the Chinese Commission for participation in the conference had been abolished. A Sino-Soviet Committee was organized by the Chinese Foreign Ministry to look after affairs which should normally have been attended to by the conference. The committee was headed by Wang Yin-tai, the Vice-Minister. It was also announced that three committees, on commerce, boundary and legal questions respectively, were to be established in Peking, and that another three committees, on the Chinese Eastern Railway, navigation rights on the Amur River, and debt and compensation questions respectively, were to be established in Mukden. The Chinese Foreign Ministry then notified the Soviet Embassy that they wished to continue the Sino-Soviet Conference and requested that Soviet representatives be appointed to sit on the committees. By this time, however, the Chinese Nationalist Government had already been established in Canton, and the centre of Sino-Soviet diplomatic relations was gradually shifted from the north to the south. To the repeated requests of the Peking Foreign Ministry, therefore, the Soviet Government paid no attention whatever. Thus concluded the affairs of the Sino-Soviet Conference.

6. Soviet-Japanese Convention

At this point it would not be out of place to dwell briefly on Soviet-Japanese relations which concerned China so much. The secret Russo-Japanese Convention of 1910 defined most specifically the spheres of their common interests in Manchuria, and declared the maintenance of the *status quo*. The Convention of 1912 added Mongolia to the delimitation of spheres of interest in Manchuria. The eastern part of Mongolia was recognized as belonging to the Japanese sphere of interest. In the Convention of 1916, Russia and Japan recognized the vital interests of each other in China, and came to an understanding for co-operative action against actions of any third power having hostile designs on them. This was almost equivalent to an alliance to maintain peace and order in the Far East, and effectively ousted American interests from Manchuria, thereby ending the Open Door Policy in practice, as far as Manchuria was concerned.

When the Soviet régime came into power, the secret Russo-Japanese Conventions were declared null and void, which, of course, alarmed Japan. She began to intervene by sending troops to Siberia, but without any success. After the withdrawal of troops from Siberia, she started an economic blockade against Soviet Russia. This was found to be a great commercial loss to Japan, especially since her interests in the fisheries of the Far East were totally impeded. Owing to the stability of the Soviet Government, diplomatic relations with other nations had been re-established. In view of this and the resumption of Sino-Soviet relations on May 31, 1924, Japan changed her foreign policy and was seeking the restoration of normal relations with the Soviet Union.

Prior to the signing of the Sino-Soviet Pact in Peking, Soviet-Japanese negotiations had been started in Changchun. Joffe suggested to the Chinese Foreign Ministry on August 27, 1922, that delegates be appointed to participate in the Changchun Conference. This was rejected by the Chinese Government, but a declaration was made both to Tokyo and Changchun, to the effect that any agreement reached in the Soviet-Japanese Conference concerning China's sovereignty and interests would not be recognized unless approval was previously obtained from China. The reply from the Japanese Government gave the assurance that Soviet-Japanese negotiations would only limit the relations between the two countries and would not affect China's sovereignty and interests in any sense. This calmed the uneasiness of the Chinese Government which considered the reply to be entirely reliable. The Soviet-Japanese Conference at Changchun ceased to function before any substantial results were obtained. After that Joffe went to Japan to continue the negotiations, but they again ended in a deadlock. The whole matter was then taken over by Karakhan, after his arrival at Peking. He once made an interesting statement to Japanese newspapermen at

Peking, commenting on an interview given by the Japanese Premier. 'This interview,' he said, 'admirably illustrates why relations between the Soviet Union and Japan have not yet been restored, for even now the Japanese Government is mistaken in its appraisal of the significance of this question. Japan imagines that, by recognizing the Soviet Union, it is making us a tremendous concession and is placing us under great obligations. But so long as Japan does not comprehend that both sides are alike interested in the resumption of mutual relations, just so long will it be difficult to attain the desired result. . . . The Soviet Union's policy is based upon the principle of full reciprocity, and we do not wish to recede from this principle. . . . We want an agreement with Japan, but we cannot make any sacrifices, just as we do not ask for any sacrifices on the part of Japan.'[10]

The signing of the Sino-Soviet Agreement hastened the conclusion of a Soviet-Japanese Treaty. Chicherin, the Commissar for Foreign Affairs, declared in October 1924 that a treaty with Japan was in sight. On January 17, 1925, the Chinese Government, on hearing that the Soviet-Japanese Treaty was about to be signed, reiterated the previous declaration to Japan and also to the Soviet Union, on the basis of Article IV of the Agreement on General Principles, signed between China and the Soviet Union.

On January 20, 1925, the Soviet-Japanese Treaty was signed at Peking by Mr. L. Karakhan for the Soviet Union and Mr. K. Yoshizawa for Japan, and thus diplomatic relations between the two countries were normally restored.

Article II of this treaty stipulated: 'The U.S.S.R. agrees that the treaty concluded in Portsmouth on September 5, 1905, remains in full force. It is agreed that all treaties, conventions and agreements outside of the above-mentioned Portsmouth Treaty entered into between Japan and Russia up to November 7, 1917, will be revised at the conference which is to take place subsequently between the governments of the contracting parties, and that they may be changed or cancelled as will be called for by the changed circumstances.' The Chinese Foreign Ministry sent a strong protest to the Soviet Government on February 11, stating that the Chinese Government would not recognize the treaty, which violated the existing Sino-Soviet Agreement. The same statement was despatched to the Japanese Minister in Peking. The Soviet Ambassador in Peking replied that such protest would have been timely if it had been made

[10] Yakhontoff, op. cit., p. 245.

twenty years ago, i.e., when the Portsmouth Treaty was contracted and (in the parts concerning China) accepted by China herself through direct agreements with Japan. Karakhan further stated that he would welcome such a protest 'if it were directed towards the protection of Chinese interests but, in this particular case, such a protest is bound to convey to the Chinese people the erroneous impression that the Soviet Government could violate the rights of China, while in reality the Soviet-Japanese Convention does not affect in any way the interests and sovereignty of China.'[11]

The Japanese Minister also replied on March 3 that the Japanese interests in Manchuria obtained through the Portsmouth Treaty had already been recognized by China as mentioned in the Sino-Japanese Treaty signed in 1905. This, being an existing Sino-Japanese Treaty, could not be affected by any controversies arising from the Sino-Russian Treaties.

Thus, the working of the Sino-Soviet Agreement was handicapped. The Soviet-Japanese Convention did not accord with the letter and spirit of the 1919 and 1920 Declarations, or with Article IV of the 1924 Agreement, according to which all treaties concluded between the former Tsarist Government and any third party affecting the sovereign rights or interests of China were to be cancelled.

[11] Ho Han-wen, op. cit., p. 363.

Chapter XI

SEVERANCE OF SINO-SOVIET RELATIONS

CONTROVERSIES over the Sino-Soviet Conference as shown in the last chapter had already strained relations between the two countries. During that time, the Peking Government had been reduced to a merely nominal body, with the rise of the Nationalist Government at Canton and another separate government in Manchuria. Left-wing activities began to seep into China, making use of the Soviet Embassy in Peking as their centre of operations. The Peking Government was at that time headed by Marshal Chang Tso-lin, a very anti-Communist warlord. He searched the Soviet Embassy, with the connivance of the Diplomatic Corps in Peking. Some important documents were seized during the raid, and more than sixty Chinese Communists, headed by Li Ta-chao, were arrested. In the south the Nanking Government found Communist activities intolerable, and checked them by purging the party. M. Borodin and General Galen, once very influential Soviet advisers, soon afterwards left China. Recognition of Soviet representatives in China was withdrawn. Thus China and the Soviet Union severed relations.

1. Question of Return of Russian Legation

After the resumption of Sino-Soviet relations on May 31, 1924, the Soviet Government proposed to China to elevate their respective Legations to Embassies. Hence M. Mikhailovitch Karakhan was made first Soviet Ambassador to China. This timely action had great significance, for the first Soviet Ambassador automatically became Dean of the Diplomatic Corps, with ambassadorial precedence over the Ministers of Britain, Japan, the United States, France, Germany and Italy.[1]

Naturally this did not please the Diplomatic Corps in Peking, who

---

[1] Teichman, Eric, *Affairs of China*, 1938, p. 62.

had tried to interfere with the resumption of normal relations between China and the Soviet Union. Then a controversy arose about the return of the Russian Legation as agreed upon in the Sino-Soviet Agreement. Owing to the stipulation of the Protocol of 1901, the Chinese Government had been unable, during the Russian Revolution, to take over control of the Russian Legation, which was located in the Legation Quarter, even though diplomatic relations between China and the new Soviet régime had not yet been established. The Protocol Powers in Peking at first asked Prince Koudachev, the Russian Minister of the Tsarist régime, to take care of the Legation, and then it came under the charge of Sir William Oudendyk, the Dutch Minister and concurrently Dean of the Diplomatic Corps in Peking. The Chinese Ministry of Foreign Affairs sent a formal note to the Diplomatic Corps on June 9, asking the return of the Russian Legation to the representative of the Soviet Government. The Diplomatic Corps, however, took advantage of the Boxer Protocol, declared that the Soviet representative should be placed in direct negotiation with the Diplomatic Corps regarding the return of the Russian Legation, and added that the Chinese Government had not authority to intervene. This declaration naturally infuriated the Chinese people. The *Waichiaopu* (Ministry of Foreign Affairs) lodged a strong protest. In order to calm public sentiment, the Diplomatic Corps addressed another note to the *Waichiaopu* as well as to the Soviet representative, asking the latter to take over the Russian Legation on the condition that the Soviet Union would still be bound by the Protocol. This was the reason why Karakhan once declared that the Soviet Union was still one of the Powers signatory to the said Protocol. It was even rumoured that before he moved into the old Russian Legation, Karakhan had agreed that, in return for being recognized as Dean of the Diplomatic Corps, he would not carry on any propaganda detrimental to the other Powers. Karakhan, however, categorically denied this after receiving bitter criticism from the Chinese community.

'As the only Ambassador to China,' said the Dutch Minister, 'Karakhan should be the dean of the diplomatic body, but since at the official receptions he was received separately and all the Ministers were received together, he never had an occasion to exercise the function. He had expressed the conviction that he would be able to obstruct all the collective activities of the diplomatic body, because complete unanimity was required for its decisions, but he was never given an opportunity to do so. The diplomatic meetings were carried on as before under my chairmanship as " Senior Minister ".'[2]

On March 17, 1925, the Diplomatic Corps in Peking passed a resolution that, according to diplomatic practice, the Ambassador should become automatically Dean of the Diplomatic Body, and that the Soviet Union should be recognized as one of the signatory Powers of the Protocol of 1901. Karakhan, after receiving instructions from Moscow on April 27, formally assumed office as Dean of the Diplomatic Corps, and a few years later all the major Powers converted their Legations into Embassies.

2. Raids on Soviet Embassy

Meanwhile the centre of Chinese political activities had shifted from the north to the south. With the establishment of the Chinese Nationalist Government in Canton, the real centre for relations between the Soviet Union and China had been transferred from Peking to Canton. Sir Eric Teichman once remarked: 'Karakhan, the Armenian, working in Peking as Soviet Ambassador, and Borodin, the unofficial but masterful Soviet agent in Canton, had all the Kuomintang generals and politicians dancing to their tunes.'[3] The Soviet Embassy in Peking remained but an empty shell which the Soviet Government still preserved for the reason that it was a hot-bed of Communist activities. For the purposed protection, Li Ta-chao, a professor of Peking National University, who later was revealed as the leader of the Chinese Communists in north China, made his headquarters in the Soviet Embassy. It seemed that he was a true believer in Marxism, as he was often found penniless after having received his salary from the university, through giving alms to his poor friends on the way home. The writer often met him in Peking. Communist activities in Peking ultimately became well known, and the Chinese authorities were very much annoyed with the existing state of affairs and decided to take immediate action.

In the early part of 1926, the anti-Communist movement in the capital was very strong. Youthful Communists who held responsible positions found it necessary to take shelter in the Soviet Embassy, which later attracted the attention of the authorities. The Chinese police, knowing of the existence of such a conspiracy, were further strengthened in their belief by the arrest of a messenger boy who delivered notices for the Communist meetings. They decided

---

[2] Oudendyk, William, *Ways and By-ways of Diplomacy*, 1939, p. 345.
[3] Teichman, op. cit., pp. 63-4.

not to delay appropriate action against those who took shelter under the protection of the status of the Legation Quarter.

The Chinese authorities took this arbitrary action against the Soviet Embassy for a number of reasons. (1) The Nationalist Government, then newly established in Hankow, had taken a stand against the Peking Government, materially assisted by the backing of the Soviet Union. The Peking Government, therefore, decided to strike back. (2) The Peking Government was believed to have been prompted by Britain, which after the massacre in Shanghai and the strike in Hong Kong had suffered tremendous setbacks both economic and political. British prestige in the Far East was seriously shaken. It was reported that Britain had persuaded the almost-disintegrated Peking Government to take action against the conspiratorial centre in the Soviet Embassy. (3) The southern revolutionary government, having won the popular sympathy through revolutionary slogans, was carrying everything before it in a northern expedition, which greatly endangered the position of the Peking Government. To regain the sympathy of the people, the Peking Government undertook to destroy Red influence. (4) Because of the dispute over the Chinese Eastern Railway, Marshal Chang Tso-lin bore a grudge against the Soviet Union, and especially against its Ambassador, Karakhan.

For these reasons, the Peking Government had been harbouring a design to undermine Soviet influence in China. On March 1, 1927, a Soviet steamer, *Pamiat Lenina*, on its way to Hankow with a cargo of tea, was detained at Pukow by some of General Chang Chung-chang's troops, consisting of White Russians. Borodin's wife and several other Soviet citizens who claimed to be diplomatic officials were discovered on board. Large quantities of Communist literature were also found. Chang Chung-chang ordered these people to be detained and transported to Tsinan under guard. Against this the Soviet Ambassador immediately lodged a strong protest.

At the same time, Chang Chung-chang's Headquarters published a statement to the effect that the Soviet Government should be held responsible for the incident, as the ship was carrying Communist leaflets in direct violation of the Sino-Soviet Agreement. The Chinese *chargé d'affaires* in Moscow was instructed to inform the Soviet Government that it was not possible to release the ship and the people on board as requested.

On March 20 the Peking authorities conducted a general search of the schools and colleges of the city and arrested a number of students. A further arrest was made on the 29th. These educational institutions in Peking had among them at the time some ten thousand Kuomintang members and six or seven hundred Communists. A list of the more important members of both parties was drawn up by the authorities and the principals of the various schools were instructed to hand them over. The terror-stricken students and intellectuals, especially the active Communists, took refuge in the Soviet Embassy.

These developments led to the search of the Soviet Embassy in Peking. The Mukden authorities first consulted with the Dutch Minister, who heartily favoured the measure, but added that Chinese troops or police were debarred from the Legation Quarter by the Boxer Protocol, and it was no small matter to act in violation of that treaty. A request for permission to do so, therefore, should come from the Chinese Foreign Ministry. Dr. Wellington Koo, the then Foreign Minister, was asked to undertake the task. Dr. Koo passed the request on to his subordinates, but no definite measures were taken.

It happened that a serious rumour of a Communist uprising was current in Tientsin, and foreign residents were fast evacuating the city. These also looked upon the Soviet Embassy as being concerned in the trouble. It was then that the Mukden authorities decided to take the situation in hand arbitrarily. The opinion of the Ministers of Great Britain and France was sought, but they refused to commit themselves. The Mukden authorities insisted that, with war going on, it was impossible to permit the existence of such a nuisance in the rear, where the army command was, and that the matter had to be dealt with somehow. The Ministers replied that they would call a conference of all representatives of countries which had a part in the Boxer Protocol. The decision arrived at by the conference was that Chinese troops and police might be allowed to enter on certain conditions; the actual working plan to be left to the discretion of the Dutch Minister. The Mukden authorities then held negotiations with the Minister of the Netherlands. The strictest secrecy was observed, so much so that, other than the Ministers themselves, not even the diplomatic circle had knowledge of the affair.

On the night of April 5, the Metropolitan Police Chief, Chen Hsing-ya, was called to the Headquarters and instructed what he should do. He was to have the necessary number of police ready early the next morning, in addition to a number of men in civilian dress who were to bear a red arm-band for identification. At the same time, he was instructed to prepare an official document, requesting the diplomatic authorities for permission to search the Dalbank, the offices of the Chinese Eastern Railway and the Boxer Indemnity Fund, all located in the Legation Quarter. He was to say that certain party men were plotting for a riot, and that the emergency required an immediate search.

Early next morning, Foreign Commissioner Wu Chin of Chang Tso-lin's Headquarters and concurrently Vice-Minister for Foreign Affairs, proceeded to the Soviet Embassy to direct the search. By 10 a.m. all necessary personnel were gathered. The document aforementioned was countersigned by the Dutch Minister at 10.20 a.m., and the search was immediately begun. The police had with them a plan, made by a foreigner, of the various grounds and buildings. With the help of the plan, the police now posted guards and the search was begun, the result of which was the apprehension of Li Ta-chao, Lu You-yu and over sixty other Communists as well as many important documents relating to the attempted conspiracy.[4] At 2 p.m. the search was still going on. 'With diplomatic zeal, the Chinese raiding party exceeded their authority and broke into the adjoining building which housed the offices of the Soviet military attaché, where they found the occupants busy consigning their archives to the flames. But the Chinese are a practical people, not to be deterred by so simple a manœuvre, and Chinese people were already on the roof pouring water down the diplomatic chimneys. The result of the raid was the seizure of a mass of documents, which, charred by fire though many of them were, revealed to the world the close association between the Russian Embassy, the Chinese Communists and many of the leaders of the Kuomintang.'[5]

On the evidence thus obtained, the Peking Government lodged a strong protest with the Soviet *chargé d'affaires*. The Soviet *chargé d'affaires* also protested on March 7 against the searching of the offices of the military attaché of the Embassy. Meanwhile, the Dutch Minister, on behalf of the diplomatic representatives, protested to the Foreign Ministry, because the search was allegedly carried beyond the prescribed limits. This last, however, was no more than a graceful gesture.

Let us confirm this extraordinary event by the following state-

[4] Chen Po-wen, *History of Russo-Chinese Diplomacy* (in Chinese), pp. 147-8.
[5] Teichman, op. cit., p. 65.

ment written by Oudendyk, the Dutch Minister, a man of authority.

'The Chinese police had reason to believe that the Soviet Embassy in Peking was the headquarters of a widespread conspiracy, not only for assisting various parties in the civil wars, but also for causing a Communist uprising in the capital. . . . They learned that the Dalbank, the Bolshevik banking institution installed in the former Russian post office, and certain buildings in the former Russian barracks occupied by employees of the Chinese Eastern Railway, were being used for revolutionary purposes and as meeting-places for Chinese Communists, and they desired to put an end to these illegal doings, which went on under the protection afforded by the status of the Legation Quarter.

'One of Marshal Chang Tso-lin's right-hand men, Mr. Wu Chin, who was then Vice-Minister of Foreign Affairs, came to see me about it. After being told that the Legation Quarter could do nothing in this matter, he asked for permission for the Chinese police to enter the Quarter and search these buildings. This request I submitted to my colleagues, who shared my opinion that it should be granted. Thereupon, on the morning of the 6th April a secretary of the Metropolitan Police requested my endorsement on a warrant for the search of the buildings in question: so I wrote on the back in English (as there was an American sentry at the western entrance of the Legation Street) that a company of Chinese police should be admitted to the Quarter at eleven o'clock. I immediately informed my colleagues of this. . . .

'Exactly at eleven o'clock a few Chinese police in plain clothes came quietly along, pushed the gate between the barracks and the Soviet bank open, passed the few women and bank clerks who were standing there chatting, and disappeared into the barracks compound. They were followed by a few more police in uniform. It took some time before the Russians began to suspect that something was up. They then hurriedly decamped, and some front doors of the bank were closed. By that time some fifty or sixty policemen had rushed the gate and disappeared from view. I watched the proceedings from the landing window in my legation, with some friends, among whom there was Captain Roque of the French Legation. Everything remained perfectly quiet for quite a while. Some six or eight passers-by stopped in the street, curious to know why Chinese police should have gone into the Soviet bank. Then a well-dressed young Chinese drove up in a ricksha. He carried an immense bag with documents, and also an attaché case. The ricksha was just turning into the gate when its occupant perceived two policemen standing inside. He quickly ordered his ricksha puller not to enter but to go straight on. He saved his life by this timely manœuvre.

'After a few minutes some of the policemen came out again, leading a very well-dressed, elderly Chinese by the arm. It was Li Ta-chao, the well-known Chinese Communist. Next in quick succession came several younger Chinese and a Chinese woman. They were placed in motor-cars and driven away. Then a number of Russians were brought out, some with their arms tied behind their backs, they were also driven away. . . . Suddenly a great column of smoke was seen rising from the western part of the barrack compound. Before long a Chinese fire engine was brought on to the scene, and a hose was laid over the building and water pumped down the chimney. This quenched the fire, but an enormous quantity of documents, and no doubt the most incriminating ones, must have meanwhile perished in the flames. . . .

'When my colleagues and I heard that these premises had been searched, we sent a written protest to the *Waichiaopu*, pointing out that the Chinese police had exceeded their authority. The raid naturally created no small sensation.'[6]

The Soviet Government was naturally very indignant over the incident. Mass demonstrations were held in many Soviet cities. A severe diplomatic protest was handed to the Chinese *chargé d'affaires* in Moscow, embodying the following four demands: (1) Chinese troops and police to retire immediately from the office of the Embassy; (2) The arrested Soviet personnel of the Embassy and employees of the Economic Investigation Bureau to be immediately released; (3) All documents taken from the office of the military attaché of the Embassy to be returned at once; (4) All articles taken by the troops and the police to be returned to the proper owners. Unless a satisfactory reply was received, the Soviet Ambassador would be recalled.

This protest having been made, the personnel of the Soviet Embassy got ready to leave. A list of names was given to the Chinese Foreign Ministry, with the request that passports be issued, which was complied with. On the morning of April 19, the Soviet *chargé*

6 Oudendyk, op. cit., pp. 348-50.

d'affaires, together with some twenty other staff members of the Embassy, entrained for Russia via Harbin. The Chinese formal reply to the Moscow protest was sent on April 16, in which all the four demands were rejected.

Upon receipt of the Chinese reply, the Soviet Government tacitly severed relations with the Peking Government, but the Chinese *chargé d'affaires* representing the Peking Government was not recalled. On the other hand, though the Soviet *chargé d'affaires* had left Peking, Soviet consuls in the Three Eastern Provinces were still at their posts. Thus diplomatic relations between Peking and Moscow were still maintained in one way or another right down to the time when the Peking Government itself went out of existence.

The prisoners still remained to be dealt with. A special court was set up for their trial. Prisoners of Chinese citizenship were first heard. The following individuals were found guilty on evidence obtained through the search and variously sentenced: Li Ta-chao, Lu You-yu and eighteen others were sentenced to death. Li died the death of a martyr, gazing heavenward with a long sigh, leaving no parting word for his family. Others were sentenced to various degrees of imprisonment. Some thirty of the rest were not tried but detained by the police.

As to the nineteen prisoners of Soviet citizenship arrested in the Soviet Embassy, as well as Borodin's wife and the three postal messengers apprehended in Pukow, the Peking Government decided that they should be tried by the Peking Supreme Court. A pre-hearing was conducted on May 10, but sentence was reserved. On July 12, the Judge of the Supreme Court exercised his authority to announce in the court that Borodin's wife and the three messengers should be set at liberty on account of the grand amnesty (in connection with the assumption of the rank of Generalissimo by Marshal Chang Tso-lin), while the others were detained for further trial. These latter did not regain their liberty till after the Peking Government toppled, when the Soviet Embassy incident was considered virtually closed.

According to the version of Oudendyk these Russian culprits owed their lives to the advice he gave to Chang Tso-lin. For shortly after the raid, he received a visit from one of Chang Tso-lin's secretaries, who told him that the arrested Russians would be treated in the same manner as the Chinese owing to the fact that the Russians were under Chinese jurisdiction. He made the following suggestion: 'That the Chinese Communists had been executed without a public trial, but with regard to the Russians the matter stood somewhat differently. . . . A proper and public trial would be necessary, in accordance with China's new laws, in the presence of the foreign Press and with proper defence for the accused.' His sound advice was apparently accepted by Generalissimo Chang Tso-lin.

3. Party Purge

The northern expedition of the Nationalist Government, which started from Canton, met with easy successes and, by July 1926, Hunan, Hupeh and Kiangsi were captured. It was then that Communist influence greatly extended along the valleys of the Pearl and the Yangtze Rivers.

A number of Soviet military and political advisers were sent from Moscow. Michael Borodin was made the chief political adviser, and Galen, also known as Bleucher, was appointed military adviser. It was not long before the virtual control of the Chinese Revolution fell into their hands, which aroused the indignation and jealousy of the Kuomintang who attempted to oust the Communists. The incident of the Chungshan gunboat on March 20, 1926, gave rise to the sudden declaration of martial law in Canton. Internal and external communications were severed. Twenty or thirty Soviet citizens in the service of the Canton Government were rounded up and deported. This immediately created a tense atmosphere, and it was thought that the Kuomintang might break with the Communist Party.

Next came the party purge in Nanking. Influential heads of the Kuomintang called a meeting on April 15, at which Wu Tze-hui, an elder member, requested the Central Plenary Executive Council to adopt drastic measures. Party purge movements were then started in Kwang-tung, Kwangsi, Fukien, Chekiang, Kiangsu and Anhuei.

The Wuhan Government, dominated by the Communist Party, at first maintained a strong opposition. At this time the Communist influence was fast spreading in Hunan and Hupeh. By June 3, an active purge was begun in Kiangsi, when the leaders of the Wuhan Government found it necessary or advisable to sever relations with the Communist Party also. The Central Executive Committee of the Wuhan Government passed a resolution on June 17 dispensing with the services of Borodin as adviser to the government, and Foreign Minister Eugene Chen was entrusted with the responsibility of asking Borodin to take his departure. Another resolution to curb the Communist Party was passed on July 15.

Borodin and the rest of the Soviets realized that their opportunity for activities in China was irretrievably gone, and the whole party left Wuhan for the Soviet Union on July 27 via Honan, Shensi and Mongolia. It was not till October that they reached Moscow. Soon after, Borodin was followed by Eugene Chen. General Galen remained behind and later set out for Shanghai, where he took boat for Japan and the Soviet Union.

After the uprisings in Canton, the Nationalist Government on the night of December 14 withdrew recognition from all the consuls of the U.S.S.R. in the various provinces and suppressed all Soviet commercial agencies. The Foreign Ministry was instructed to put this order into execution, in conjunction with the authorities concerned.

Recognition of Soviet consulates having been withdrawn, the Soviet Government requested the German Government to instruct the consuls of the latter country· in China to take charge of the Soviet consulates as well as to look after the protection of Soviet citizens. This was agreed to by the Nationalist Government, provided no political or diplomatic duties were included.

When news of the withdrawal of recognition of Soviet representatives on the part of the Nationalist Government reached Moscow, it brought about a very unfavourable reaction. Chicherin, the Foreign Commissar of the Soviet Government, telegraphed B. Kozzovsky, the Soviet Consul in Shanghai, who had not yet left, to inform Quo Tai-chi, the Chinese Commissioner for Foreign Affairs, that the Soviet Government had never recognized the Nanking Government and, for that reason, refused to consider the Nanking Government's note of July 15.

The Soviet Government also alleged that the Nanking Government was working under the influence of foreign imperialists to the disadvantage of the Chinese people as a whole. It also denied having participated in the uprising.

After the establishment of the Nationalist Government in Canton, in spite of the close relations with the U.S.S.R., no diplomatic recognition was formally given, which enabled the Soviet Government to ridicule any move on the part of the Nationalist Government and to refuse severance of relations. However, the Nationalist Government from that time on simply paid no attention to what the Soviet Union had to say.

Among the documents relating to the incident is a telegram to

General Chiang Kai-shek from Madame Sun Yat-sen who was in Moscow at the time. A translation of this is appended hereto:

'I was on the point of starting for home from Moscow when I learned of your proposal to sever relations with the Soviet Union and to exclude Soviet consuls from the country. Should this proposal of yours be put into practice, it would not only mean national suicide, but would isolate the Party and the Country from all possible sources of help. Future history will brand you guilty of ruining the Party and the Country. Had you a fraction of the foresight of the late Dr. Sun Yat-sen, or did you not entirely forget his last command to co-operate with the Soviet Union, could you have blindly fallen into the snare of self-destruction like this? I hope you will carefully weigh the matter and I expect you to awake and withdraw your proposal; otherwise I should be compelled to stay here for the present as a protest against such faithless and suicidal policy. On whatever points you think are difficult of settlement or inducing dispute, I firmly believe the Soviet Union will be glad to negotiate with us for a peaceful solution in order that the revolution may be brought to a success.'[7]

It should be finally added that, whether recognition came from the Nationalist Government or not, Soviet consuls in north China continued to function right down to 1929—the year of the Chinese Eastern Railway dispute—when diplomatic relations were finally severed.

[7] Chen Pao-wen, op. cit., p. 157.

Chapter XII

THE SINO-SOVIET CRISIS OF 1929

THE agreement for the joint management of the Chinese Eastern Railway between the Soviet Union and China in 1924 was a makeshift, which did not remove one of the major bones of contention between the contracting parties. Friendly relations between them were nominally resumed with the signing of the Peking and Mukden Agreements, to which the Railway Agreement was but a supplementary document, but in fact the Soviet Government gained more and more power over the railway till finally its management practically passed into Soviet hands.

Meanwhile, Communist activities were being carried on in the railway zone through the agency of Soviet diplomatic channels. The search of the Soviet Embassy in Peking, dealt with fully in the foregoing chapter, precipitated the beginning of strained relations between the two countries.

The Sino-Soviet crisis of 1929 caused an open conflict, bringing to China a humiliating defeat. Such a consequence could have been easily foreseen from the start, since China had no clear objective and had made no adequate preparations.

1. Taking Over of the C.E.R.

In the recall of the Soviet Embassy officials, the Soviet consular staff and Soviet commercial representatives in various parts of China were not included. In Harbin the police received confidential information that a conference of the Third International was to be held in the Soviet Consulate on May 27, 1929. A raid was launched on its premises while the conference was in progress. Among the participants were a small number of Soviet officers and employees of the Chinese Eastern Railway. The suspicions of the police were first aroused by the fact that all doors of the consulate were closed. When they got in, they found that most of the documents had been burnt in the stove. But the remaining documents and those in the stove not yet consumed were confiscated, translated and published by the Nanking Government.[1]

At that time the controversy about the respective rights and privileges over the railway between China and the Soviet Union was still in progress. The situation was becoming more tense daily.

The Sino-Soviet Agreement which stipulated that there should be an equal number of Soviet and Chinese directors with equal executive power was never carried out. The Soviets were holding an overwhelming portion of the administrative power in their hands. For instance, out of the eighteen divisions of the railway, the heads of fourteen were Soviet citizens, and only four Chinese. The Manager and one of the two Assistant Managers were Soviet citizens. The Chinese share of control over the railway was but nominal. Proposals were made by the Chinese side to remedy these differences in a joint conference; but the answers were invariably prevaricative. A last concessional arrangement was offered by the Chinese on March 27, 1929, embodying their minimum conditions, but it was also rejected.

Now came the opportunity for the Chinese authorities to take high-handed measures. Finding many of the Russian officers of the railway involved in left-wing activities, the Government of the Eastern Provinces telegraphed the Central Government for instructions and was allowed to act at its own discretion. Given a free hand, the Provincial Government ordered that the railway be taken over. At the same time, the telegraphic lines of the railway were also forcibly taken over by the Provincial Government. The Soviet Manager ·and Assistant Manager, together with fifty-nine members of the higher Soviet executives of the railway, were dismissed and deported. The dismissal and deportation were carried out so abruptly and hastily that it created adverse reactions among other Soviet employees on the railway, who numbered more than 20,000. They perpetrated strikes and sabotage. It also created a false impression in other countries to the effect that the dismissal of.the Soviet Manager of the railway was a prelude to the taking over of the railway.

On the following day after the consulate had been searched, the government received a long-distance telephone message from Vladivostok intimating that the Soviet authorities had already

[1] See *Documents with reference to the Sino-Russian Dispute*, 1929, pp. 18-65.

lodged a protest with regard to the incident with the Chinese Consul General in Vladivostok. On May 31, a formal note of protest was delivered, in which it was said that the arrested persons were employees of the Soviet Government and the Chinese Eastern Railway, or other Soviet citizens in the consulate on busineess regarding passports and visas. The note demanded the immediate release of the persons detained and the restoration of documents and properties, stating further that the Chinese Legation and consulates in the Soviet Union would no longer be accorded diplomatic privileges. Another note of warning was handed to the Chinese *chargé d'affaires* in Moscow, signed by Karakhan. Moreover, a separate protest was delivered to young Marshal Chang Hsueh-liang by the Soviet Consulate in Mukden on July 13. After that the Chinese diplomatic and consular officials in the Soviet Union were on their way back to China.

2. Soviet Ultimatum

Unexpectedly the Soviet Government commissioned Chelieplanhoff as Envoy Extraordinary to fly to China for negotiations. His plane was delayed on the way and he arrived at Irkutsk on July 15, expecting to arrive at Harbin on the 17th. However, while Chelieplanhoff was yet on his way, a note in the nature of an ultimatum was signed and delivered to the Chinese Government by Karakhan on July 13, which demanded a satisfactory answer in three days. The three main points of the note were:

1. A conference should be called without delay to settle all questions pertaining to the Chinese Eastern Railway.

2. All illegal actions against the Chinese Eastern Railway perpetrated by the various Chinese Government Departments should be stopped.

3. All citizens of the Soviet Union in detention were to be immediately released, and the Chinese Government should stop all oppressive actions against Soviet citizens and organizations.

'The Government of the Soviet Union,' added the note, 'hopes the Mukden Government and the Government of the Republic of China will carefully consider the serious consequences of opposing these proposals made by the Soviet Government. The Soviet Government expects a reply from the Chinese Government to the above-mentioned items within three days, and wishes to state in advance that, failing to receive a satisfactory reply the Soviet Government will be forced to adopt other measures to safeguard the rights and privileges of the Soviet Union.'[2]

The situation had now come to a most critical stage. War could have broken out between China and the Soviet Union at any time. Partial military mobilization was anticipated. The Chinese Government's reply to the Soviet ultimatum was telegraphed to the Chinese *chargé d'affaires* in Moscow to be delivered to the Soviet Government. The English translation of the full text is given below:

'Since the signing of the Sino-Russian Provisional Agreement in 1924, diplomatic relations between the two countries have been firmly established. The Chinese Government and people according to their traditional sense of world brotherhood have at all times endeavoured to meet the Soviet Government and people with a spirit of equality and mutual assistance. In recent years, however, it has been repeatedly discovered that Soviet Russia has been conducting organized propaganda and other activities to instigate the Chinese people to take destructive measures against the interests of the Chinese Government and society, thus compelling the government to take such steps as are necessary for the maintenance of peace and order in the country.

'The authorities of the Three Eastern Provinces in ordering the search of the Soviet consulate at Harbin, and in taking such steps as already have been taken with reference to the Chinese Eastern Railway, have but in view the prevention of the sudden occurrence of incidents that are detrimental to the peace and order of the country. They are emergency measures the government has been forced to take, and the local authorities have been extremely careful in localizing the incident.

'The National Government of China has repeatedly received reports from the Three Eastern Provinces to the effect that the Soviet Manager and other important Russian officials of the Chinese Eastern Railway from the very beginning have never observed the terms of the 1924 Sino-Russian Agreement on the provisional management of the Chinese Eastern Railway. For the past several years, the said Manager and others have on numerous occasions acted illegally and exceeded their lawful authority, making it impossible for the Chinese officials of the railway to carry out their duties according to the agreement. Furthermore the Soviet members often utilized the said railway for

[2] See text in the *Sino-Russian Crisis*, pp. 35-9.

propaganda, thereby intentionally violating the stipulations of the Sino-Russian Agreement.

'For these reasons, the authorities of the Three Eastern Provinces are constrained to take this necessary action against the Chinese Eastern Railway. That we are not responsible for the violation of the Sino-Russian Agreement and the agreement concerning the provisional management of the railway is very obvious.

'Again, from the reports of our Embassy and consulates in Russia, we have learnt that the Soviet Government has arrested more than one thousand of our merchants without any provocation whatsoever. Most Chinese merchants there have been reduced to wretched circumstances owing to Soviet oppression. The Chinese Government, on the contrary, has always been broadminded in its relations with Soviet merchants and Soviet commercial organizations in China; and has never entertained any prejudice against Soviet nationals. The arrest of certain Russians and the raid on certain Russian institutions by the authorities of the Three Eastern Provinces are entirely necessary for the purpose of preventing anti-revolutionary propaganda and for maintaining peace and order.

'The National Government of China does not propose the following conditions as counter-demands. But if the Soviet Government will

1. Release all the Chinese merchants arrested and detained by the Soviet Government, except those who, being involved in law suits, are guaranteed by the Chinese Embassy or consulates to remain in Russia; and

2. Give such adequate protection and facilities as the Chinese merchants in Russia are entitled to,

then the National Government of China will be ready at the appropriate time to take similar measures towards the arrested Soviet agents and the closed office buildings.

'In conclusion, the Chinese Government and people have always cherished the hope that the Soviet Government will, of its own accord, correct its past improper actions. As regards the present case, we hope the Soviet Government will respect China's law and sovereignty and refrain from submitting proposals contradictory to the actual facts of the case.'[3]

By this time relations between China and the Soviet Union

[3] *China Year Book*, 1929-30, p. 1221.

had come to a deadlock, and the Chinese Government felt that it was useless to bandy words any further, and accordingly made all military preparations within the limits of self-defence. At the same time, the Chinese Foreign Ministry drafted a public manifesto proclaiming to the world at large the real and actual facts of what had transpired. Evidence of secret activities on the part of the Soviet Union, disclosed during the search of the Soviet consulate in Harbin, were also made public. The Chinese manifesto was published on July 19 simultaneously through the Chinese Legations in various countries and in the form of a telegram from the Central Government to Dr. Wang Chung-hui, who was instructed to publish its contents at the Hague Conference.

3. Melinikoff-Tsai Negotiations

Following the Soviet note severing diplomatic relations, the Soviet representatives in China had been immediately recalled. Just before he left for Russia, the Soviet Consul General in Harbin, Melinikoff, called on Tsai Yun-shing, Commissioner of Foreign Affairs, requesting an interview with Governor Chang Tso-hsiang of Kirin to discuss the Chinese Eastern Railway incident. The request was granted, and the interview was arranged for July 24 at Changchun. The outcome of the interview was considered satisfactory, and Melinikoff entrained for Moscow the following day, making it known to Commissioner Tsai that as soon as he arrived he intended to work for the opening of a conference to discuss Chinese Eastern Railway questions. On July 28, Melinikoff telegraphed Tsai from Chita, asking the latter to proceed there for discussions.

At about the same time, a telegram was retransmitted by the Commander of the Chinese Eastern Railway military guards in Manchuli, from the Soviet Military Command, in which it was stated that the Soviet Union, being desirous to negotiate with China concerning the Chinese Eastern Railway affair, and with a view to resuming international communication, had appointed Melinikoff as representative for the discussions, and hoped that China would also send Commissioner Tsai Yun-shing for the same purpose. Thereupon Commissioner Tsai set out for Kirin for instructions, in the meantime reporting to the Central Government. He was instructed to proceed to the appointed place in the company of Li Shao-keng, Director of the Chinese Eastern Railway. They were met by Melinikoff at the third midway station building. Rather detailed opinions were exchanged both in regard to the railway and on the subject of communication over the national boundaries. The result was considered satisfactory. Following the discussion, Melinikoff immediately made a report to the Soviet Government and prepared to set out for Moscow to lay the whole affair before the government, suggesting that a properly appointed representative should be sent to open a formal conference with China. As to railroad communication between Europe and Asia, it was decided that such should be resumed even before the conference opened, in view of the mediation proffered by the consuls of the different Powers concerned.

The above-mentioned Tsai-Melinikoff conversation took place on the evening of July 30. A second talk was scheduled for the morning of August 1. This did not take place on account of both representatives falling ill. On the afternoon of August 2, Melinikoff entered Chinese territory and overtook Tsai at Manchuli. However, this discussion led to nothing. The next day Melinikoff sent his secretary to call on Tsai and inform him that instructions had been received from the Soviet Government for transmission of the following three points to the Chinese Government:

1. The personnel of the Chinese Eastern Railway to be reinstated, and the prevailing system of management restored.
2. Soviet troops should enjoy the right to protect the railway.
3. Supervision over the Far Eastern Bank to be removed.

It was added that should the Chinese Government agree to these proposals, the Soviet Union would be willing to send representatives for a Sino-Soviet conference, and that railway communication over the border could be resumed in advance. Tsai promised to transmit the message, and on the same night he telegraphed it to Marshal Chang Hsiao-liang and Governor Chang Tso-hsiang. On the morning of August 4, a reply was received intimating that the proposed conditions were detrimental to the sovereignty of China and could not be agreed to. This answer was passed on to Melinikoff, and the Tsai-Melinikoff conversation was postponed.

The Chinese Foreign Ministry formally appointed Chu Shao-yang as Plenipotentiary on July 26, and he at once proceeded from Nanking to Manchuli for negotiations with the Soviet authorities. He arrived there on August 6, but the authorities avoided meeting him.

Unable to meet Melinikoff, Chu telegraphed to Karakhan, requesting that a Soviet representative be sent for negotiations. On the morning of the 9th, Karakhan called and talked with Chu over the telephone, stating that his government was ready to open negotiations on condition that the items given in the ultimatum be accepted as a basis for discussion, and requesting Chu to furnish a guarantee in writing. Thus Chu had no choice but to return to Nanking.

4. Germany's Mediation

Soon after the disruption of friendly relations, Soviet Russia set about mobilizing troops and invading the Chinese border. In view of the grave situation, the French Government had previously intimated its willingness to mediate, but nothing more was heard of this offer. The Chinese Foreign Ministry then telegraphed Chiang Tso-pin, Chinese Minister in Germany, instructing him to enquire from the Soviet diplomatic representative in that country why such actions were taken. The reply was that the Soviet Government knew nothing about the affairs referred to along the border, and that, provided Chinese troops did not invade Soviet territory, Soviet military forces would not begin the attack. It was stipulated that White Russian troops in China should be disbanded, otherwise the responsibility for all the encounters which might occur would have to rest with the Chinese Government. When the Chinese Minister pointed out actual instances of Soviet troops opening attacks on China, the Soviet reply was that the entrance of Soviet troops into Chinese territory was caused by the need for self-defence against White Russians who opened fire on them first. Should China be willing to dissolve the armed White Russians and stop all menaces, the Soviet Government would be willing to restrict similar actions.

On August 27 the Foreign Ministry prepared a reply, which was delivered through the Chinese Minister in Germany, who was instructed to get in touch with Soviet diplomatic representatives from time to time. Meanwhile the German Government offered its services as mediator of peace, for which purpose it had previously sought the opinion of both sides. On August 27 the German Government formally proposed that both countries should publish a joint manifesto, embodying the following four points:

1. All questions should be settled in accordance with the provisions of the Sino-Soviet Agreement, both countries immediately appointing fully empowered representatives for discussions.

2. Conditions in respect of the Chinese Eastern Railway should be adjusted on the basis of the Sino-Soviet Agreement and the Soviet-

Mukden Pact, previously agreed upon by the representatives of both sides.

3. The Soviet Union should nominate one candidate for the post of Manager and Assistant Manager of the railway respectively for appointment by the Board of Directors. The Soviet Government should instruct all Russian employees of the railway to observe strictly Article VI of the Sino-Soviet Agreement.

4. Both sides should set free all persons apprehended in connection with the incident.

The Moscow Commissariat of Foreign Affairs replied through its Minister in Germany that the Soviet Government agreed in principle to the proposal, but suggested the following alterations:

1. The conference should be called to settle the outstanding disputes in accordance with the Sino-Soviet Agreement of 1924. The Provisions of Clause IX of the Sino-Soviet Agreement should be observed, especially in regard to the redemption of the Chinese Eastern Railway.

2. All outstanding disputes connected with the railway should be settled at the conference.

3. The appointment of the Soviet Manager and Assistant Manager of the railway should be made simultaneously with the publication of the joint manifesto.

4. Both governments were to instruct their respective employees of the Chinese Eastern Railway to observe strictly Article VI of the 1924 Agreement.

5. Both sides were to set free immediately all persons apprehended since May 1, 1929, in connection with the incident.

The Chinese Government did not agree to these points, neither would the Soviet Government give way. Another deadlock seemed to be near, but Germany finally succeeded in persuading the Soviet Government to make certain concessions. Even this did not save the situation, for the Chinese Government insisted on the exact original terms; with these the Soviet Government was so dissatisfied that it did not reply. So the German good offices did not bring any result. The Soviet Government, in order to avoid the blame for the rejection of the proposed mediation, instructed its Ambassador in Berlin to convey to the Chinese Minister that the Soviet Union was ready to open direct negotiations with China. The Soviet Union was reluctant to accept mediation by a third party, but welcomed direct negotiations.

5. Military and Naval Engagements

Shortly after the disruption of the negotiations, Soviet troops occupied three strategic towns near the border on August 12. Concerning the Chinese preparations, Reuter reported that Chinese troops in the area numbered only 1,300 men, and that it was impossible for such a small band to resist any attack.

Marshal Chang Hsueh-liang did not order the mobilization of his 60,000 troops for defence till August 15—three days after the Soviet troops had actually occupied three Chinese towns. Neither did Governor Chang Tso-hsiang proceed to Harbin to direct the defence before August 22.

The captain of one of the Chinese gunboats asserted that he was aware of the grave insufficiency of ammunition and commissariat supplies. Commander Han Kwang-ti also complained of an insufficient number of men, and antiquated armaments.

In addition to the occupation of the three towns already noted, Soviet troops attacked and captured Mishan Hsien on August 23, Wang-ching Hsien on the 28th, Suiping Hsien on September 19, Tungkiang Hsien on October 12, and Funchin Hsien on November 1.

With regard to the battle of Tungkiang, the Soviets alleged that the Chinese opened fire first, and they lodged a protest through the German Minister. As a matter of fact the Government of the Eastern Provinces gave a strict order to the armies under its authority not to open fire on any account, and the military reverses suffered were partly due to this order.

In October fighting was resumed. The Chinese possessed only seven river gunboats, confiscated from Germany at the end of the World War, while the Soviet flotilla was immeasurably stronger. In addition, the Soviets had eighteen planes. Early in the morning of October 12, the Soviet Navy opened fire on the Chinese flotilla, in which attack nine gunboats, eighteen planes and three thousand cavalry and infantry participated. The upshot of the encounter was that Tungkiang fell to the Soviets, and the Chinese suffered a loss of two gunboats and 400 men.

The Chinese Government lodged a protest against the occupation of Tungkiang, through the German Government. At the same time the Soviet Government also lodged a protest through the German diplomatic representative in China, which the Chinese Government refused to accept, insisting that the offensive was taken by the Soviets.

6. Peace Movements

On October 9 the German Government again tendered its good offices, suggesting that both countries should cease reprisals and immediately release prisoners. The Soviet Government turned down this offer and took the stand that 'no Soviet national would be permitted to negotiate with the Chinese Government, nor would mediation by any third party be acceptable unless the Soviet demands were met'.

The Chinese Government then issued a second manifesto in English on October 25 to all the signatories of the Kellogg Pact, stating that the Soviets had assumed the offensive while responsible spokesmen on both sides were consulting a third party. The manifesto further held the Soviet Government responsible for all losses and damage caused to Chinese life and property.[4]

The general reaction to this Chinese manifesto was far from sympathetic. It looked as if China was to find herself isolated. The advance of Soviet forces was accelerating. On November 17 the Soviets were making use of 60 cannons, 20 planes, a number of armoured tanks and three divisions of infantry in the attack against Dalainor.[5] The Chinese brigade there was surrounded and completely wiped out. Of the total number of 7,000 only about 1,000 escaped with their lives. Two of the three battalion commanders died in action, the other was wounded, and the renowned Brigade Commander Han Kwang-ti was killed. Simultaneously with the attack on Dalainor, the Soviet forces encircled Manchuli, which, after the occupation of the former, was so effectively cut off, that it also fell. Brigade Commander Liang Chung-chia in charge of its defence was killed in action.

The anxiety of the Chinese Government was increasing. A statement of past incidents was again issued to all the signatories of the Kellogg Pact with the request that sanctions be applied against the Soviet Union. Britain, France and the United States, the signatories of the pact, seeing that their respective interests in China would thus be endangered, delivered a note to the Chinese, as well as the Soviet Government, requesting them to stop military activities forthwith, and pointing out that since both countries were signatories to the Kellogg Pact, it behoved them to desist from war at once.

---

[4] *China Year Book*, 1929-30, p. 1229.
[5] Chang Hsueh-liang's report to the Nanking Government on the fall of Manchuli dated August 24, 1929.

The Chinese Government expressed readiness to comply with this request, while the Soviet Government considered this act as unfriendly on the part of the three Powers concerned, and announced its decision to refuse the mediation of any third party in the settlement of the affairs of the Chinese Eastern Railway. A second note was sent to the Soviet Government by the United States, with equally unfruitful results.

Left to fight its battle alone, the Chinese Nationalist Government felt itself incompetent for the task. It would do nothing but hint to the Government of the Eastern Provinces that it should look for an opportunity to negotiate peace with the Soviet Union. Thereupon the Provincial Government instructed Tsai Yun-shing to try to get in touch with the Soviets. Tsai sent a Soviet employee of the Chinese Eastern Railway from Harbin to Khabarovsk to see the Soviet Consul General, Simanovsky, and to express China's hope for peace. The Soviet Consul General then sent a special train for Tsai to meet him at the fourth midway station, and the two representatives had a conversation in Kwanchengtze. Tsai also telegraphed Karakhan, who wired Simanovsky to negotiate with Tsai.

Meanwhile the Nationalist Government seemed to have admitted the expediency of permitting the local authorities to deal directly with the Soviet Union. The reason for this was two-fold. First, being on the country's border, the North-eastern Provinces were weighed down by complicated international relations, and all Sino-Soviet negotiations were influenced by Japan. At the time, Japan strongly recommended local negotiations with the Soviet Union. Secondly, since the publication of the Chinese manifesto of October 23, the Soviet Government had been apprehensive of intervention by Japan.

Even after the fall of Manchuli and Dalainor, the Nationalist Government did not give up hope of intervention on the part of a third Power. On the 24th, a telegram was despatched to various Chinese Legations containing a statement of past events for transmission to the respective governments to which they were accredited. A proposal was also made through the German Government to form an investigation committee, whose chairman was to be a citizen of a third country. To this proposal the Soviet Government replied that Marshal Chang Hsueh-liang had already accepted the conditions suggested by the Soviet Government, and therefore there was no necessity to set up such a committee.

The British, French and American Governments issued a note on

December 1 requesting the two governments concerned to stop military activities. Both governments replied on December 3, but the Soviet note was very stiffly worded and asserted that direct negotiations were being carried on with the Mukden Government regarding the Chinese Eastern Railway. Hence no intervention from a third party was admissible. With neither a definite objective nor sufficient preparations to start with, the Nationalist Government had now to suffer the consequences.

7. Khabarovsk Convention

After a week's conference a provisional agreement was made, and Tsai returned to Mukden to report on his mission. The draft agreement was generally approved by the Government of the Eastern Provinces, and Tsai was told to proceed to Khabarovsk to sign it. This consisted of ten articles, accepting the Soviet demands in their entirety. (See full text in Appendix A.)

Some sort of a protocol seemed to have been signed by the representatives of the Soviet Government and the Mukden Government, for the latter commissioned Tsai Yun-shing and Li Shao-keng to proceed for this purpose on November 30. Reference was also made in the Khabarovsk Treaty to the existence of the Kwanchengtze Protocol, signed on December 3. The latter, however, was never published, but incidental evidence may be gathered from a telegraphic report from Nanking in the Shanghai Press, which reads as follows:

'Chang Hsueh-liang telegraphed the National Government to the effect that arrangements had been made by Tsai Yun-shing with the Soviet representatives, viz.: (1) A new railway Manager and Assistant Manager were to be appointed by the Soviet Government: the ex-Manager was to be given another post on the railway; (2) The question of responsibility and blame to be decided by investigations made by a personnel from each side; no participation by a third party to be admitted; (3) The Sino-Soviet controversy to be settled by a Sino-Soviet conference. The Nationalist Government was requested to make a decision thereon and appoint an envoy for formal negotiations. Upon receipt of this telegram, General Chiang Kai-shek called an urgent meeting of the government heads, at which Chiang decided to accept these terms *in toto*, in view of prevailing internal troubles.'[6]

[6] *Shun Pao*, Shanghai, December 8, 1929.

In other words, China capitulated unconditionally. The negotiations had, by this time, arrived at a riper stage. On December 10, Tsai Yun-shing proceeded to Khabarovsk, where a preliminary conference was held on the 16th. Discussions were concluded by December 22, when the Khabarovsk Convention was signed.

From then on the Chinese authorities did their best to carry out the conditions specified in the convention. Their successive steps are enumerated below.

Chang Hsueh-liang wired to the Central Government on December 25 a request that the latter should telegraph the Chinese Consuls General and other consular officials in Vladivostok and Blagoveshchensh in accordance with Article 5 of the Convention.

About 1,200 Soviet prisoners were released from the detention quarters in Harbin and north Sungari. The thirty-seven Soviet prisoners arrested during the search of the Soviet consulate in Harbin, who were the tinder, were also freed, in observance of Article 3 of the Protocol.

The newly appointed Soviet Manager and Vice-Manager of the Chinese Eastern Railway arrived at Harbin on December 31.

The Soviet Manager and Assistant Manager of the railway assumed office on January 4, 1930. One of the first acts in their new capacity was the appointment of a large number of Soviet personnel to serve on the railway.

With the signing of the Draft Agreement, the Khabarovsk Convention was brought to a close, and the Soviet Government accordingly wound up military activities along the border. But the Nationalist Government was greatly dissatisfied with the contents of the treaty, for not only did it reinstate Soviet monopoly over the Chinese Eastern Railway, but also gave the Soviet Union a favoured position in other matters. When the treaty was published, public opinion greatly objected on the ground that the reversion of the Chinese Eastern Railway to its *status quo ante* was nothing less than admission on the part of the Chinese Government of its errors in instituting the changes. The Soviet personnel of the railway, therefore, enjoyed extra protection from the provisions of the treaty. The Soviet Government also succeeded in arresting Chinese citizens in the U.S.S.R. as a ransom for the release of Soviet prisoners. Moreover, the Soviets were then given the opportunity to interfere in the administration of the Chinese Eastern Railway. The discussions relating to Sino-Soviet trade questions were also beyond the usual limits for such negotiations. The Nationalist Government then issued a manifesto, revoking all articles not directly concerned with the Chinese Eastern Railway. As to those in respect of the railway, the Nationalist Government declared its intention to meet the Soviet Union in another conference to make necessary and suitable revisions.

In addition to publishing a manifesto, the Chinese Foreign Ministry deprived its representative of his post and subjected him to further investigations.

The Khabarovsk Convention thereupon ended the deplorable Sino-Soviet strain lasting seven months. During this time, China suffered tremendous losses in life and property as a result of many military and naval encounters with the Soviet Union, as well as a grievous loss of national prestige, and gained nothing but the unfair conditions imposed by the treaty. It was estimated that Chinese casualties, military and civilian, exceeded 10,000, and property valued at $1,000,000,000 was lost.

The complete capitulation of China to the Soviet terms in the restoration of the *status quo ante* of the management of the Chinese Eastern Railway ended the former contention of equal employment of nationalities between the two countries. Apart from this, as stipulated in Article 4 of the convention, the Soviets succeeded in getting rid of the White Guards in Manchuria, which they had so much hated.

This leaves for consideration the Sino-Soviet Conference in Moscow for the settlement of other issues and the ratification of draft agreements, which forms the main subject of the next chapter.

PART III

CHINA AND THE SOVIET UNION
1931-1950

Chapter XIII

RESUMPTION OF SINO-SOVIET RELATIONS,
DECEMBER 12, 1932

THE Khabarovsk Convention opened the way for a formal Sino-Soviet Conference, to which the Nationalist Government intimated its readiness to send plenipotentiaries. Moh Teh-hui was appointed chief delegate upon the recommendation of Marshal Chang Hsueh-liang, and he set out for the Soviet Union on May 1, 1930, arriving at Moscow on the 9th. The Soviet Government appointed Karakhan plenipotentiary to the conference. After numerous meeting and conversations, the conference was to be started on October 11, 1930. But the discussions could make no headway, owing to a conflict of views arising out of an interpretation of the Khabarovsk Protocol concerning the question of recognition. Then the conference was deadlocked almost as soon as it was convened. Informal negotiations then proceeded laboriously, with the result that the conference was again opened on December 4, 1930. Meantime, the Nationalist Government telegraphed Moh to return to China for consultation, and it was not till March 21 of the following year that he set out for Moscow again.[1] One impasse after another threatened to ground the conference altogether, and on September 18, 1931, a most untoward affair happened—the Manchurian incident —as a consequence of which China was unable to maintain her sovereign rights over the Chinese Eastern Railway. The Soviet Government then postponed the conference indefinitely. But it was

---

[1] Ho Han-wen, op. cit., p. 423.

also due to the Manchurian incident that formal relations between China and the U.S.S.R. were resumed.

1. Sino-Soviet Relations Since the Manchurian Incident

As soon as news of the Manchurian incident reached Moscow, the Soviet Vice Commissar of Foreign Affairs, Karakhan, called upon the Chinese Representative, Moh Teh-hui, expressing the opinion that the incident was another reason why China and the Soviet Union should resume relations. Moh, however, had not received news of the incident, and refused to discuss the matter on the ground that he had not received instructions from the Chinese Government. The preliminary negotiations, therefore, produced no results.

By the time that news of the incident had spread all over the Soviet Union, Karakhan had been approached by the Japanese Ambassador, Hirota, and his subordinates. Hirota even suggested the conclusion of a non-aggression pact with the Soviet Union, and Matsuoka, on his way to Europe, had an interview with Karakhan with the same object in mind.[2] As it happened, however, all this was of no avail, for Soviet and Japanese interests in Manchuria were always diametrically opposed to one another. On the side of China, although there were expressions of opinion that relations with the Soviet Union should be resumed, yet no formal statement had been made. The reason for this was that China had been expecting assistance from the capitalist countries. In order to court their pleasure, it had forgotten that diplomacy should of necessity be independent and not subject to the influence of one country to another. Clever manipulations always win success in international relations.

In 1932 the Chinese Government realized that the Sino-Japanese question had reached a deadlock. The League of Nations began its debate on the Lytton Report on December 6 and listened to the arguments by Dr. Wellington Koo and Mr. Yosuke Matsuoka, representing China and Japan respectively. The speech of the British Foreign Minister, Sir John Simon, emphasized the arguments in favour of Japan to such an extent that Mr. Matsuoka was reported to have remarked that 'Sir John Simon had said in half an hour, in a few well-chosen phrases, what he—Matsuoka—had been trying to

[2] *Bulletin of Waichiaopu*, January 15, 1933, p. 5.

say in his bad English for the last ten days!'[3] It was at once reported by the American Press as a strongly pro-Japanese speech which would lead the Assembly to shelve the Lytton Report. The Chinese Government's faith and hope in the League of Nations was very much shaken. But it was not until June 6, 1932, that the Central Executive Committee of the Kuomintang passed a resolution to resume relations with the Soviet Union. The strictest secrecy was enjoined. Instructions were cabled to Dr. W. W. Yen, First Chinese Delegate to the Assembly of the League of Nations, to use his discretion in negotiations with the Soviet representative in Geneva on the question of resumption of relations between China and the Soviet Union. Both sides came to an understanding that relations should first be resumed. It was then that Dr. Lo Wen-kan, Chinese Foreign Minister, stated to Press representatives 'the activities of Matsuoka will be completely nullified. Things to prove this will happen in ten days.' This was one of the few instances where the Chinese Government used secret diplomacy in the conduct of its foreign relations.

As for the Soviet Union, its motive for resuming relations with China was none other than the realization of its policy of peaceful foreign relations and development of commercial interests. The Soviet Union wished to resume relations with countries bordering on the Pacific in order that she might be able to deal with Far Eastern problems. Probably she also hoped to stir up war between Japan and the United States. Regarding the resumption of Sino-Soviet relations, Litvinov had this to say: '. . . At this time, the beginning of the difficulties in the Far East is closely related to the absence of diplomatic relations between the countries bordering the Pacific. There is no doubt about this claim. . . .'[4] The general situation prevailing at that time may be understood from the above quotation.

2. Reasons for Resumption of Sino-Soviet Relations

China and the Soviet Union had for a long period maintained good-neighbour relations. Both countries have common interests in the Far East and should therefore seek mutually favourable trade

---

[3] Royal Institute of International Affairs, *Survey for 1933*, p. 492. See also Henry L. Stimson, *The Far Eastern Crisis*, 1936, p. 224. (In Stimson's book, it was mentioned that China was represented by Dr. W. W. Yen in the delegation, but actually Dr. Wellington Koo took China's seat at the Council table, for Dr. Yen purposely yielded on this occasion for diplomatic reasons, though he was still the First Chinese Delegate.)

[4] *Bulletin of Waichiaopu*, January 15, 1933, p. 6.

relations. The Sino-Soviet Agreement had already established a foundation for equality and reciprocity between the two countries. Resumption of diplomatic relations would morally oblige the Soviet Union not to recognize 'Manchukuo'. The resumption of relations with the Soviet Union would therefore tend greatly to lessen the crisis in the Far East.

Both China and the Soviet Union could fundamentally change and improve their respective traditional policies. In the past, relations between the two countries were chiefly political; economic relations were little developed. Had the Tsarist Government tried to improve economic relations with China, its position in China and the Far East would have been very much stronger and far superior to that of any other country. On the other hand, Japan would never have been able to occupy her position in the Far East, and the Soviet Union would have inherited a much greater economic advantage. A strong economic tie is the key to political and diplomatic success. China and the Soviet Union had therefore a common interest to exert themselves towards this end.

From the viewpoint of China, the Sino-Soviet Agreement was no doubt a failure; but no less was it a failure from the Soviet viewpoint. For the Soviet Government had counted upon immediate recognition as the price of the voluntary relinquishment of the advantages aforementioned. But recognition by China became immaterial while the Soviet Government could not recede from its declarations.

3. Soviet Diplomacy

It is said that Soviet diplomacy moves in a 'curve-line'. But is there a country that carries on a 'straight-line' diplomacy? The basic principles of Soviet diplomacy have been declared to be equality and reciprocity as well as racial self-determination.

In the first and second declarations signed by Karakhan, the Soviet Union announced its intention to give up voluntarily all treaty rights obtained from China by the Tsarist Government, including extraterritoriality, and unconditionally to return the Chinese Eastern Railway. In return it was suggested that China should exclude White Russians from her territory as a *quid pro quo*. In this way, it was hoped that new treaties based upon the principles of equality and reciprocity might be signed. Unfortunately the first declaration did not reach the Chinese Government until later. When a copy did arrive, it was disregarded.

In spite of this, both the Sino-Soviet Agreement and the Mukden-Soviet Pact were based upon the aforementioned declarations. The status of the Chinese Eastern Railway was, however, not determined by them since it had assumed that of a Sino-Soviet commercial enterprise. According to the unofficial explanation given by the Soviets, the Chinese Government was unable to protect that line alone without being molested by other Powers, therefore it was converted into a joint enterprise. Did China really confess that she was so feeble? Would the Soviet ' curve-line' diplomacy follow ·the same track as other imperialistic Powers after Sino-Soviet relations had been resumed?

Despite inevitable suspicion, things ran quite smoothly as far as the Chinese Eastern Railway was concerned. The railway was netting huge profits after the Sino-Soviet crisis of 1929. The outbreak of the Manchurian incident put the Soviet Union in a dilemma. The refusal of the Soviet Government to transport Chinese troops on the line free of charge had to be withdrawn at the request of the Japanese army. Other controversies made the railway almost impossible to run. During that time, the Soviet-Japanese relations became very much strained, and the Soviet people thought that the Japanese manœuvre was merely the prelude to a second attack on the Soviet Union. In such strained circumstances, it was only natural that the Soviet Government would be pleased to renew its friendship with China.

4. Sino-Soviet Relations Formally Resumed

When Dr. W. W. Yen approached M. Litvinov in Geneva on the question of resumption of Sino-Soviet relations, the astute Soviet diplomat knew that this was the very thing his government desired. He therefore rushed back to Moscow for instructions. Naturally the question was favourably received there, and before long Litvinov returned to Geneva. He held a ten-minute conversation with Dr. Yen on December 12, 1932, at 5 p.m., at the end of which the two representatives exchanged notes, and relations between the two countries were formally resumed.

The documents are given hereunder :

1. Exchange of notes:
' In pursuance of our recent conversations during our pleasant meetings at Geneva, I am duly authorized to inform you that,

being desirous of promoting in the interests of peace friendly
relations between our two countries, the Government of —— has
decided to regard normal diplomatic and consular relations as
having been re-established as from to-day.'

2. *Dr. W. W. Yen's declaration:*
  'I am very gratified to be the instrument of China in the restoration of diplomatic and consular relations with the Soviet Union.
It was my feeling when I came to Geneva as the Chinese delegate
to the Disarmament Conference that normal relations should be
restored between the two great nations on the shores of the Pacific
in the interests of peace. That feeling was also shared by M.
Litvinov.
  'For some time it was realized that resumption of relations
between the two countries could no longer be delayed, and the
presence of M. Litvinov was considered an excellent opportunity
to bring this about.
  'The publication of the Lytton Report, in which references were
made to the Soviet Union and the suggestion to invite the United
States and the Soviet Union to participate in the deliberations of
the Committee, made more obvious the desirability of the re-
establishment of normal relations.
  'The Chinese Government and the Chinese people are very
sincere in their decision to cultivate friendly relations with their
great neighbour, and they are convinced these feelings are
reciprocated.'

3. *M. Litvinov's declaration:*
  'I have to-day exchanged notes restoring diplomatic relations
between the U.S.S.R. and China. This normal act hardly requires
an explanation, but what does require one is the rupture of
relations between States, or the refusal to maintain relations-
phenomena which constitute an infringement on normal international life and sometimes danger to peace.
  'There is no need to dwell on the events which led to the rupture
between the U.S.S.R. and China. These were not due to Soviet
initiative, and I am certain that no one in China to-day can think
that the regrettable events which led to the rupture of relations
were any benefit to China.
  'Beyond a doubt the beginning of the present troubles in the
Far East was in no small degree due to the fact that not all the

States situated on the shores of the Pacific Ocean had been maintaining diplomatic relations with one another.

'The people of the Soviet Union feel the greatest sympathy towards the Chinese people and towards their efforts to maintain independence with sovereignty, and to achieve an equality status. The Soviet Government has given repeated proofs of its friendly attitude towards China. Alone among the extraterritoriality and other rights and privileges wrung from China by Tsarist imperialism, she agreed to transform the railway concession into a commercial concession under joint management.

'These feelings of disinterestedness and friendship guided the Soviet Government when it established relations with China in 1924. These feelings, and not temporary considerations, have dictated to-day the restoration of relations.

'The Soviet Union has its hands unfettered by any secret political combinations and agreements, consequently the improvement of relations with one country is not a means of rendering worse relations with another. Only such a policy can genuinely assist in strengthening general peace. Only when all States maintain relations with each other shall we be able to speak seriously of international peace pacts and agreements, and the creation of universally recognized authoritative international organizations.

'In conclusion, I am convinced that all sincere friends of peace and international co-operation will learn with satisfaction that resumption of relations between our two great States has taken place.'[5]

5. Mutual Appointment of Ambassadors

With the resumption of Sino-Soviet relations, Dr. W. W. Yen was appointed Ambassador to the Soviet Union. Dr. Yen started for Moscow from Geneva on March 1, 1933, and arrived at the latter city on the 5th. On March 9 he presented his credentials, making a speech, an extract from which is given below:

'Mr. President of the Central Executive Committee of the Union of Soviet Socialist Republics:

'You will recall that it was during my stewardship of the Ministry of Foreign Affairs of the Chinese Government that a Presidential mandate was issued on September 23, 1920, to suspend

[5] Archives of the Ministry of Foreign Affairs, Chungking.

the recognition of the Russian Minister and consuls of the Tsarist régime, thereby paving the way for the establishment of diplomatic relations with your government. Unfortunately in the last few years the relations between our two States were somewhat strained, but happily our ancient friendship has been restored. This is the more gratifying to me, because I served again as the medium of my government that brought about this historical event.'[6]

To this M. Kalinin, the Chairman of the Central Executive Committee of the U.S.S.R., replied in a speech which expressed his gratification and satisfaction at the resumption of Sino-Soviet relations. He added that Dr. W. W. Yen would obtain confidence and assistance from the Soviet Government during his tenure of office in the execution of his duties.

At the same time M. Dimitri Bogomoloff was appointed Soviet Ambassador to China. On delivery of his credentials to Mr. Lin Sen, President of the Republic of China, Nanking, May 2, 1933, Bogomoloff made an appropriate speech.

President Lin Sen replied in a speech of cordial welcome.

The consensus of opinion at that time seemed to be that the resumption of Sino-Soviet relations centred around the consideration of Red potentialities. It should be borne in mind, however, that Communism thrives best in a country where there is economic unrest. Mere contact with the Soviet Union will not make a country go Red. Karl Radek once said: 'A revolution cannot be brought into a country in the bag of a tourist; revolution cannot be imported; it must be produced internally.'[7] As a matter of fact, left-wing activities were in full swing at a time when no relations had existed between China and the Soviet Union for many years.

It should also be noted that, after the signing of the 1924 Agreement, many Sino-Soviet questions were outstanding. These questions were pending settlement in the Sino-Soviet Conference. When the Sino-Soviet Conference was postponed indefinitely on account of the Manchurian incident, all these questions were shelved. The resumption of Sino-Soviet relations was initiated by the Soviet Union but was eagerly pursued by China. In the opinion of Dr. W. W. Yenn, who was in charge of the negotiations, China could very likely have obtained better terms if she had been less anxious.

[6] Archives of the Ministry of Foreign Affairs, Chungking.
[7] Bulletin of Waichiaopu, January 15, 1933.

Dr. Lo Wen-kan, the then Foreign Minister, was hard pressed by the Kuomintang party to resume relations with the Soviet Union without delay as a threat against Japan. He therefore sent several telegrams to Dr. Yen asking him to approach M. Litvinov at Geneva to bring the resumption of relations to a successful conclusion without discussing any terms. Hence Dr. Yen could hardly do otherwise but carry out the instructions of his government. Dr. Lo clearly told Press representatives at that time that ' before relations could be resumed with the Soviet Union, a non-aggression pact must first be mutually agreed upon '. For at first, China hoped that the desire for a non-aggression pact would meet with a sympathetic reception and that Soviet officials in China would desist from their Communist activities and that a solution of all pending questions between the two countries would be reached. The Soviets, however, insisted on an unconditional resumption of diplomatic relations before discussing a non-aggression pact. For some reason, however, this non-aggression pact did not materialize after the resumption of relations. The writer, in the capacity of the Commissioner of Foreign Affairs for Sinkiang Province, accompanied Dr. Lo Wen-kan from Urumchi to Novo-Sibirsk, Siberia, to meet Dr. W. W. Yen, who came purposely from Moscow to meet Dr. Lo. He recalled that the question of a non-aggression pact with the Soviet Union was freely discussed by them. Dr. Lo was very cordially received in Soviet territory because he was responsible for the reopening of the diplomatic relations between the two countries. The original draft of the non-aggression pact was not mutually agreed upon and signed until August 21, 1937, shortly after the Sino-Japanese conflict which will be fully dealt with in another chapter.

Chapter XIV

MONGOLIAN PEOPLE'S REPUBLIC

As previously stated, when the Living Buddha died in 1924, Outer Mongolia was converted into a Republic and again became a protectorate of the Soviet Union. From the beginning, Soviet influence was naturally hostile to the Lama monasteries. The Soviet authorities made good use of the Buriat Mongols, who had set up their Autonomous Republic in 1923, to further their influence over Mongolia, particularly in the anti-clerical campaign.

Soviet-Mongol trade became closer and intertwined after the establishment of the Mongol Industrial and Commercial Bank which was practically under Soviet control. All foreign firms in Outer Mongolia had to close down in 1928. Soviet trade showed a steady rise towards a virtual monopoly. Very few travellers were allowed to visit the country, and from 1924 visas for Outer Mongolia could be obtained only at Moscow or Ulan Bator, the capital of Mongolia, formerly known as Urga. Little, therefore, was known at the time in China or the outside world as to what was going on in Outer Mongolia after this dramatic change of government. It was only after the signing of the Sino-Soviet Treaty of Friendship and Alliance on August 14, 1945, that China recognized the independence of Outer Mongolia.

1. Collectivization of Outer Mongolia

The Mongolia People's Republic was and still is a mystery. The actual feeling of the Mongols towards the new scheme is not clear. However, Outer Mongolia may be considered a most successful experiment in collectivization. Such a transition from feudalism to a Soviet form of administration is one of the most incredible developments in the Far East.

According to Karl Marx, Communism can arise only in a country where industries are fully developed; but the nomadic Mongols who live in a most primitive way are far from being industrialized. Yet when the office of the Living Buddha ceased to function, and after a few short years under Soviet influence, the Mongols began to appreciate Communist ideas, and even worshipped Marx and Lenin in their sacred shrines. Perhaps economic conditions in Outer Mongolia favoured collectivization, because the overwhelming majority of the nomadic Mongols have no idea of the possession of land, which is a great help to affiliation. The only possessions among the Mongols are livestock. It is only necessary to divide up their livestock and collectivization is done, or almost done.

The Soviet Union formerly recognized China's suzerainty over Mongolia. But with the proclamation of the People's Revolutionary Government by a number of Mongols and a predominant group of Soviet citizens who established local soviets, the Soviet influence became manifest. However, a *coup d'état* broke out on August 30, 1924, when the leader of the left-wing, the Buriat Ricino, and other high officials were expelled.[1]

After that a new constitution was inaugurated on November 21, 1924. The Government of the People's Republic belonged then to the labouring class. Land and natural resources were nationalized, and a State monopoly in foreign trade was introduced.[2]

The M.P.R. had diplomatic relations only with the Soviet Union with its representative in Moscow. Its foreign contacts had been reduced to a minimum after the exclusion of representatives of other countries.

2. Soviet Aid to Outer Mongolia

The constitution, promulgated in 1924, is in effect a replica of the constitution of the U.S.S.R. The M.P.R. elects no president, but is ruled by an executive committee as in the U.S.S.R. The members of the executive committee are very much in sympathy as well as in close contact with the U.S.S.R. There is not in existence any organized method of control by the Soviet Union, but its prestige is being maintained and is even steadily growing because of the help which is rendered by the Soviet Union to the Mongols, both technically and financially. The U.S.S.R. has won the confidence of the Mongols by making them loans without interest and also by assisting them to modernize their economy. Owen Lattimore once wrote: 'Outer

[1] Haslund, A., *Tents in Mongolia*, 1924.
[2] Beloff, Max, *The Foreign Policy of Soviet Russia*, 1947, Vol. I, p. 244.

Mongolia was first made a victim of Tsarist Russian imperialism and then set free by the non-exploitative policy of the Soviet Union towards the Mongol People's Republic, the granting of loans without interest, economic aid, technical help, and the creation of an army trained and equipped by the Soviet Union but not officered by the Soviet Union or under its orders.'[3]

Attempts have been made at forms of 'collectivization' suitable to a pastoral economy, where no industrial or agricultural economy is in existence to carry out the Soviet programme. The rights of personal property have, of course, been severely limited. Such a drastic measure has seriously affected the country's economy, as countless livestock were allowed to die off. During the collectivization, many Mongols attempted to cross over into Inner Mongolia. The collectivization policy was, however, abandoned, and a new policy substituted after the revolt of 1932. It was the visit of the Prime Minister Gendun to Moscow in 1932 that brought about this change.

It was later revealed that transport in Mongolia was greatly improved by Soviet aid, and a railway was constructed between Ulan Bator and Kiakhta. Also the economic condition of the country has been improved a great deal.

3. Outer Mongolia After the Manchurian Incident

After the Manchurian incident, September 18, 1931, part of Inner Mongolia fell into Japanese hands. In order to strengthen their position, the Japanese tried to improve means of communication in the occupied territories. They completed new railway lines, but solely for military purposes. It was generally believed that the situation in Outer Mongolia was far more important than that in Siberia. The frontier of Siberia was fortified, whereas that of Outer Mongolia was considered precarious. Had the Japanese attacked Outer Mongolia, they could have proceeded from Kiakhta to Verhne Udinsk within a few hours, cutting the Trans-Siberian Railway.

The Soviet Government was only too well aware of these long-cherished ambitions of Japan. Shortly after the Manchurian incident, the M.P.R. was instructed to close its frontiers with neighbouring countries. Military camps and air bases were constructed in Urga, with Soviet commanders permanently stationed there. Mongolian youths were given military training, and aviation schools were established. Nearly all the military and civil administrations

[3] Lattimore, Owen, *Inner Asian Frontiers of China*, London, 1940, p. 101.

were headed by Mongols, assisted by Soviet citizens. War preparations were in full swing, since the M.P.R. feared that Outer Mongolia might be the Japanese target.

Later, various border incidents happened between Outer Mongolia and 'Manchukuo'. On January 24, 1935, an incident took place at Khalkhine, a small station on the Outer Mongolian-'Manchukuo' border.[4] The 'Manchukuo' authorities claimed that the area was 'Manchukuo' territory, while the M.P.R. asserted that the Manchurian occupation was a violation of Outer Mongolia's border. Both sides agreed to enter into negotiations by calling a conference which took place on June 3, but without result.

Meanwhile another serious incident occurred at the Sumbur outpost on June 23, where employees of the Japanese army were arrested by Outer Mongolia border guards.[5] Later, a mixed Outer Mongolian-'Manchukuo' commission was formed to investigate all border incidents.

Following the break-up of another conference which was held at Manchuli in October, the Bulum Dersu incident took place in the south-west of Lake Buir-nor on December 19, 1935.[6] It was alleged that the Japanese-'Manchukuo' forces on the border first attacked the Outer Mongolian guards, and caused some casualties. The Outer Mongolian Government lodged a note of protest warning 'Manchukuo' of the grave consequences, the responsibility for which would rest with 'Manchukuo' and the Japanese Government whose forces were alleged to have taken a direct and active part in the attacks. The 'Manchukuo' authorities delivered a counter-protest claiming that the incident actually occurred on 'Manchukuo' territory, and that should any similar clash occur in the future, 'Manchukuo' would be compelled to act in self-defence.

After the Bulum Dersu incident and subsequent minor ones, both the Outer Mongolian and the 'Manchukuo' Governments came to realize that the numerous border disputes could be settled only by creating a mixed border commission to investigate all the circumstances leading up to the incidents, as well as to fix ways and means for preventing further conflicts. The matter, naturally, was brought to the attention of the respective sponsors, namely the Soviet Union and Japan.

It was proposed to form a mixed boundary commission to settle all border disputes between Outer Mongolia and 'Manchukuo'.

[4] *Izvestia*, January 25, 1935.
[5] ibid., June 24, 1935.
[6] ibid., December 20, 1935.

Litvinov, the Soviet Commissar for Foreign Affairs, expressed his opinion that inasmuch as the Japanese had proposed establishing a joint commission of representatives of the U.S.S.R. and 'Manchuku' for the demarcation of the Soviet-'Manchukuo' border, similar commissions for the redemarcation of the Outer Mongolia-'Manchukuo' border could be established. Later, however, the Japanese Ambassador, Ota, found it difficult to conduct negotiations on this question with the Soviet Government without knowing the exact nature of the relations existing between the U.S.S.R. and Outer Mongolia.

Notwithstanding that further explanations were made in such plain words, the Soviet Government felt determined to come to Outer Mongolia's aid in the event of her being attacked by a third party, but the proposed mixed border commission never materialized.

4. The Soviet-Outer Mongolia Protocol

In view of the incessant incidents on the Mongolia-'Manchukuo' border, relations between Outer Mongolia and the Soviet Union had become much closer both militarily and economically. On December 11, 1935, a delegation from the Mongolian People's Republic, including Gendun, the Prime Minister, and Dermid, the Minister of War, went to Moscow to hold a conference with Stalin and Voroshilov with the object of making plans for resisting Japan-'Manchukuo' aggression.

On March 12, 1936, a Protocol of mutual assistance was concluded at Ulan Bator between the representative of the U.S.S.R., M. Tairov, and the M.P.R., represented by M. Amor, chairman of the small khural, and M. Gendun, Premier and Foreign Minister. The Moscow newspapers published the text of the Protocol on April 8, in which mutual assistance by all means was pledged for averting and preventing any military attack by any third State upon the U.S.S.R. or the M.P.R. (See full text in Appendix B.)

When the Protocol became known in China, the Chinese authorities immediately protested to the Soviet Government declaring: 'Outer Mongolia being an integral part of the Republic of China, no foreign State has the right to conclude with it any agreement or treaty.' The note finally declared that the Chinese Government could, under no circumstances, recognize such a Protocol, and was in no wise bound by it.

The Soviet Government replied to the Chinese note on the following day through its Commissar for Foreign Affairs, Litvinov, to the effect that it could not agree with the Chinese interpretation of the Protocol, and therefore could not recognize the Chinese protest as justified. It was emphasized in the Soviet note that neither the fact of signing the Protocol nor its separate articles violated in the slightest degree the sovereignty of China over Outer Mongolia, and that it did not admit nor contain any territorial pretensions whatsoever on the part of the U.S.S.R. in relations to China or the M.P.R. The signing of the Protocol did not introduce any change in the formal as well as the actual relation which existed between the U.S.S.R. and China as well as between the M.P.R. The Soviet Union then affirmed that the Peking Agreement of 1924, which suffered no harm through the conclusion of the Protocol, still retained its force.

The Chinese Government naturally found the Soviet reply unsatisfactory, and two more strong protests were lodged on April 11 and June 4, 1936, reiterating the stand of the Chinese Government as enunciated in its first note of protest.

The Chinese note particularly objected to the Soviet Union quoting the conclusion of the Soviet-Mukden Agreement as a precedent, recalling that the Chinese Government protested to the then Soviet Ambassador on September 25 and October 11, 1924, against the signing of the said agreement and that it was only ratified subsequently by the Chinese Government as an annex to the Sino-Soviet Agreement of 1924 as a *quid pro quo* to M. Karakhan's note of March 6, 1924, informing the Ministry of Foreign Affairs that the last of the Red troops had been withdrawn from Outer Mongolia.

5. Outer Mongolia Becomes an Independent State After the Sino-Soviet Treaty

Considerable significance was given to the arrival of Marshal Choy Bol-san, Prime Minister of the M.P.R., in Moscow on July 4, 1945, coinciding with the visit of T. V. Soong, the Chinese Prime Minister and Foreign Minister, to Moscow. The Soviet Minister to Mongolia, I. A. Ivanoff, accompanied Marshal Choy who was welcomed with equally high honours and enthusiasm as T. V. Soong.

The M.P.R. declared war on Japan on August 10, 1945, immediately following the Soviet declaration of war against Japan. The Sino-Soviet Treaty of Friendship and Alliance, signed in Moscow on August 14, 1945, contained an exchange of notes as follows:

'In view of the desire repeatedly expressed by the people of Outer Mongolia for their independence, the Chinese Government declares that after the defeat of Japan, should a plebiscite of the Outer Mongolian people confirm the desire, the Chinese Government will recognize the independence of Outer Mongolia with the existing boundary as its boundary.'

Such a concession exceeded what Russia surrendered to Japan during the Russo-Japanese War in 1904. Nevertheless, it was clearly stipulated in the Yalta Secret Agreement that 'the *status quo* in Outer Mongolia shall be preserved'. China could hardly do otherwise than give in.

After Japan's formal surrender on August 14, Soviet forces marched into Manchuria and made her an easy prey. In the midst of Soviet removals of Japanese assets in Manchuria as war booty, it was reported that the Mukden Arsenal, having been greatly enlarged by Japan during her occupation, had been given to Marshal Choy Bol-san as a token of Soviet appreciation for his help in crushing the Japanese. It was believed that Mongolian cavalry had been sent to the battlefield, acting jointly with the Soviet troops under Marshal Rodion Y. Malinovsky in a drive through western Manchuria. Other industrial equipment and war booty, seized by the Soviets in Manchuria, had also been reported to have been presented to Marshal Choy. Thus the Mongols were enabled to attain a high degree of militarization and become a power to be reckoned with on the Continent.[7]

On October 20, the M.P.R. voted by plebiscite on whether it wanted to remain a nominal part of China or become independent. All Outer Mongolia's population, numbering about 900,000 men and women, of eighteen years old or over, were eligible to vote. Mr. Lei Fa-chang, Chinese Vice-Minister of the Interior, arrived at Ulan Bator as the Chinese Government observer of the plebiscite. The return of votes in Ulan Bator alone was 24,683 to nil in favour of independence. The complete returns showed that the Mongols had cast 483,291 votes in favour of independence without a single vote against. That is to say, all the ballot papers were marked 'yes'.[8]

It was generally believed that the plebiscite was merely a formality. At any rate, the Chinese Government were only giving up something they did not really possess.

[7] *New York Times*, October 3, 1945.
[8] ibid., October 24, 1945.

The Nationalist Government in Nanking announced on January 5, 1946, that China had recognized the independence of Outer Mongolia as the result of a plebiscite. Through this recognition, China let go a piece of territory not less than 1,600,000 square miles.

In the early part of February 1946, eight Mongols, headed by the Deputy Prime Minister of the M.P.R., Chimitodovki Surungab, made their first formal visit to Chungking, China's war capital, in return for the visit of Mr. Lei Fa-chang, Vice-Minister of the Interior. They were received by the Chinese Foreign Minister, Wang Shih-chieh, as citizens of a foreign country. It was quite an historical event but an embarrassing moment for the Nationalist Government.

'The Mongols took offence because the band played only the Chinese national anthem and only the Chinese flag was displayed. It was eventually explained to them that nobody here knew that the M.P.R. had the same national anthem as the Soviet Union. Nor did anybody know what flag had been designed for the republic.

'The Vice-Minister for Foreign Affairs, Lhamasuruna, drew a picture of Mongolia's new flag. Foreign Office observers watched attentively, eager to repair their morning blunder.

'Mongolia's flag has three vertical stripes. The middle stripe is blue and the two side ones are red. On the stripe nearest the staff are three mystical symbols in gold, dating from the time of Genghis Khan. Reading from top to bottom are a star, flame, sun, moon, triangles, two fishes in a circle and another triangle. On both sides of these devices are two pillars representing boundaries. The fishes stand for watchfulness. The triangle signifies righteousness.'[9]

The Chief Delegate of the M.P.R., Surungab, concluded an amity pact with China on February 13, 1946, in Chungking, when diplomatic relations between the two countries were established. Notwithstanding both countries had agreed to exchange diplomatic envoys with the rank of minister extraordinary and plenipotentiary, in actuality this did not materialize. As things are now, Outer Mongolia has only a diplomatic representative in Moscow.

A treaty of amity and mutual aid between the U.S.S.R and M.P.R. was signed in Moscow on February 27, 1946. Its terms consisted of three clauses: 1. Joint consultations to be made if one of the two

[9] *Chicago Daily News*, February 9, 1946.

countries be militarily threatened by a third party.   2. Military and other aid to be given in the event of an armed attack by a third party.   3. Withdrawal of supporting troops when no longer needed.[10]

In June 1946, the M.P.R. informed the United Nations Secretary, General Trygve Lie, that it intended to apply for membership of the United Nations Organization.   An application was sent by Marshal Choi Bal-san, Prime Minister and Foreign Minister, in which it was stated that the M.P.R. had fully sided with the United Nations in the struggle against Fascist aggressors and declared war against Japan on August 10, 1945, giving the M.P.R. grounds for entertaining high hopes that the U.N.O. would take into account the contribution of the Mongolian people to the cause of the U.N.O. and include a representative of the M.P.R. in the Far Eastern Commission.[11]   The Security Council's Committee reviewed the application on August 29, and the session lasted for eight hours.   The result was the delegates of the U.S.S.R., Brazil, Mexico, China, France and Poland voted in favour of Outer Mongolia's request, whereas America, Britain and Holland voted against it.   Finally it was agreed to ask the M.P.R. for further information as to her position.

On October 26, 1946, Marshal Choi Bal-san delivered an address to all members of the Council of Foreign Ministers asking Japan to pay war reparations.   A copy of this address was later sent to the chairman of the Far Eastern Commission, Major-General McCloy in Washington, setting forth the claims of the M.P.R. to reparations from Japan.

On August 18, 1947, the Security Council of the United Nations rejected the M.P.R. application for membership.   The Chinese delegate, though he had supported M.P.R.'s claim the year before, rejected it during the discussion, on the ground that Outer Mongolia was not a peace-loving country.   The news had already spread that Mongolian troops were invading eastern Sinkiang.

The Chinese public, while admitting the loss of Outer Mongolia, were deeply concerned about the political situation in Inner Mongolia.   Though a certain degree of political autonomy could be granted to Inner Mongolia, it must nevertheless be under Chinese sway.   It seemed that insistence upon Mongolian unity by the M.P.R. foreshadowed a formal proposal that the area of Inner Mongolia should be added to the Republic, namely Outer Mongolia.

Mr. James F. Byrnes, American Secretary of State, once stated:

[10] *New York Times*, February 28, 1946.
[11] ibid., October 26, 1946.

'No question should have arisen concerning the status of Inner Mongolia, because Inner Mongolia was generally recognized as an integral part of Chinese territory.'[12] This statement quietened existing rumours.

On October 8, 1949, the M.P.R. severed relations with the Nationalist Government in Canton, as was reported from the Tass News Agency in a despatch from Ulan Bator, which synchronized with the recognition of the Peking People's Government.

6. Peitashan Incident

On June 5, 1947, the eastern part of Sinkiang was invaded by the cavalry troops of Outer Mongolia, which penetrated more than 200 miles into the province with the aid of aircraft. The town of Peitashan in eastern Sinkiang was attacked. Fighting was going on, and government troops were resisting. The incident was kept secret for five days before it was revealed. China lodged a protest through her Ambassador in Moscow with the U.S.S.R. and the M.P.R. through its minister in Moscow over the invasion of Chinese territory in Sinkiang as being 'no ordinary frontier incident'. The Chinese Government viewed the matter with deep concern, contemplating the despatch of General Pai Chung-hsi, a Chinese Moslem, to Sinkiang to give necessary directions to local authorities.

Another like protest on July 10 was lodged with both the U.S.S.R. and the M.P.R. on the alleged attack against Chinese positions in Sinkiang. A brief communiqué on the protest to the U.S.S.R., read: 'The Chinese Government has, after careful investigation of facts, reiterated the previous Chinese protest against the aerial attack made by the Soviet military planes on Peitashan.'

Concerning the new protest to the M.P.R., an official source made the following statement:

'1. When the Chinese Government recognized the independence of Outer Mongolia, it was agreed then the existing boundaries of Outer Mongolia should be the boundary of that country after its independence. As Outer Mongolia was part of China up to that moment, the legal existing boundary is the one defined by the Chinese Government before that date. . . . Peitashan is clearly on the side of the boundary line, and within the territorial limits of Sinkiang province. This is substantiated by the fact that Chinese

[12] *United Press*, Washington, February 12, 1946.

police and troops are assigned by the Sinkiang provincial
authorities to guard and patrol the district. It was the case before
the independence of Outer Mongolia; it has been so ever since.

'2. Troops of Outer Mongolia had penetrated over twenty kilometres of Chinese territory to make an attack on Chinese troops
stationed at Peitashan. Such a grave situation certainly cannot
be regarded as an ordinary incident.

'3. Even if the military attack of June 5 be regarded as having
originated from a so-called "boundary incident", why did the
Outer Mongolian Government fail to seek a peaceful settlement
in accordance with international practice and the terms of the
United Nations Charter?

'Why did the Outer Mongolian Government despatch the forty-
eight-hour ultimatum to the local Chinese garrison and immediately afterwards launch an attack on Chinese troops there?
The conduct of Outer Mongolia clearly indicates that she has no
regard either for peace or for international law observed and
respected by other nations.

'4. From June 6 to 30, 1947, Outer Mongolian forces continued
to violate Chinese territory and launch attacks on Chinese troops.
Military planes from Outer Mongolia also repeatedly flew over
Chinese territory for purposes of observation, bombing and
strafing.

'5. Besides demanding punishment of those responsible for the
attack and guarantees against any further occurrence of a similar
attack and reserving the right to claim damages, the Chinese
Government insists that the Outer Mongolian Government must
immediately order the withdrawal of its troops from Sinkiang.'

The Tass Agency in Moscow denied that planes with Soviet mark-
ings were taking part in the fighting. They asserted that the craft
were Outer Mongolian as their emblem was the same as the Soviets'.
Tass stated 'China's allegations were not in accordance with facts,
and represented a provocative fabrication.'[13] However, no comment
was received from the Chinese Government on the Tass denial.

Meanwhile General Pai was urged by the Sinkiang Government to
postpone his trip to Sinkiang because of complications in Tihwa and
opposition from 'certain quarters'.

The Outer Mongolian Government issued a statement in which it
was stated that Chinese forces had violated Mongolian territory, and

[13] *New York Times*, June 14, 1947.

which denied alleged Mongolian penetration of Chinese territory. An abstract of the statement is produced hereunder:

'A detachment of Chinese troops crossing the border of the M.P.R. encamped about fifteen kilometres from the border and began to dig in and build fortifications, at the same time making raids on the Mongolian frontier post permanently located in this area. When the Chinese armed detachment which had unlawfully invaded the territory of the M.P.R. was discovered, the Commander of the Mongolian frontier guard, wishing to prevent a conflict . . . sent a negotiator to the Commander of the Chinese detachment, demanding that they clear out of Mongolian territory. The Chinese Commander refused to comply with the lawful demand. Furthermore . . . the Mongolian negotiator was detained by the Chinese while the Chinese detachment continued to remain on the territory of the M.P.R.

'In view of this the Mongolian frontier guard was compelled to take measures to drive out the raiders from their country's territory. A Mongolian border detachment, supported by several aircraft of the Mongolian air force, drove the Chinese detachment off the territory of the M.P.R.

'In this action the Mongolian frontier guard did not cross the border into Chinese territory.'[14]

The Mongol charges were denied by the Nanking Government as 'absolutely false'. Government spokesman, Hollington K. Tong, announced at a Press conference that 'there could be no dispute concerning the fact that Peitashan lies within the Province of Sinkiang and therefore is in Chinese territory. Both before and since the signing of the Sino-Soviet Treaty of 1945 there had always been a Sinkiang police station at Peitashan, manned by a small Chinese police force together with Chinese sentry posts.'[15] Official Chinese quarters admitted that the Outer Mongolian claim of Peitashan as lying within its borders made the whole incident more difficult to settle. The Soviet reply to the second Chinese note of protest was received on August 5, but its contents were not revealed. Although the Sinkiang frontier has been quiet since, it still remains a subject of controversy.

[14] *Soviet News*, June 17, 1947.
[15] *North China Daily News*, June 24, 1947.

Chapter XV

SALE OF THE CHINESE EASTERN RAILWAY

B Y the Sino-Soviet Agreement of 1924, the Chinese Eastern Railway was given the plain status of a joint government enterprise. A conference should have been held, its task being to settle the amount of and conditions governing the redemption as well as the procedure for the transfer of the Chinese Eastern Railway. Pending the redemption of the railway, the management was to be in the hands of a board of five Chinese and five Soviet directors with equal rights.

The Soviet Union suggested that disputes upon which the Chinese and Soviet directors failed to reach an agreement should be referred to the two governments for a just and amicable settlement, whereas the Chinese Government proposed that such outstanding problems could easily be settled through arbitration by neutral experts. The Soviet Union was very much opposed to the Chinese proposal, fearing that it would lead to intervention by imperialist nations. Finally the Soviet Union's original suggestion was agreed upon. When the scheme was put into practice, the result was that there were too many disputes arising from both sides to be referred to their respective governments for amicable settlement.

Since then, the railway has been working quite smoothly, and making huge profits. As Russia—both the Tsarist and the Soviet régime—was never eager to have China redeem the railway, the final settlement for the redemption was delayed by her consistent policy of procrastination. Then came the Manchurian incident on September 18, 1931, which totally changed the situation, enabling the Soviet Union to ignore China's position with regard to the railway and finally leading to its sale by the Soviet Government.

1. Soviet Union's Concession to Japanese Aggression

The Japanese made their initial success in South Manchuria all of a sudden on September 18, 1930. On November 19, Hirota, then Japanese Ambassador in Moscow, addressed a note to the Soviet Commissar of Foreign Affairs, asking the Soviet Government to pursue a policy of strict neutrality in view of the fact that the Imperial Government of Japan had maintained a policy of non-interference during the Sino-Soviet crisis in 1929 by refusing to transport Chinese troops to the Manchuli station. The note went on to say that the Japanese army had no intention of interfering with the Chinese Eastern Railway, and gave an assurance that Soviet interests would be well protected. Litvinov, then Soviet Commissar of Foreign Affairs, made a reply the following day, expressing his satisfaction that the Japanese Government had given repeated assurances to safeguard the interests of the Chinese Eastern Railway, and, in turn, the Soviet Government promised to maintain strict non-interference with this Manchuria crisis.[1]

Having learned that the Soviet Government would not interfere with Japanese military operations along the railway line, the Japanese began to transport their troops over the railway. The Chinese Eastern Railway Company then received a note from the Japanese command at Harbin, suggesting that the charge for transportation of Japanese troops over the entire line should be reduced to fifty per cent of the usual rate. This matter, however, together with other questions, was brought to Moscow for negotiations between Karakhan and Hirota. On the question of transporting Japanese troops, though the Japanese Government denied knowledge of a proposal from the Japanese command for a reduced rate of transportation charge, they requested the Soviet Government to grant permission to transport Japanese troops as before. To this, Karakhan yielded by making a statement that permission would be granted 'by way of exceptional and temporary measures' in view of special circumstances referred to by the Japanese Government.[2] Such generosity on the Soviet side enabled Japan to carry out a large-scale military campaign in North Manchuria and bring the whole of Manchuria under her control.

On the establishment of the puppet state of 'Manchukuo', the Soviet Government promised to hoist the 'Manchukuo' flag on the Chinese Eastern Railway after accepting Li Shao-keng as successor to the former President, Mo Teh-hui. The Soviet Government was so interested in the preservation of peace in the Far East that it

[1] *Soviet Union Review*, Vol. X, January 1932, p. 19.
[2] ibid, April 1932, p. 94.

accepted the Soviet-'Manchukuo' system and forgot the railway was a joint Sino-Soviet enterprise. Trading on the conciliatory attitude of the Soviet Government, the Japanese took advantage by intruding farther and farther, finally bringing the railway into complete chaos.

2. Chaos in Chinese Eastern Railway

The Soviet authorities knew they had no chance against the well-armed Japanese, but, on the other hand, they were astute enough to remove most of the rolling stock from the railway, which was the crux of the whole trouble. The Japanese Government, at first too busy handling their affairs in the newly established 'Manchukuo', had no time to deal with the question of the rolling stock removed by the Soviet authorities. But as soon as the remnant Chinese forces in North Manchuria had been subdued and Jehol taken, then the Japanese paused and began to turn their eyes to the Chinese Eastern Railway.

On April 12, 1933, Li Shao-keng, the 'Manchukuo' President of the railway, delivered a note of protest to the Soviet Vice-President, Stephen Kuznetzoff, demanding the immediate return of the rolling stock then detained in Siberia.[3] Kuznetzoff set the matter aside. Whereupon the Vice-Minister of Communications of the 'Manchukuo' Government at Changchun was sent to Harbin to proceed with the negotiations, but again without success.[4] On April 8, a blockade of Manchuli was carried out by 'Manchukuo'. Against this Kuznetzoff and the Soviet Consul-General at Harbin immediately protested. On April 12, Japan-'Manchukuo' troops at Manchuli suddenly detained the International Wagons-lits from Moscow to Vladivostok. Li Shao-keng then delivered an ultimatum to Kuznetzoff, demanding that he forward a message to Moscow for the return of the detained rolling stock, namely 83 locomotives, 190 passenger cars and 3,200 freight cars, within a period of thirty days.[5] On April 13, another blockade was effected on the Soviet customs at Suifenho (Pogranitchnaya), and all trains leaving Suifenho for Manchuli had to be inspected. No locomotives or cars were allowed to pass through to the Soviet territory.

On April 16, Karakhan lodged a note of protest through Ota, the Japanese Ambassador in Moscow, stating that the detained rolling

[3] *Bulletin of Waichiaopu*, May 15, 1933, p. 149.
[4] ibid, p. 152.
[5] Wu You-san, *Russo-Japanese Relations* (in Chinese), 1938, p. 84.

stock was the property of the Soviet Union and not of the railway.[6] Much evidence was produced to prove that the locomotives in question were purchased by the Tsarist Government from the United States for Russian railways, and that they were assembled in the railway workshops at Vladivostok and Harbin and afterwards passed on to Russian railways. The Japanese Government was never ready to recognize the Soviet possession of the Chinese Eastern Railway, though documents were exchanged between the 'Manchukuo' President and the Soviet Vice-President, each presenting the opinion of their respective governments.

At the same time, the 'Manchukuo' authority, on account of the fact that the Soviet Union had not released the cars seized some time before but continued seizing more cars, disconnected the line between the Soviet Union and 'Manchukuo' at Suifenho station. According to Sokolnikov's protest dated June 5, handed to Ota, the Japanese Ambassador, it was stated that on May 31, Saito, Japanese official of the 'Manchukuo' Ministry of Communications, led a number of police to Suifenho station, demanding that the station master cut off the communication between the Chinese Eastern Railway and the Ussuri Railway.

3. Soviet-Japanese Parley

In view of the increasing difficulties over the Chinese Eastern Railway, the Soviet Government found that there was no other remedy except to offer for sale their interests in the Chinese Eastern Railway. So rumours of the Soviet proposal to sell the railway to Japan were current before the expiration of the ultimatum. On May 2, 1933, Litvinov directly proposed to Ota the intention of the Soviet Government to sell the Chinese Eastern Railway to settle the outstanding question once and for all.

On May 11, Litvinov, through the Tass Agency, declared: 'During the negotiations between Ota, the Japanese Ambassador, and myself, I did mention that the actions of the "Manchukuo" authorities caused serious difficulties to the Chinese Eastern Railway and aggravated controversies between Japan, "Manchukuo" and the Soviet Union. In order to arrive at some possible solution, I therefore suggest that there may be a chance for "Manchukuo" to redeem the Chinese Eastern Railway; that is to say, the Soviet Government would sell the interests of the Chinese Eastern Railway

[6] *Current Affairs Monthly* (in Chinese), Vol. XI, No. 5, 1933, p. 305.

to " Manchukuo " which is considered as one of the radical methods of solving the present difficulties.'[7]

4. China's Protests

When the rumour of the sale of the Chinese Eastern Railway reached China, she was, of course, annoyed at the Soviet action. The Chinese public were rather puzzled at such an event occurring only a few days after the arrival of the new Soviet Ambassador to China, following the resumption of formal relations between the two countries.

The Chinese Embassy in Moscow was instructed to present a note to the Soviet Government to that effect and to ask whether there was any truth in the rumour. Karakhan, the Vice-Commissar of Foreign Affairs, assured the Chinese Ambassador, D. W. W. Yen, that no such sale was contemplated, and the rumour was flatly denied.

It was only two days later that Litvinov gave an interview to the Tass Agency, confirming his proposal for the sale of the railway to Japan. He argued that the Soviet Government had never conceded to China the right of purchasing the railway before due time, nor had it entered into any obligation to refrain from selling the railway to any third party.

He further stated that:

' The Chinese Government or the powers under its control have ceased to be actual partners with the U.S.S.R. in the Chinese Eastern Railway since over eighteen months ago. They have been deprived of this possibility by causes not dependent upon the U.S.S.R., and are unable to exercise their rights or discharge their undertakings in terms of the Peking and Mukden Agreements. On the strength of these agreements, the Government of China is obliged to maintain representatives on the Board of the railway, but no such representative has been on the Board for the past eighteen months.'[8]

On May 13, the Chinese Government instructed Dr. W. W. Yen to lodge a strong protest with the Soviet Government against the steps being taken for the proposed sale of the railway.

[7] *Current Affairs Monthly*, Vol XIII, No. 6, p. 485.
[8] *Bulletin of Waichiaopu*, May 1933, p. 190.

Litvinov, it was reported, told the Chinese Ambassador that the Soviet sale of the railway was rather favourable to China, in that the railway could not be removed to Japan after purchase, and that as China had expected to recover Manchuria, she would ultimately get the railway back without paying the Soviet Union for it. Litvinov also attempted to explain Karakhan's misstatement by saying that the latter was not *au courant* with the question. It was believed that Karakhan's transfer to the Embassy in Turkey soon after was due to the Chinese Ambassador's expression of dissatisfaction with him, in that he had given assurances contrary to facts on this important diplomatic question.

On the following day, the *Waichiaopu* made public the contents of the protest. The note began with a reference to the conversation which Dr. Yen had with Karakhan on May 11, and to the statement given out by Litvinov during the Press interview of the same day regarding the proposed sale of the Soviet interest in the railway.

The note recalled the memorandum written by Dr. Yen and delivered to the Commissariat of Foreign Affairs on May 9, in which the relative position of the Chinese and Soviet Governments in respect of the Chinese Eastern Railway as determined by the agreement of 1924 was set forth.

Meanwhile Karl Radek wrote that the Soviet 'is not deceiving China' when offering to sell the Chinese Eastern Railway to Japan. He went on to say: 'The Chinese *bourgeoisie*, which are losing one region after another without attempting to resist the invaders, think that the Soviets should preserve the Chinese Eastern Railway for them, thereby suffering material losses, risking the lives of her employees and hazarding international conflicts.'[9]

The Chinese vigorous and well-founded protest put the Soviet Government in a dilemma. The reply was deferred until June 19. The Chinese Ambassador sent another note on June 25, but both sides agreed not to publish them. Thereafter, China made no further protests to the Soviet Government, which was enough to arouse suspicion.

5. Motives of Proposed Sale of Railway

When the Soviets proposed to sell the railway, the Japanese Government pretended to be indifferent and unconcerned. For they believed

[9] *Izvestia*, May 20, 1933.

that if they did not maintain a cool and calm attitude, their anxiety would be exposed, thereby causing the Soviet authorities to raise the price deliberately. For this reason the Soviet proposal dated May 2, 1933, met with indifference. It was not until May 23 that the meeting of the Japanese Cabinet decided to persuade 'Manchukuo' to consider the sale offer. At the same time, four principles were laid down: (1) To investigate, first of all, whether the Soviet Union had the right to claim ownership of the railway; (2) To consider whether, according to the Sino-Soviet and the Mukden-Soviet Agreements of 1924, the Soviet Government had merely the joint administrative power over the Chinese Eastern Railway, now that the Soviet Government was willing to transfer such vested administrative power to 'Manchukuo' which, in turn, was also willing to pay an appropriate sum; (3) That 'Manchukuo' should purchase the mining rights belonging to the railway from the Soviet Union; (4) That the procedure of conducting the sale and effecting the payment should be by persuading 'Manchukuo' to take up negotiations with the Soviet Union. On the same day an *aide-memoire* was despatched to 'Manchukuo'. The 'Manchukuo' Government therefore sent a formal reply to the U.S.S.R.: (i) deciding to accept the offer; (ii) hoping that Japan would mediate in the matter; (iii) suggesting that the locale for negotiations be Tokyo. The Japanese Government was kept informed to the same effect.[10]

On May 29 Ota, the Japanese Ambassador at Moscow, formally notified the Soviet Commissariat of Foreign Affairs that the Soviet Government should open negotiations with 'Manchukuo', Japan acting as mediator. He further stated that such discussion should be settled politically but not technically; in other words the Chinese Eastern Railway had depreciated in value after the Manchurian incident and, therefore, the selling price could not be based upon the initial cost.

On June 3, a reply from the Soviet Government was made through Sokolnikov, then Vice-Commissar of Foreign Affairs, accepting the Japanese suggestion and also proposing June 26 as the first date for opening negotiations. The Soviet Government agreed to send delegates to Tokyo for the purpose.

At 2 p.m. on June 26, 1933, negotiations for the sale of the railway were formally inaugurated at the residence of the Japanese Vice-Foreign Minister. The Soviet delegation was headed by Yurenev, Soviet Ambassador at Tokyo, while the Japanese was headed by

[10] *Current Affairs Monthly*, Vol. IX, No. 1, 1933, p. 5.

Count Uchida, Japanese Foreign Minister, "Manchukuo' being headed by Ting Shih-yuan, its Minister at Tokyo, and Chuichi Ohashi, 'Manchukuo' Vice-Foreign Minister, and the Chinese Eastern Railway was represented by Shang Jui-ling. Opening speeches were read by the three parties in a cordial atmosphere. It seemed that the Soviet Government had already implied *de facto* recognition of 'Manchukuo', tactfully created by Japan.

On June 28, a second conference was called to discuss the necessary procedure of calling meetings, whereas at the third conference, held July 3, actual negotiations for the sale of the railway began. Both parties submitted their representations. The Soviet proposals were: (a) they would sell all properties belonging to the railway with the exception of the detained rolling stock which belonged to the Soviet Union; (b) the purchase price of the railway was set at a total amount of 250,000,000 gold roubles, of which 210,000,000 gold roubles was the cost of building the railway, and 40,000,000 gold roubles the cost of the railway land and forests; (c) the method of payment: half of the purchase price, i.e., 125,000,000 gold roubles, to be reimbursed in the form of commercial merchandise by four instalments within a period of two years, whereas of the other half (125,000,000 gold roubles), one quarter was to be paid in cash, while the remaining amount was to be paid in security bonds issued by 'Manchukuo', guaranteed by the Japanese Government, bearing interest at four per cent per annum, to be redeemed within a period of three years; (d) a special agreement to be entered into affording special privileges for the transport of Soviet goods, Soviet citizens and Soviet employees of the railway after its transfer.

The 'Manchukuo' counter-proposals were as follows: (1) 'Manchukuo' to pay 50,000,000 yen for the purchase, the way and time of payment to be specially arranged for thereafter; (2) the transfer to be effected within three months after the signing of the agreement; (3) the Soviet Government to be responsible to the former shareholders, bond holders and any other creditors; (4) documentary records with regard to the railway and its auxiliary enterprises to be handed over to 'Manchukuo'.[11]

The difference of opinion between the two parties was substantial and wide; the price was the main stumbling-block. The Soviet Government asked for 250,000,000 gold roubles, but 'Manchukuo' offered to pay only 50,000,000 yen, which was equivalent to only 40,000,000 gold roubles according to the exchange rate at the time,

[11] *Current Affairs Monthly*, Vol. IX, No. 2, 1933, p. 5.

being merely one-sixth of the sum asked for by the Soviet Government.

At the fourth conference on July 5, Yurenev, the Soviet representative, demanded sole Russian ownership of the railway. The 'Manchukuo' representatives categorically rejected Yurenev's claim, which had much to do with the price because, had it been accepted, then 'Manchukuo' would have to pay the full value of the railway. Both parties stood their ground and negotiations came to a standstill.

6. Controversies Over Ownership

With regard to the ownership of the Chinese Eastern Railway, the question is indeed complicated. The original contract of 1896 clearly stipulated in Article 1 that the shares of the Chinese Eastern Railway Company could be acquired only by Chinese and Russian subjects. On account of this contract, the Chinese Government was to invest 5,000,000 kuping taels towards the funds of the Russo-Chinese Bank for helping to construct the railway. Article 7 of the 1896 contract again stipulated that 'the day when the line is finished and traffic is in operation, the Company will make to the Chinese Government a payment of five million kuping taels'.[12] The latter has never been paid.

After the Russian Revolution of 1917, the newly established Soviet Government nationalized the Russo-Asiatic Bank. Then the two Karakhan Declarations of 1919 and 1920 clearly abandoned all the Russian rights and interests in the Chinese Eastern Railway acquired by the Tsarist Government. But when the Chinese Government entered into negotiations for Chinese recognition of the Soviet Government in November 1922, Jóffe claimed sole Soviet ownership of the railway. China did not accept the Soviet claim of sole ownership, nor did 'Manchukuo' recognize it. The 'Manchukuo' delegates claimed that 'Manchukuo' was the legitimate successor of Chinese rights in Manchuria, and they believed that the Soviet Government had surrendered the entire ownership of the railway in favour of China by virtue of the Karakhan declarations.

The Soviet Government, on the contrary, claimed sole ownership in view of the fact that the railway was constructed by the toiling masses of Russia with their hard-earned money.[13] The Chinese Government, however, claimed that the entire work was carried out

[12] Contract for the Construction and Operation of the Chinese Eastern Railway, September 8, 1896.
[13] Litvinov's statement of May 11, 1933.

by Chinese labourers who were paid with Romanoff rouble notes. Supervision and the building of the steel structures were exceptions. Such a contention was actually brought forward by the 'Manchukuo' delegates who asked for compensation for the losses of the Manchurian people who all suffered immensely through the Soviet repudiation of the Romanoff rouble notes which had been earned during the construction and operation of the railway.[14]

7. Controversies Over Price

After much contention over the question of ownership, both parties refrained for lack of relevant documents from touching this knotty problem, and proceeded to discuss the only outstanding question— the sale price.

The original agreement of 1896 provided that the price to be paid for the redemption of the railway should cover the capital cost of construction plus all the losses which the operation of the railway might incur up to the time of redemption. According to this stipulation, the price would be about 800,000,000 gold roubles, half of the amount being the capital cost of construction and the other half the accumulated operating losses. The Tsarist régime deliberately spent money in such a lavish way during the construction that as a result the average per mile cost was three times what it should have been. The sole aim was to make China's redemption almost impossible. To build the railway at that time would probably have cost only 120,000,000 gold roubles.[15]

The Soviets offered to sell the railway for 210,000,000 gold roubles plus 40,000,000 for timber and other concessions, making a total of 250,000,000 gold roubles, which was, therefore, less than the original cost, but was twice as much as the cost of reproduction. The Japanese counter-offer was 50,000,000 yen, being about twenty per cent of the sum asked for, which was obviously based upon the supposed negligible value of that railway.

After a long adjournment of the negotiations, the Soviets brought the price down to 200,000,000 gold roubles. But the Japanese stuck to the suggested price of 50,000,000 yen, stating that it would be equivalent to the amount of 200,000,000 gold roubles at a rate of exchange fixing one quarter of the silver yen to one gold rouble.[16]

[14] Information Bulletins, *Manchukuo*, Foreign Office, 1933-4, No. 81, p. 10.
[15] Wang, C. C., op. cit.
[16] Yavdynsky, J. A., *The Chinese Eastern Railway Problem in Contemplation of Law*, Shanghai, 1934, p. 8.

Since the Soviet Government showed its unwillingness to sell the Chinese Eastern Railway for 50,000,000 yen, many complications arose, all unfavourable to the railway. Brigandage along the railway became very serious, while sabotage, train-wrecking and burning of stations were of frequent occurrence. Railway properties were seized, railway employees were killed or kidnapped, and trains raided by armed force. No attempt was made to keep order along the line, as it was generally known that the more trouble, the cheaper the price. In spite of these difficulties, the railway was still able to run at a profit, as reported by the Soviet General Manager.

What proved fatal was that the Japanese were quickly constructing parallel lines to the Chinese Eastern Railway, which would render it valueless and impossible to run at a profit. The 'Manchukuo' authorities even bluntly told the Soviet Government that the completion of the 'Manchukuo' railway system would cause further dwindling of the profits of the Chinese Eastern Railway, and that, in a year or two, the railway would find it impossible to balance income with expenditure.[17] Besides, the White Russians in Manchuria were becoming very active, and it was told that they had received special assistance from the Japanese. Frontier incidents were also of frequent occurrence, which were directly connected with the railway dispute, bringing about a deadlock of the Tokyo conference. The Soviet Government began to realize the truth of Hirota's statement that ' as long as the Chinese Eastern Railway is not sold, the feeling of animosity will continue to exist '.[18] Therefore the Soviets could hardly do anything but face realities and try to get something out of it before it was too late.

On February 26, 1934, the Soviet Government lowered its price to 200,000,000 yen instead of 200,000,000 gold roubles asked previously. It was also agreed to accept one-half of the amount in Japanese goods. The 'Manchukuo' delegation thought the price was still too high, but they made a counter-offer on April 26, by raising their price from 50,000,000 yen to 100,000,000 yen, including 30,000,000 yen for allowances given to the discharged employees of the railway. To this Yurenev did not consent. On May 25, Yurenev deducted another 10,000,000 yen from their last offer, making the purchase price 190,000,000 yen, whereas the allowance for the discharging of railway employees was to be paid by the buyer. The 'Manchukuo' delegation did not accept this either.

[17] Information Bulletins, Manchukuo, Foreign Office, 1933-4, No. 81, p. 15.
[18] China Weekly Review, February 24, 1934.

On June 23, Hirota tried to compromise by telling Yurenev that 'Manchukuo' would bear the discharging allowances, but the purchase price was still fixed at 100,000,000 yen. The Soviet Ambassador declined the new offer, but on June 28 he expressed the view that the Soviet Government would again reduce the price, from 190,000,000 yen to 170,000,000 yen. Hirota made an increased offer of 120,000,000 yen on July 23, but this did not meet with the approval of the prospective seller. On July 30, Yurenev again lowered his previous offer, to 160,000,000 yen, of which one-third would be accepted in merchandise. The proposal was again turned down by the buyer. On August 13, Ohashi, the 'Manchukuo' delegate, held another conference with Yurenev, but without result. The following day Ohashi left Tokyo, and the negotiations were brought to a deadlock as both parties rejected further concessions.[19]

Inasmuch as both parties railed at each other, there was apparently no hope for a resumption of negotiations. Actually it was not so. One was willing to effect a quick sale, while the other was quite ready to buy. Both merely played for time by bargaining over the purchase price.

It was true enough that the Japanese Foreign Minister again mediated by asking for the reopening of the conference. Hirota informed Yurenev on September 6 that the last offer of 120,000,000 yen would be increased to 130,000,000 yen. The Soviet Ambassador, although he did not agree to this sum, nevertheless expressed his desire to make a further concession. He duly informed Hirota on September 12 that it was the desire of the Soviet Government to seek a just settlement and not to continue the bargaining over the price. The Soviet Government had already suffered a great loss on the last offer of 160,000,000 yen on July 30, because such a figure was far below the cost of construction. If the suggested price could be concluded once and for all, the Soviet Government would again be willing to reduce the price, to 145,000,000 yen. Then Hirota immediately put the price up to 140,000,000 yen, the difference of which was only 5,000,000 yen. The Japanese indicated clearly that it was not willing to make further concessions. Thereupon on September 19, Yurenev expressed the acceptance of the Soviet Government to Hirota's last offer with the understanding that the allowances for discharged Soviet employees were not included.

[19] Wu You-san, op. cit., pp. 115-16.

8. Conclusion of Conference

After both parties had agreed on the purchase price, negotiations were carried on without any further hindrance, with only one exception, namely the question of Japanese guarantee of payment by 'Manchukuo'. Finally, Hirota agreed to this.

On March 23, 1935, all arrangements were ready, and the agreements, together with the protocols and notes, were duly signed at the residence of the Foreign Minister in Tokyo. Those who represented Japan were headed by Hirota, the Foreign Minister, and Shigemitsu, the Vice-Minister; Yurenev, the Soviet Ambassador, represented the U.S.S.R.; Ting Shih-yuan, 'Manchukuo' Minister to Japan, and Chuichi Ohashi, 'Manchukuo' Vice-Foreign Minister, represented 'Manchukuo'; Wu Tze-seng, Counsellor, together with a Soviet Director, represented the Chinese Eastern Railway. The signatures were no fewer than fifty.

Important items of the agreement were as follows:

On the date of the signature of the agreement, the U.S.S.R. ceded to 'Manchukuo' the rights concerning the Chinese Eastern Railway at a purchase price of 140,000,000 yen. One-third of that sum, i.e., 46,700,000 yen, to be paid in cash, of which 23,300,000 yen was to be paid simultaneously with the signing of the agreement, while the remaining 23,400,000 yen was to be paid in four instalments over three years at the simple interest of three per cent per annum to be paid in the form of Treasury Bonds of the 'Manchukuo' Government. Exchange was fixed in Swiss francs to safeguard the possible fluctuation of the yen. Another two-thirds of the purchase price, i.e., 93,300,000 yen to be discharged in the form of payments for goods in instalments over three years. The price of the goods, produced or manufactured in 'Manchukuo' or Japan, to be settled by the Soviet Trade Representation with subjects or juridical bodies of Japan or 'Manchukuo'. Delivery of the goods thus purchased to be effected during six equal periods of six months constituting the said three years. Deliveries in each period not to exceed in value the sum of 15,550,000 yen.

With regard to the locomotives and freight cars removed by the Soviet authorities into Soviet territory from North Manchuria in 1933, it was stipulated in Article XI of the agreement that they were not necessarily to be returned. The U.S.S.R. was held responsible for claims made by shareholders, bond holders and creditors of the railway prior to 1917. The dismissal of Soviet employees and the discharge allowance amounting in total to 30,000,000 yen were well arranged in detail. The form of Japan's guarantee of the payment, in money and in goods, was made effective by the exchange of notes between Japan and the U.S.S.R. (See full text in Appendix B.)

Since 'Manchukuo' was not financially able to buy the Chinese Eastern Railway, the sum had to be raised in Japan entirely by bonds. In fact, the first cash instalment was borrowed from the syndicate banks of Tokyo and Osaka. The property and the income of the railway had to be used as security. Upon the formal signing of the agreement for the transfer of the Chinese Eastern Railway, the whole line of 1,700 kilometres, costing more than 160,000,000 gold roubles, was completely taken over by 'Manchukuo', which announced at that time that the railway was to be renamed the 'South Manchurian Railway', controlled by the South Manchurian Railway Company. Thus the long dispute over the Chinese Eastern Railway was brought to a close.

Chapter XVI

SOVIET INFLUENCE IN CHINESE TURKISTAN
(SINKIANG)

AFTER the signing of the Treaty of St. Petersburg in 1881, events in Chinese Turkistan were comparatively quiet. Additional agreements with Russia concerning national boundaries and frontier trade were signed. During the Russian Revolution of 1917, White Russian troops poured into Chinese Turkistan for shelter. It was due to the merit of Governor Yang Tseng-hsin that the White-Red contests, as took place in Outer Mongolia, did not spread to the westernmost frontier of China. When Yang was assassinated in 1928, Chin Shu-jen succeeded him. Shortly after his two years' reign, an Islamic revolt, headed by General Ma Chung-yin, a young Tungan commander, broke out. In order to put down the rebels, Chin had to depend on ammunition from the U.S.S.R., and for this reason he was compelled to sign a secret agreement with the Soviet authorities, conceding to the U.S.S.R. many privileges which his predecessor had refused to grant. He was overthrown by a *coup d'état* on April 12, 1933. Sheng Shih-tsai was elected Military Governor by the Maintenance Committee.

Soviet influence was then mainly confined to trade as the Soviets had not concerned themselves with Chinese politics. In 1934 the Tungan forces under Ma Chung-yin besieged Urumchi (Tihwa), capital of the province, and brought it to the verge of surrender. The military authorities could not help following the example of the late Governor by asking for immediate and effective aid from the Soviets in order to drive out the formidable foe. The Soviets responded by sending Red troops and bombing planes to chase away the rebels, and thus they saved Urumchi from peril. From then on, Soviet influence in the province greatly increased. Owing to geographical proximity, Chinese administrative policy was bound to gravitate towards the Soviet Union. The air route from Chungking to Moscow, passing through Urumchi as the mid-station, gave further significance to this orientation. Moreover, Soviet arms sent to China followed the old Silk Road. Thus Sinkiang again became important, and its powerful neighbour—the Soviet Union—began to play an important role in that part of the world.

1. Brief Description of Chinese Turkistan

Chinese Turkistan or Sinkiang lies north of Tibet and India, and south of Central Asia. Historically, Sinkiang was annexed to China as early as the Han Dynasty, about two hundred years before Christ. At that time, the land known as 'Hsi-yu', or the Western Regions, consisted of thirty-six separate kingdoms, and there were many inhabitants of Aryan blood. These thirty-six kingdoms broke up into fifty-five, but all were located in the southern part of Sinkiang, being divided by the famous Tienshan, the celestial mountain.

North of Tien-shan, the country belonged to the Mongols and the Turks known as 'Hsiung-nu' and 'Wu-sun' respectively. It was not until the Manchu Dynasty, about the latter part of the eighteenth century, that the Emperor Kang Hsi went three times in person to drive off the Jungarians and the Kazaks, and the present vast regions north and south of the Tienshan ranges were incorporated into the Chinese domain. Hence the present Sinkiang, with Urumchi in the centre as the capital, Kashgar in the south, Altai in the north, Ili (Kuldja) in the west and Hami in the east, comprises not only old 'Hsi-yu' but also the land formerly owned by the Mongols and the Turks.

The importance of Sinkiang to China can be gauged by its geographical and economic position. Sinkiang is 1,200 miles from east to west and 1,000 miles from north to south. It has an area of approximately 600,000 square miles, which is about one-third of China proper, more than one and a half times as big as Manchuria, and bigger than the British Isles, France and Germany together.[1]

Notwithstanding the extent of such a vast stretch of land, the country is very sparsely populated. It has a population of only about 2,500,000 people, which is an average of four to a square mile. This is considered the most sparsely populated region in the Chinese Empire.

The tribes in that province are very much differentiated. There are at least fourteen distinct races: Chinese, Manchus, Mongols,

[1] Wu, Aitchen K., *Turkistan Tumult*, 1940, p. 261.

Moslems or Uighurs, Tungans, Kasaks, Hsipei (Manchus from Mukden), Sao-lun (Manchus from Heilunkiang), Chahar (Mongols from Kalgan), Kirghiz, Torgut Mongols, Tatars, Tadjiks and White Russians. In addition to these races, there are Russians, Britons, Swedes, Afghans, Persians, Indians, Jews, Aryan Turks, and other nationalities; indeed, so many that Sinkiang has earned for itself the epithet of a 'living ethnological museum'. Such a condition is seldom found anywhere else in the world.

In spite of the many races with diverse languages and different social customs, they can be easily classified according to religion, Buddhists on the one hand and Islamists on the other, each so remote from the other as to be fated to bicker and war. The Chinese, Manchus and Mongols adhere to Buddhism, while the Moslems, Tungans, Kasaks, Tadjiks and Tatars are of the faith of Islam. Of these two and a half million people, only about 200,000 are Chinese, being nigh to ten per cent of the population, while the Moslems and Kasaks are in an overwhelming majority. Though the Chinese are in a minority, the whole province is always under the control of the Chinese.

2. Sinkiang and the Russian Revolution

Sinkiang was the first to feel the repercussions of the Russian Revolution in 1917 owing to its geographical proximity. Thousands of White Russians had to retreat to Sinkiang, not only using it as a shelter, but also using it as a base to gain a foothold in order to continue the struggle.

The attitude taken by Governor Yang Tseng-hsin towards the Russian Revolution was one of strict neutrality. But how to maintain this neutrality along more than a thousand miles of frontier was quite a problem. A slight favour given to one party might lead to complications with the other. With shrewdness and sagacity, Yang was able to intern the raiders, impede the incursions of Soviet troops into Sinkiang, and thus extricate himself from a perilous situation.

In November 1917 the Russian Consul at Tacheng (Tarbagatai) demanded of the local Chinese authorities passage through Tacheng for a division of Russian troops under the command of General Annenkov in order to attack Red forces in Samara. The demand was resisted on the ground that it was a violation of the spirit of neutrality hitherto strictly observed by the Chinese authorities.

Moreover, Samara was adjacent to Ili; should the Red forces be informed of the contemplated move of General Annenkov's troops through Tacheng, they would launch an attack on Ili to forestall the advance, which would cause irreparable damage to Ili. Hence the White troops were persuaded to take the passage through Semipalatinsk in Russian territory and bypass Sinkiang.

Failing to get consent for the passage of his troops through Tacheng, Annenkov secretly despatched agents to Chinese territory for the purpose of recruiting Chinese nationals for his army. This unexpected action naturally met with opposition from the Chinese authorities, who protested to the Russian Consul and prohibited their citizens from joining the White Russian forces.

The White Russians insisted on securing a passage through Tacheng on pretext of protecting the Russian Consulate there. But it was a fact that Russians residing in Chinese territory had sustained practically no losses. So the Chinese local authorities, under the instruction of Governor Yang, informed the Russian Consul that Russian nationals in Sinkiang would be well protected, and the presence of Russian troops would be unnecessary.

Meanwhile the White and Red Armies encountered each other with the result that the White Russian forces were utterly defeated and, in order to save their lives, were compelled to retreat into Chinese territory. Fighting continued upon the frontier. Then the problem of taking care of such large numbers of refugees confronted the Chinese authorities. It was about the same time that the Peking Government sent troops to Outer Mongolia where they were encountered by the White Russian army headed by Baron Ungern Sternberg.

Governor Yang's policy was to observe strict neutrality during the White and Red struggle, for he feared Annenkov even more than the Reds, the former being young and restless and quite capable of trying to occupy the northern parts of Sinkiang. The Governor, however, succeeded in removing Annenkov from the scene not by military power but by his own stratagem.

The difficulties confronting the Governor during this crisis were complicated by the fact that the Tsarist Government and its representatives in China were still legally recognized by the Chinese Government. Sinkiang, however, made no blunder in violating its strict neutrality, leaving the Reds no pretext to infringe the integrity of Chinese territory in their pursuit of White Russian forces. It was estimated that no fewer than one hundred thousand defeated

Russian soldiers and refugees crossed the border and retreated into Sinkiang for safety during the course of the Russian Revolution.

3. Exchange of Consulates between Sinkiang and U.S.S.R.

In accordance with Article I of the Sino-Soviet Agreement of 1924 providing for the immediate re-establishment of normal diplomatic and consular relations between the two contracting parties, the Soviet Government at Omsk appointed an envoy to Sinkiang to discuss the question of the re-establishment of the five Russian consulates in Sinkiang.

Negotiations with the Soviet representatives were conducted on a basis of complete reciprocity, and for every consulate which the Soviet authorities established in Sinkiang, there was the reciprocal establishment of a Chinese consulate on Soviet territory in Central Asia, where thousands of Chinese nationals had, for a long time, been deprived of any protection.

The Soviet authorities could not but agree to the first Chinese proposal, and an exchange of notes finally took place on October 6, 1924. The Soviet authorities promised to give the necessary housing for the establishment of the Chinese consulates in Central Asia, and the Sinkiang authorities agreed to hand over the old Russian consulates to the Soviet representatives. Thus the Soviet Consulate-General at Urumchi was matched by the Chinese Consulate-General at Tashkent, while Soviet consulates at Tarbagatai (Tacheng), Ili, Altai and Kashgar were matched by Chinese consulates at Semipalatinsk, Alma Ata, Zaisan and Andijan respectively.

4. Ili Trade Agreement

When the Soviet régime became stabilized after the 1917 Revolution, repeated efforts were made to enter into regional trade agreements with Sinkiang. The Ili Trade Agreement was considered an important diplomatic document in the modern history of Sinkiang. Tremendous losses to Chinese revenues occurred every year on account of the Treaty of St. Petersburg in 1881, by which Russian goods passing through the northern and southern routes into Sinkiang were free of duty. Later, British imports into the same area, under the most favoured nation clause, enjoyed similar privileges.

Upon the fall of the Tsarist régime and the coming to power of the

Soviets, it was pertinent to consider the revision of these unilateral agreements. It happened that the periodical decennial revision of the treaty expired in 1921. The Sinkiang Governor lost no opportunity of seizing the moment to revise the treaty and other corresponding regulations for fear that the treaty would be automatically renewed for another period of ten years.

A Chinese delegation was appointed to proceed to Tashkent, where it conferred with the Soviet commercial representatives in the early part of 1920. The Soviet representative proposed that Sinkiang should not permit the formation of White Russian organizations. Also a Soviet representative should be permitted to reside in Ili. Further, Russian refugees in Sinkiang should be sent back to their own country and the arms seized from the retreating Russian soldiers should be returned to the Soviet Government. The Chinese delegates counter-proposed that due protection should be accorded Chinese nationals residing in Soviet territory, restrictions on immigration law be modified, and that a Chinese trade representative be permitted to reside at Alma Ata. Regarding the stationing of a Soviet trade representative at Ili, the Chinese delegates expressed their opinion that the Soviet authorities should first agree to conclude a provisional trade agreement based on the principles of equality and reciprocity. The Russian refugees and interned soldiers would be persuaded to return to their homeland provided the Soviet authorities would promulgate an order of amnesty. The seized arms would be returned only when a legally constituted government had been established and recognized by China.

A second conference took place at Ili to continue negotiations. The Soviet representatives conceded to the Sinkiang authorities the right to impose a duty on goods imported into Ili from Soviet territory. After some lengthy discussions, the Ili Trade Agreement was signed on May 27, 1920.

The agreement was in three parts. Part I, relating to trade and commerce, provided for the mutual establishment of commercial and foreign affairs bureaux, the designation of trade routes, and customs duties levied on goods from Soviet territory into Ili or vice versa, and the adoption of passports for nationals of both countries who crossed the frontier on business.

Part II dealt with the repatriation of interned White Russian troops and refugees in Sinkiang. The Soviet authorities declared the existence of the amnesty recently promulgated. The Ili authorities, therefore, agreed to the appointment of a Soviet commission to Ili to effect jointly with the Ili foreign affairs bureau the repatriation of the interned soldiers and refugees.

Part III concerned the question of losses sustained by Chinese nationals as a consequence of the Russian Revolution. The Soviet representatives declared that as the Soviet authorities had established an Investigation and Compensation Bureau, it would be more convenient for the Chinese authorities to take up the matter with the said Bureau. The Soviet representatives consented to transmit the Chinese demands to the Soviet authorities at Tashkent in order that an amicable settlement might be reached.

The Ili Trade Agreement thus paved the way for the recovery of China's lost sovereignty caused by treaty relations with Tsarist Russia. Practically speaking, it not only concerned Ili but was enforced in other parts of Sinkiang as well. There were several attempts by the Soviets between 1922 and 1924 to have the Sinkiang authorities agree to a modification of the Ili Trade Agreement. In September 1923 a tentative agreement was reached by the two contracting parties for replacing the Ili Trade Agreement—the latter to be declared null and void. This tentative draft was submitted to Peking for formal sanction. Later, the Sinkiang authorities received instructions from Peking authorizing them to sign the agreement with slight modifications. The Soviet Government found the modifications unsatisfactory, and its representatives put off the settlement of the question under discussion. Meanwhile the Sino-Soviet Agreement on General Principles was signed in Peking on May 31, 1924. The two contracting parties agreed to await further action on the part of their respective governments.

The Sino-Soviet Conference, though opened, was without any concrete result. Diplomatic relations between China and the Soviet Union were further strained over the dispute about the Chinese Eastern Railway in 1929. Sinkiang also underwent a marked change in internal politics. Governor Yang Tseng-hsin, who had ruled Sinkiang in absolute peace for seventeen years, was assassinated, and the administration passed into the hands of Chin Shu-jen.

5. Soviet-Sinkiang Provincial Trade Agreement

The Islamic Revolt in Sinkiang between 1930 and 1934, headed by a young Tungan, General Ma Chung-yin—a rising considered but second in importance to the Yakub Beg Rebellion of 1868—had a great deal to do with the ever-increasing Soviet influence in Sinkiang.

The writer was in Sinkiang during this period, and was 'not only an eyewitness of, but an actor as well, in the revolt.'[2]

When Urumchi, the provisional capital, was under the direct attack of Ma Chung-yin, Chin Shu-pen, without the knowledge of the Central Government, secretly entered into a provisional trade agreement with the Soviet authorities in the form of an exchange of notes for the purpose of receiving arms from the Soviets.

These notes with four annexes attached were signed at Tihwa on October 1, 1931, by M. Slavusky representing the Soviet Government, and Chen Chi-shan representing the Provincial Government of Sinkiang. The text of the notes and the annexes which were revealed after the downfall of Shin Shu-jen by a *coup d'état* on April 12, 1933, appear in Appendix B.

The phrase 'existing laws and regulations' in Article I of the Trade Agreement is vague and indistinct. Article II seems advantageous to the interests of Sinkiang, but the power rests with the Soviet authorities. Moreover, foreign trade is a state monopoly in the Soviet Union, so Chinese merchants in Sinkiang can have little to say regarding the quality or quantity of their goods to be exported to the Soviet Union. Again, the goods would be further restricted by the 'existing laws of the Soviet Union'. By Article III, Soviet citizens and commercial bureaux enjoy the right to trade freely in the five 'areas' mentioned. The word 'areas' is indefinite and subject to various interpretations. It might be interpreted as the metropolitan areas of the five cities or it might also be taken to embrace the jurisdictional limits of the five areas mentioned, which would include a much larger area. Article V which provides for the payment of a uniform tax by the Soviets as paid by Chinese merchants is no contravention of international practice. Article VI relates to the supply of Soviet machinery and provision of technical experts for the reconstruction of Sinkiang. It should be borne in mind that by virtue of this stipulation, Soviet influence and economic hold in Sinkiang would naturally expand in proportion to the assistance rendered. Article VII reveals the right to decide upon the kinds of goods to be given in the appended list which may be revised yearly to suit the economic conditions of the two contracting parties. Suffice it is to say that the Soviet Government is virtually given the power to supervise the kinds of goods to be imported into and exported from Sinkiang. Annex II gives the Soviet Government

---

[2] Review of *Turkistan Tumult*, by Sir G. Macartney, *Royal Central Asian Journal*, April 1940, p. 234.

the right to establish financial bureaux in the four leading cities of Sinkiang. Thus the economic domination of Sinkiang by the Soviet Union was made preponderant.

As the Provisional Agreement had never been recognized by the Central Government, legally speaking, relations between Sinkiang and the Soviet Union were then bound by the Ili Trade Agreement of 1920 and the Sino-Soviet Agreement of 1924. Chin Shu-jen was subsequently imprisoned by the Nanking Government for having signed an agreement with a foreign Power without the consent of the Central Government.

6. Soviet Influence in Sinkiang

Soviet economic domination of Sinkiang following the exchange of the notes was quite manifest. The Soviets organized their trade in Sinkiang by means of the Sinkiang-Soviet Trading Co. Prior to this, goods reached Sinkiang from the coastal provinces first through the Peiping-Suiyuan Railway, and then by camel from Paotow to Tihwa. Since the completion of the Turk-Sib Railway, the U.S.S.R. has been in a better position to trade with Sinkiang. In addition, the Sinkiang paper tael depreciated considerably after the Islamic Revolt, and customs duties levied on goods imported from Soviet territory were based on the Sinkiang paper tael which was almost valueless.

The overthrow of Chin Shu-jen led to the inauguration of a maintenance committee in Tihwa which elected Sheng-Shih-tsai as Military Governor. This was later approved by the Central Government. Ma Chung-yin, the ambitious young Tungan leader, had retreated to Suchow, Kansu province. On hearing of the downfall of Chin Shu-jin he thought it best to take the governorship of the province. He led his strong forces westward and captured Kucheng without much resistance. The writer was then asked to head the Peace Mission to Kucheng to talk peace with the Tungan general. An offer to the latter to go to south Sinkiang as the Commander-in-Chief was gladly accepted at the outset, but later he was convinced by his advisers that he could take the capital with ease by resorting to force. After the encounter, he was defeated owing to the presence of White Russians and Manchurian troops from the capital—something beyond his expectations. The successive appointments by the Central Government of General Hwang Mu-sung and Foreign Minister Dr. Lo Wen-kan, to pacify the province from further civil war brought no result; in fact, it worsened the situation.

After a brief rest at Turfan, Ma Chung-yin recruited more soldiers from those of his own creed and attempted another attack on the capital in the early spring of 1934. His troops were exceedingly brave, and they occupied nearly all the strategic points on the outskirts of Tihwa. The fall of the capital seemed imminent. Besides, General Chang Pei-yuen of Ili mobilized his troops and marched towards the capital in co-operation with Ma Chung-yin for the overthrow of the Tihwa Government. Chang immediately seized the main road between Tacheng and the capital, an act which was very detrimental to Sheng, who had now no communications either to the north or west where the trade route ran. Sheng's position was so desperate that he could ask for no immediate assistance except from the Soviet Union.

How the Soviet authorities came to the rescue is still a mystery. It was reported that several thousand Soviet troops, equipped with tanks, artillery and aircraft, entered the Altai area. These troops were not in the uniform of the Red Army, and were not officially part of it. Later the White Russians in the province were incorporated into this force, but were subsequently disbanded for their unreliability.

It was due to Soviet military aid that the seige of Tihwa was immediately lifted, and Ma Chung-yin finally fled and crossed into Soviet Turkistan at Irkeshtan from Kashgar. General Chang Pei-yuan committed suicide when he met a strong force which ambushed his men on the way in a narrow valley. With the timely intervention of the Soviet forces, the so-called Eastern Turkistan Republic, which was proclaimed in Kashgar, was also put an end to. Sinkiang was finally brought under control, and many meaningless sanguinary battles were thus avoided. It was quite true that ' Sheng owed nothing to Nanking, but much to Moscow, for the assistance which had enabled him to triumph over Ma Chung-yin '.[3]

It has been stated that in the conversation between M. Stalin and Dr. Sun Fo at Moscow in April 1939, Stalin explained to Sun Fo why the Soviet Government helped General Shang Shih-tsai of Sinkiang province to check the advance of Ma Chung-yin, for the first was legally appointed by the Chinese Central Government, whereas the latter advanced to the province on his own accord. Furthermore, it was reported that the Japanese were backing Ma Ching-yin, supplying him with ammunition and money. Should Ma Ching-yin capture Sinkiang with the Japanese behind the scene,

[3] Teichman, Sir Eric, *Journey to Turkistan*, 1939, p. 105.

then Soviet Central Asia would be threatened. Therefore a prompt response was given to Shang Shih-tsai, who asked for immediate military assistance, by sending two brigades of Soviet troops disguised in Chinese military uniform to demolish the formidable force of Ma Chung-yin. Such troops were instantly called back as soon as the task had been carried out. The Soviet Government, therefore, directly helping Shang Shih-tsai, who had no connections with the Soviets whatsoever, was indirectly helping the Chinese Government to quell the rebels. The financial aid for the reconstruction of industry could be looked upon in the same way.[4]

Soviet influence was formerly confined to economic matters such as the monopolization of import and export trade. Since then, its influence has also developed along political and military lines. Soviet 'advisers' were appointed to key positions throughout the military and civil organization of the province. A secret loan was contracted from which the Sinkiang authorities received a credit of 500,000 gold roubles, a large supply of arms, ammunition and aeroplanes. In return, the Soviets secured natural products such as cotton, raw hides, wool, sheep and astrakhans from Sinkiang.

Another revolt was reported in Tihwa in 1937, in which many officials were involved. The Moslems of the south, who had already advanced to Karashar intending to strike a serious blow at Tihwa, attempted to intrigue with members of the Provincial Government. The uprising was again put down with the aid of Soviet forces. It was said that the Soviets were deeply interested in supporting a legal régime which was friendly to the Soviet Government.

The next phase was the rise of an 'anti-imperialist' or rather 'anti-British' movement in south Sinkiang, bordering on northern India. It was at this time that Sir Eric Teichman of the British Embassy in China was sent by the British Government to Tihwa to investigate and negotiate with the local authority.

In 1939 it was reported that edicts were issued in Khotan and Yarkand ordering all foreigners, meaning in practice British-Indian traders, to surrender their goods and leave the country within a week. The British Consulate General at Kashgar was boycotted, and its couriers were molested along the trade route from India.[5] A message from Delhi ran: 'Thirty-three British-Indian refugees, including nine women and twelve children who had been deported from Sinkiang have arrived at Gilgit frost-bitten and destitute. . . .

[4] Lecture by Dr. Sun Fo, at Hongkong University, October 12, 1941.
[5] *The Times*, March 25, 1939.

Propaganda against "imperialists", as British-Indian subjects are described in Sinkiang, continues as strong as ever.'[6] The British Consul General tried to visit Tihwa in July 1939 to discuss the situation with the provincial authorities, but his plan was finally abandoned.

The preponderance of Soviet influence in Sinkiang naturally alarmed Japan. Hirota, the Japanese Foreign Minister, once made a speech concerning the 'Sovietization of Sinkiang'.

Molotov replied in his speech to the Seventh All-Union Congress of Soviets condemning the slanderous rumours maliciously made by Japan, and emphasizing that 'the Soviet Union considers as incompatible with its policy the seizure of foreign territories, and is an absolute adherent of the independence, integrity and sovereignty of China over all her parts including Sinkiang'.[7]

The Sino-Japanese conflict brought Sinkiang to the first line of defence. Sinkiang's loyalty to the Central Government was strengthened by Soviet sympathy towards China. A concrete manifestation was the reported contribution of ten aeroplanes and 1,000,000 winter uniforms to Chinese soldiers which was decided upon at the All-Sinkiang Congress attended by 6,000 delegates representing fourteen races of people on October 8, 1938.

7. Sino-Soviet Land and Air Routes via Sinkiang

Sinkiang is still regarded as the most important gateway between the two continents, for it is separated from China by vast deserts and from India by the world's highest ranges. But between Sinkiang and Russia there are no natural geographical barriers. Moreover, the people of Chinese and Russian Turkistan are mainly of the same race and language. The overland route of communication between Asia and Europe must pass through Chinese Turkistan and Russian Turkistan. The close tie was again accentuated by the completion of the Turk-Sib Railway in 1930.

The Chinese are not unconscious of the important role of Chinese Turkistan as a western outlet of the country. The existence of the Silk Road for the last two thousand years alone proves the importance which has always been attached to this province. A feeble effort to restore the Silk Road was made in 1933 by the Central Government with the aid of the famous Swedish explorer, Dr. Sven

[6] *The Times*, June 1, 1939.
[7] *Documents for 1934*, p. 410.

Hedin. The Sino-Japanese conflict had also accelerated the completion of the Kansu-Sinkiang Highway covering a distance of 1,172 kilometres, from which connection can be made across Sinkiang with the Soviet Union.

At the end of 1937, the construction of the Kansu-Sinkiang Highway was pushed on with feverish haste under far more difficult conditions than ordinarily, for the supply of essential materials and motor oil had been largely curtailed when the coastal provinces were occupied by Japan. The road had to be completed rapidly in order that the most urgently needed materials and supplies from the Soviet Union could be imported by that route. Some 100,000 civilians guarded by soldiers were mobilized to work on the project so that by the end of 1938 the road was ready for traffic. The highway between China and the U.S.S.R. started from Holkutz, on the border of Ili, passing Tihwa, Lanchow, Sian, Hanchung and Chengtu, and finally reached Chungking, a total distance of 5,274 kilometres.

Hundreds of modern trucks, tanks and armoured cars used to run daily on these highways. Besides, camel caravans as well as mule carts were added to the scene for carrying petrol and military supplies across Sinkiang from the Soviet Union when the Indo-China railroad and the Burma Road were closed. All Soviet munitions destined for China had to be transported over this route.

Another historic feature which brought Sino-Soviet relations closer was the inauguration of the Chungking-Moscow airline after the signing of an agreement for the formation of the Sino-Soviet Aviation Company on September 9, 1939. The total distance is divided into three sections, namely Chungking-Hami, Hami-Alma Ata and Alma Ata-Moscow. The Chungking-Hani line was operated by the Ministry of Communications of the Chinese Government, the Hami-Alma Ata line by the newly organized Sino-Soviet Aviation Company with its abbreviation 'Hami-Ata', and the Alma Ata-Moscow line by the Communication organ of the Soviet Government.

The Eurasia Aviation Company, a Sino-German concern, had previously opened an air service between Berlin and Shanghai—a five days' journey with only Sinkiang as its midway stop. Owing to strained relations between the U.S.S.R. and Germany, the Company was compelled to suspend its air service. As the Chungking-Moscow line was a Sino-Soviet concern, it ran quite smoothly after its inauguration.

The Sino-Soviet Aviation Company has a capital of 1,000,000 U.S.

dollars, divided into 1,000 shares, subscribed by the two parties on a fifty-fifty basis. The Germans held only one-third of the interests in the Eurasian Aviation Company, while the Americans in the China National Aviation Corporation had an interest of forty-five per cent. The Board of Directors of the Company consisted of three Chinese and three Soviet citizens, who elected a President of Chinese citizenship and a Vice-President of Soviet citizenship.

The geographical position of Sinkiang is such as to encourage its inclination towards the U.S.S.R. Moreover, Sinkiang is actually economically dependent upon the U.S.S.R. and imports therefrom all machines and equipment. At the same time all the natural products from Sinkiang have to be sent to the U.S.S.R. for barter. There is no other alternative. The control of the market and transportation of goods by the Soviet authorities is no doubt the cause of Soviet influence in the province of Sinkiang.

8. Political Changes in Sinkiang

Throughout the role played by Governor Sheng Shih-tsai for ten years, it had been his policy to be anti-imperialistic and pro-Soviet. The provincial three-year plan of reconstruction was instituted with Soviet advisers, and at one time a brother of Mao-Tse-tung was made Commissioner of Finance. When the U.S.S.R. signed a Non-Aggression Treaty with Nazi Germany in August 1939, Sinkiang was supporting Soviet actions in the west and China's resistance to Japan in the east. But when the Tripartite German-Italian-Japanese Alliance was announced in September 1940, the Sinkiang Government also changed its attitude, commenting that the two imperialist forces, namely the German-Italian-Japanese Axis and the Anglo-Americans, would soon come to an open clash.

Sheng Shih-tsai continued to support the Nationalist Government, then in Chungking. The signing of the Soviet-Japanese Non-Aggression Pact in April 1941 and the Nazi attack on the Soviet Union had drawn Sinkiang closer than ever to the Central Government and even went so far as to get it away from the Soviet Union. The Nationalist troops were despatched to the province in October 1943, when a 'Soviet garrison' was withdrawn from Hami without any incidents. Soviet engineers were also withdrawn from the province, and all the machinery and pipes from Wusu oilfields were dismantled and shipped back to the Soviet Union. By that time Sheng had shifted his allegiance to Generalissimo Chiang Kai-shek.

The control of Sinkiang foreign relations returned to the Central Government for the first time since 1927.

American interests in the development of Sinkiang began in April 1943 with the opening of a U.S. Consulate in Tihwa. The British Government also maintained a consulate in the capital. Curious to say, both the American and British Consuls, Mr. Horace Smith and Mr. W. Graham, who had been sent to Tihwa, were the writer's colleagues in Changtu, Szechuan province, at that time. Not only that, Dr. Chaucer Wu, now Ambassador to Chile, and the writer also changed their posts as from Foreign Commissioner for Sinkiang to that for Szechuan and Sikong. It seemed that Chinese aid in the province had supplanted that of the Soviets, who apparently were determined to withdraw from the province.

Sheng Shih-tsai, who once was sympathetic to the Communists, was removed and replaced by Mr. Wu Tsung-hsin, appointed from Chungking. Then a revolt occurred in Ili in November 1944 with the establishment of the 'Eastern Turkistan Republic'. The revolt also affected the districts of Tacheng and Altai. It was not until January 1946 that a compromise was concluded between the representative of Ili and General Chang Chih-chung representing the Central Government, giving special privileges in the matter of autonomy to the people of Sinkiang.

From July to December 1947, there were numerous attacks from Outer Mongolia in the Altai district, particularly Peitashen. It should be remembered that the Altai formerly belonged to Kobdo in Outer Mongolia. It was not annexed to Sinkiang until the year 1922. Peitashan is located in Eastern Sinkiang near Kucheng or Chitai, the gateway from the Chinese interior to Sinkiang. Should Kucheng be threatened, then communications to Tihwa would be interrupted.

It might be added here that Sinkiang went over to the Communists in September 1949, and the Sinkiang Provincial People's Government was established in December 1949 with Pao Erh-han and Saifudin, Chairman and Vice-Chairman. The Sinkiang Military Headquarters which were inaugurated on the same day were headed by General Peng Teh-huai and General Chang Chih-chung, Chairman and Vice-Chairman of the North-west Military and Administrative Committee respectively.[8]

[8] New China News Agency, London, December 28, 1949.

Chapter XVII

SOVIET ATTITUDE TOWARDS THE SINO-JAPANESE CONFLICT

THE Sino-Japanese conflict started at Lukouchiao, known as the Marco Polo Bridge, on July 7, 1937. Before the incident there were eight successive conferences between Kawagoe, the Japanese Ambassador to China, and Chang Chun, the Chinese Foreign Minister. The Japanese insisted on Hirota's Three Principles, namely Sino-Japanese co-operation, anti-Comintern and economic collaboration. Negotiations, however, turned out a failure when Japan produced seven vigorous demands and China put forth five counter demands on the Chengtu and Pei-hai incidents which broke out during the conference, although these were finally settled as local cases in 1936.[1]

Then followed the Sian coup, when Generalissimo Chiang Kai-shek was held a captive in December 1936. The outbreak of popular indignation at his incarceration, and the nation-wide rejoicings among the Chinese at his release, naturally inspired the admiration and aroused the jealousy of the Japanese militarists, who realized that China was on the road ot national unification. Hence an attempt to strike a fatal blow was in progress.

The Soviet attitude towards China during her war of resistance was vital. No one could deny that China depended largely on Soviet support. Nevertheless, it was also due to China that the Soviet Union was saved from Japanese attack. As the U.S.S.R. is a nation with territory in both Asia and Europe, both flanks were liable to be attacked. China's refusal to join the anti-Comintern pact, and her armed resistance against Japan, certainly eased the plight of the U.S.S.R. and saved her from war.

1. Bogomoloff-Sun-Wang Parley

Considerable interest and significance had been attached to the

[1] Author's personal interview with Governor Chang Chun at Chengtu, March 8, 1943.

preliminary talks in Shanghai beginning March 1937, between M. Bogomoloff, Soviet Ambassador to China, and Dr. Fun, Fo, President of the Legislative Yuan. Bogomoloff was reported to have criticized the Chinese Government for having put forward impractical terms which hindered the progress of negotiations regarding the commercial treaty. Bogomoloff returned to Moscow and came back to China in April 1937, bringing with him three new proposals:

(1) China should take the initiative in proposing a Pacific Peace Conference; (2) China and the Soviet Union should enter a Non-Aggression Pact; (3) China and the Soviet Union should sign a Mutual Assistance Pact. These Soviet proposals were put to the Chinese Government with a promise that the Soviet Government would be willing to float a machinery loan to China for the supply of ammunition in the sum of $50,000,000 in Chinese currency.

The Chinese Government, however, came to the conclusion that the first proposal would not be effective, as Japan would very likely refuse to participate in such a conference; also should Japan participate, she would present unreasonable demands; or else 'Manchukuo' might also send delegates to the peace conference, which would only embarrass China. The second proposal, for a Non-Aggression Pact, was drafted in 1933. It was then re-studied and thought possible. Negotiations for a Sino-Soviet Mutual Assistance Pact were not even considered, because responsible Chinese political circles did not regard such a military understanding as expedient, in view of China's desire to maintain peaceful relations with Japan. The Japanese, however, must have got wind of the Soviet offer through their active intelligence service, because unprovoked hostilities were immediately started by them regardless of China's peaceful intentions.

The Lukuochiao incident broke out during the Lushan Conference, called by Generalissimo Chiang Kai-shek. Though the incident was at first hoped to be local, the Chinese Government was willing to discuss the mutual assistance pact with the Soviet Union. Bogomoloff hinted that he had no authority to enter into immediate negotiations, but would report to Moscow. He even expressed his opinion that Chinese official circles were not in full accord, and that an antagonistic attitude towards the Soviet Union still prevailed. He did not believe that the Chinese would resist on all fronts, owing to the lack of military and economic preparations, and he predicted that the incident would end in a week or two.

After the outbreak of hostilities in Shanghai on August 13, 1937, the situation became exceedingly grave. Bogomoloff still did not believe that China would be able to resist on all fronts. Negotiations, however, were started between M. Bogomoloff and Dr. Wang Chung-hui, Chinese Foreign Minister. Both believed that the proposed Pacific Peace Conference was out of the question, and they concluded and signed the Non-Aggression Pact at Nanking.

Since peace is the basic foreign policy of the Soviet Union, it is natural she would propose to create 'collective security' in the Pacific. The Soviet proposal, however, received a cold reception in other countries that still held views antagonistic to the Soviet Union, which soon discerned that the time had not yet come for a collective security pact in the Pacific owing to the opposition of imperialistic Powers. To protect herself, the Soviet Union had, therefore, to depend upon self-defence and do everything in her power to aid the victims of aggression.

2. Sino-Soviet Non-Aggression Pact

The Soviet attitude towards China in the Sino-Japanese conflict was most cordial and sympathetic, more so than that of any other country. The Sino-Soviet Non-Aggression Pact was concluded on August 21, 1937, six weeks after the Lukouchiao incident, and eight days after the hostilities in Shanghai on August 13. As early as 1933, Dr. W. W. Yen, Chinese Ambassador to Moscow, had started negotiations with Litvinov, the Soviet People's Foreign Commissar, for the conclusion of a Non-Aggression Pact. Had the Chinese authorities been more far-sighted, they would have immediately approved the pact.

Not until China sounded the bugle of resistance did Sino-Soviet relations take a new turn. The decision of the Soviet Union to sign the pact with China certainly gave the latter spiritual and moral support. In letter, this pact was limited to non-aggression and non-assistance in aggression, but in spirit it laid the foundation for a permanent friendship between the two countries. (See full text in Appendix B.)

Both China and the Soviet Union were member States of the League of Nations as well as signatories to the Pact of Paris. When signing the Sino-Soviet Non-Aggression Pact, neither China nor the Soviet Union had forgotten its obligations under the League and the Pact of Paris.

The pact on the one hand provided for non-assistance to the

aggressor, either against China or the Soviet Union, and on the other, strengthened the guarantee of collective security in the Pacific. This reflected the same spirit in which China refused to participate in the 'anti-Comintern pact', refraining from assisting Japanese aggression against the Soviet Union.

3. Soviet Attitude to League of Nations

Early in 1932 the U.S.S.R. refused to give information to the Lytton Commission of Enquiry on the Manchurian incident, trying to preserve complete neutrality and maintaining its own rights. The U.S.S.R. also regarded the Powers in the League of Nations as tending to encourage the Japanese advance into Manchuria by not taking a definite stand against aggression.

After the Soviet Union joined the League of Nations in September 1934, the Soviet delegate repeatedly advocated the extension of assistance to China and the application of sanctions against Japan. The U.S.S.R. expressed the hope that some sort of machinery for collective security in the Pacific should be worked out.

In his speech in the League of Nations, September 28, 1936, Litvinov, the Soviet Commissar of Foreign Affairs, mentioned the fact that 'the larger the area included in the pact, the greater the guarantee of security'. He argued in the Assembly that Article XVI of the League Covenant should be enforced. It was his report declaring that 'the event constitutes a breach by Japan of her obligations towards China and towards other States under these treaties', which recommended the calling of the Brussels Conference.

It is to be remembered that in 1937 the Australian Prime Minister, Lyons, proposed a conference of Powers having interests in the Far East to be held in London with the hope of working out some kind of agreement for collective security in the Pacific. The Soviet Government immediately supported the Australian proposal, desiring to make the Covenant more precise by concluding a regional pact as proposed in the Australian project. Through its Foreign Commissar in the League, Litvinov, the Soviet Government even thought of 'bilaterial pacts of mutual assistance' of all nations concerned.

In the course of the League conference, Litvinov defended the rights of small nations, urging the Communist parties of the various States to give up their anti-democratic attitude and seek collaboration with other democratic parties in the form of a 'popular front'.

4. Soviet Attitude to Brussels Conference

In 1937 the U.S.S.R. was invited to the Nine-Power Treaty Conference at Brussels, although she was not a signatory to the said treaty. Litvinov in his opening speech gave warning to the conference in the following sarcastic tone:

'When it is a question of an aggressive attack by one State against another, and if that attack has been in some measure successful, there is nothing easier than for an international organization, in order to gain a momentary success, to say to the aggressor: "Take your plunder, take what you have seized by force, and peace be with you," and to say to the victim of aggression: "Love your aggressor; resist no evil." But while that may constitute a superficial success of the conference, it does not represent the victory of peace or the victory of the peace-loving countries. Such successes can only provoke new cases of aggression, giving rise to new conferences, and so on without end.'[2]

Before the close of the Brussels Conference, Soviet commentators already saw that nothing would be accomplished by the conference, as shown by the following passage.

'The composition of the Brussels Conference, even in the case of Japan's absence, makes it impossible, in advance, for the conference to reach any positive decisions. Its basis for activity under these conditions can result only in empty chatter, under cover of which the Japanese militarists will continue their criminal war against the Chinese people.'[3]

Much blame was placed on Britain for her policy of appeasement vis-à-vis Japan. The failure of the Brussels Conference was also due to the fact that Japan remained outside, making it difficult to take any action on the basis of the Nine-Power Treaty. Italy also took part in it in order to disrupt it from within, while Germany stood on one side to play the part of beneficent intermediary.

In spite of the fruitless efforts at mediation, the declaration of the Brussels Conference on November 24, 1937, showed general support for the Soviet Union.

[2] *The Conference of Brussels*, p. 34, published by the Department of State, Washington, D.C., 1938.
[3] *Pravda*, October 28, 1937.

Though a non-signatory nation and non-participatory in the Nine-Power Treaty of Washington, 1922, the Soviet Union took no less interest than other Powers in upholding the said treaty, and such a friendly attitude enhanced the spirit of collective action in support of China by condemning Japanese aggression.

5. Soviet Material Aid to China

Has the Soviet Union helped China during the latter's war of resistance? 'In actual fact,' declared Dr. Wang Chung-hui, the Chinese war-time Foreign Minister, 'Soviet Russia has been continually giving us plenty of material and technical assistance so as to increase our power of resistance both at the front and in the rear.'[4]

The first Soviet loan to China was $100,000,000 in Chinese currency, but no agreement was signed. In the latter part of 1937, Bogomoloff was recalled, and General Yang Chieh accompanied him to Moscow with the hope of negotiating another loan. This was found difficult, because the Soviet Government had already supplied twenty-four Chinese divisions with $100,000,000 worth of arms, and the agreement for such a loan was still in abeyance. Voroshilov, Soviet Commissar of War, expressed the opinion that the first loan should be cleared before discussing another.

At the request of Generalissimo Chiang Kai-shek, Dr. Sun Fo arrived in Moscow in March 1938 to negotiate the second loan. He took up the matter with Stalin, who suggested that the first loan be $50,000,000 U.S. currency, and the second loan another $50,000,000. Sun Fo expressed the opinion that though the amount was large, it was still insufficient for China's resistance, and he wished the second loan to be increased to U.S. $100,000,000. Stalin promised to float a third loan should the second one become exhausted. So an agreement for the first and second loans was signed at Moscow by General Yang Chieh in May 1938.

The second Soviet loan was practically exhausted by November 1938, one month after the evacuation of the Chinese Government from Nanking to Hankow. After that, no ammunition was received. The Soviet Ambassador to China promised to report to Moscow a request for floating another loan, but this had no result. Meanwhile Chiang Kai-shek urged Sun Fo to proceed to Moscow again. He

[4] Wang Chung-hui, "China's Foreign Policy," *The China Quarterly*, Autumn number, 1940.

arrived there in April 1939, which was just at the time of Italy's
occupation of Albania. He waited to see Stalin for some weeks, but
without avail, despite the best efforts of Litvinov, Soviet Commissar
for Foreign Affairs. On May 2, Litvinov was relieved of his office,
and Molotov succeeded him. On May 13, Sun Fo was received at
the Kremlin where Stalin, in his usual good spirits, was present.
Talking in a very frank manner, Stalin asked Sun Fo whether he
was in need of another loan. At this question, Sun Fo handed over
a prospectus in which the proposed loan was put at U.S. $150,000,000.
The discussion lasted almost two hours. At length Stalin said
bluntly: 'You may have a loan of any amount you require without
putting forward any reasons.' Asked as to the procedure, Stalin
replied: 'For the signing of the agreement you have to negotiate
with Mikoyan (Soviet Commissar of Trade), while as to the ammunition you can talk with Voroshilov (Soviet Commissar of War).'
Thus the loan agreement and also the Commercial Treaty were both
signed in June 1939. The loan was to be reimbursed by Chinese
goods such as tea, wool, tungsten ore, etc., and the period was
extended to thirteen years. The interest was fixed at three per cent,
and the Chinese dollar at its pre-war value was accepted.[5]

General Yang Chieh, Chinese ex-Ambassador to Moscow, stated
in an interview: 'Soviet loans to China have all been settled as
barter agreements based on U.S. currency. The Soviet authorities
asked me to fix prices on all ammunition delivered to China instead
of waiting for instructions from the Chinese Government. I therefore laid down the principle that all Soviet makes ought to be
cheaper than American products, to which they generally agreed.
Altogether six instalments of ammunition, amounting to 60,000 tons,
were sent to China through the port of Odessa in the Black Sea
between 1937 and 1939.'[6]

There were also large numbers of Soviet engineers and pilots
arriving at Lanchow. About 1,500 car-loads of Soviet bombs had
reached Lanchow through Sinkiang. Edgar Snow, a noted author
on China, witnessed hundreds of trucks of Soviet make bringing
military supplies, mostly bombs, torpedoes and shells for planes and
artillery, across the desert from Chinese Turkistan. No fewer than
2,000 camels and pack animals were engaged in carrying gasolene

[5] Author's personal interview with Dr. Sun Fo at his residence, Hongkong,
August 29, 1941.
[6] Author's personal interview with General Yang Chieh at his residence,
Chungking, October 29, 1941. General Yang was murdered in Hongkong on
September 19, 1949—believed to be a political assassination.

from the Soviet Union as fuel for trucks along the historic 'Silk Road' now actually converted into the 'Red Route'.[7]

Dr. Wellington Koo, then Chinese Ambassador to France, who arrived at Vichy in July 1940, told a Pressman that 'China is now using 20,000 camels to carry military supplies across Chinese Turkistan from the Soviet Union after the closing of the Burma Road and the railway in French Indo-China'.[8]

It was generally believed that the great victory of Taierchuang in April 1938 was mainly due to modern equipment which came from the Soviet Union. The Chinese aviators, once reported to have flown to Tokyo to drop pamphlets, were said to have been accompanied by Soviet airmen. At that time there were about 200 Soviet aviators in China, many of them stationed in Chungking and Chengtu, helping Chinese in the construction of air bases. Besides, a sufficient air force was kept in Lanchow, to maintain the balance of strength in the western part of China.

Soviet material aid not only continued but also increased in quantity. All munitions were sent to Chungking and then distributed to the Chinese armies, including the Communist forces.

The Soviets actually came to China's rescue, rendering far more aid than Britain and America together. Before the Pearl Harbour incident Britain and American aid to China in the form of ammunition was very limited, while that accorded to Japan at the same time was considerable. For instance, in March 1938, America sold war materials to China worth $200,000, but those she sold to Japan in the same month reached the value of $900,000. Dr. W. W. Yen expressed the same opinion early in 1940, during his stay in America, saying, 'Soviet Russia has rendered, perhaps more than any other Power, material aid to China, in the form of arms, ammunition and planes.'[9]

6. Commercial Treaty

During that time relations between the two countries were most friendly and cordial. Generalissimo Chiang Kai-shek received much praise from Soviet journals. General Yang Chieh was appointed Chinese Ambassador to Moscow to succeed Dr. T. F. Chiang in June

---

[7] Edgar Snow, "Will Stalin Sell Out China?" *The China Weekly Review*, p. 372, May 11, 1940.
[8] *South China Morning Post*, Hongkong, July 28, 1940.
[9] *Pacific Affairs*, September 1940, p. 265.

1938. He was received by Stalin—an honour which few of the diplomatic representatives in Moscow enjoyed.

However, there had been no other pact concluded until the signing of a new Commercial Treaty. Sun Fo was responsible for the conclusion of this treaty. He took two trips by air to Moscow in 1938 and 1939 to negotiate a treaty with the Soviet authorities.

The actual date of the signing of the Commercial Treaty in Moscow was June 16, 1939, between Sun Fo and Mikoyan. The treaty was ratified by the Soviet Union on January 5, 1940, and by China on January 23. It is notable that Moscow published the treaty, whereas the Nationalist Government withheld publication.

The full text of the Commercial Treaty consists of fifteen articles. Articles I-IV treat of the importance and exportation of goods and the stipulation of customs duties, in which the 'most favoured treatment' is mentioned. Articles V-X treat of the navigation of steamers. Either of the contracting parties has the right of fishing in common waters both in sea and river. Articles XI-XII deal with the position of merchants and the necessity for the Soviet Government to establish a trade as stipulated in the constitution of the Soviet Union; the trade representation consisting of one representative and two vice-representatives to be attached to the Soviet Embassy located in the Chinese capital, receiving the same diplomatic privileges enjoyed by other members of the Embassy. Articles XIII-XV concern the duration of the agreement for three years, after which it could be prolonged for another two years, provided neither party gave any notification three months before its expiration. The exchange of the treaty was made in Chungking after its ratification by both contracting parties. Besides, there is an annex with regard to the exercise of authority as well as the treatment of the Soviet trade representation stationed in the Chinese capital and its branches in Tientsin, Shanghai, Hankow, Canton and Lanchow.

Dr. Wang Chung-hui once made the remark that 'similar in spirit to the political treaty of non-aggression of August 1937 this trade pact forges another link in the chain of Sino-Soviet friendship'.[10] It was generally believed that the conclusion of the aforesaid commercial treaty might have eased negotiations in obtaining Soviet credits to China to facilitate the enlargement of Chinese purchases of war materials. (See full text in Appendix B.)

[10] *The China Quarterly*, Autumn number, 1940, p. 42.

Chapter XVIII

SOVIET-JAPANESE RELATIONS

THERE was no doubt that Sino-Soviet relations were bound to affect other nations, particularly Japan. Similarly, changes in Soviet-Japanese relations affected China. Owing to their geographical proximity and inter-connection, it seemed that relations between China, the U.S.S.R. and Japan formed an inseparable whole. A study of Sino-Soviet relations would be incomplete, therefore, which did not mention Soviet-Japanese relations.

1. Amur Incident

Before the Japanese militarists started any action against China, they wanted to test the strength of the Soviet Union which was pregnant with internal trouble at that time. So in June 1937 they started the Amur incident near Blagoveshchensk, where the writer was Chinese Consul-General at the time. The Japanese occupied deltas in the middle of the Amur River, claiming them to be in 'Manchukuo' territory. The Soviet authorities promptly sent troops to the scene with three gunboats to check the Japanese, stating that the deltas were clearly Soviet land. Both exchanged fire, and it was reported that the Soviets sustained some casualties, and that one gunboat was hit and sunk. The hostilities did not last long before the Soviet forces were ordered to withdraw. One of the disputed deltas was immediately occupied by 'Manchukuo' troops as the Soviet Government allowed the matter to drop. This gave clear evidence to Japan that there would be no likelihood of Soviet intervention if she started a campaign. Scarcely a month had passed when the Lukouchiao incident broke out, being obviously part of a prearranged plan.

2. Changkufeng Incident

The Changkufeng incident, which occurred on the Soviet-'Manchukuo' border near the Hassan Lake in July 1938, was a direct Soviet challenge to Japan-'Manchukuo'. In the beginning the crisis was so grave that many observers believed that this would turn out to be a second Lukouchiao, and would develop into a Soviet-Japanese war. The situation appeared so serious that Vladivostok, where the writer had in the meantime been transferred, had a black-out for two weeks. Shortly after the installation of air-raid sirens, Soviet planes appeared in the sky to chase enemy planes. The Japanese alleged that Soviet planes had flown to the Korean ports of Seishin and Rashin with the intention of bombing bridges.

Changkufeng is a strategic village commanding a view of Rashin Bay in Korea and the Soviet naval base at Possiet. The 'Man-chukuo' Government, on receiving a report that about forty Soviet soldiers had entered 'Manchukuo' territory to engage in systematic operations for occupying the area near Changkufeng, lodged a note of protest with the Soviet Union. Tokyo filed another protest, back-ing up 'Manchukuo's' demand that the Soviet troops should be withdrawn. The protests were reported to have been rejected. The incident was intensified by the fact that a Japanese gendarme was shot dead in the disputed territory, and that the frontier was violated by a Soviet plane. Tokyo lodged a second protest, demanding the immediate withdrawal of Soviet soldiers and refuting the assertion that Changkufeng was Soviet territory.

Litvinov made a statement in which he accused Mamoru Shige-mitsu, the Japanese Ambassador to Moscow, of using threats in his diplomacy. He placed a map before the Japanese Ambassador, stating that this map, being attached to the Hunchun Treaty of 1869, definitely established that the disputed area was in Soviet territory. Shigemitsu contested the genuineness of the map which was not published anywhere. Tokyo also revealed that Korean villages at the base of Changkufeng Hill had held semi-annual festivals in March and September on the top of the hill, but had never been molested by the Russian or Soviet authorities.

Therefore the crux of the whole dispute lay on the authenticity of the Hunchun Treaty map produced by the Soviet Commissar. Shigemitsu then suggested that the question of the border be set aside for the time being, but that the *status quo ante* be restored by the evacuation of Soviet troops. The proposal, however, was flatly rejected by Litvinov.

Border clashes were of daily occurrence on the Changkufeng Hill for two weeks. Each side claimed possession of the top of the hill.

The city of Vladivostok was under general mobilization. Wounded soldiers from the front thronged the hospitals. The battle was a real operation of modern warfare, and casualties on both sides were heavy.

The Japanese Government then proposed the establishment of a border commission representing Japan, 'Manchukuo' and the Soviet Union for settling outstanding disputes. The Soviet authorities insisted that the map was valid and should be respected. Tokyo contended that the map was drawn up from rough surveys and could not be considered as accurate, irrespective of its authenticity, and nothing, therefore, could be done until re-demarcation had been effected.

A mutual 'face-saving' formula for the settlement of the Changkufeng incident was finally advanced by Japan on August 4. The proposal was that the Japanese should withdraw from the disputed territory provided the Soviets would not reoccupy it, leaving the area as a virtually neutral zone pending the re-demarcation by a joint commission. The Soviet Union was also anxious to localize the border clashes by converting the disputed territory into a buffer zone.

The Soviet-Japanese truce agreement was finally reached on August 11. Both Soviet and Japanese troops had to remain in the positions held at midnight, August 10, local time. A mixed commission of four persons, composed of two Soviet representatives and two others nominated by Japan and 'Manchukuo', had to deal with the re-demarcation of the frontier.

At midday on August 11, the opposing forces laid down their arms along the entire front where, at Changkufeng, the Japanese and Soviet troops were entrenched only sixty metres apart. An armistice was signed locally on the following day between the respective Soviet and Japanese commanders. One of the significant sequels of the armistice was the removal of Marshal Bleucher from his post as Commander-in-Chief of the Far Eastern Red Army, believed to be a direct result of the Changkufeng incident.

The armistice furthermore affected the Japanese campaign in China, for when the Soviet Union accepted the Japanese offer of compromise, the Japanese, knowing there would be no more clashes between the Soviets and themselves, transferred a portion of their troops on the Soviet-'Manchukuo' border to strengthen their forces in south China.

3. *Nomonhan Incident*

Of all the border incidents occurring in those years with almost monotonous regularity, the Nomonhan incident of July 1939 was the most serious, for not only was it a direct clash between Inner and Outer Mongolia, but a clash between Japan and the Soviet Union.

Nomonhan is an oasis in the Gobi Desert, whose rich pastures have always been coveted by Mongolian nomads. The territory on both sides of this obscure frontier is inhabited by Mongols who, through no fault of their own, found themselves divided, part of the country being under Soviet and part under Japanese protection.

The Mongols of Inner and Outer Mongolia formerly moved their flocks and herds freely from one pasture to another. Now they were confronted with a rigid frontier. The Outer Mongolian Government naturally thought that with the weapons they had acquired from the Soviet Union they were strong enough to open the Nomonhan pastures to Mongolian cattle. Early in 1936 Stalin told Roy Howard in an interview that if Japan ventured to attack the Mongolian People's Republic, seeking to destroy its independence, the Soviet Union would have to assist the M.P.R. in the same way as the Soviet Union had helped the M.P.R. in 1921.[1] The Japanese, however, knew that there would be no conflict in Manchuria, but that the Soviet threat might be a prelude to a struggle in Mongolia.[2]

An inevitable clash on the 'Manchukuo'-Mongolian border finally occurred in the neighbourhood of Lake Buir on May 28, when 39 Outer Mongolian aeroplanes were shot down, and 150 Mongolians were killed, according to a statement issued by the Japanese head-quarters in Hsinking, the capital of 'Manchukuo'. It was reported that the Outer Mongolians attacked the Japanese when 1,000 Outer Mongolian troops, supported by five tanks and 70 aeroplanes of Soviet make, crossed the frontier near Lake Buir but were repulsed by the Japanese land and air forces. The Japanese Press accused the Soviet Union of instigating the trouble with the intention of assisting the Chinese by a diversion in the north, or just to test the 'Manchukuo' defences.[3]

Reviewing relations with Japan in regard to the Nomonhan

---

[1] *Moscow Daily News*, March 6, 1936.
[2] Gunther, John, *Inside Asia*, 1939, p. 168.
[3] *The Times*, London, May 30, 1939.

incident, Molotov, the Soviet Premier and Foreign Minister, gave the following warning to Japan when he delivered a speech to the Supreme Council on May 31, 1939.

'Japanese threats against Outer Mongolia are funny and non-sensical. There is a limit to all this nonsense; it is time for the Japanese to cease all provocations. Owing to our pact of mutual assistance with Outer Mongolia, we will defend the Outer Mongolian borders like our own.'[4]

Another big Soviet-Japanese air battle was reported on the 'Manchukuo' border on June 24. The report alleged that sixty Soviet planes crossed the frontier and were attacked by Japanese machines. The battle was said to have taken place over the Khalka River, which flows into Lake Buir and then formed the boundary between 'Manchukuo' and Outer Mongolia for about one hundred miles.[5]

But according to a Soviet report from the Mongolia-'Manchukuo' front, 60 Japanese fighting machines crossed the frontier from 'Manchukuo' into the M.P.R. near Lake Buir. They were chased by 50 Soviet-Mongolian aeroplanes, and a fierce battle raged for two hours, during which 25 of the Japanese aeroplanes were brought down. All the Soviet-Mongolian machines returned to their base except three which were missing.[6]

It was officially reported in Moscow that fifteen Japanese-'Manchukuo' bombers, escorted by fighters, again violated Outer Mongolian territory on June 29 near Lake Buir; but, meeting with anti-aircraft fire and Mongol-Soviet fighters, they dropped a few bombs aimlessly and returned to 'Manchukuo' territory.[7]

On July 3, a telegram from Tokyo stated that heavy fighting was going on near the Khalka River where a strong force of Japanese started their offensive and attacked a hill where the Outer Mongolian forces were in occupation of Nomonhan. The Tokyo report stated that Japanese Press despatches from Khalka River claimed that 4,000 Mongolian troops were surrounded and annihilated, and 30 tanks and 10 aeroplanes were captured in that day's dog fight.[8]

Moscow papers, however, gave the Soviet account that all Japanese attacks on Nomonhan and Burdobo were repulsed with severe losses:

[4] *The Times*, June 1, 1939.
[5] ibid., June 27, 1939.
[6] ibid., June 27, 1939.
[7] ibid., June 30, 1939.
[8] ibid., July 5, 1939.

in the three days' fighting, 45 Japanese aircraft, 50 tanks and eight guns were put out of action, and the casualties among the Japanese and 'Manchukuo' troops were numbered about 800.

On August 20, the very day of signing the Soviet-German trade agreement, the Soviet-Mongolian troops at Nomonhan carried through a counter-attack on the Japanese-'Manchukuo' forces and won a considerable victory.

Then gradually ground fighting on the 'Manchukuo'-Mongolian border died down, though air fighting still continued. It was noted that there had been no exchange of notes between the two governments about this fighting, as the dispute was between the two 'puppet' régimes of Outer Mongolia and 'Manchukuo', and it seemed that neither government wished to aggravate the affair. Nevertheless, both sides had learned some valuable military lessons as well as tested each other's strength. The announcement made in Moscow on August 30 of the award of more than 9,000 decorations to military officers in the Red Army for their bravery during military operations on the Outer Mongolian frontier meant that the fighting had come to an end.[9] It was recalled that, basing their claims upon the number of successes on the ground and in the air in a series of actions, the Soviet Government did not intend to do more than beat off attacks on their positions by Japan-'Manchukuo' forces, and were satisfied with the outcome of the hostilities. Then a truce was officially announced in Moscow, and the agreement for the truce was signed between Togo and Molotov on September 15, 1939.

It was agreed that a commission consisting of two representatives of the Soviet-Mongolian side and two representatives of the Japanese-'Manchukuo' side should be organized at the earliest possible date in order to establish the precise frontier line between the M.P.R. and 'Manchukuo'.[10]

Later, Tokyo made public that 'Japanese casualties in the recent fighting on the borders of "Manchukuo" and Outer Mongolia reached a total of 18,000 killed and wounded'.[11] The Japanese War Office admitted that the Soviet forces were not only numerically but mechanically far superior to theirs, and the lesson for Japan from the Nomonhan battle was the need for better mechanization. They described the struggle from May to September as the 'longest and

[9] The Times, August 31, 1939.
[10] ibid., September 16, 1939.
[11] ibid., October 4, 1939.

bitterest fought between the two chief adversaries since they came to grips in the Russo-Japanese War of 1904 '.[12]

The Nomonhan incident on the borders of Outer Mongolia was completely settled in Moscow on June 9, 1940, in an agreement by which the 'Manchukuo'-Mongolian boundary between Japan and the Soviet Union was re-demarcated. The Nonomhan Border Commission held more than ten meetings in China in November and December 1939, and at Harbin in January 1940. Almost five months later, the line of the frontier at Nomonhan was finally agreed to by Togo and Molotov as a sign of improvement in relations.

4. Soviet-Japanese Trade

Before the Manchurian incident, Soviet exports to Japan exceeded imports. Soviet raw materials such as lumber, fish, oil and so on were exchanged for manufactured goods, ships, chemicals and cement, or for purchasing Japanese machinery. Soviet-Japanese trade was greatly curtailed after Japanese expansion in north Manchuria. After the Sino-Japanese conflict and the conclusion of the Sino-Soviet Non-Aggression Pact, the Soviet Union abstained from giving assistance of any kind to Japan, living up to the letter and spirit of Article XI of the Non-Aggression Treaty.

Soviet trade with Japan fell off considerably, including exports of coal and iron from Japanese concessions in Sakhalin. In 1936 the Soviet Union shipped war materials, largely pig-iron, to Japan, but after 1937 it was recorded that no war materials were exported. Soviet-Japanese trade dwindled almost to zero mark after the payments from the sale of the Chinese Eastern Railway were completed. Nothing had developed by the time actual trade negotiations began in 1940.

After the signing of the Neutrality Pact in April 1941, the first concrete result was the Soviet-Japanese Commercial Convention in June, providing for an exchange of goods to the value of 60,000,000 yen.[13] The pact defined both tariff and commercial procedures between the two nations, and it was the first time these had ever been mentioned, although general principles of commercial relations had been laid out in the 1925 treaty. The new convention called for a one-year barter agreement with plans to expand the shipping service between Vladivostok and Japan.

[12] Quoted in an article, "Soviet Far Eastern Policy", *Pacific Affairs*, September 1940, p. 266.
[13] *New York Times*, June 13, 1941.

5. Fisheries Convention

The grant to Japan of rights to fish in Russian waters was made in the Portsmouth Treaty and recognized in the Peking Convention of 1925. The fisheries convention provided for certain open and certain close areas. In the former, the Japanese were given equal rights to fish or obtain fishing lots with Russians, whereas the latter were granted to the Japanese without auction. The convention, signed on January 23, 1928, was effective for a period of eight years, to be revised or renewed for subsequent periods of twelve years. Controversies often arose over the Japanese demand for more fishing lots and on the exchange rate of the rouble for payment of the leases.

As Japan signed the anti-Comintern pact with Germany, the Soviet Union refused to renew the convention expiring in 1936. An extension for only one year was later allowed. In November 1938 negotiations were again opened. The Japanese asked for a prolongation of a further eight years. The Soviet Government was not inclined to give such favourable terms to Japan on the ground that many outstanding questions, particularly the last payment on the sale of the Chinese Eastern Railway, still remained unsettled.

However, an agreement was finally signed at Moscow in April 1939, extending the duration of the convention to December 21, 1939. Before its expiration, a new temporary agreement, providing for the extension of the existing fishing modus vivendi for another year, that is, to December 31, 1940, was signed. The Soviet Government, in view of the last payment on the railway having been settled, agreed to insert a clause in the new agreement for a long-term fisheries treaty in 1940, and negotiations for such a treaty were to be continued later on.

The rapid expansion of Soviet fishing operations in recent years, as evidenced by the grouping of a number of lots, met with some apprehension from the Japanese. Naturally the Soviet Union was unwilling to permit the Japanese to fish in Soviet waters, their objection being based on treaty obligations.

The extension of the modus vivendi concerning Japanese fisheries in Sakhalin and Kamchatka was signed on January 21, 1941, for another year to December 31, 1941. Even if the Soviet Union had not renewed the fisheries convention after 1941, the economic effect on Japan would not have been great, as it would only have meant a loss of 30,000,000-50,000,000 yen every year, and unemployment of about 20,000 workmen. The fisheries convention was again renewed for another year to the end of 1942 by an agreement concluded between Mr. Sato, new Japanese Ambassador to U.S.S.R. and M. Vyshinsky, Soviet Assistant-Commissar of Foreign Affairs, at Kuibyshev, March 20, 1942.

6. Sakhalin Concessions

After the Japanese intervention in the Russian Far East, they operated oil and coal in northern Sakhalin. Then concessions were granted to the Japanese for a period of forty to fifty years. There were various controversies over the Sakhalin concessions about the labour supply and the general regulations for their operation.

While Japan was at war with China, the Soviet Union presented all kinds of hindrances, making it almost impossible for the Japanese to work either oil or coal in northern Sakhalin. Numerous protests were exchanged between them in the early part of 1939. The Japanese charged the Soviet authorities with obstructing operations, whereas the Soviet Union charged the Japanese with the breach of concession contracts, particularly the violation of Soviet labour regulations.

7. Anti-Comintern Pact

The Italo-German-Japanese Anti-Comintern Pact was signed in November 1937, three days after the opening of the Brussels Conference. The pact was commented on in Moscow as being the formation of a *bloc* of aggressors, with the intention of effecting a new re-division of the world. It was thought that the action, though evidently aimed at the U.S.S.R., was primarily against England, France and the United States.

The tripartite anti-Comintern alliance had in common not only ideological claims, but also specified territorial claims against the Soviet Union by Germany from the west and Japan from the east. But when Germany and Italy reaffirmed their alliance by signing a military pact, Japan hesitated to participate.

The signing of the Soviet-German Pact on August 23, 1939, came as a sudden shock to Japan, making the tripartite anti-Comintern pact almost meaningless. Though the Japanese Government protested to Germany that it was a direct violation of the spirit of the anti-Comintern agreement, they did not intend repudiating the latter.

On September 27, 1940, Japan adhered to the tripartite military alliance with Germany and Italy by signing a new axis pact in Berlin in which mutual assistance was pledged one to the other. The pact certainly caused great concern to the Soviet Union, which was moving towards accommodation with Japan.

Molotov's visit to Berlin in October was responsible for Germany bringing about closer relations between the U.S.S.R. and Japan. The new Japanese Ambassador, Lieutenant-General Yoshitsugu Tatekawa, presented his credentials in Moscow on October 28, 1940, with an earnest hope of concluding a non-aggression pact with the Soviet Union. Simultaneously, the Soviet Union's intention was to stay out of war and remain in strict neutrality.

8. Soviet-Japanese Neutrality Pact

The conclusion of the Soviet-Japanese Neutrality Pact on April 13, 1941, alarmed not only China, but also the world at large. The Soviet recognition of 'Manchukuo', concluded in the Soviet-Japanese Neutrality Pact, was a most regrettable act from China's standpoint. For the Japanese declaration of her recognition of 'The Mongolian People's Republic' was no doubt harmful to the interest of the Chinese people. As a result of this pact, Japan was able to withdraw 100,000 troops from Manchuria to be used against China, and, at the same time, to enhance Japan's diplomatic position.

Soon after the conclusion of the Soviet-Japanese Neutrality Pact, Mr. Shao Li-tze, Chinese Ambassador to Moscow, was informed by the Soviet Government that the pact did not affect China, much less influence Soviet foreign policy towards her. Moscow also assured Chungking that 'Soviet policy towards China has not changed, especially in regard to material aid to China'.[14] Further, the pact never touched upon the question of assistance to China.

The conclusion of a neutrality pact with Japan was for her own safety. The Soviet Union predicted that Germany would make war on her. She was, therefore, just as anxious as Japan to conclude a sort of non-aggression pact to keep the latter out of war in the Far East in case she was attacked by Germany in the west. Events turned out to be as anticipated, for Germany attacked the Soviet

[14] *The United Press*, Chungking, April 16, 1941.

Union with all her might on June 22, 1941, without warning or ultimatum.

The Chinese public then began to realize that the reason for the Soviet Union concluding the neutrality pact was merely a desire to protect herself. She was not in any way endangering China's interests. Bitter criticism among the Chinese gave way to whole-hearted sympathy towards the Soviet Union.

During the first half of the year 1941, the Soviet Union was kept busy in resisting Germany. It was only natural that Soviet aid to China was greatly reduced and even temporarily suspended on account of the serious pressure encountered on the whole Soviet front. In spite of this, relations between China and the Soviet Union remained cordial and friendly. Though the seat of the Soviet Government was temporarily removed to Kuibyshev in October 1941, co-operation among the American, British, Soviet and Chinese people was intensified.

9. Denunciation of Soviet-Japanese Neutrality Pact

The Soviet Japanese Neutrality Pact, concluded by Mesuoka, Japan's Foreign Minister, on his visit to Moscow, was declared null and void by the Soviet Government on April 5, 1945. Molotov received the Japanese Ambassador, Mr. Sato, that very afternoon, making the following statement in the name of the Soviet Government:

'The Pact of Neutrality between the Soviet Union and Japan was concluded on April 13, 1941—that is before the attack by Germany on the U.S.S.R. and before the outbreak of war between Japan on the one hand and Great Britain and the United States of America on the other.

'Since that time, the situation has radically changed. Germany attacked the U.S.S.R., and Japan—Germany's ally—helped the latter in her war against the U.S.S.R.

'In addition, Japan is fighting against the United States of America and Great Britain, which are the allies of the Soviet Union. In such a situation, the Pact of Neutrality between Japan and the U.S.S.R. has lost its meaning, and the continuance of this pact has become impossible.

'On the strength of the aforesaid, and in accordance with Article 3 of the pact mentioned, which envisages the right of denunciation one year before the expiration of the five-year period of validity of the pact, the Soviet Government by the present statement announces to the Japanese Government its desire to denounce the pact of April 13, 1941.'[15]

When it was made known, Dr. Wang Shih-chieh, Minister of Information, stated that, from the point of view of morale, this would prove a serious blow to Japan, hastening the complete collapse of the Japanese forces and removing all barriers between the Soviet Union and China. It was generally believed, at the same time, that the Soviet Union would precipitate war with Japan in the Far East if requested by the San Francisco Conference of the United Nations.

It is interesting to note that, only two days prior to the abolition of the Soviet-Japanese Neutrality Pact, the Soviet Government appointed A. A. Petrov as Soviet Ambassador to China, a post which had been vacant for some time after the departure of A. S. Paniush-kin, the former Soviet Ambassador. This was a sign of a new turning-point in Sino-Soviet relations. Owing to the existence of the Soviet-Japanese Neutrality Pact, China and the Soviet Union could not come together at various meetings of the Four Powers. That is why the Chinese and Soviet delegates did not sit together at Dumbarton Oaks, and why they were not represented simultaneously at any international conference prior to the denunciation of the Neutrality Pact. After its denunciation, the Ambassadors of the two countries in Washington held conferences together, which action won the praise of the United Nations and gave satisfaction to the Chinese public.

On August 8, 1945, the Soviet Foreign Commissar, Molotov, handed the following statement to the Japanese Ambassador, Sato, for transmission to his government:

'After the defeat and capitulation of Hitlerite Germany, Japan remains the only great Power which still stands for the continuation of the war.

'The demand of the three Powers, the United States, Great Britain and China, of July 26 for the unconditional surrender of the Japanese armed forces was rejected by Japan. Thus the proposal made by the Japanese Government to the Soviet Union for mediation in the Far East has lost all foundation.

[15] *New York Herald Tribune,* April 6, 1945.

'Taking into account the refusal of Japan to capitulate, the Allies approached the Soviet Government with a proposal to join the war against Japanese aggression and thus shorten the duration of the war, reduce the number of casualties and contribute towards the most speedy restoration of peace.

'True to its obligation as an Ally, the Soviet Government has accepted the proposal of the Allies and has joined in the declaration of the Allied Powers of July 26.

'The Soviet Government considers that this policy is the only means able to bring peace nearer, to free the people from further sacrifice and suffering and to give the Japanese people the opportunity of avoiding the danger of destruction suffered by Germany after her refusal to accept unconditional surrender.

'In view of the above, the Soviet Government declares that from to-morrow, that is from August 9, the Soviet Union will consider herself in a state of war against Japan.'[16]

10. Occupation of the Kuriles and Southern Sakhalin

The Soviet Union entered the war against Japan on August 9, a few days before Japan's surrender. In his V-J Day broadcast, Stalin told his people that the Soviet Union would regain southern Sakhalin and the Kuriles, lost to Japan in 1904. James F. Byrnes, the U.S. Secretary of State told newsmen at a Press conference on September 4 that the United States was not opposed to the presence of Russians on the Kuriles and southern Sakhalin, and the matter would have to be settled some time in the future. Early in 1946 Japanese reports from the Kuriles and southern Sakhalin stated that Russian occupation troops seemed to contemplate a permanent stay, because they brought in their families with them. Dean Acheson, then the U.S. Under Secretary of State, said on January 22 that the Russian occupation was merely temporary, whereas the Tass News Agency in Moscow announced on January 25 that it had been authorized to disclose that the Yalta Agreement clearly stated that after the war was over that Kuriles would be handed over to the Soviet Union and that southern Sakhalin and its adjacent islands would be also returned.

Secretary Byrnes, answering questions of newspapermen, disclosed that the military Chiefs of Staff had full knowledge of it at the time Russia entered the war, and said he saw no reason why the agree-

[16] *Information Bulletin,* August 11, 1945.

ment should not be published now. *Izvestia*, the Soviet official paper, revealed after the publication of the Yalta Agreement that it should convince the world ' once again with what scruples and accuracy the U.S.S.R. fulfils her treaties and agreements '. The Japanese Foreign Office, however, stated that Japan was not bound by the Yalta Agreement, and could therefore make her claim on her sovereignty over the Kurile islands and southern Sakhalin despite Soviet intentions of making them part of Soviet territory.[17]

[17] *The Times*, London, December 22, 1949.

Chapter XIX

SINO-SOVIET TREATY OF FRIENDSHIP AND ALLIANCE, AUGUST 14, 1945

SINO-SOVIET relations remained cordial and firm throughout the troublous time when China was at war with Japan. Soviet aid to China was very great, particularly at the outset of the Sino-Japanese conflict, when China was fighting alone. When, however, the Soviet Union was attacked by Germany, she had to concentrate all her forces against that formidable foe, leaving hardly any time or energy to deal with the situation in the Far East. Hence Sino-Soviet relations after June 1941 were uneventful. When the European War ended in May 1945, the Japanese forces seemed still strong enough to hold out the prospect of lasting a year or two before being subdued.

The Yalta Secret Agreement was signed on February 11, 1945, between Roosevelt, Churchill and Stalin to draw the Soviet Union into war with Japan. The agreement was only revealed a year later. Shortly after, the famous Sino-Soviet Treaty of Friendship and Alliance was signed in Moscow by representatives of the two countries, truly an epoch-making event in the Far East.

1. T. V. Soong's Visit to Moscow

During the San Francisco Conference, the Chinese and Soviet delegates seemed to have many views in common, and T. V. Soong, Chinese Premier and Foreign Minister, did not deny the current rumour that he meant to visit Moscow immediately after the conference. *Ta Kung Pao*, the leading newspaper in Chungking at the time, suggested in an editorial that a supreme measure of autonomy should be accorded to Outer Mongolia as well as to the small races in Sinkiang. Alternatively Outer Mongolia might be recognized as an independent State. Simultaneously a Sino-Soviet Pact should be concluded on a friendly basis. Just as the Rush-Bagot Agreement between America and Canada had regulated frontier arrangements, so should the attempt be made to work out a Sino-Soviet Non-Garrisoned Frontier Pact. An editorial of the *New York Herald Tribune* stressed the significance of T. V. Soong's visit to Moscow. He was going to discuss Sino-Soviet relations and frontier problems in north China with the Soviet authorities, and this would affect the future peace of Asia.

T. V. Soong's retinue included Shen Hung-leh, Minister of Agriculture and Forestry; Chien Chong-chow, Vice-Chairman of the National Resource Commission; Chang Fu-yun, Director-General of the Customs; Colonel Chiang Ching-kuo, son of Generalissimo Chiang Kai-shek; Victor Hoo, Vice-Minister of Foreign Affairs; Liu Chieh, Minister-Counsellor of the Chinese Embassy in Washington; Pu Tao-min, Director of the Western Asia Department, Foreign Office; and Liu Tze-yung, Commissioner of Foreign Affairs for Sinkiang province. Soong left Chungking on his way to Moscow on June 27, and arrived there on the 30th. Molotov greeted the party at the military aerodrome. Soong was immediately received by Stalin with great cordiality, and Fu Ping-chang, the Chinese Ambassador to Moscow, and A. A. Petrov, the Soviet Ambassador to China, who had come along with T. V. Soong, were all present. Soong declared : ' I have full confidence in Sino-Soviet cordiality and friendship which should be a direct contribution to the establishment of peace.' On July 1, Soong and his party were entertained by Molotov in the ' Bolshoi Theatre', and the Chinese national anthem was sung in his honour. Next day Soong was invited by Molotov to the Kremlin.

T. V. Soong's second interview with Stalin took place on July 3 at 8 p.m., and lasted quite a long time. On July 4, Kalinin, Chairman of the Supreme Soviet of the U.S.S.R., received Soong and Hoo, the last mentioned acting as interpreter. The third interview with Stalin was on the 7th, and that same day Soong had an interview with Harriman, American Ambassador to Moscow. On the 10th a fourth interview was granted by Stalin where T. V. Soong, Fu Ping-chang, Victor Hoo and Chiang Ching-kuo were in attendance. The meeting lasted two hours and rapid progress was made. Though the Chinese Delegation held it to be strictly confidential, the atmosphere of the meeting was cheerful and friendly. The fifth interview was held on the 12th. As it was known to be the last conference, the session was a long one and lasted from 11 p.m. until early next morning. The Chinese participants were Soong, Fu, Hu and Chiang, while the Soviet Government was represented by Stalin, Molotov, Losovsky (Deputy People's Commissar of Foreign Affairs) and Petrov. It was learned that, throughout the interview, Soong was anxious to keep everything secret. Not the slightest bit of news leaked out even among his closest associates, and this caused them to be much dissatisfied. On the Soviet side, Stalin was sole judge, and whenever any concession had to be made his word was final.

On the evening of the 13th, Stalin entertained Soong and his party in the Kremlin. Owing to the departure of Stalin and Molotov for the Three Power Conference in Berlin, a statement was made public by the two parties declaring the discussion to have been successful and full of mutual understanding. Soong and his party left Moscow for Chungking on the 14th after a stay of twelve days. He kept in constant touch with Sir Archibald Clark Kerr and Mr. Averill Harriman, the British and American Ambassadors at Moscow, during the conference. He was accompanied by Petrov on his homeward journey, and he reiterated his belief that the new Sino-Soviet Agreement in the making would be the corner-stone of everlasting peace in the Far East.

It is interesting to note that Soong came by a specially chartered American plane with American pilots and crew, and the whole trip from Chungking to Moscow took only two and a half days, stops being made at Calcutta and Teheran. When interviewing Stalin, Soong spoke English with the help of an English interpreter.

2. Soong's Second Visit to Moscow, Accompanied by Wang Shih-chieh, Newly Appointed Foreign Minister

Soong visited Moscow again in August. He, after having resigned his concurrent post as the Foreign Minister, left Chungking on the 5th accompanied by the newly appointed Foreign Minister, Dr. Wang Shih-chieh. The retinue was the same as on the last trip, with the addition of General Hsiung Shih-hui, High Commissioner of the North-Eastern Provinces. The party arrived at Moscow on the 7th together with Petrov, the Soviet Ambassador to China. Soong called on Stalin that same evening, and they continued the conversation the following day. Each meeting lasted almost two hours. Molotov and Wang, Soviet Foreign Commissar and Chinese Foreign Minister respectively, met the same day. In the evening, Molotov held a Press Conference, stating the Soviet Government had handed a declaration to Sato, the Japanese Ambassador, and had kept British,

American and Chinese Ambassadors fully informed. He even went so far as to say that war would soon come between the Soviet Union and Japan, and that a new treaty with China would be concluded.

Dr. K. C. Wu, Vice-Minister of the Foreign Ministry in Chungking, called on the *chargé d'affaires* in the Soviet Embassy and expressed his gratification at the Soviet's declaration of war against Japan. On the 13th a secret conference was held between Soong and Molotov, and in the evening Stalin gave a farewell dinner in honour of Soong and Wang. Stalin again received Soong and Wang on the 14th for the third time, and on the same day Moscow broadcast that the Sino-Soviet Treaty of Friendship and Alliance had been concluded, and that it would be made public as soon as it had been ratified by the two countries concerned. Soong left Moscow the same day via Washington on his way home while Wang and the party left Moscow on the 15th and arrived in Chungking on the 20th.

3. Signing of Sino-Soviet Treaty

The Sino-Soviet Treaty of Friendship and Alliance was signed by Molotov and Wang Shih-chieh representing their respective countries in the Kremlin on August 14, 1945. During the signing of the treaty, Stalin stood behind Molotov to watch him sign, while Soong stood beside Wang. The whole treaty, together with other related documents, will be found in Appendix C.

To hasten the ratification of the newly concluded Sino-Soviet Treaty, the Legislative Yuan in Chungking held an extraordinary meeting at the Headquarters of the Nationalist Government on August 24. Dr. Sun Fo, President of the Legislative Yuan, presided over the discussion and told the seventy-two members present that the Supreme National Defence Council had approved the treaty and had asked the members to discuss it. Dr. Wang Shih-chieh explained points raised by the members of the Legislative Yuan concerning the treaty. Sun Fo stressed that the conclusion of the Sino-Soviet Treaty had opened the way for the making of new treaties with other nations and laid the foundation of a new era of friendly relations between the two countries. After two hours of deliberation and debate, the Sino-Soviet Treaty of Friendship and Alliance was unanimously approved by the Legislative Yuan, though some of the members were rather reluctant. But they knew that there was no use in opposition since the treaty had already been approved by the Supreme National Defence Council.

While addressing the joint meeting of the Supreme National Defence Council and the Central Executive Committee of the Kuomintang on August 23, General Chiang Kai-shek made the following remarks:

> 'The re-establishment of China's territorial and administrative integrity in the Three North-Eastern Provinces, the recovery of Formosa and the Pescadores and the restoration of the independence of Korea are the most important aims of the national revolution. Failure to realize these aims will mean that our national independence and freedom will never be restored and the goal of our armed resistance never be reached.'

Stressing the fact that the Principle of Nationalism, as expounded by Dr. Sun Yat-sen, aims at the safeguarding of world peace and national stability, Chiang said that Outer Mongolia should be granted independence and Tibet autonomy. Outer Mongolia, owing to its secludedness, he explained, is different from other outlying provinces, and has long been regarded as a 'brother State'. In fact, since the setting up of the Peking Government, Outer Mongolia has become an independent entity. In view of this, Outer Mongolia should be formally granted independence, so that relations between these two peoples could become all the more cordial and friendly. As for Tibet, it was decided at the Sixth National Kuomintang Congress to grant her autonomy. Should the Tibetan people now make known their aspiration for independence, the government would not hesitate to accord them a full autonomous status. In the enforcement of the Principle of Nationalism, Chiang continued, the Chinese Government and people must give every possible assistance to other nations which possess self-government and the spirit of independence in attaining their ends. In this connection he pointed out that Burma, Thailand and Indio-China should also receive help in their struggle for independence in accordance with the letter and spirit of the Atlantic Charter and the Three People's Principles.

After the Sino-Soviet Treaty had been approved by the Legislative Yuan, the Nationalist Government ratified the treaty and related documents on August 25 and authorized the publication of their full texts. The Soviet Government also ratified the treaty on August 25.

4. Comments on Sino-Soviet Treaty

Hailing the signing of the Sino-Soviet Treaty as an epoch-making event, the Chinese people were very much puzzled that the Sino-Soviet Treaty which was signed on August 14 was followed next day (August 15) by President Truman's announcing the unconditional surrender of Japan. Two atomic bombs had been dropped on Hiroshima and Nagasaki in Japanese territory on August 6 and 9 respectively, causing great terror and destroying thousands of lives, an event unprecedented in history. The Soviet Government declared war on Japan on August 8, and the world received news of Japan's surrender on August 10th. Yet China had to sign the Sino-Soviet Treaty notwithstanding that the war was wellnigh over.

It is true the Soviet Union would, in any case, have been in a position to invade Manchuria whether the Chinese signed the treaty or not. Without a treaty, the Soviet Union could only have invaded Manchuria on its own initiative, whereas, with a treaty, the Soviets were invited by the Chinese Government to participate in bringing about the subsequent declaraton of 'war booty' on Japanese assets in Manchuria. Knowing the war was already at an end, the Chinese Foreign Minister had to sign the treaty without any hesitation simply because the Yalta Secret Agreement was in existence wherein it was clearly stated that Soviet claims should be unquestionably fulfilled after Japan's defeat.

There was also some illusion concerning General Chiang Kai-shek's speech after signing the treaty. Instead of making it public that China was compelled to sign, he made out that it was the aim of the late Dr. Sun Yat-sen, in accord with the Principle of Nationalism, that Outer Mongolia should be granted independence. Not only that, he even spoke of Tibet's autonomy. This seemed a most inappropriate time to refer to such a thing as it might mislead other races in the border province. Sun Fo said that 'the great significance of the treaty lies in its being a guarantee for a durable peace in the Far East. The treaty ensures China's immunity from any future Japanese attempt at aggression for thirty years, giving China sufficient time to complete her plans of reconstruction and industrialization and raising herself to the position of a really powerful nation.' He emphasized that the stipulation in the treaty that any moral or material assistance which might be rendered to China by the Soviet Union would be rendered to the Central Government as the National Government of China, and that the Soviet Union would not interfere in the internal affairs of China was the greatest contribution to Chinese unity.[1]

Wang Shih-chieh said to the Pressmen: 'What makes me particularly happy is that, in the lengthy discussions of so many problems, there was not a single moment in which either one of the two sides did not try to understand sympathetically the viewpoints of the other. This was because there is a desire, equally strong on both sides, for the closest co-operation, and an enduring mutual regard. . . . As Generalissimo Stalin has assured me, these agreements will benefit not only China and Russia, but all Asia and the world at large.'[2]

World diplomats who were responsible for working out the future of Asia could breathe a sigh of relief at the Sino-Soviet understanding. The first official reaction came from James Byrnes, the then Secretary of State for the U.S.A., who issued a formal statement saying: 'I believe that the new treaty between China and Soviet Russia and the accompanying agreements constitute an important step forward in the relations between China and Russia. We were kept informed of the progress of the deliberations in Moscow, and we welcome this development as a practical example of continuing unity and mutual helpfulness which should characterize the acts of the members of the United Nations in peace as well as in war.'[3]

The Sino-Soviet Treaty was based on a give-and-take policy. The terms which seemed favourable to the Soviet Union were:

1. China recognized the independence of Outer Mongolia.
2. Joint management of the Chinese Changchun Railway for thirty years, upon which the directorship would be awarded to a Soviet citizen.
3. China to make Dairen a free port and its harbour-master to be a Soviet citizen.
4. China to lease to the U.S.S.R., free of charge, one half of all port installations and equipment for a term of thirty years.
5. China to agree to the joint use of Port Arthur as a naval base.
6. China to entrust to the U.S.S.R. the defence of the naval base where the U.S.S.R. has the right to maintain its army, navy and air forces.

---

[1] *National Herald*, Chungking, August 27, 1945.
[2] ibid., August 30, 1945.
[3] Central News Agency, Washington, August 27, 1945.

On the other hand, the terms which seemed favourable to China were:

1. Non-interference in China's internal affairs.
2. The U.S.S.R. to agree to give its military supplies and other material resources entirely to the National Government as the Central Government of China.
3. The U.S.S.R. to re-affirm its respect for China's full sovereignty over the Three Eastern Provinces, and to recognize their territorial and administrative integrity.
4. The U.S.S.R. to confirm its intention not to interfere with the internal affairs of Sinkiang.
5. The Chinese Changchun Railway, with all its properties, to be transferred, without compensation, to China after the expiration of thirty years.
6. The withdrawal of Soviet troops from Manchuria within three months of Japan's capitulation.

From the above, it will be noted that China yielded much more than she gained. Recognition of the territorial and administrative integrity of the Three Eastern Provinces and non-interference with China's internal affairs should have been a matter of course and hardly worth mentioning. The reason China paid such a high price was that she wished to win the friendship of the Soviet Union. Should outstanding problems have remained unsolved, then Sino-Soviet relations would have ceased to be cordial and friendly. As far as China was concerned, should she trust the Soviet Union as her permanent friend, such surrender might not mean much, though it should be remarked that the giving of independence to Outer Mongolia had practically taken away the national boundary, thus creating a direct menace to Inner Mongolia. One particular clause which occurred in the exchange of notes should be noted: 'The Chinese Government will recognize the independence of Outer Mongolia with the existing boundary as its boundary.' This statement is far from clear and will, probably, give cause for future dispute.

On the other hand, should China deem the Soviet Union her enemy, then yielding or non-yielding would not prevent the Soviet Union from coveting, and, in any case, China would have had no guarantee of security. As to the Soviet, should she consider China her friend and ally, the possession of these privileges or not would

have been of little importance compared with the inestimable blessing of a real friendship with China.

In conclusion, after the signing of the Sino-Soviet Treaty, the
Soviet position in Outer Mongolia became unquestionably secure.
Further, the Soviet Union gained a dominant position in Manchuria,
particularly in the Liaotung Peninsula, where she was superior in
the military sense.

5. Release of Yalta Secret Agreement

Long before the Yalta Conference, or even earlier than the
Teheran one, the American Government was of the opinion that,
since the post-war position of the Soviet Union in Europe would be
a dominant one, she should be given every assistance, and every effort
should be made to win her friendship. At the same time, they had
to consider relationship with the Soviets for carrying on the war
in the Pacific. If only the Soviets would be willing to join the Allies
in the war against Japan, this would bring it to a rapid end and
would save thousands of lives and much material destruction. On
the other hand, if the war in the Pacific had to be prosecuted without
the aid of the Soviet Union, then untold difficulties would arise, as
well as a serious prolongation of hostilities.

This state of affairs led to Roosevelt's talks with Stalin, first at
Teheran and much later at Yalta. At the Teheran Conference, it
was reported that Stalin expressed the opinion that Anglo-American
successes in the Pacific would not all be welcomed by the Soviet
Government. He then explained that the heavy encounters with
Germany on the western frontier prevented his joining in the
Pacific War against Japan as the Siberian forces were in sore need
of reinforcements. This was the first time that Roosevelt and
Churchill heard Stalin speak disparagingly of Japan. On Churchill
putting a question regarding Soviet future territorial interests, Stalin
replied: 'There is no need to speak at the present time about Soviet
desires, but when the time comes, we will speak.'[4]

During the friendly talk between the Big Three at the Teheran
Conference, it was reported that Churchill was the first to bring
up the question since he thought that the Soviets might be aiming
at warm-water ports. Thereupon Roosevelt mentioned the possibility
of their being given access to the port of Dairen in Manchuria.

[4] Sherwood, Robert E., *The White House Papers of Harry L. Hopkins*, Vol II,
p. 784.

Stalin forthwith made the point that the Chinese might be very much against such a proposal, to which Roosevelt retorted that they would agree if Dairen became a free port under international control, as he had, a few days before, brought up the question with Generalissimo Chiang Kai-shek in Cairo.

When a joint message was sent by Roosevelt and Churchill to Chiang as to what was going on at the Teheran Conference, nothing was said of Stalin's own statement about entering the war against Japan. This is believed to have been deliberately omitted for fear that such monstrous news might leak out in Chungking and cause untold damage to the Allies.

It was not long before Roosevelt sent a cable to Stalin asking for another conference after the former's national election. Nothing could be better than to quote the following passage from Hopkins's own pen on the genesis of the Yalta Conference:

'As early as the middle of September 1944, the President was contemplating a second conference with Stalin and Churchill. There were a variety of pressing problems which the President believed warranted a conference, and both Churchill and Stalin were agreeable to the conference. Churchill was, indeed, insistent on it. The reasons were obvious. . . . Although at Teheran Stalin had made a firm commitment in so far as Soviet participation in the war against Japan was concerned, that needed to be clarified as to precise dates and the extent of Soviet participation. . . . Our whole policy towards the Far East needed a thoroughgoing understanding, particularly so far as the Soviet Union was concerned. We knew from Teheran that the Russians wanted certain things as a condition to their declaring war on Japan, or, at any rate, they said they wanted them, as it was extremely important for the U.S. in particular, in view of our historic relationship with China, to protect China's interests in these negotiations. . . . Things regarding the Far East had to be settled, otherwise we might find the three Allies going their separate ways. . . . I told the President as soon as the discussion started that there was not a chance of getting Stalin out of Russia at this time . . . we might as well make up our minds first at least to go to some convenient point in Russia—preferably in the Crimea. The President was not opposed to this . . . he postponed all discussion of the place until after the election was over. . . . The President got a message from Stalin saying he understood the President was willing to go to the

Crimea, and suggesting Yalta as a desirable place. . . . All of the President's close advisers were opposed to his going to Russia. . . . When they descended on the President to urge him not to go, the President wavered again. . . . I am sure the President would wind up by going to the Crimea . . . the election being over, he would no longer be disturbed about it for political reasons.'[5]

Roosevelt sailed by S.S. *Quincy* and arrived in the Grand Harbour of Valetta on February 2, 1945. The rest of his journey was made by air. After his arrival at Yalta, the first meeting was held in the President's study at Livadia, and later they moved down to the Grand Ballroom for the formal conference.

It was at the Teheran Conference that Roosevelt had already 'agreed the most if not all of the Soviet claims, the restoration of possessions and privileges taken by the Japanese from the Russians in the war of 1904'.[6] The Yalta Conference merely gave it final shape to which Stalin said bluntly that the agreement must be conducted in utmost secrecy. Stalin told Roosevelt that twenty-five divisions needed transferring across Siberia, and the time needed would be three or four months. Roosevelt said that when this movement of troops had been completed, he would send an officer to Chungking via Moscow to inform Chiang of the existence of the agreement. Stalin then insisted that this agreement must be put in writing containing the statement:

'The heads of the three Great Powers have agreed that these claims of the Soviet Union shall be unquestionably fulfilled after Japan has been defeated.'

Thus the Yalta Secret Agreement was duly made and signed by Roosevelt, Churchill and Stalin on February 11, 1945, the text of which is shown in Appendix C. At the time, China knew nothing about it, and the Chinese public were very much puzzled as to why T. V. Soong took all the trouble to go to Moscow twice for the signing of the rather humiliating treaty known as the Sino-Soviet Treaty of Friendship and Alliance. It was not till February 11, 1946, that the secret agreement was made public simultaneously in Washington, London and Moscow, exactly one year after.

When the news reached China, it caused a shock to the Chinese

[5] Sherwood, op. cit., Vol. II, p. 835.
[6] ibid., p. 841.

public, giving rise to comments and reactions on all sides. The spokesman for the Chinese Foreign Office, Mr. Ho Feng-shan, made the following statement:

> 'As China is not a party, she was and is not bound by it in this connection, but the Sino-Soviet Agreement of August 14, 1945, is binding on both Russia and China.'[7]

The Yalta Secret Treaty was made public only ten days after an agreement reached by the Political Consultative Conference on January 31, 1946, in Chungking representing various parties. General Chiang Kai-shek had ended up with a very determined speech. Then, suddenly the Yalta Secret Treaty was revealed. This gave an opportunity for anti-Communist elements to start a students' demonstration against the Soviet Union as well as the Chinese Communist Party. Offices of a Communist organ, *Hsing Hwa Daily Herald*, and the Democratic Press owned by the China Democratic League, were wrecked by the demonstrators, and this showed the hatred between the Kuomintang and Communist Parties. Without the revelation of the Yalta Secret Treaty, the political development in China might have been quite different. To pacify public sentiment, Chiang declared in a memorial service that the Sino-Soviet Treaty of Friendship and Alliance must be respected, and urged the people to exercise greater control and not to go beyond the limits of law.

The Yalta Agreement gave the Soviet Union more gains for less effort than any similar pact of modern times. Stalin expressed at Yalta the hope that the U.S.S.R. would enter the war against Japan within two or three months after Germany had surrendered. The reason for setting this time-table was that twenty-five divisions had to be transported across Siberia to the Far East, and this would take time. The Soviet Union did declare war on Japan, August 8, 1946, exactly three months after Germany's capitulation on May 7 of that year. Soviet forces entered Manchuria on August 9, when Japan was preparing to surrender. Soviet troops took part in the Far East War exactly six days, and had met with almost no resistance when the Japanese surrendered on August 14.

In return, the Yalta Agreement gave the Soviet Union absolute possession of the Japanese Kurile Islands, stretching in a long arc from the Japanese home island of Hokkaido north to the Soviet Kamchatka Peninsula. Moreover, the Yalta Agreement restored to

[7] Press Conference in Chungking, February 20, 1946.

Russia all the territory and rights she had lost to Japan as a result of the Russo-Japanese war in 1904. In addition, Outer Mongolia was recognized as an independent Republic. So she gained at Yalta more than she lost in the Russo-Japanese War.

The Yalta Agreement had been kept 'top secret' after its signing because the Big Three thought that if the news reached Chungking it would cause tremendous damage to the Allies. Since the publication of the Agreement, there has been considerable criticism both in China and abroad, and the question has been asked why Roosevelt agreed to its terms. Those who were close to the late President and knew his mind, consider his acquiescence quite reasonable. They were of the opinion that it was the only course he could have taken through the advice of the experts in his government, both military and diplomatic. For Roosevelt thought he must have Russian aid in order to defeat Japan, and no cheaper price could be obtained than that contained in the Yalta Agreement. It was generally believed that, even though beaten in their own home islands, the Japanese would still be able to carry on the fighting in Manchuria for many months and presumably years to come. They had large ammunition dumps, and the fighting spirit of the Kwangtung Army in Manchuria was very strong. Roosevelt was convinced that, without a large-scale Russian attack on the rear, it was almost impossible to drive the enemy out of Manchuria. The war would then drag on for years.

It was estimated by General George C. Marshall, then Chief of Staff, that the United States would need to send about a million men to Manchuria, an army almost certain to suffer extremely heavy casualties, to bring the Japanese to their knees, had not the Russians joined in the Pacific War. Before the President made his decision, not one among his advisers but thought that Russian aid was necessary to defeat the Japanese in Manchuria. Two important factors could not be foreseen. First the perfecting of the atomic bomb, and second the utilization of the Japanese Emperor to bring about total surrender. During the Yalta discussion, the atomic bomb was still in the experimental stage, and Roosevelt had no idea when the new weapon would be available. It was not until after a successful test in New Mexico on July 10, 1945, that the scientists working on the project knew for certain that a mightily destructive weapon was ready for use. Fearing that Russia's price for entering the Pacific War might rise if it became evident that the Japanese were going to resist to the end, Roosevelt took no chances, but signed the Yalta

Agreement. Those who feared that the Japanese would continue to fight on the continent even after being beaten on their home islands, failed to take into account that the war could be brought to a quick end by using the Emperor to facilitate surrender and subsequent control of Japan.

Another important factor was the state of health of the late President when he undertook the tedious journey to the Crimea. 'A photograph had been taken in July before his departure for the Pacific tour, in which he appeared haggard, glassy-eyed and querulous.' He had to wear leg braces for his nation-wide broadcast from Seattle. When Robert E. Sherwood saw Roosevelt eight months after, he was shocked by the almost ravaged appearance of his face. When Admiral King went aboard to greet the arrival of the United States President in the Grand Harbour of Valetta on February 2, he was alarmed at his condition, as it was less than two weeks since he had seen him at the Inauguration.[8]

Only after a meeting lasting seven days, covering a wide range of grave matters, did Roosevelt make sundry concessions. He accepted the Russian veto in the Security Council of the United Nations, and he agreed to the Soviet Union having two additional votes in the General Assembly. Had he not been tired out and anxious to end the negotiations, he certainly would not have given in so meekly. It was the opinion of Roosevelt that, when the time came, he would be able to explain and straighten out the whole matter with Chiang, but, alas, this hope died with him.

6. Controversies on Taking Over Manchuria

The withdrawal of Soviet troops after Japan's defeat was to commence within three weeks and end within three months. This agreement had been initialled by both parties in the minutes, though it was not contained in the agreement. When the Soviets declared war on Japan and invaded Manchuria on August 8, they met with hardly any resistance, and there was only a few days fighting before Japan gave in. Then took place the systematic confiscation and selective removal of industrial machinery in Manchuria by Soviet forces, declared to be war booty and sorely needed to replace the enormous damage caused by the German invasion. It was intended to complete the removal by December 3, the date set for the withdrawal of Soviet forces from Manchuria. The Russians took all function-

[8] Sherwood, op. cit., p. 841.

ing power-generating and transforming equipment, electric motors, experimental plans, laboratories and hospitals. Of machine tools, they took the newest and the best. After removal, Chinese mobs took the opportunity of robbing and pillaging in the extreme.

A. Question of Withdrawal of Soviet Troops

On October 1, 1935, A. A. Petrov, the Soviet Ambassador to China, handed a memoir to T. V. Soong, President of the Executive Yuan, to the following effect:

1. The Soviet military authorities had commenced to withdraw Soviet troops from Manchuria.

2. The main Soviet forces would start their withdrawal in the latter part of October, and it would be completed by the end of November.

3. The Soviet Government had appointed Marshal Malinovsky as Envoy Plenipotentiary to take up discussions concerning the withdrawal of Soviet troops from Manchuria.

The Ministry for Foreign Affairs then sent a despatch to the Soviet Embassy informing them that thirteen divisions of the Chinese army would sail from Kowloon by American steamers to Dairen and land there. The Soviet Embassy, however, considered the sending of Chinese troops to Manchuria through the port of Dairen a violation of the Sino-Soviet Treaty, and therefore expressed their opposition. Dr. Wang Shih-chieh, the then Foreign Minister, made the following declaration to the Soviet Ambassador on October 9:

' The Chinese Government will fulfil its obligations as stipulated in the treaty, but the port of Dairen is Chinese territory which should be strictly under Chinese control with restrictions. The Chinese Government cannot view the sending of her troops to Manchuria via Dairen as a violation of the treaty.

' The aim of sending troops to Manchuria is to maintain order and suppress any reaction. Such work is now undertaken by the Soviet troops, but as soon as withdrawal takes place, then responsibility will rest on the Chinese army.'

The Soviet reply, however, stated that, according to the Sino-Soviet Treaty, Dairen was a commercial port for use in transporting goods, not troops. The landing of troops at Dairen would constitute a violation of the treaty, and the Soviet Government would be very much opposed to it.

Thus the negotiations were at an impasse until Generalissimo Chiang Kai-shek received the Soviet Ambassador in person. He expressed his eager desire to send troops to Manchuria via Dairen, and said that he expected the Soviet Government to give port facilities for the transport of such troops. He asked the Ambassador to forward a message to Generalissimo Stalin stating that owing to the friendship that existed between the two countries, it was hoped the Soviet Government would render such assistance irrespective of Dairen being Chinese territory as safeguarded by the treaty. If the Chinese troops could not land at Dairen, then it would be impossible to despatch troops to Manchuria.

After a few days the Soviet Ambassador forwarded a reply from the Soviet Government stating that, according to the treaty, Dairen was a commercial port, and they could not agree to the landing of troops in Dairen. It would be regrettable to violate the treaty, and Generalissimo Stalin held the same view.

The great majority of the officials sent to Changchun in the autumn of 1945 to commence taking over Manchuria were compelled to return to Peiping. The situation seemed to improve following negotiations with the Soviet authorities, and Chinese officials again went to Changchun. The municipal governments of Changchun, Harbin and Mukden and a few provincial ones were taken over. Chinese national troops were flown to Changchun, and other Chinese troops also succeeded in marching from Shanghaikwan to Mukden. However, the taking over of industrial enterprises had hardly started.

The Chinese Government, therefore, had to abandon the plan of sending troops to Dairen. As a result of negotiations between General Hsiung Shih-hui, High Commissioner of the North-Eastern Provinces, and Marshal Malinovsky in Manchuria, it was agreed that China would send troops to Yingkao and Hulutao. All transport would be supplied by the United States, and the landing troops would be entirely Chinese. In view of the existence of Japanese troops and police forces from 'Manchukuo' in Manchuria, the Chinese Government was very anxious to maintain order by sending troops there during the taking over of the administration.

At this juncture, the Chinese Communist army had already taken Yingkao, and so it was out of the question to land there. The next idea was to send troops to Mukden and Changchun by air, and the Soviet authorities were asked to disarm the unrecognized forces in and around the respective aerodromes and to give due protection to the staffs sent beforehand. In case the Peiping-Mukden Railway was required for transporting troops, the Soviet authorities were asked to give all possible facilities. These proposals were put forward by the Foreign Ministry, and a postponement of one more month until January 3, 1946, for the completion of the withdrawal was requested.

The Soviet Government accepted China's request for one month's postponement, and again the Chinese Government confirmed the decision made in Changchun by both parties that the Soviet troops should make a complete withdrawal not later than February 1, 1946.

When the time for withdrawal expired, it was learned that the Soviet troops had not been entirely withdrawn. The Foreign Ministry was reported to have informed the Soviet Embassy that during the withdrawal in some districts in Manchuria, the Chinese authorities were not informed, and it asked later for the dates of withdrawal to be notified in every district so that peace and order should be maintained.

It was further proposed by the Soviet Embassy that complete withdrawal should be postponed to the end of April in view of the wintry weather which produced all kinds of hindrance and hardship for the withdrawing troops. April would be definitely better to effect a withdrawal, and to this the Foreign Ministry agreed. Ultimately the total withdrawal of Soviet troops from Manchuria was completed on May 3, 1946.

B. Question of Taking Over Dairen and Port Arthur

On March 7, 1947, the Soviet Ambassador addressed a memorandum, in person, to the Foreign Ministry asking the Chinese Government to establish a civil administration in the naval base of Port Arthur and the port of Dairen in accordance with the Sino-Soviet Treaty. The memorandum urged the Chinese Government to take effective measures for the Chinese Changchun Railway to be jointly owned by the two countries.

Dr. Wang Shih-chieh, the Foreign Minister, however, told the Soviet Ambassador that the reason why the Chinese Government could not take over Dairen and establish a civil administration both in Dairen and Port Arthur was that there were armed anti-government forces in the vicinity. It was the intention of the Chinese Government to send troops to land in Dairen, and the only reason why this did not happen was that the Soviet Government would not admit them. The Chinese Government had then negotiated with the Chinese Communists for them to take over the important cities along the Chinese Changchun Railway, but without result. Wang further stated that Dairen was Chinese territory, and that it had never been stipulated in the Sino-Soviet Treaty that China would not be allowed to land troops at this port. The treaty terms called for thirty years' joint control in the common aim of security against Japan. Over such a long term of years, it would be absolutely necessary for China to send troops via Dairen from time to time.

According to a communiqué from the Foreign Ministry, 'the declaration of Dairen as a free port, under the treaty, only signified that commodities in transit through that port should be exempt from duty, and had no bearing whatever on the question of stationing of Chinese troops in that port'.

The Soviet Government would only permit Chinese police to enter Dairen, provided their number and the places where they should be quartered were agreed upon between the two parties. It, however, could not agree to the entry of Chinese troops into Dairen on the ground that a state of war had not yet been terminated and Dairen should therefore still be subjected to military supervision established in the Port Arthur naval base area.

In the opinion of the Foreign Ministry, the Chinese Government was fully entitled to send troops to Port Arthur and maintain them there as, according to the treaty, the entire Port Arthur naval base area was set aside for the 'joint use' of the two countries. The Chinese Government could not, therefore, accept the Soviet interpretation.

The Chinese Foreign Ministry then addressed a communiqué to the Soviet Embassy on March 31, stating that the Chinese Government intended to send officials, troops and police within a short time to Dairen and Port Arthur, by land and sea, to establish a civil administration there, as it would be impossible to take over Dairen and Port Arthur without the aid of military force.

This did not meet with the approval of the Soviet Government. In reply, the Soviet Embassy sent another memorandum stating that, with regard to the sending of Chinese troops to the naval base of Port Arthur and the port of Dairen, it was clearly stated in Articles IV and VI in the agreement on Port Arthur, that the Chinese Government had entrusted to the Soviet Government the defence of the naval base. The Soviet Government might erect such installations as were necessary for their defence, and the Soviet Government could maintain in that region their army, navy and air force and determine their location. It had also been mutually agreed that Port Arthur, which existed only as a naval base, would be used by

Chinese and Soviet military and commercial vessels. As regards Dairen, the war against Japan had not ceased; there was still no peace treaty signed with Japan. In accordance with the agreement concerning Dairen, the military supervision or control established in Port Arthur would cover the port of Dairen.

The Foreign Ministry stated that 'while it is true that the Sino-Soviet Treaty subjects that city to the military supervision of the Port Arthur naval base area "in case of war against Japan", it is undeniable that Japan has, for more than a year, been under Allied occupation following her unconditional surrender, and that the war against Japan no longer, in actuality, exists. And even in case of war against Japan, the Chinese Government is not precluded by any provision of the Sino-Soviet Treaty from sending troops to Dairen.'

Numerous meetings were held between the Chinese Foreign Minister and the Soviet Ambassador, but they ended in deadlock. The Foreign Minister reiterated that (1) In laying down that Port Arthur should be used only by Chinese and Soviet military and commercial vessels the intention had been to prevent any third party from using it and not to hinder the Chinese Government. (2) Though there was still no treaty with Japan, neverthless war against Japan had ceased. The landing of Chinese troops at Dairen should not, therefore, be prohibited. In fact, supervision of Dairen by Port Arthur should only continue as long as the war with Japan existed. In any case, even if war still existed, it could not be considered detrimental by the Russians for Chinese troops to enter Dairen.

Public sentiment in China demanded that the Chinese Civil Administration should be under the protection of its own military and police force. China had just been emancipated from the foreign yoke, and the Chinese people would certainly oppose the Chinese Civil Administration being again put under foreign control.

On May 12, 1947, the Chinese Government notified the Soviet Embassy that a Chinese investigation mission under General Tung Yen-ping had been despatched to Port Arthur and Dairen by Chinese gunboat to prepare for the establishment of a Chinese Civil Administration there.

General Tung Yen-ping's mission arrived at Port Arthur on June 3. They made an inspection, but it was reported that they did not receive 'the promised assistance' from the Soviet authorities. The Mission left Port Arthur after a stay of ten days, without much success.

On June 25, the Chinese Government announced that 'the recent Chinese mission of inspection to Dairen and Port Arthur was a failure because of Soviet non-co-operation, and it gave notice that it considers itself free, at any time, to exercise the right to send troops to the two ports'.[9]

The Tass News Agency, however, published a counter statement saying, 'as early as December 1945 and January 1946, the local Soviet authorities had notified the Chinese representative that the necessary aid would be given so as to establish a Chinese administration at Dairen. Though the Chinese Government had approached some officials, not one of them came to Dairen to take up the post. The Soviet Government sent further notes in December 1946 and March 1947, but failed to get a reply from the Chinese Government. Therefore the allegation of Soviet obstruction was contrary to fact. Likewise, the Chinese announcement that the failure of General Tung Yen-ping's tour of inspection was due to lack of co-operation on the part of the Soviets was also a fabrication, and contrary to the actual facts.'[10]

During the Soviet occupation, Dairen, by far the best port, was used exclusively by the Soviets. In December 1946 a 348-ton United States naval boat, the U.C.I. 1090, which was at Dairen on a second routine courier mission carrying diplomatic mail and supplies for the United States Consulate in Dairen, together with two American newspapermen, was barred from the port after receiving an oral ultimatum from the local Soviet military officials.

The Soviet Government rejected the United States protests of January 3 and August 14, 1947, against the failure to reopen the Manchurian port of Dairen to international commerce. The United States contended that, according to the treaty, only in war-time could the Soviets have any military control over Dairen, yet the war had already been over for two years. Washington, however, had been informed that Moscow was not obliged to turn over Dairen to Chinese civil control and open the port to world commerce till the Japanese Treaty had been signed. The Soviet reply, dated August 26, to the American note of August 14, read as follows:

'In reply to the Embassy's note No. 689 of August 14 on the question of the opening of Dairen for international commerce, the Soviet Foreign Office have the honour to refer to its note

---

[9] *North China Daily News*, Shanghai, June 26, 1947.
[10] *Pravda*, Moscow, July 11, 1947.

No. 103 of February 27, 1947, in which it was stated that the status of Dairen is defined by the special Soviet-Chinese Agreement regarding Dairen. of August 14, 1945.

' As is known, in accordance with that agreement, Dairen during the existence of a state of war with Japan falls under the régime which has been set up in the naval base of Port Arthur.

' Inasmuch as the state of war with Japan is not terminated because there is as yet no peace treaty with Japan, naturally the régime of the naval base continues to prevail over Dairen.'

Dairen, thereupon, became the bone of contention between the Soviet Union and the United States. The Soviets, at the outset, permitted U.S. Courier vessels to call at Dairen and deliver mail and supplies for the American Consulate there until March 1947, when they banned further admissions.

C. Question of the Soviet Removal of Japanese Assets

An account of the controversy which arose on the taking over of Manchuria would not be complete without mentioning briefly the dismantling of machinery and its removal to the Soviet Union. The Chinese Government had decided that Japanese public and private properties, together with Japanese-owned enterprises in China, should be confiscated in order to compensate for China's losses during the war. As early as September 3, 1945, the Foreign Ministry had sent despatches to the American and Soviet Embassies asking their particular help in this respect, and only then to instruct their troops to protect Japanese-owned enterprises, including factories, mines, and transportation facilities before being handed over to the Chinese authorities. This was a step considered necessary to avoid any destruction, hiding or removal by the Japanese. The Soviet Government protested against this measure and declared in a memorandum addressed to the Chinese Government on January 21, 1946, that the Chinese North-Eastern Provinces which had rendered services to the Japanese army would be regarded by the Soviet Union as war booty of the Soviet forces.[11]

In view of the existing Sino-Soviet friendship, the Soviet Government suggested the organization of a joint Sino-Soviet Company for the management of Japanese enterprises, particularly coal mines, power plants and iron and steel industries, etc., in Manchuria. The Soviet Government further agreed to hand over to China a part of

[11] *United States Relations with China, 1944-1949,* p. 597.

the Japanese enterprises which were regarded as war booty. The Chinese Government considered 'this claim of the Soviet Government as far exceeding the scope of war booty as generally recognized by international law and international usage'. The Chinese Government also found it impossible to agree to the Soviet proposal of joint operation as beyond the provisions of the treaty.

Though reluctant, the Chinese Government felt inclined to comply with the Soviet wish. It discussed the possibility of so-called 'economic collaboration', but reiterated that the law applying to a Sino-foreign company must be abided by. It was suggested that further negotiations should be carried on at Changchun between the two parties. In any case, final agreement could only come after the withdrawal of Soviet troops. There were many difficulties in the way of the Sino-Soviet economic collaboration. There was the Soviet theory of war booty that prevented unanimity of views on some fundamental principles. Moreover, many of the Japanese industrial installations had been dismantled. Even so, the terms were discussed for a Sino-Soviet joint company to operate coal mines, iron and steel industries, oil refining, chemical and cement industries as well as power plants. They were to cover a period of thirty years, after which time all enterprises would revert to the Chinese Government without compensation. The situation, however, grew worse, for most of the installations and machines had, by that time, been removed to Soviet territory.

It was understood by the United States Government that exclusive government control over Manchuria enterprises would be limited to the railways as laid down in the Sino-Soviet Treaty. The United States Government was somewhat disturbed on receiving reports that discussions were under way which might result in the establishment of exclusive Sino-Soviet control over industrial enterprises in Manchuria. It was the opinon of the United States Government that negotiations for agreements between China and the Soviet Union would be contrary to the principles of the Open Door policy. The United States Government then instructed its Embassies in Chungking and Moscow to present that view to the Chinese Government and the Government of the U.S.S.R. respectively. A British protest to the same effect was also presented to the Soviet Foreign Commissar by the British Embassy in Moscow on March 9, 1946.

In June 1946, E. W. Pauley was sent by the American Government as the personal representative of the President to investigate Japanese assets in Manchuria. The Mission arrived at Changchun to make the necessary investigations, and it was the opinion of Pauley that all Japanese properties in Manchuria should be transferred to the Chinese authorities. He made a complete list of what had been removed to the Soviet Union, and his estimate of direct damage was U.S. $858.1 million.[12] The Mission returned to Washington in July and made a report to the President on Japanese assets in Manchuria.

In Pauley's report it was stated: 'Japanese assets in Manchuria did not belong solely to the Soviet Government. Other nations, too, are logical claimants. . . . Moving this equipment has destroyed a large part of its original value, and the installations from which this equipment was removed have in many cases become total losses.'[13]

The Soviet Press in Moscow strongly opposed the report made by Pauley, and stated that the report itself was full of falsity and fabrication. The estimate made by Pauley that the total loss to Manchuria would run up to United States $2,000 million was categorically denied by the Soviet authorities, who claimed that all materials and equipment removed were war products which the Soviet Government had the full right to seize, it being in the first place Japanese military property, but now Red Army war booty. The Soviet estimate of the value of their removals from Manchuria is U.S. $97 million.[14] The Soviet Government further accused Pauley of having maliciously mingled together war booty and reparations.

[12] Jones, F. C., *Manchuria Since 1931*, p. 230.
[13] *United States Relations with China*, p. 603.
[14] Byrnes, J. F., *Speaking Frankly*, p. 225.

ADDENDUM.—A one-year trade pact between the Manchurian People's Democratic Authorities', headed by Kao Kang, and the Soviet Union was announced in Moscow on July 31, 1949. It was noted that the Soviet Union would deliver to Manchuria industrial equipment, motor vehicles, oil, textiles, paper and medicines. In return, Manchuria agreed to supply the Soviet Union with soybeans, vegetable oil, maize and rice. The National Government in Canton strongly protested against the Soviet-Manchurian trade pact as violating the Sino-Soviet Treaty of 1945.

Chapter XX

RISE OF THE CHINESE COMMUNIST PARTY

THE Nationalist Government of China gained its power after the overthrow of the north China warlords while the People's Government, newly set up in Peking, in turn overthrew the Kuomintang (hereafter abbreviated to KMT). The Chinese Communist Party (hereafter abbreviated to KCT for Kungchantang) did not reach political importance until Dr. Sun Yat-sen, founder of the KMT, accepted its co-operation and thereupon reorganized his Party in 1924. The KCT, knowing itself to be far from mature at the outset, succeeded in fostering its own growth within the KMT.

The rapid growth of the KCT made the KMT members uneasy and apprehensive. The Nationalist Government at Nanking ordered a purge and issued a proclamation stating that if the KCT wished to dominate the Party, it would mean the end of co-operation. In spite of the Party purge, membership of the KCT grew steadily. Within a few years, the KCT had built up an army formidable enough to challenge the very rule of the KMT.

It was only after the Sino-Japanese conflict that the KCT made a declaration announcing its allegiance to the KMT. The two parties, however, worked harmoniously only for a short time in the struggle against the common foe. Dissensions and frictions were soon revived, and open armed conflicts occurred where the armies of both parties came into contact. An attack by KMT troops on the New Fourth Route Army and its disbandment was the first fuse that put the whole country ablaze.

After Japan's surrender in August 1945, there was a fresh attempt at collaboration between the two parties. The Political Consultative Conference was convened in October with representatives of all parties and independents. The situation looked very promising, and there was definite agreement on reorganization and reconstruction. Chinese people were overjoyed at China's unity. But scarcely had a month passed when the two parties fell out and again resorted to arms.

309

General George C. Marshall, who was in China acting as a mediator between the two parties, went to Lushan eight times in 1946 to confer with General and Madame Chiang Kai-shek who were spending the summer there. In spite of Marshall's best efforts, the two parties failed to come together. The Nationalist Government then ordered all members of the KCT to evacuate from various cities, and it soon captured Yenan, the Communist capital, without meeting much resistance. Before long, the tide changed, and not only was Yenan retaken, but the whole of Manchuria gradually fell into the hands of the KCT.

The KCT troops immediately threatened north China, where General Fu Tso-yi signed a truce and allowed them to enter Peking and Tientsin without bloodshed. Generalissimo Chiang Kai-shek announced his retirement and asked General Li Tsung-jen to act for him.

The Peace Missions to north China, headed by Dr. W. W. Yen and General Chang Chih-chung respectively, both proved a failure. With the fall of Nanking the Nationalist Government moved its capital to Canton, but did not stay long. The KCT troops went in hot pursuit, and within eight months the Nationalist Government had to move its capital four times, namely, to Canton, Chungking, Chengtu and Taipeh. In the end the Nationalist Government retreated to Taiwan with the intention of fighting to the bitter end.

1. Birth of Chinese Communist Party

Chinese Communism is believed to have been introduced to China after the success of the Russian Revolution by two well-known Chinese scholars—Chen Tu-hsiu and Li Ta-chao—both professors at the National Peking University. The first was imprisoned for many years, and was only set free after the Sino-Japanese conflict. He died in Szchuan on May 24, 1942. In his late years he changed his opinions, becoming first a Trotskyist, and later, as shown in recently published letters to his friends, a true democrat. The latter lost his life at the hands of Marshal Chang Tso-lin, as has been fully described in a foregoing chapter.

Early in 1916, Chen Tu-hsiu published several periodicals for promoting an emancipation of thought among the Chinese people, particularly his *Hsin Ching Nien* (the *New Youth*) which specially appealed to Chinese young people. This gave birth to the Chinese students' movement in 1919 in Peking. It may be recalled that in that year the Versailles Peace Conference completely disregarded China's rights and interests, even though China was an ally of the victorious Powers. China's disillusionment came suddenly and unexpectedly, so that when Russia, then a young Communist republic only two years old, made its declaration to China, voluntarily abolishing all unequal treaties contracted by the Tsarist Government and offering to retrocede all territorial concessions, Chinese intellectuals flocked into the open arms of the Soviets.

The National Peking University, then headed by the late Tsai Yuan-pei, a great scholar and philosopher, was noted for its inclinations and sympathies. Both Chen Tu-hsiu and Li Ta-chao held chairs there. In 1920 these two professors founded a society for the study of Marxism in Peking. Contemporaneously, another society of the same nature was organized in Shanghai, known as the ' Young Socialist League '. Both bodies attracted large numbers of intellectuals and students, and were the forerunners of the KCT.

Mao Tze-tung, leader of the Chinese Communist Party, was in 1919 associated with Li Ta-chao at Peking University. It was at the University that he met Chen Tu-hsiu, who had a greater influence over him than anyone else.[1]

Chen Tu-hsiu had established contact with Moscow as early as 1919 and sent representatives to the Soviet capital to solicit Chinese membership in the Third International, known as the Comintern.[2] Mr. Marling, an energetic and persuasive representative of the Comintern, arrived at Shanghai in 1920 and arranged to organize a Chinese Communist Party. Chen then called a conference of all sympathizers the following May, and the Communist Party of China was inaugurated. It already included other intellectuals who were in sympathy with Communist ideas.

2. Sun Yat-sen-Joffe Declaration

In 1922 M. Joffe went to Peking to attempt to reach an understanding with China. At that time Dr. Sun Yat-sen was heading a government in Canton, organized to oppose the Peking Government, which was then the internationally recognized Government of China.

Unfortunately for Dr. Sun, soon after he became President of the Canton Government, General Chen Chiung-ming turned against him. The breach between them originated from a difference of opinion. Dr. Sun wanted to start a northern expedition at once, by

[1] Edgar Snow, Red Star Over China, 1937, p. 154.
[2] Yakhontoff, Chinese Soviets, 1934, p. 70-1.

means of which he intended to unify the country by force, whereas General Chen strongly doubted the wisdom of the plan. The discord developed into open revolt on the part of Chen, and Dr. Sun had to flee from Canton.

Meanwhile, finding that he could not make any headway with the Peking Government, Joffe left Peking for Shanghai on January 16, 1924, *en route* to Japan, ostensibly to recuperate his health, but actually to see what he could do in Japan. Dr. Sun also arrived at the same city from Canton. There the two important figures met several times and discussed the general situation in China, and the outcome was the following declaration authorized for publication on January 26, 1924, under the joint signatures of Sun Yat-sen and Joffe:

'During his stay in Shanghai, Mr. Joffe has had several conversations with Dr. Sun Yat-sen, which have revealed the identity of their views on matters relating to Chinese-Russian relations, more especially on the following points:

1. Dr. Sun Yat-sen holds that the Communistic order, or even the Soviet system, cannot actually be introduced into China, because there do not exist here the conditions for the successful establishment of either Communism or Sovietism. This view is entirely shared by Mr. Joffe, who is further of opinion that China's paramount and most pressing problem is to achieve national unification and attain full national independence, and regarding this great task, he has assured Dr. Sun Yat-sen that China has the warmest sympathy of the Russian people, and can count on the support of Russia.

2. In order to clarify the situation, Dr. Sun Yat-sen has requested of Mr. Joffe a reaffirmation of the principles defined in the Russian note to the Chinese Government, dated September 27, 1920. Mr. Joffe has accordingly reaffirmed these principles and categorically declared to Dr. Sun Yat-sen that the Russian Government is ready and willing to enter into negotiations with China on the basis of the renunciation by Russia of all the treaties and exactions which the Tsardom imposed on China, including the treaty or treaties and agreements relating to the Chinese Eastern Railway.

3. Recognizing that the Chinese Eastern Railway question in its entirety can be settled only at a competent Russo-Chinese Conference, Dr. Sun is of opinion that the realities of the situa-

tion point to the desirability of a *modus vivendi* in the matter of the present management of the railway. And he agrees with Mr. Joffe that the existing management of the railway should be temporarily reorganized by agreement between the Chinese and the Russian Governments without prejudice, however, to the true rights and special interests of either party. At the same time, Dr. Sun Yat-sen considers that General Chang Tso-lin should be consulted on the point.

4. Mr. Joffe has categorically declared to Dr. Sun Yat-sen (who has fully satisfied himself as to this) that it is not and has never been the intention and purpose of the present Russian Government to pursue an imperialistic policy in Outer Mongolia or to cause it to secede from China. Dr. Sun Yat-sen, therefore, does not view an immediate evacuation of Russian troops from Outer Mongolia as either imperative or in the real interest of China, the more so on account of the inability of the present government at Peking to prevent such an evacuation being followed by a recrudescence of intrigues and hostile activities by White Guardists against Russia and the creation of a graver situation than that which now exists.

' Mr. Joffe has parted from Dr. Sun Yat-sen on the most cordial and friendly terms. On leaving Japan, to which he is now proceeding, he will again visit the south of China before finally returning to Peking.'[3]

This declaration signalized the advent of that fraternalization between the KMT and the KCT which is of paramount importance in the history of Chinese Communism. As a result of this joint declaration in which Dr. Sun sought Soviet support, the KCT practically won official recognition, and the Party increased in influence and membership.

3. Reorganization of KMT

Before the joint declaration, Dr. Sun Yat-sen sent Liao Chung-kai to approach Joffe and ask for Soviet aid for the establishment of a military academy in Canton to strengthen the position of the KMT. Embittered by repeated failures and disgusted with the refusal of recognition of his government by the Powers, Dr. Sun Yat-sen, praising the remarkable success of Lenin as well as the iron discipline of the Bolshevist Party, invited Soviet advisers to Canton.

[3] *China Year Book*, 1924, p. 863.

With the agreement and approval of Moscow, Michael Borodin, who had been sent by the Third International to Turkey to assist Kamel in State reforms, but had later been expelled from the country, came to China to be a political adviser. General Galen (Bleucher) was sent as head of a military mission. The KMT was completely reorganized following on the Soviet example. Party principles were defined, and unity and discipline were strengthened.

The first National Congress of the KMT was held at Canton, January 15, 1924, where Borodin, in the capacity of adviser, was present. There were twenty-four members of the Central Executive Committee to which several Communist members, including Li Ta-chao, Tan Pin-san, Mao Tze-tung, Ch'u Chiu-pei, etc., were admitted. A resolution for the organization of the Nationalist Government was unanimously passed during the session. Li Ta-chao announced the complete acceptance of KMT principles, policies and discipline by the KCT. He made the point, however, that this joining of the KMT and participation in the National Revolution was an individual choice by members, there being no idea of the fusion of the two groups.

There were quite a few members in the KMT who were opposed to the admission of the KCT into the Party, but Dr. Sun Yat-sen, in view of the fact that they had accepted the Three People's Principles, overruled the dissent. Nevertheless, friction between the KMT and the KCT appeared at the outset of their co-operation.

The Central Executive Committee at that time appointed three secretaries to look after the Party affairs. These were Tan Pin-san for the Organization Department, Tai Chi-tao for the Propaganda Department, and Liao Chung-kai for the Labour Department. Both Tai and Liao were busy with other political functions, but Tan seized the opportunity to grasp power through his influential position for the benefit of the KCT. Before long, the KCT were practically monopolizing all the important positions in the party as well as the lower ranks of the district organizations. Consequently, public opinion became controlled by the KCT, and nearly all important KMT documents were drawn up by the KCT. Borodin once submitted to the Committee a resolution in favour of land distribution, but was impeded by Tai Chi-tao, who thought it would never work in China.[4]

A military academy was established at Whampoa. This was

---

[4] Author's personal interview with the late Tai Chi-tao, who was the President of the Examination Yuan, Chungking, May 27, 1942.

administered by Liao Chung-kai, as founder, Borodin adviser, and Chiang Kai-shek principal; the last named at the time was making a tour of inspection in Moscow. Chiang resumed office in April 1924, but the actual planning and direction of the academy was in the hands of Borodin, who was largely responsible for its creation and administration. It was a most important institution, as history later was to show. Here it was that high-spirited young men were imbued with the ideas and ideals of world revolution and national emancipation for China. The northern military expedition that brought the KMT supreme power over the whole country owed its success to Soviet trained officers from the military academy at Whampoa.

When the reorganized army defeated the forces of General Chen Chiung-ming, Dr. Sun Yat-sen was lying critically ill at the hospital of the Peking Union Medical College. On hearing news of the victory, it is said that he was so exultant that he burst into tears.

Dr. Sun Yat-sen wrote and despatched a letter to the Central Executive Committee of the Soviet Union, dated March 12, 1925, within a few hours of his demise:

'I am suffering from an incurable disease of the body, but my heart turns towards you, towards my Party, and the future of my country. You are the leaders of a free union of republics. This free union of republics is the world inheritance bequeathed to the oppressed peoples by the immortal Lenin. Peoples suffering from imperialism will safeguard their freedom by it, and will emancipate themselves from an international system based upon ancient orders of enslavement, war and injustices by it. What I leave behind me is the Kuomintang. I hope the Kuomintang will, in the process of completing the historical work of emancipating China and other oppressed nations from the imperialistic system, co-operate with you. Fate has forced me to lay down my work uncompleted, and to hand it over to my true comrades who strictly observe the principles and instructions of the Kuomintang to continue the work of the revolutionary movement so that China, reduced by imperialists to the position of a semi-colonial country, may become free. With this object in view, I have instructed the Party to be in constant contact with you. I firmly believe in the continuance of the support which you have hitherto accorded to my country. Taking leave of you, dear Comrades, I want to express the hope that the day will soon come when the U.S.S.R. will welcome a friend and ally in a mighty free China, and that, in the great struggle for the liberation of the oppressed peoples of the world, these two great nations will go forward to victory hand in hand.

(*Signed*) SUN YAT-SEN.'[5]

At the time of the death of Dr. Sun Yat-sen in 1925, Borodin was at the height of his influence and enjoyed the complete co-operation and whole-hearted support of the KMT leaders. He had a big staff of both Soviet and Chinese citizens at the residence in Hankow which he used as his headquarters.

4. *Ups and Downs of KCT*

As early as 1925, when Communist influence was at its height, the seed of dissension with the KMT had already been sown. Slowly but unobtrusively the KMT was splitting into two wings—the moderate right and the radical left. Wang Ching-wei, then chairman of the Canton Government, or the Nationalist Government as it was called, was the leader of the left wing, while the right wing had not firmly and definitely consolidated itself; Chiang Kai-shek had not as yet emerged into sufficient prominence to take the helm.

In March, Chiang Kai-shek declared martial law over Canton, cut off communications, occupied all government offices by force, disarmed suspected troops and dismissed the Soviet advisers.[6]

However, the northern military expedition planned by Dr. Sun Yat-sen before his death could not be successfully carried out without the help of Soviet personnel. Thus a reconciliation took place. Communists were readmitted and Soviet advisers were reinstated.

The northern military expedition met with easy success. Hankow and Nanking fell to the Nationalists. Shanghai, the stronghold of the Powers, was in a turmoil of union strikes. The seat of the Nationalist Government was then in Hankow. In April 1927 Chiang Kai-shek, having succeeded in winning the support of the Shanghai bankers, set up another government in Nanking. A Party purge was again proclaimed.

The KCT also issued a manifesto on July 13 announcing that they had withdrawn their representatives from the Nationalist Government, but would continue to collaborate with the true revolutionary members of the KMT.

In August 1927 the Fourth Army stationed at Nanchang went over

[5] See also Yakhontoff, op. cit., p. 204.
[6] ibid., p. 73.

to the Communists. These troops were known as the best fighters among the KMT troops. Some fifteen thousand soldiers were enlisted into the KCT and formed the nucleus of the Chinese Communist Army.

The KCT Central Executive Committee empowered Mao Tze-tung to organize a movement at Changsha, and Chu Teh joined him there in May 1928. A reorganization of the forces followed in which the Communist Fourth Route Army was created.

The first Congress of the Chinese Communists was held in Juichin, Red capital of Kiangsi province, on November 7, 1931. The Congress passed the Provisional Constitution of the All China Soviet Republic and elected Mao Tze-tung as President. He had been the chief Communist leader since 1928.

The Chinese Communists, having consolidated a position in the south of Kiangsi, captured Changsha on July 27, 1930, in the hope of finding an outlet to the sea for the growing Soviet areas. Though they held Changsha only ten days, their power was further strengthened, and additional Soviet areas were founded. By this time, nearly the whole province of Kiangsi, as well as extensive sections along the borders of Hunan, Hupeh, Anhuei, Fukien and Kwangtung, were under Soviet administration.

5. Anti-Communist Campaigns

The KMT Central Executive Committee met in Nanking in November 1930. In view of the rapid extension of power of the KCT, it was then decided that this power must be checked at all costs. A military campaign was then started, known later as the First Campaign, being followed by the Second, the Third, the Fourth and the Fifth Campaigns.

In the Third Campaign, Generalissimo Chiang Kai-shek took personal command, as he was determined to eradicate the Communist Army by force. Before he set out for Nanchang, he despatched a circular telegram stating that he would not return to Nanking alive unless he succeeded in exterminating the Communists. The clever strategy adopted by the Communist Army, however, prevented Chiang from obtaining any immediate success.

The Lushan Conference held in July 1933, over which Chiang Kai-shek presided, was summoned to discuss how to devise effective ways and means to exterminate the Communists. A water-tight blockade was set up to encircle the Soviet areas. In subsequent months, the

Communists suffered great hardships owing to the complete lack of salt. A belt of pill-box fortifications was also built around the territory.

Meanwhile, there was an incident in Fukien in November 1933. General Tsai Ting-kai, the renowned Commander of the Nineteenth Route Army, instead of resuming operations against the Communists as instructed, was carrying on some sort of collaboration following his withdrawal from Shanghai. As a consequence, a People's Government was established in Foochow. But the People's Government was short-lived, and was overthrown by the Nationalist forces.

As a result of successive military campaigns conducted by Chiang Kai-shek, the Chinese Communists suffered heavily in men. Their supply of ammunition dwindled. A military conference was called at Juichin, and they decided to withdraw from Kiangsi to northern Shensi. The long trek of an army of 90,000 men started in October 1934. It took the Chinese Communists a full year to reach their destination—the Shensi-Ninghsai region.[7]

6. Sian Coup

After the Communist vanguards arrived in northern Shensi, an incident of far-reaching consequence took place in Sian, capital of Shensi province. Marshal Chang Hsueh-liang retired to Sian with his whole army after the Japanese had overrun Manchuria. His army was known as the *Tungpei* or North-Eastern Army. These troops were ordered by Generalissimo Chiang Kai-shek to a station in the north-western part of China after their retreat, and for the previous two years they had been employed in safeguarding the situation.

A slow awakening to the fact that they had not fired a single shot to repel the invaders, but were merely continuing civil wars in China, seemed to dawn on the *Tungpei* Army, especially on the younger officers. Discontent gradually developed into mutiny. On December 7, 1936, Chiang Kai-shek landed at the Sian aerodrome in a giant plane. Five days later he became Chiang Hsueh-liang's captive and was confronted with eight demands. Chiang was asked to promise (1) the abandonment of civil war and co-operation between the KMT and the KCT; (2) a defined policy of armed resistance against any further Japanese aggression; (3) dismissal of certain 'pro-

---

[7] Author's personal interview with Mr. Chou En-lai at Chungking, December 6, 1941.

Japanese' officials in Nanking, and adoption of an active diplomacy for creating closer relations with Great Britain, America and the Soviet Union; (4) reorganization of the *Tungpei* and *Hsipei* armies on an equal footing with Nanking's forces; (5) greater political freedom for the people; and (6) the creating of some sort of political structure at Nanking.[8]

Ironically, the Communists, instead of taking the opportunity to do away with their arch enemy, came into the picture as mediators. Several important Communist leaders, including Chou En-lai, vice-chairman of the KCT Military Council, arrived at Sian. Chiang at first refused to discuss any programme. Later he was convinced that not only his captors but also the Communists were ready to work under his leadership in resisting Japanese aggression. During these meetings, a truce was reached between Chiang and the KCT. Arrangements were speedily made, and Chiang was set free after three weeks' detention. Immediately after his return to Nanking, the tone of the Kuomintang Government underwent a marked change. No longer was there any talk of exterminating the Communists. The Press was instructed to refrain from using any obnoxious terms against the Communists.

7. *Border Region*

In May 1937 the KCT passed a resolution on the tasks of the National Anti-Japanese United Front. They agreed to reorganize the 'Red Army' as the 'National Revolutionary Army', which was to be submitted to the orders of the High Command and to transform Soviet districts into special areas. Both the KMT and the KCT made changes in their policies. China for the first time offered resistance to Japanese aggression as a united nation.

In December 1937, the KCT declared that they joined hands with the KMT 'not only for the purpose of resisting Japan but also for the building of a new China.'[9] Soon the Red Army partisans in the south were organized into the New Fourth Route Army.

The KCT had by this time established the so-called 'Border Region' in Yenan, Shensi province, and this gave considerable concern to the public as a sign of dissension between the KCT and the Central Government. In an interview given to the Delegates of the World Students Association, July 12, 1938, Mao Tze-tung explained

[8] Snow, op. cit., pp. 427-8.
[9] Mao Tse-tung, *The New Stage*, published in English by the New China Information Committee, Chungking, 1939.

the nature of the Border Region as nothing but 'a democratic anti-Japanese stronghold'. He further pointed out that the Border Region was intended to set a good example and to make the Chinese people understand that democracy is the only road to national salva-tion and reconstruction. He welcomed any one from all corners of the globe to come and see what was going on in the Border Region. In the Border Region, a government was set up. The masses were organized, engaging in all kinds of anti-Japanese activities. The economic system in the Border Region was also different from that of the Chungking Government. The people were taxed by a progres-sive system; other taxes imposed by the former government were all abolished. The Border Region Government also enforced the system of election of the personnel of all ranks.

The Eighth Route Army achieved military successes in south Shensi, while the New Fourth Route Army also achieved something in guerilla warfare. Both armies expanded so fast that they attracted the recruitment of irregulars.

8. New Fourth Route Army Affair

In the latter part of 1939 there were reports of friction and even open conflict between the KMT and the KCT. The Eighth Route Army was accused of having directed their guerilla warfare against the Nationalist armies instead of the invaders.

With regard to friction, Mao Tze-tung, in an interview with Chinese Pressmen in Yenan on September 11, 1939, admitted political differences. He urged the convocation of a National Assembly and the adoption of full democratic practice. He charged General Chang Yin-wu of Hopei and General Chin Chi-yung of Shantung with being responsible for the conflict, and said that they had fought against the Eighth Route Army more frequently than against the enemy.[10] A telegram was finally sent out from Yenan to the Nationalist Government, asking for the cancellation of 'precautionary measures'. Mao said bluntly: 'We know that in our war of resistance we must co-operate instead of taking precautions against each other. We, the Communists, bitterly oppose this friction which reduces our strength, but if we are badly oppressed, we shall be obliged to take necessary measures.'[11]

[10] China Weekly Review, May 11, 1940.
[11] Mao Tse-tung's interview with the Chinese correspondents of the Central News Agency and other newspapers, September 11, 1939. Pamphlet published in Chinese.

The Chinese people were deeply concerned over the dispute between the KCT and KMT. The Nationalist Government put forward a plan on July 16, 1940, which provided that the Border Region should be renamed 'the Northern Shensi Administration', and the New Fourth Route Army in southern Kiangsu should be the Hopei-Charhar-Northern-Shantung-Northern-Shensi area. The plan was to become effective within one month.

The KCT agreed to remove their New Fourth Route Army in southern Kiangsu, but hoped their troops in northern Kiangsu would be allowed to remain to fight the common foe. On December 9, 1940, Generalissimo Chiang Kai-shek issued a manifesto ordering the removal of the New Fourth Route Army not later than December 31. Several members of the People's Political Council, who were afraid of open conflict, sent a joint telegram to Chiang Kai-shek asking him to reconsider the matter for the sake of the country. The High Command, however, remained firm in its decision, and felt confident of being able to deal with the situation.

An armed clash finally broke out and brought defeat to the New Fourth Route Army, whose commander, Yeh Ying, was arrested. Though the New Fourth Route Army was disbanded by the Nationalist Government, in reality the Central Revolutionary Commission of the KCT appointed a new commander to replace Yeh Ying, and the New Fourth Route Army was reorganized into seven divisions.

The affair of the New Fourth Route Army aggravated the initial frictions between the two parties irreparably. Chou En-lai, the Communist leader, tried to settle the differences, but without success. The KCT put forward twelve written and eight oral suggestions which their representative, Lin Chu-han, took to Chungking. Later, they received counter-proposale from the Nationalist Government. The latter took cognizance of only four armies with ten divisions of approximately 100,000 men who were recognized out of the 570,000 regulars that the KCT claimed to have under arms. Chou En-lai, however, declared: 'To disband several hundred thousand anti-Japanese troops, as the National Government demands, is beyond reason. If we accepted these demands, it would be equivalent to aiding the enemy.' He then considered that the only correct ways for rescuing China from her plight were the reorganization of the Government and the High Command, and the establishing of a coalition government and a high United Command.

Between 1941 and 1945 Chou En-lai and Tung Pi-wu, two Communist leaders, were staying at Chungking acting as liaison officers between the KMT and KCT but without achieving much.

9. Political Consultative Conference

After the signing of the Sino-Soviet Treaty on August 14, 1945, followed on the self-same day by Japan's formal surrender, Generalissimo Chiang Kai-shek invited Mr. Mao Tse-tung, Chairman of the Central Committee of the KCT, to come to Chungking to discuss matters of national interest. Mao arrived at Chungking on August 28, and had a number of talks with Chiang. Meanwhile, representatives of both parties were appointed. The KMT representatives were Dr. Wang Shih-chieh, General Chang Chun, General Chang Chih-chung and Mr. Shao Li-tze, while the KCT representatives were Mr. Chao En-lai and Mr. Wang Jo-fei.

The representatives of both parties met and conferred on many occasions and reached a number of conclusions. It was agreed that the period of political tutelege should be brought to an early conclusion, and that a constitutional government should be inaugurated. The first preliminary measure would be the convocation of a political consultative conference to which all parties and non-partisan leaders should be invited to exchange views and discuss questions relating to peaceful national reconstruction and the convocation of the National Assembly.

It was at that time, after the resignation of General Patrick J. Hurley, American Ambassador to China, that General George C. Marshall was appointed as U.S. President Truman's representative to China. His mission was to mediate between the two major parties in order to reach an agreement. As a result of his efforts both parties yielded to some extent, paving the way for a final settlement. He, however, did not participate in the discussions of the Political Consultative Conference (PCC).

Prior to the convening of the PCC both parties agreed to the cessation of hostilities. It was suggested that a Committee of Three, composed of a representative of each party with General Marshall as chairman, should be formed to discuss the questions arising out of the cessation of hostilities. General Chang Chun and Mr. Chou En-lai were appointed representatives of the KMT and KCT respectively, and they held their first meeting on January 7, 1946, in the presence of General Marshall.

The PCC was formally opened on January 10, 1946, with thirty-six members in attendance, representing the KMT, KCT, Democratic League, Youth Party and non-party delegates. A final agreement was reached on January 31 after a tenth meeting. The whole situation was at last clarified, and the conference formally closed after Generalissimo Chiang Kai-shek had delivered a speech for the occasion which greatly moved members present. The National Assembly was fixed to be convoked on May 5, 1946. It seemed that everything was going on very nicely, and the Chinese public were exalted at the promise of a united China. The Diplomatic Corps in Chungking were also pleased with the political situation, thinking that China would now be able to avoid civil strife and march forward on the road to reconstruction.

Unfortunately, immediately after the aforesaid settlement, there were murmurs from malcontents among the irreconcilable elements of the KMT. Numerous disquieting events happened; there was an attack by alleged KMT plain-clothes men at a mass meeting on the drilling-ground in Chungking, which was being held to celebrate the success of the PCC; there was police interference with minority party delegates to the PCC. The worst incident was a ruthless raid on the KCT newspaper premises in Chungking during a students' demonstration. All this served to strengthen the fear that irreconcilable elements in the KMT were incurably opposed to the PCC.

Meanwhile the KMT called meetings of the Central Executive Committee (CEC) at Chungking to discuss and pass PCC resolutions. Although the PCC resolutions had been approved *in toto* by the CEC, the irreconcilable elements in the KMT requested the revision of the principles regarding the basis of the Draft Constitution. Both the KCT and Democratic League were greatly concerned, and they opposed any major changes in the resolutions which had been agreed upon by authorized representatives of all parties. In consequence, another deadlock arose, and the National Assembly which was scheduled to convene on May 5 was postponed until November 15. The KCT even refused to nominate members of the State Council for the purpose of reorganizing the government.

10. Wild Conflict Between KMT and KCT

The crux of party differences was how to bring hostilities to an end after the cease-fire order, to come into effect on January 13. The whole military situation rested on the question of army reorganization. The Nationalist Government brought down their forces to ninety divisions within six months, while the Communist army was reduced to twenty divisions as agreed upon. The Nationalist Government also expressed the hope that as soon as reorganization was complete, the nation's entire armies should be further reduced to fifty or sixty divisions.

The Communists agreed in principle, hoping the proportionate strength of the various forces would be maintained, and that separate localities for garrisons would be arranged. It was later agreed that these questions should be discussed by a Three-Man Military Sub-Committee on which General Chang Chih-chung and Mr. Chou En-lai were appointed representatives for their respective parties with General Marshall as the third member.

An agreement on a basic plan for military reorganization was signed on February 25, 1946, by Chang, Chou and Marshall, and this marked a new page in China's political history. The terms of the agreement included the reduction of Nationalist forces to ninety divisions and the Communist army to eighteen divisions within a period of twelve months. Then there would be further reduction to fifty Nationalist divisions and ten Communist divisions containing not more than fourteen thousand men in a division. After the signing of the agreement, an Executive Headquarters was established in Peking to carry out the army reorganization plan.

Then came the controversy in Manchuria. The cease-fire order did not mention that certain parts of China would not be included. When the Soviet troops were about to withdraw from Manchuria, Marshall urged that an Executive Headquarters field team in Manchuria should be organized to prevent clashes between the two opposing forces. The Nationalists, however, were not willing to agree, though the Communists approved. It seemed that the Nationalists were determined to occupy the whole area, although they were not in a position to do so. Not until Marshall's departure for Washington did General Chiang agree to the entry of an Executive Headquarters field team into Manchuria, and even then there was further delay. Meanwhile the Communist troops in Manchuria increased beyond bounds. Most of them were despatched from Chefoo and Lungkao, seaports of Shantung, in native boats and junks, to Manchuria. The Communist forces were able to take with them weapons and military supplies formerly possessed by the Japanese army.

The Nationalist Government had not the means to occupy Manchuria in the face of Communist opposition. Lieutenant-General

Albert C. Wedemeyer, who was in China as Commanding General, reported to Washington that the Nationalist Government would not be able to stabilize the situation in north China until a satisfactory settlement could be achieved with the Communists. The reason why General Wedemeyer came to this conclusion was that Nationalist Government corruption and malpractices had created serious discontent among the local population.

The Communist forces occupied Changchun on April 18 after the withdrawal of Soviet troops. The Nationalist military position in Manchuria grew weaker. But some reinforcements were made and Szepingkai, a strategic town, was retaken on May 19, and Changchun also fell to the Nationalists on May 23. After these successes, the Nationalists thought they could settle the problem by force and so were not willing to compromise with the Communists. General Chiang's long absence from Nanking through his summer stay in Lushan and the open resumption of the military campaign in Manchuria made the situation more critical.

In spite of the unco-operative attitude and constant warnings of the KCT, the Nationalist Assembly was convened at Nanking on November 15, 1946. Delegates of the KCT and Democratic League were not present. Moreover, the names of the Youth Party and independents were submitted only on the eve of the opening. Chou En-lai issued a statement declaring the opening of the National Assembly to be contrary to the PCC resolutions and affirmed that the KCT could not recognize the Assembly. He further said that the door to negotiations was definitely slammed by the KMT.

On November 11, 1947, the Nationalist Government notified the Communist delegation in Nanking that its presence was no longer desired. Chou En-lai and fourteen others departed for Yenan on November 19 by Marshall's private plane. Before their departure, General Marshall gave a farewell party at the American Embassy at which he particularly thanked a Mr. Chang, Chou En-lai's interpreter, for his untiring service during the conference. Thereupon a joyous clamour arose for attacking Yenan, the Communist capital. Marshall, however, opposed it strongly, saying that if such an attack was made a reality he would terminate his mission.

General Marshall's position was very difficult as he had to display patience. Soon he became convinced that 'twenty years of intermittent fighting between the two factions, during which the leading figures had remained the same, had created such deep personal bitterness and such irreconcilable differences that no agreement was possible '.[12] When the writer had an interview with General Marshall in the American Embassy, Chungking, Marshall said frankly that he would never rely on reports from either the Nationalist Government or the Communists, and he had his own way to find out the truth.[13]

On January 6, 1947, General Marshall was recalled and appointed Secretary of State in America. He was succeeded by Dr. J. Leighton Stuart as American Ambassador to China. Before leaving China, General Marshall issued a statement through the State Department complaining of ' the opposition of the dominant group of the KMT who have been opposed to almost every effort I have made to influence the formation of a genuine coalition government and the efforts of a definite liberal group among the Communists who would put the interest of the Chinese people above ruthless measures to establish a Communist ideology in the immediate future. . . . The salvation of the situation would be the assumption of leadership by the liberals in the government and in the minority parties, a splendid group of men, but who as yet lack the political power to exercise a controlling influence.'[14]

From now on, the Nationalist Government waged war on an increasing scale. Yenan, the Communist capital, which had largely been evacuated, was finally taken by Nationalist forces on March 19. On April 19 the election of a President took place in the National Assembly at which General Chiang Kai-shek was elected, and later General Li Tsung-jen was made Vice-President, after keen competition.

In July intense fighting between the Nationalists and the Communists occurred in two major battles at Paoting, capital of Hopei, and Szepingkai, a strategic town near Changchun. The main Nationalist troops were slowly approaching the stronghold of Szepingkai, the garrison of which, under General Chen Min-jen, held out nineteen days against Communist assaults. Nationalist troops entered Szepingkai on June 30. There was some real fighting at Szepingkai as the Communist forces were said to have battered Szepingkai with more than 100,000 artillery shells. Though the Nationalists regained Szepingkai, the Communists appeared to retain the offensive in southern Manchuria. Communist forces were more

---

[12] Dean Acheson's letter to President Truman, July 30, 1949, *U.S. Relations with China*, p. xii.
[13] Author's personal interview with General Marshall at Chungking, February 1, 1946.
[14] *United States Relations with China*, Annex. 113, pp. 687-8.

active and stronger, not only in Manchuria but in every part of China. Yenan was soon retaken by Communist forces in spite of Chiang's having previously paid a visit of inspection there. The Nationalist forces became weaker and weaker despite full mobilization of manpower and resources by the government.

The Communists started a new drive in Manchuria on September 30. After the recapture of Szepingkai on March 12, 1948, by the Communists, many other important cities in Manchuria fell to them, among them Kirin, Changchun and Mukden. The Nationalist troops equipped with the most modern American weapons, suffered heavy losses in the field and were unable to achieve their objectives.

Outside Manchuria, Communist forces occupied Loyang in April, Kaifeng in June, Tsinan in September, Chinchow in October and Hsuchow in December. The 'all out' war given by Chiang Kai-shek proved of no avail. The Communists declared Chiang and his aides 'war criminals' who should face trial.

On January 8, 1949, the Nationalist Foreign Minister requested the foreign Powers to act as intermediaries in an invitation to the KCT to negotiate for the restoration of peace. The U.S. Government replied on January 12 that the U.S. Government, after having made every effort to assist the Chinese in bringing peace to China immediately after the Japanese surrender, considered that it had no alternative but to withdraw from its position as an intermediary.

General Fu Tso-yi of the Nationalists in north China gave up after the fall of Tientsin on January 15, 1949. Peking thus changed hands on January 31 without bloodshed. On January 21, Chiang announced his retirement and left Nanking for Fenghua, his birthplace, and Li Tsung-jen automatically took his place just a few days before the fall of Peking.

General Li then sent an unofficial peace mission, headed by Dr. W. W. Yen, to fly to Peking to arrange for the subsequent reception of an official peace mission. The KCT announced an eight-point peace plan as the basis of a settlement. This included strict punishment of war criminals and the abolition of the KMT constitution. The official peace mission, headed by General Chang Chih-chung, proceeded to Peking on April 2 and held discussions with the KCT peace delegates, who were headed by Mr. Chou En-lai.

The Nationalist Government at Nanking was informed of the terms of the KCT. These set a deadline for April 20, and the KMT were requested to accept without change or reject the draft agreement presented by the KCT. The Nationalist Government considered this draft was based upon the previous eight-point proposals, and this was tantamount to unconditional surrender. An extension of the time limit was requested. There were contradictory views among KMT leaders, but they finally rejected the draft agreement, and requested a cease-fire order for further negotiations. The KCT informed the Nationalist peace delegates at Peking that, if no reply was received by April 20, or if the reply was a rejection of the terms, the KCT would consider the negotiations ended.

On April 20, at midnight, the KCT forces crossed the Yangtze River, a crossing which turned out to be 'ridiculously easy', and occupied Nanking on April 22. The Nationalist Government hurtried to remove its capital to Canton. The occupations of Hangchow (May 4), Hankow (May 16), Shanghai (May 25), Sian (May 29) and Tsingtao (June 2) by the Communist forces followed one another in quick succession.

Changsha was handed over to the Communists on August 4 by Governor Cheng Chien, an elderly KMT member, without any fighting. Foochow, capital of Fukien province, fell to the Communists on August 16, and Amoy on September 23. In the north-west, Lanchow, the capital of Kansu province, which was under heavy Communist attack, changed hands on August 28, while Sining, capital of Chinghai province, fell on September 3. Ninghsia gave in on September 22. The Moslem troops, believed to be the best fighters in the north-west, were determined not to fight a civil war. In turn, Sinkiang, the westernmost part of China, also went over to the Communists on September 28.

The Communist drive on Canton went at such a speed that the Nationalist Government was compelled to evacuate Canton, and made Chungking and Taipeh successively its two new capitals. The Communist forces entered Canton on October 15, 1949. Kweilin, capital of Kwangsi province, was occupied on October 21, and Kweiyang, capital of Kweichow province, on November 14.

Szechwan, though possessing formidable natural barriers, was now exposed to Communist attack. The Communist forces expanded steadily westwards after the fall of Canton. The fall of Chungking was announced on December 1 when the Nationalist Government removed its capital to Chengtu. This could not hold out either, and it fell to the Communists on December 8. Sikang province, the last Nationalist military base on the mainland, also went over to the

Communists. General Chiang Kai-shek flew to Taipeh, the new capital for the Nationalist Government, while General Li Tsung-jen took plane to America to undergo an operation. In Yunnan province, Governor Lu Han issued a proclamation pledging his loyalty to the Peking Government on December 10. By the end of 1949, the Communist forces had conquered the whole mainland, with the exception of Hainan Island,[15] Tibet and Formosa.

11. Recognition of Chinese People's Republic

The Chinese People's Political Consultative Conference held in Peking with an attendance of more than 600 delegates, brought into being the Chinese People's Republic. Mao Tse-tung, Chairman of the KCT, was elected chairman of the 'Central People's Government of the People's Republic of China' on September 30, 1949. Six vice-chairmen, namely Mme Sun Yat-sen, née Soong Ching-ling, widow of the founder of the Chinese Republic, Mr. Chang Lang, Chairman of the China Democratic League, General Chu Teh, Commander-in-Chief of the Communist armies, Mr. Kao Kang, Chairman of the Regional Government of Manchuria, Mr. Liu Shao-chi, member of the Communists' inner circle, and Marshal Li Chai-sum, Chairman of the KMT Revolutionary Committee.

Mao Tse-tung formally proclaimed the inauguration of the new régime. Peiping was given back its old name of Peking, and was adopted as the capital of the new republic. The Chinese calendar was abolished and replaced by the European one. A new national flag of five yellow stars on a red background was adopted. A popular song, 'The March of the Volunteers', was provisionally made the new national anthem.

Mao declared: 'This government is willing to establish diplomatic relations with any foreign government which is willing to observe the principles of equality, mutual benefit and mutual respects of territorial integrity and sovereignty.' A message was sent to all foreign diplomatic representatives in China inviting recognition of the new régime. Chou En-lai was appointed by the Central People's Government Council as Premier of State Administration and con-currently Minister for Foreign Affairs.

The Soviet Government recognized the Chinese People's Republic on the day following its inauguration, and simultaneously broke off relations with the Nationalist Government then in Canton.

[15] Chinese Communist forces landed on Hainan Island, April 17, 1950.

A telegram sent to Chou En-lai by M. Gromyko, Soviet Deputy Foreign Minister, is produced in part hereunder:

'Having examined the proposal of the Central People's Government of China, the Soviet Government, invariably striving to maintain friendly relations with the Chinese people, and confident that the Central People's Government of China expresses the will of the overwhelming majority of the Chinese people, informs you that it has decided to establish diplomatic relations between the Soviet Union and the People's Republic of China and to exchange Ambassadors.'

The Nationalist Government, however, decided to sever relations with the Soviet Union on October 3. The *Waichiaopu* issued a statement saying, 'This recognition was not only an act of aggression against China, but also a threat to the peace and security of the Far East.'

After Soviet recognition, Bulgaria, Rumania, Yugoslavia, Czechoslovakia, Poland and Hungary followed suit on October 3.

On October 5, General Reshchin, who was the Soviet Ambassador to the Nationalist régime in Nanking and Canton until his recall in May, was newly appointed as the Soviet Ambassador in Peking. Mr. Wang Chia-hsiang was appointed Chinese Communist Ambassador to Moscow.

Moscow sources hinted that the Communist Government would review the treaties concluded with foreign countries by the Nationalist Government and, according to their nature, would revise, annul, or recognize them. The Sino-Soviet Treaty of Friendship and Alliance is, practically, the only treaty of a detrimental character known to have been concluded by the Nationalist Government.

The British view on recognition of the Peking régime was expressed by Sir Terence Shone on December 2 in the political Committee of the United Nations General Assembly that the question of recognition of the Chinese Communist régime should be decided on the facts and should not be influenced by like or dislike of the Government in question.

Burma recognized the Peking régime on December 15 following the severance of diplomatic relations with Burma by the Chinese Nationalist Government. Burma, in fact, was the first non-Communist country to recognize Communist China. The Korean Democratic People's Republic also appointed a new Ambassador to Peking.

India recognized the Communist régime on December 30. Mr. K. M. Panikkar who was Indian Ambassador in Nanking has been appointed to Peking. Pakistan's recognition of the Peking régime was effected on January 4, 1950. She is the third non-Communist Government to give full recognition to the Peking Government.

British recognition of the Peking régime finally came on January 6. It had been generally anticipated. Significantly enough, formal recognition took place three days before the Colombo Conference of the Commonwealth Foreign Ministers, which began on January 9. Recognition of the Nationalist Government was officially withdrawn.

The British Government note was delivered to the Communist Foreign Minister, Chou En-lai, by Mr. W. Graham, the British Consul-General in Peking. An abstract thereof follows:

'H.M.'s Government in the United Kingdom of Great Britain and Northern Ireland, having completed their study of the situation resulting from the formation of the Central People's Government of the People's Republic of China, and observing that it is now in effective control of by far the greater part of the territory of China, have this day recognized the government as the *de jure* government of China. In these circumstances, His Majesty's Government, in response to Chairman Mao Tse-tung's proclamation of October 1, 1949, are ready to establish diplomatic relations on the basis of equality, mutual benefit, and mutual respect of territory and sovereignty, and are prepared to exchange diplomatic representatives with the Central People's Government.'

The Nationalist Foreign Minister, Dr. George Yeh at Taipeh, announced his government's decision to recall its diplomatic mission in London.

Ceylon and Norway recognized the Peking régime on the same day as the British recognition. Denmark and Israel also accorded *de jure* recognition to the People's Republic of China on January 9.

Afghanistan, Finland, Viet Nam and Sweden accorded their recognition in January, while Switzerland and Holland followed suit in February and March respectively. The People's Republic of China and the Mongolian People's Republic have also exchanged Ambassadors. The first Mongolian Ambassador arrived at Peking in June.

Chapter XXI

SINO-SOVIET TREATY OF FRIENDSHIP, ALLIANCE AND MUTUAL ASSISTANCE, FEBRUARY 14, 1950

In September 1949 the Chinese Communist Party announced that it would recognize, revise or annul, according to their nature, the treaties concluded with foreign countries by the Kuomintang. The Sino-Soviet Treaty of 1945, a very different document from any other concluded by the Nationalist Government, would be included in this review. Therefore after the formal recognition of the Chinese People's Republic by the Soviet Union, it became necessary for Mao Tze-tung to try to find ways to revise or annul the notorious 1945 Treaty. Out of this came the new Sino-Soviet Treaty of Friendship, Alliance and Mutual Assistance. Not only does this new treaty govern the present relations between the two countries, but future relations will largely depend upon it.

1. Mao Tze-tung's Visit to Moscow

In the eyes of the average Chinese, there could never be real friendship between China and the U.S.S.R. so long as the 1945 Treaty continued in force. Its revision or nullification, however, would have been no easy task unless Mao Tze-tung had taken the opportunity to see Stalin in person and persuade him that the best course for the Soviet Union to pursue would be to renounce its gains of 1945. It so happened that at the time when Mao was ready to negotiate, Stalin's seventieth birthday was approaching. Mao seized this chance to visit Moscow on the pretext of celebrating the occasion, but in reality he wished to discuss the whole range of Sino-Soviet relations *tête-à-tête* with the Soviet leader.

On December 16, 1949, Mao Tze-tung arrived in Moscow accompanied by Professor Chen Po-ta and other retinue. The Soviet Ambassador to Peking, N. V. Roshchin, also accompanied him. He was met by Molotov and other high officials of the Soviet Government at the railway station, and was received by Stalin on the same day. The forthcoming meeting between Mao and Stalin had already been hailed by the Communist paper in Peking as 'a meeting that will change world history' or 'the Great Event of 1949' and it seemed that some mutual understanding had already been agreed upon.

The reception in the Kremlin in celebration of Stalin's birthday was attended by visiting delegations from China and European countries. *Pravda* made some distinction between China and most of the other countries. The East European countries were all described as 'Peoples' democracies which have here set out on the road of building Socialism', but China was mentioned as a country which had so far simply 'thrown off the yoke of colonial oppression'. Mao Tze-tung, when he addressed the large meeting in the Bolshoi Theatre in Moscow, spoke as the head of an equal State, for he referred to the Soviet Union as 'our great ally'.

In answering a Tass correspondent's questions, Mao Tze-tung stated that the length of his sojourn in the U.S.S.R. depended on the time required to settle outstanding problems of the existing Treaty of Friendship and Alliance, a request for Soviet credits and a trade agreement. Mao Tze-tung's long stay in Moscow and the later arrival of Chou En-lai on January 20, 1950, seemed to indicate that either the conference was near its completion or some hard bargaining was still going on.

2. Signing of Treaty

The Thirty-Year Sino-Soviet Treaty of Friendship, Alliance and Mutual Assistance was signed in Moscow on February 14, 1950, by Chou En-lai and Vyshinsky representing their respective countries. (See full text in Appendix D.) The speech made by Chou En-lai after signing the treaty is reproduced in part hereunder.

'The significance of the treaty and agreements between China and the Soviet Union is of particular importance for the revived People's Republic of China. This treaty and these agreements will help the Chinese people to realize that they are not alone, and will help in the restoration and development of Chinese economy.

'The agreements between China and the Soviet Union on the

Chinese Changchun Railway, Port Arthur and Dairen, the agreement on granting credits to China, and also the exchange of letters on the transference gratis to the Chinese Government by the Soviet Government of property acquired in Manchuria from Japanese owners and on transference gratis of buildings in the former so-called military cantonment in Peking, which agreements constitute a demonstration of great friendship on the part of the Soviet Government and Generalissimo Stalin, undoubtedly will evoke the greatest enthusiasm among the Chinese people.'

In reply, A. Y. Vyshinsky made the following remarks, in brief:

'The Treaty of Friendship, Alliance and Mutual Assistance signed to-day between the Soviet Union and the People's Republic of China expresses the striving of both our peoples for eternal friendship and co-operation for the good of our countries, for the strengthening of peace and the security of the nations.

'Of great and important significance is the agreement on the Chinese Changchun Railway, Port Arthur and Dairen. The agreement points out that since 1945 radical changes have occurred in the situation in the Far East which permit a new approach to the question of the Chinese Changchun Railway, Port Arthur and Dairen. Every article of this agreement bespeaks the high respect on the part of the Soviet Union for the national independence and the national rights and interests of the Chinese people, and bespeaks the grandeur of the principles of Soviet foreign policy. The determination of our peoples to develop and consolidate economic and cultural ties between the Soviet Union and China and to render each other economic assistance formed the basis of the agreement on the granting of long-term economic credits by the Soviet Union to the People's Republic of China.'[1]

Stalin not only gave a dinner in the Kremlin honouring Mao Tze-tung and Chou En-lai but also attended a banquet given by Wang Chia-hsiang, Ambassador of the Chinese People's Republic to Moscow, to celebrate the signing of the treaty. The reception was held at the Metropole Hotel in Moscow, and this was the first time for Stalin to dine out at a public hotel since he took over power twenty-seven years before. This was regarded as an indication of the anxiety of the Soviet leader to show Mao Tze-tung, the Chinese

[1] New China News Agency, London, February 28, 1950.

Communist leader, the maximum courtesy.[2] Both Mao and Chou left Moscow for China on February 17.

3. Important Terms in Treaty

Contemporary Sino-Soviet relations are governed by this new pact. Notes were exchanged to the effect that both governments guaranteed the independent status of the Mongolian People's Republic as a result of the referendum of 1945, and the establishment of diplomatic relations between the two Republics. Further notes were exchanged affirming that the corresponding treaty and agreements concluded on August 14, 1945, had become invalid. Both parties agreed jointly to prevent any repetition of aggression by Japan or any other state which might unite with Japan, directly or indirectly, in acts of aggression. In case any party was attacked by Japan or any State allied with her, the other party would immediately render military or other assistance with all the means at its disposal. The Chinese Changchun Railway, Port Arthur and Dairen would be returned to the Chinese People's Republic after the signing of the peace treaty with Japan, or not later than at the end of 1952. Soviet troops would then be withdrawn from the Manchurian naval base of Port Arthur. The Soviet Government further agreed to grant long-term credits amounting to 300,000,000 American dollars at one per cent interest over a period of five years for the purchase of industrial equipment from the Soviet Union. The note also declared that the Soviet Government would hand over to the Chinese People's Republic, without compensation, property acquired by Soviet economic organizations from Japanese owners in Manchuria, and all buildings of the former military settlement in Peking.

The new treaty also stated that both parties would consult each other in regard to all important international problems, and would render each other every possible economic assistance to carry out the necessary economic co-operation. Pending the transfer of the Chinese Changchun Railway, the new existing position of the Sino-Soviet joint administration would remain unchanged. The order of filling posts by both sides would be established, being filled alternately after the coming into force of the treaty.

The installations in the naval base of Port Arthur would be handed over to China immediately upon the conclusion of a peace

[2] The *Daily Mail*, February 16, 1950.

treaty with Japan. In connection with this, the Chinese Government would compensate the Soviet Union for the expense incurred in the restoration effected since 1945. A joint Sino-Soviet Military Commission would be established within three months upon the coming into force of the present treaty. Pending the withdrawal of Soviet troops, the zone of billeting of Soviet troops in the area of Port Arthur would remain unchanged. The question of Port Dairen would be further considered upon the conclusion of a peace treaty with Japan.

With regard to the loan amounting to 300,000,000 American dollars granted to China by the Soviet Union, it was to be made available over a period of five years and was to be used for purchasing machinery and equipment from the Soviet Union. The Chinese People's Government agreed to redeem the credits, as well as interest on them, in actual goods and hard currency in the course of ten years, i.e., one-tenth every year and the first payment to be effected not later than December 31, 1954. It is interesting that both countries negotiated the loan in terms of American dollars.

Sceptics noticed that the treaty was identical in form and wording with those which the Soviet Union had previously concluded with Eastern European satellites, and it was suspected that there might be other secret clauses. Why else had two months been spent in discussion? They wondered why the question of Chinese expansion into south-east Asia had not been brought up. Others thought that the loan was very meagre in view of the vast need of China's ravaged economy.

On the other hand, Communist sympathizers believed that China could never become a satellite of the Soviet Union, nor Mao Tze-tung a Chinese Tito. While in Moscow he described the Soviet Union as 'our friendly ally'. They argued that it was absurd to put China in the same category as Eastern European countries in view of the size and population of the Chinese Empire. The smallness of the loan might be a sign of the tightness of Soviet economy, though its value has since been diminished by the revaluation of the Soviet rouble announced shortly after the grant of the loan. In any case this would be a first loan; further loans might be made as required. The Soviet Union had given generously to China during the war years.

These were the terms presented to China after two months' hard bargaining between Mao Tze-tung and Stalin. The rumours that China was leasing seven additional ports to the Soviet Union in exchange for Soviet support of Chinese expansion into south-east Asia proved unjustified. Treaty rights which the Soviet Union had won from the Nationalist Government in 1945 were returned to the Chinese People's Government. This was a big saving of face for China as the new treaty redressed the old.

Soviet assistance to the Chinese People's Government was further justified by the signing of the Sino-Soviet Sinkiang Pact and the Sino-Soviet Civil Aviation Agreement on March 27, 1950, at Moscow. The first was to organize two joint stock companies for the exploitation of oil and non-ferrous minerals for thirty years, while the latter was to organize a civil aviation company operating on three routes between Peking and Chita, Irkutsk and Alma-Ata for ten years. All expenses and profits were to be shared equally. Care had been taken to show that the agreements, particularly on the part of management, were on a basis of strict equality.

A Sino-Soviet trade agreement and an agreement on an exchange of goods for 1950 were signed in Moscow on April 19, 1950. Under the agreement on the exchange of goods, the Soviet Union promised to supply equipment, while China supplied raw material. A protocol was also signed on the same day concerning the delivery to be made by the Soviet Union to the Chinese People's Republic in 1950-2 of equipment and materials, in accordance with the credit granted under the agreement of February 14, 1950. (See also Addendum, p. 308.)

4. Comments on Treaty

Roosevelt's surrender during the Yalta Conference resulted in the sale of China's interests. Naturally this did not please Chiang Kai-shek, who was reported to have been greatly disturbed at the President's singular failure to keep him informed. It was only common sense for the Kuomintang leaders to think that since others were trying to please Stalin at China's expense they themselves could do the same. By the time the Chinese mission left Chungking for Moscow for the signing of the treaty, atomic bombs had been dropped on Japan's soil and the world had already heard the joyful news of Japan's surrender. The mystery still remains why an almost unneeded treaty should have been signed when the collapse of the common enemy was already in sight. What a curious coincidence that the signing of the treaty fell on the same day as Japan's surrender—August 14, 1945!

Such was the Nationalist Government's pacific attitude towards the Soviet Union. The Nationalist leaders thought that the peaceful relationship of thirty years with the U.S.S.R. was China's only need, particularly as the Soviet Government had given an assurance that whatever assistance was extended to China would be given only to the Nationalist Government. The price paid to the U.S.S.R., though high, was only a trifle as compared with the Soviet assurance not to give aid to another opposing party. Secondly, there probably was a feeling of being bound by the Yalta Secret Agreement. The Nationalist leaders, however, failed to realize that should China refuse to sign in view of a change in the situation, the Allies would be in hearty agreement. Nevertheless, the Yalta Agreement and the 1945 Treaty were both blots on the pages of modern history.

Nothing would have been better than for the Soviet Union to repudiate the treaty. Rumours were even current in Moscow that there would be a revision of the treaty by the Peking régime before the visit of Mao Tze-tung to the Kremlin. As regards the new treaty it is premature to predict whether its provisions will be kept. But the Chinese People's Government will have to be on their best behaviour towards the Soviet Union for the next two years for fear that promises might be revoked. Should the Soviet Union fail to keep its promises by the end of 1952, not only would there be general dissatisfaction among the Chinese, but the Chinese People's Government, one of the signatories, would lose the support of the people. China, though unable to force her formidable neighbour to fulfil the treaty obligations, could hesitate to come to the rescue of the Soviet Union if the latter were at bay.

The military implications of the treaty also need further study. What will happen if the Soviet Union is again attacked by Germany, or if China clashes with Britain on the question of Hongkong or with France on the matter of Indo-China? And what will be the Soviet attitude if Outer Mongolia has another border dispute with China as has happened heretofore?

In a communiqué it was stated that the question of Port Dairen ' must be further considered upon the conclusion of a peace treaty with Japan '. The question of compensating the Soviet Union for expenses incurred at Port Arthur since 1945 may be one of the main factors which will lead to further disputes unless one Power dominates the other. Consultation on all important international problems and the carrying out of economic co-operation may also lead sceptics to suppose that China's sovereignty is being infringed.

Should the parties fail to agree on any important international problem, what would then be the outcome? There is also in the communiqué a vague expression recognizing the independence of Outer Mongolia 'with its existing boundary as its boundary', as contained in the old treaty. This may lead to further dispute.

The invalidating of the Sino-Soviet Treaty of 1945 simultaneously nullified the Yalta Secret Agreement which was so detrimental to China. No matter how legitimate it might have been for the Soviet Union to ask a price for entering the war against Japan, it caused, nevertheless, great bitterness in Sino-Soviet diplomatic relations. Other Powers could have undone Yalta only by war. The Soviet Union alone could offer redress. The Soviet's actual gains in Manchuria under the 1945 Treaty were, at any rate, limited. But the benefits to be won from the sympathy and appreciation of the Chinese populace are beyond bounds. It goes without saying that the degree of China's gratitude will be in proportion to the generosity of the Soviet Union. Although no mention was made in the new treaty of the machinery taken away from Manchuria as war booty or of the withdrawal from Dairen, which matter would be 'further considered' on the conclusion of a peace treaty with Japan, the Soviet Union has made some show of generosity by offering much and demanding little. One thing seems sure: the Soviet Union will fulfil all treaty obligations and keep her promise to return the Chinese Changchun Railway, Port Arthur and Dairen to China by 1952 at the latest, to win the confidence and gratitude of the Chinese people which would obviously be a great asset to the Soviet Union.

5. Future Trend of Sino-Soviet Relations

It is extremely curious that China and Russia or the Soviet Union have never been, in the real sense, at war. History contains no reference to Sino-Russian or Sino-Soviet war. The common frontier extends from north-eastern Manchuria to the west of Outer Mongolia and still farther west to Sinkiang, a line measuring more than 3,000 miles. This must surely be the longest frontier in the world. It is no hindrance to peace. Rather is it a guarantee of perpetual friendship betwixt the two countries. Soviet aid to China during the Sino-Japanese War was enormous, and, what is even of greater importance, it was the first aid given to China before the Pearl Harbour incident. Without the Soviet Union's timely aid, China would not have been able to resist Japan.

The U.S.S.R. is a country with territories in both Asia and Europe. What she feared most was a simultaneous attack from both sides when the German-Japanese anti-Comintern pact was in force. China's refusal to join the anti-Comintern pact and her armed resistance against Japan eased the critical situation of the U.S.S.R.

The conclusion of a pact first with Germany and later with Japan by the U.S.S.R. removed the threat of attack from both west and east. It was a great achievement on the part of Soviet diplomacy.

The Soviet-German hostilities changed the situation entirely. It seemed that the Soviet Union had passed the peak of her ascendancy. Not only in the west were the German, Finnish and Rumanian forces attacking her, but in the east, along the Manchurian border, Japan was waiting for the chance to strike a serious blow.

The reason why the Soviet Union did not attack Japan earlier can be explained thus: why should she pull other people's chestnuts out of the fire? Besides, the price might have been too heavy, as Japan was a formidable foe. The Soviet leader was not so naïve as to let his government, created by himself, plunge into a war that would bring no ultimate victory.

When Japan was stuck in China's quagmire, she tried to come to terms with the Soviet Union. What the Soviet Government was interested in at that time were the nullification of the tripartite anti-Comintern pact, cancellation of the fisheries convention, and, most of all, the nullification of the Portsmouth Treaty concluded after the Russo-Japanese War of 1905. She could not imagine things turning out so favourable that what she lost to Japan would be restored and the *status quo* in Outer Mongolia be preserved as the outcome of the Yalta Secret Agreement and later be fulfilled by the Sino-Soviet Treaty of 1945. The Soviet Union won an easy victory over Japan, just when the latter was about to surrender, as the war lasted only six days. It was indeed the climax of Soviet history. With the downfall of the Nationalist Government and the establishment of the Chinese People's Republic in Peking, the Soviet Union no longer feared encountering another powerful nation. As a result, future friendly relations between the two countries should help to maintain everlasting peace in the Far East.

Generally speaking, Sino-Soviet relations have always played an important part in the diplomatic and political history of both countries. Notwithstanding that the leaders of the two countries did have frequent dissensions and serious differences from time to time, and the methods of administration were quite opposite in character, the two peoples themselves have never shown any hatreds or prejudices whatsoever. On the contrary, they are much alike in many ways, and, if not prevented, will make the friendliest neighbours.

The Soviet Union harbours the same races within her borders as does China. In Central Asia, particularly Transcaucasia, there will be found not only many strange tribes but also Uzbeks, Tadjiks, Kazaks and Kirghiz who are of the same origin as those in Sinkiang. All along the Sinkiang frontier, such Turkish tribes wander at will because they know there is no national boundary.

So long as the Soviets and the Chinese develop no religious or racial hatred such as happens in other lands, there is every chance of a friendly spirit expanding between the two. Even if the leadership and administration of either country change from time to time, becoming either ideological or otherwise, nevertheless the character and traditions of the two nations remain the same and, for this reason, these two mighty peoples in the uttermost East should become even more friendly in the future.

6. Relations Between U.S.A., U.S.S.R. and China

The relations, geographical and political, between the United States and China make it obvious that the maintenance of peace and order in Asia depends not only upon friendly relations between the Soviets and the Chinese but also upon genuine co-operation between the United States and the Soviet Union, these being the only two great Powers remaining after the Second World War. The American people should learn more about the Soviets and vice versa. The late Wendell Wilkie thought America should co-operate with the Soviet Union in peace time as she did during the successful and heroic defence of Stalingrad in 1942. He stated that the Soviet Union 'is a dynamic country, a vital new society, a force that cannot be by-passed in any future world'.[3] Sumner Welles once also wrote optimistically: 'There are no traditional or material grounds for antagonism between the Russian people and the people of the United States.'[4]

Since the United States has no longer a monopoly of atomic bombs, the international control of this disastrous weapon seems more vital than ever. If the two great Powers cannot come to terms, then they will start a race in the production of atomic bombs, and, once pro-

[3] *One World*, 1934, p. 68.
[4] *The Time for Decision*, p. 318.

duced, such things tend to be used suddenly. The division of the world into two camps, instead of its integration into a whole, would surely destroy the last remnant of our civilization. It is true, 'We must remain at peace or die.'[5]

On this point Stalin, when interviewed by Stassen of the American Republican Party, stated that though the economic systems differed, the two countries had never been at war but, on the contrary, were close allies. Stalin went on to say that if the two different systems could co-operate so well in war-time, why could they not do so in time of peace? Answering Stassen's query regarding reciprocal willingness to co-operate, Stalin emphasized that the Soviet Union was quite willing to work with the Western Powers.

Another Stalin statement, in reply to Henry Wallace's open letter in May 1948, was that 'peaceful settlements of disagreements between the U.S.S.R. and the U.S.A. are not only possible but are also absolutely essential in the interest of general peace'. The statement repeated Stalin's belief in the possibility of the peaceful co-existence of Capitalism and Communism, in spite of differences in their economic systems and ideologies.[6]

These three big countries in the Pacific area, the United States, the Soviet Union and China, all desire peace. Right down the ages these three countries have never resorted to war with one another, but have fought shoulder to shoulder to resist aggression. Such resistance is significant enough to warrant the continuation of peace. Welfare in the Pacific World depends entirely on Soviet-American co-operation. China remains an important factor with regard to co-operation and her future national policy would affect it.

It would not be wrong, therefore, to say that China's future will determine that of the Pacific. Nothing better could happen than for China to become a bridge for Soviet-American co-operation. At the same time, she would be in a position to keep a strict watch over Japan and prevent that country from becoming an armed menace in the Pacific as once she was. In this way, China could perform a double act of valuable service to the rest of the world.

How do the three countries stand to-day? In the last ten years, Soviet diplomacy has been strikingly successful. The Soviet Union has become one of the strongest nations on earth. The so-called popular front, the Iron Curtain, the cold war, and what not, are all

[5] Opening address of the fourth United Nations Day by General Romulo, President of the Assembly, October 24, 1949.
[6] *The Times*, February 21, 1950.

recent inventions of the Soviet Union. Must she prolong and
expand the revolution into a world ferment? Failing to bring
about world revolution, would the Soviet system be vanquished by
capitalist powers? Will the Soviet Union and her satellites gradually
weaken, or will the capitalist powers become so strong as to destroy
her? Surely such sentiments are born of dread and fantastic imagination. Remove the ugly fears and suspicions and there is no
earthly reason why two totally different systems should not exist side
by side in harmony. It would be extremely dangerous for the Soviet
Union to attempt another encounter with the capitalist world. Now,
at any rate, the Soviet Union is enjoying a spell of peace and stability with all her satellites round her. She has, indeed, the largest
unbroken area of land in the world. Why should she run the risk
of attempting a world revolution, the success of which would be
more than doubtful? If capitalist countries are bound to fall, let
them fall like ripe plums. It is unnecessary for her to hasten their
downfall. Moreover, the Soviet Union lost so many people during
the last global war that she may not be prepared to start another
duel.

Consider now the position of the United States. What a great
international responsibility is hers to-day! Think of the vast
financial aid she is according to many countries ruined by war.
Without Marshall Aid, many European countries would have turned
Communist. Indeed, at the last general election in Italy, not very
long ago, the Communists nearly got in. As for France, there was
a time when three weeks went by and still she could not set up a
government. The uproar by the Communist deputies in the Paris
Assembly in March 1950 almost put an end to Parliament. As for
Britain, the crisis is still on, and the devaluation of the pound
sterling has produced a fall in the standard of living, affecting every
Englishman. The recent Fuchs case has revealed the existence of
an extensive spy ring in the heart of London. Even in America, the
Government thought it necessary to arrest eleven Communist leaders
and sentence them to imprisonment. Serious strikes followed one
another in rapid succession. Moreover, land exploitation and aerial
development in the Arctic have brought the United States and the
Soviet Union into juxtaposition and made them rival neighbours.
No longer holding the monopoly of atomic bombs, the United States
has to realize that she has no hope of winning an easy war. The
only sensible way for her is to try to reach an understanding with
the Soviet Union without any irritating challenging attitude.

With regard to Communist China, the picture is outstandingly clear. The duty of the People's Government is to seek first and foremost the welfare and interests of the people. The Communist Government has won such vast territory within so short a time that the only way to restore order and bring conditions back to normal is to gain the help and co-operation of educated and experienced men from all walks of life, whether partisans or not. The great defect of the Kuomintang régime, at the time of its domination, was that intellectuals and experienced men were ousted from office simply because they were not members of the party. Indeed, the party itself was divided into cliques with the result that all the power was concentrated in a few hands. The Chinese Communists would be well advised not to make the same blunder. On the contrary, all men of ability, both at home and abroad, should be invited to play an active part in the reconstruction of the nation. So far as science and industry are concerned, China is far behind the times. She can pass through the difficult phase of reconstruction only if the world is at peace. Should another global war break out, China, a weak nation but one whose territory is of great strategic importance, would inevitably become a battlefield for other Powers. No matter which side won, China would be the first to suffer ruin. Therefore, the future of the Pacific World depends upon Sino-Soviet relations, now in the making. The foreign policy of the People's Government will not only determine the success or failure of China herself but influence the welfare of the world at large.

7. Future of Asia

The point of greatest danger to peace in the Far East does not lie so much in China as in lands like south-east Asia and Korea. Tension started when France restored the throne Viet Nam to Bao Dai. This action received the assent of both Britain and America. On the other hand, the Soviet Union and the Chinese People's Republic recognized Mo Chi-minh as head of Viet Nam. As to South Korea, this is even more vulnerable. It is an arena which has long been recognized as strategically disadvantageous to America. Seoul, the capital of Korea, is only 3,000 miles from Alaska, and thus is well within bombing range. These are powder magazines which, if lighted, will set the whole of Asia ablaze. The huge Chinese colony in Siam, the terror in Malaya, the unrest in Burma, the exis-tence of Communists and near-Communists in India and of adherents of the Soviet doctrine in Pakistan have all been important factors in bringing about the present chaos. Indeed, the great region of Asia, consisting of more than half the world's population, is in a constant state of change.

Mobilized and armed Communist forces in Asia are conservatively calculated at nearly five and a half million men, disposed over an area of approximately 8,600,000 square miles with a population of 650 million. Guerrilla warfare is going on even in the Phillipines.[7] This spontaneous tide of revolt is derived from poverty and desperation which resulted from the last war. It may bring ultimate disaster, and the whole of the Far East may succumb to it. There seems to be no way to extinguish the mighty conflagration as the struggle against Colonialism is becoming sterner than ever. The very effective cold war has spread from Europe to Asia with such velocity that it has almost turned into a 'hot war'.

As far as devastated and depleted China is concerned, it would be better for her to stay somewhat aloof. For if the oppressed peoples are fighting for national independence, they will surely succeed by following the right course. It is as unnecessary to help them as to attempt to accelerate the growth of crops by pulling at them. China's duty is to minimize the cold war in Asia instead of making it hotter.

Though the Middle Kingdom is no more a wounded dragon, she remains a sleeping lion. When the sleeping lion awakens, it will startle the world. Remember that one in every five on earth is a Chinese. China has no right to interfere in the affairs of neighbouring peoples. This would be against her peace-loving tradition. Interference might result in war, and, once a global war is started, no country can tell what will be the outcome.

The world's fundamental problem to-day is how to get the U.S.S.R. and the U.S.A. to co-operate both in Europe and Asia. The setting up of the East German Republic in Europe, the reported Soviet offer to return the Kuriles to Japan, and the growing Japanese criticism of irksome American occupation may further separate the world into two rival camps, Capitalist and Communist. Would it not be advisable to ask a third nation, friendly to the Soviet Union, to act as mediator, and have all cards put on the table so that differences can be levelled out? The United Nations Organization has, so far, failed to accomplish much for world peace. The U.S. Government should be ready to accept any reasonable compromise even if, in

---

[7] The *Sunday Times*, March 19, 1950.

some instances, it may not be favourable to them. An old Chinese saying goes: 'A chivalrous warrior will cut off an arm to save his body.' It is high time for America to make such a decision. After all, it is a fantastic illusion to think that the world can be dominated by one nation. The only solution is the co-existence of the two systems of administration which should and could exist concurrently in this world. Communist China, after showing a co-operative attitude, could perhaps be called upon as a mediator to cut the Gordian knot confronting the world to-day. Now that Communist China is in alliance with the Soviet Union, she has raised her standard and prestige, becoming number two of the Communist bloc and second only to the Soviet Union. She may ultimately be in the position to take up this mighty duty for the benefit not only of the Asiatic peoples, but of all mankind.

APPENDICES

Appendix A

SINO-SOVIET AGREEMENTS, MAY 31, 1924

AGREEMENT ON GENERAL PRINCIPLES FOR THE SETTLEMENT OF THE QUESTIONS BETWEEN THE REPUBLIC OF CHINA AND THE UNION OF SOVIET SOCIALIST REPUBLICS

THE Republic of China and the Union of Soviet Socialist Republics, desiring to re-establish normal relations with each other, have agreed to conclude an agreement on general principles for the settlement of questions between the two countries, and have to that end named as their Plenipotentiaries, that is to say:

His Excellency the President of the Republic of China:
VI KYUIN WELLINGTON KOO.
The Government of the Union of Soviet Socialist Republics:
LEV MIKHAILOVITCH KARAKHAN.

Who, having communicated to each other their respective full powers, found to be in good and due form, have agreed upon the following Articles:

Article I. Immediately upon the signing of the present Agreement, the normal diplomatic and consular relations between the two Contracting Parties shall be re-established.

The Government of the Republic of China agrees to take the necessary steps to transfer to the Government of the Union of Soviet Socialist Republics the Legation and Consular buildings formerly belonging to the Tsarist Government.

Article II. The Governments of the two Contracting Parties agree to hold, within one month after the signing of the present Agreement, a Conference which shall conclude and carry out detailed

347

arrangements relative to the questions in accordance with the principles as provided in the following Articles.

Such detailed arrangements shall be completed as soon as possible and, in any case, not later than six months from the date of the opening of the Conference as provided in the preceding paragraph.

Article III. The Governments of the two Contracting Parties agree to annul at the Conference as provided in the preceding Article, all Conventions, Treaties, Agreements, Protocols, Contracts, et cetera, concluded between the Government of China and the Tsarist Government and to replace them with new treaties, agreements, et cetera, on the basis of equality, reciprocity and justice, as well as the spirit of the Declarations of the Soviet Government of 1919 and 1920.

Article IV. The Government of the Union of Soviet Socialist Republics, in accordance with its policy and Declarations of 1919 and 1920, declares that all Treaties, Agreements, et cetera, concluded by the former Tsarist Government and any third party or parties affecting the sovereign rights or interests of China, are null and void.

The Governments of both Contracting Parties declare that in future neither Government will conclude any treaties or agreements which prejudice the sovereign rights of either Contracting Party.

Article V. The Government of the Union of Soviet Socialist Republics recognizes that Outer Mongolia is an integral part of the Republic of China, and respects China's sovereignty therein.

The Government of the Union of Soviet Socialist Republics declares that as soon as the questions for the withdrawal of all the troops of the Union of Soviet Socialist Republics from Outer Mongolia—namely—as to the time limit of the withdrawal of such troops and the measures to be adopted in the interests of the safety of the frontiers—are agreed upon at the Conference as provided in Article II of the present Agreement, it will effect the complete withdrawal of all the troops of the Union of Soviet Socialist Republics from Outer Mongolia.

Article VI. The Governments of the two Contracting Parties mutually pledge themselves not to permit, within their respective territories, the existence and/or activities of any organizations or groups whose aim is to struggle by acts of violence against the Governments of either Contracting Party.

The Government of the two Contracting Parties further pledge themselves not to engage in propaganda directed against the political and social systems of either Contracting Party.

Article VII. The Governments of the two Contracting Parties agree to re-demarcate their national boundaries at the Conference as provided in Article II of the present Agreement, and pending such re-demarcation, to maintain the present boundaries.

Article VIII. The Governments of the two Contracting Parties agree to regulate at the aforementioned Conference the questions relating to the navigation of rivers, lakes and other bodies of water which are common to their respective frontiers, on the basis of equality and reciprocity.

Article IX. The Governments of the two Contracting Parties agree to settle at the aforementioned Conference the question of the Chinese Eastern Railway in conformity with the principles as hereinafter provided:

1. The Governments of the two Contracting Parties declare that the Chinese Eastern Railway is a purely commercial enterprise.

The Governments of the two Contracting Parties mutually declare that with the exception of matters pertaining to the business operations which are under the direct control of the Chinese Eastern Railway, all other matters affecting the rights of the National and Local Governments of the Republic of China—such as judicial matters, matters relating to civil administration, military administration, police, municipal government, taxation and landed property (with the exception of lands required by the said Railway)—shall be administered by the Chinese Authorities.

2. The Government of the Union of Soviet Socialist Republics agrees to the redemption by the Government of the Republic of China, with Chinese capital, of the Chinese Eastern Railway, as well as all the appurtenant properties and to the transfer to China of all shares and bonds of the Railway.

3. The Governments of the two Contracting Parties shall settle at the Conference as provided in Article II of the present Agreement, the amount and conditions governing the redemption as well as the procedure for the transfer of the Chinese Eastern Railway.

4. The Government of the Union of Soviet Socialist Republics agrees to be responsible for the entire claims of the shareholders, bondholders, and creditors of the Chinese Eastern Railway incurred prior to the Revolution of March 9, 1917.

5. The Governments of the two Contracting Parties mutually agree that the future of the Chinese Eastern Railway shall be determined by the Republic of China and the Union of Soviet Socialist Republics, to the exclusion of any third party or parties.

6. The Governments of the two Contracting Parties agree to draw up an arrangement for the provisional management of the Chinese Eastern Railway, pending the settlement of the questions as provided under Section 3 of the present Article.

7. Until the various questions relating to the Chinese Eastern Railway are settled at the Conference as provided in Article II of the present Agreement, the rights of the two Governments arising out of the Contract of August 27/September 9, 1896, for the Construc-

tion and Operation of the Chinese Eastern Railway, which do not conflict with the present Agreement, and the Agreement for the provisional management of the Chinese Eastern Railway, and which do not prejudice the sovereign rights of China, shall be retained.

Article X. The Government of the Union of Soviet Socialist Republics agrees to renounce the special rights and privileges relating to all Concessions in all parts of China acquired by the Tsarist Government under various Conventions, Treaties, Agreements, et cetera.

Article XI. The Government of the Union of Soviet Socialist Republics agrees to renounce the Russian portion of the Boxer Indemnity.

Article XII. The Government of the Union of Soviet Socialist Republics agrees to relinquish the rights of extra-territoriality and consular jurisdiction.

Article XIII. The Governments of the two Contracting Parties agree to draw up simultaneously with the conclusion of a Commercial Treaty at the Conference as provided in Article II of the present Agreement, a Customs tariff for the two Contracting Parties in accordance with the principles of equality and reciprocity.

Article XIV. The Governments of the two Contracting Parties agree to discuss at the aforementioned Conference the questions relating to the claims for the compensation of losses.

Article XV. The present Agreement shall come into effect from the date of signature.

In witness whereof, the respective Plenipotentiaries have signed the present Agreement in duplicate in the English language and have affixed thereto their seals.

Done at the city of Peking this Thirty-first day of the Fifth month of the Thirteenth year of the Republic of China, which is the Thirty-first day of May, One thousand nine hundred and twenty-four.

(*Seal*) V. K. WELLINGTON KOO.
(*Seal*) L. M. KARAKHAN.

AGREEMENT FOR THE PROVISIONAL MANAGEMENT OF THE CHINESE EASTERN RAILWAY

The Republic of China and the Union of Soviet Socialist Republics mutually recognizing that, inasmuch as the Chinese Eastern Railway was built with capital furnished by the Russian Government and constructed entirely within Chinese territory, the said Railway is a purely commercial enterprise and that, excepting for matters appertaining to its own business operations, all other matters which affect the rights of the Chinese National and Local Governments shall be administered by the Chinese authorities, have agreed to conclude an agreement for the Provisional Management of the Railway with a view to carrying on jointly the management of the said Railway until its final settlement at the Conference as provided in Article II of the Agreement on General Principles for the Settlement of the Questions between the Republic of China and the Union of Soviet Socialist Republics of May 31, 1924, and have to that end named as their Plenipotentiaries, that is to say:

His Excellency the President of the Republic of China:
VI KYUIN WELLINGTON KOO.
The Government of the Union of Soviet Socialist Republics:
LEV MIKHAILOVITCH KARAKHAN.

Who, having communicated to each other their respective full powers, found to be in good and due form, have agreed upon the following Articles:

Article I. The Railway shall establish, for discussion and decision of all matters relative to the Chinese Eastern Railway, a Board of Directors, to be composed of ten persons, of whom five shall be appointed by the Government of the Republic of China and five by the Government of the Union of Soviet Socialist Republics.

The Government of the Republic of China shall appoint one of the Chinese Directors as President of the Board of Directors, who shall also be the Director General.

The Government of the Union of Soviet Socialist Republics shall appoint one of the Russian Directors as Vice-President of the Board of Directors, who shall also be the Assistant Director General.

Seven persons shall constitute a quorum, and all decisions of the

Board of Directors shall have the consent of not less than six persons before they can be carried out.

The Director and the Assistant Director General shall jointly manage the affairs of the Board of Directors and they shall both sign all the documents of the Board.

In the absence of either the Director General or the Assistant Director General, the respective Governments may appoint another Director to officiate as the Director General or the Assistant Director General (in the case of the Director General, by one of the Chinese Directors, and in that of the Assistant Director General, by one of the Russian Directors).

Article II. The Railway shall establish a Board of Auditors to be composed of five persons, namely, two Chinese auditors, who shall be appointed by the Government of the Republic of China and three Russian Auditors, who shall be appointed by the Government of the Union of Soviet Socialist Republics.

The Chairman of the Board of Auditors shall be elected from among the Chinese Auditors.

Article III. The Railway shall have a Manager, who shall be a national of the Union of Soviet Socialist Republics, and two Assistant Managers, one to be a national of the Republic of China and the other to be a national of the Union of Soviet Socialist Republics.

The said officers shall be appointed by the Board of Directors and such appointments shall be confirmed by their respective Governments.

The rights and duties of the Manager and the Assistant Managers shall be defined by the Board of Directors.

Article IV. The Chiefs and Assistant Chiefs of the various departments of the Railway shall be appointed by the Board of Directors.

If the Chief of a Department is a national of the Republic of China, the Assistant Chief of the Department shall be a national of the Union of Soviet Socialist Republics, and if the Chief of the Department is a national of the Union of Soviet Socialist Republics, the Assistant Chief of the Department shall be a national of the Republic of China.

Article V. The employment of persons in the various departments of the Railway shall be in accordance with the principle of equal representation between the nationals of the Republic of China and those of the Union of Soviet Socialist Republics.

Article VI. With the exception of the estimates and budgets, as provided in Article VII of the present Agreement, all other matters on which the Board of Directors cannot reach an agreement shall be referred for settlement to the Governments of the Contracting Parties.

Article VII. The Board of Directors shall present the estimates and budgets of the Railway to a joint meeting of the Board of Directors and the Board of Auditors for consideration and approval.

Article VIII. All the net profits of the Railway shall be held by the Board of Directors and shall not be used pending a final settlement of the question of the present Railway.

Article IX. The Board of Directors shall revise as soon as possible the statutes of the Chinese Eastern Railway Company, approved on December 4, 1896, by the Tsarist Government, in accordance with the present Agreement and the Agreement on General Principles for the Settlement of the Questions between the Republic of China and the Union of Soviet Socialist Republics of May 31, 1924, and in any case, not later than six months from the date of the constitution of the Board of Directors.

Pending their revision, the aforesaid statutes, in so far as they do not conflict with the present Agreement on General Principles for the Settlement of the Questions between the Republic of China and the Union of Soviet Socialist Republics and do not prejudice the rights of sovereignty of the Republic of China, shall continue to be observed.

Article X. The present Agreement shall cease to have effect as soon as the question of the Chinese Eastern Railway is finally settled at the Conference as provided in Article II of the Agreement on Gneral Principles for the Settlement of the Questions between the Republic of China and the Union of Soviet Socialist Republics of May 31, 1924.

Article XI. The present Agreement shall come into effect from the date of signature.

In witness whereof, the respective Plenipotentiaries have signed the present Agreement in duplicate in the English language and have affixed thereto their seals.

Done at the city of Peking this Thirty-first day of the Fifth month of the Thirteenth year of the Republic of China, which is the Thirty-first day of May, One thousand nine hundred and twenty-four.

> *(Seal)* V. K. WELLINGTON KOO.
> *(Seal)* L. M. KARAKHAN.

DECLARATION I

The Government of the Republic of China and the Government of the Union of Soviet Socialist Republics declare that immediately after the signing of the Agreement on General Principles between the Republic of China and the Union of Soviet Socialist Republics of May 31, 1924, they will reciprocally hand over to each other all the real estate and movable property owned by China and the former Tsarist Government and found in their respective territories. For this purpose each Government will furnish the other with a list of the property to be transferred.

In faith whereof, the respective Plenipotentiaries of the Governments of the two Contracting Parties have signed the present Declaration in duplicate in the English language and have affixed thereto their seals.

Done at the city of Peking this Thirty-first day of the Fifth month of the Thirteenth year of the Republic of China, which is the Thirty-first day of May, One thousand nine hundred and twenty-four.

(<i>Seal</i>) V. K. WELLINGTON KOO.
(<i>Seal</i>) L. M. KARAKHAN.

DECLARATION II

The Government of the Republic of China and the Government of the Union of Soviet Socialist Republics hereby declare that it is understood that with regard to the buildings and landed property of the Russian Orthodox Mission belonging as it does to the Government of the Union of Soviet Socialist Republics, the question of the transfer or other suitable disposal of the same will be jointly determined at the Conference provided in Article II of the Agreement on General Principles between the Republic of China and the Union of Soviet Socialist Republics of May 31, 1924, in accordance with the internal laws and regulations existing in China regarding property-holding in the inland. As regards the buildings and property of the Russian Orthodox Mission belonging as it does to the Government of the Union of Soviet Socialist Republics at Peking and Patachu, the Chinese Government will take steps to immediately transfer same as soon as the Government of the Union of Soviet Socialist Republics will designate a Chinese person or organization, in accordance with the law and regulations existing in China regarding property-holding in the inland.

Meanwhile the Government of the Republic of China will at once take measures with a view to guarding all the said buildings and property and clearing them from all persons now living there.

It is further understood that this expression of understanding has the same force and validity as a general declaration embodied in the said Agreement on General Principles.

In faith whereof, the respective Plenipotentiaries of the Governments of the two Contracting Parties have signed the present

Declaration in duplicate in the English language and have affixed thereto their seals.

Done at the city of Peking this Thirty-first day of the Fifth month of the Thirteenth year of the Republic of China, which is the Thirty-first day of May, One thousand nine hundred and twenty-four.

(Seal) V. K. WELLINGTON KOO.
(Seal) L. M. KARAKHAN.

DECLARATION III

The Government of the Republic of China and the Government of the Union of Soviet Socialist Republics jointly declare that it is understood that with reference to Article IV of the Agreement on General Principles between the Republic of China and the Union of Soviet Socialist Republics of May 31, 1924, the Government of the Republic of China will not and does not recognize as valid any agreement, treaty, et cetera, concluded between Russia since the Tsarist régime and any third party or parties, affecting the sovereign rights and interests of the Republic of China. It is further understood that this expression of understanding has the same force and validity as a general declaration embodied in the said Agreement on General Principles.

In faith whereof, the respective Plenipotentiaries of the Governments of the two Contracting Parties have signed the present Declaration in duplicate in the English language and have affixed thereto their seals.

Done at the city of Peking this Thirty-first day of the Fifth month of the Thirteenth year of the Republic of China, which is the Thirty-first day of May, One thousand nine hundred and twenty-four.

(Seal) V. K. WELLINGTON KOO.
(Seal) L. M. KARAKHAN.

DECLARATION IV

The Government of the Republic of China and the Government of the Union of Soviet Socialist Republics jointly declare that it is understood that the Government of the Republic of China will not transfer either in part or in whole to any third Power or any foreign organization the special rights and privileges announced by the Government of the Union of Soviet Socialist Republics in Article X of the Agreement on General Principles between the Republic of China and the Union of Soviet Socialist Republics of May 31, 1924. It is further understood that this expression of understanding has the same force and validity as a general declaration embodied in the said Agreement on General Principles.

In faith whereof, the respective Plenipotentiaries of the Governments of the two Contracting Parties have signed the present Declaration in duplicate in the English language and have affixed thereto their seals.

Done at the city of Peking this Thirty-first day of the Fifth month of the Thirteenth year of the Republic of China, which is the Thirty-first day of May, One thousand nine hundred and twenty-four.

(Seal) V. K. WELLINGTON KOO.
(Seal) L. M. KARAKHAN.

DECLARATION V

The Government of the Republic of China and the Government of the Union of Soviet Socialist Republics jointly declare that it is understood that with reference to Article XI of the Agreement on General Principles between the Republic of China and the Union of Soviet Socialist Republics of May 31, 1924:

1. The Russian share of the Boxer Indemnity which the Government of the Union of Soviet Socialist Republics renounces, will after the satisfaction of all prior obligations secured thereon be entirely appropriated to create a fund for the promotion of education among the Chinese people.

2. A special Commission will be established to administer and allocate the said fund. The Commission will consist of three persons, two of whom will be appointed by the Government of the Republic of China and one by the Government of the Union of Soviet Socialist Republics. Decisions of the said Commission will be taken by unanimous vote.

3. The said fund will be deposited as it accrues from time to time in a Bank to be designated by the said Commission.

It is further understood that this expression of understanding has the same force and validity as a general declaration embodied in the said Agreement on General Principles.

In faith whereof, the respective Plenipotentiaries of the Governments of the two Contracting Parties have signed the present Declaration in duplicate in the English language and have affixed thereto their seals.

Done at the city of Peking this Thirty-first day of the Fifth month of the Thirteenth year of the Republic of China, which is the Thirty-first day of May, One thousand nine hundred and twenty-four.

(Seal) V. K. WELLINGTON KOO.
(Seal) L. M. KARAKHAN.

Declaration VI

The Government of the Republic of China and the Government of the Union of Soviet Socialist Republics agree that they will establish equitable provisions at the Conference as provided in Article II of the Agreement on General Principles between the Republic of China and the Union of Soviet Socialist Republics of May 31, 1924, for the regulation of the situation created for the citizens of the Government of the Union of Soviet Socialist Republics by the relinquishment of the rights of extraterritoriality and consular jurisdiction under Article XII of the aforementioned Agreement, it being understood, however, that the nationals of the Government of the Union of Soviet Socialist Republics shall be entirely amenable to Chinese jurisdiction.

In faith whereof, the respective Plenipotentiaries of the Governments of the two Contracting Parties have signed the present Declaration in duplicate in the English language and have affixed thereto their seals.

Done at the city of Peking this Thirty-first day of the Fifth month of the Thirteenth year of the Republic of China, which is the Thirty-first day of May, One thousand nine hundred and twenty-four.

(*Seal*) V. K. Wellington Koo.
(*Seal*) L. M. Karakhan.

Declaration VII

The Government of the Republic of China and the Government of the Union of Soviet Socialist Republics, having signed the Agreement on General Principles between the Republic of China and the Union of Soviet Socialist Republics of May 31, 1924, hereby agree, in explanation of Article V of the Agreement for the Provisional Management of the Chinese Eastern Railway of the same date, which provides for the principle of equal representation in the filling of posts by citizens of the Republic of China and those of the Union of Soviet Socialist Republics, that the application of this principle is not to be understood to mean that the present employees of Russian nationality shall be dismissed for the sole purpose of enforcing the said principle. It is further understood that access to all posts is equally open to citizens of both Contracting Parties, that no special preference shall be shown to either nationality, and that the posts shall be filled in accordance with the ability and technical as well as educational qualifications of the applicants.

In faith whereof, the respective Plenipotentiaries of the Governments of the two Contracting Parties have signed the present Declaration in duplicate in the English language and have affixed thereto their seals.

Done at the city of Peking this Thirty-first day of the Fifth month of the Thirteenth year of the Republic of China, which is the Thirty-first day of May, One thousand nine hundred and twenty-four.

(*Seal*) V. K. WELLINGTON KOO.
(*Seal*) L. M. KARAKHAN.

EXCHANGE OF NOTES

Peking, May 31, 1924.

MR. L. M. KARAKHAN,
Extraordinary Plenipotentiary Representative of the Union of Soviet Socialist Republics to the Republic of China, Peking.

DEAR MR. KARAKHAN,
On behalf of my Government, I have the honour to declare that an Agreement on General Principles for the Settlement of the Questions between the Republic of China and the Union of Soviet Socialist Republics having been signed between us to-day the Government of the Republic of China will, in the interest of friendship between the Republic of China and the Union of Soviet Socialist Republics, discontinue the services of all the subjects of the former Russian Empire now employed in the Chinese army and Police forces, as they constitute by their presence or activities a menace to the safety of the Union of Soviet Socialist Republics. If you will furnish my Government with a list of such persons, the authorities concerned will be instructed to adopt the necessary action.

I have the honour to remain,
Yours faithfully,
V. K. WELLINGTON KOO.
Minister for Foreign Affairs of the Republic of China.

Peking, May 31, 1924.

DEAR DR. KOO,
I have the honour to acknowledge the receipt of the following note from you under this date:

'On behalf of my Government, I have the honour ', etc.

In reply I beg to state, on behalf of my Government, that I have taken note of the same and that I agree to the proposition contained therein.

> I have the honour to be,
>> Very truly yours,
>>> L. M. KARAKHAN.
>>>> *Extraordinary Plenipotentiary Representative of the Union of Soviet Socialist Republics to the Republic of China.*

AGREEMENT BETWEEN THE GOVERNMENT OF THE UNION OF SOVIET SOCIALIST REPUBLICS AND THE GOVERNMENT OF THE AUTONOMOUS THREE EASTERN PROVINCES OF THE REPUBLIC OF CHINA

September 20, 1924.

The Government of the Union of Soviet Socialist Republics and the Government of the Autonomous Three Eastern Provinces of the Republic of China desiring to promote friendly relations and regulate the questions affecting the interests of both Parties, and to that end named as Plenipotentiaries, that is to say:

The Government of the Union of Soviet Socialist Republics:
NIKOLAI CYRILOVITCH KOUZNETSOFF.
The Government of the Autonomous Three Eastern Provinces of the Republic of China:
CHEN TSIAN, LUI JUN-HUAN and JUN SHI-MIN.

The above-mentioned delegates, having communicated to each other their respective full powers found to be in good and due form, have agreed upon the following Articles:

Article I. Chinese Eastern Railway

The Governments of the two Contracting Parties agree to settle the question of the Chinese Eastern Railway as hereinafter provided:

1. The Governments of the two Contracting Parties declare the Chinese Eastern Railway is a purely commercial enterprise.

The Governments of the two Contracting Parties declare that with the exception of matters pertaining to the business of operations which are under the direct control of the Chinese Eastern Railway, all other matters affecting the rights of the national and local governments of the Republic of China, such as judicial matters, matters relating to civil administration, military administration, police, municipal government, taxation and landed property (with the exception of lands required by the Chinese Eastern Railway itself) shall be administered by the Chinese Authorities.

2. The time limit as provided in Article XII of the Contract for the Construction and Operation of the Chinese Eastern Railway of August 27, 1896, shall be reduced from eighty to sixty years, at the expiration of which, the Chinese Government shall enter gratis into possession of the said Railway and its appurtenant properties.

Upon the consent of both Contracting Parties the question of a further reduction of the said time limit (that is, sixty years) may be discussed.

From the date of signing the present Agreement the Government of the Union of Soviet Socialist Republics agrees that China has the right to redeem the Chinese Eastern Railway. At the time of redemption the two Contracting Parties shall determine what the Chinese Eastern Railway had actually cost, and it shall be redeemed by China with Chinese capital at a fair price.

3. The Government of the Union of Soviet Socialist Republics agrees in a Commission to be organized by the two Contracting Parties to settle the question of the obligations of the Chinese Eastern Railway Company in accordance with Section 4 of Article IX of the Agreement on General Principles for Settlement of the Questions between the Union of Soviet Socialist Republics and the Republic of China, signed on May 31, 1924, at Peking.

4. The Governments of the two Contracting Parties mutually agree that the future of the Chinese Eastern Railway shall be determined by the Union of Soviet Socialist Republics and the Republic of China to the exclusion of any third party or parties.

5. The Contract for the Construction and Operation of the Chinese Eastern Railway of August 27, 1896, shall be completely revised, in accordance with the terms specified in this Agreement, by a Commission of the two Contracting Parties in four months from the date of signing the present Agreement.

Pending the revision, the rights of the two Governments, arising out of said Contract, which do not contradict the present Agreement, and do not prejudice China's rights of sovereignty, shall be maintained in force.

6. The Railway shall establish for discussion and decision of all matters relating to the Chinese Eastern Railway a Board of Directors composed of ten persons, of whom five shall be appointed by the Union of Soviet Socialist Republics and five by the Government of China.

China shall appoint one of the Chinese Directors as President of the Board of Directors, who shall be *ex officio* the Director General.

The Union of Soviet Socialist Republics shall appoint one of the Russian Directors as the Vice-President of the Board of Directors, who shall also be *ex officio* the Assistant Director General.

Seven persons shall constitute the quorum, and all decisions of the Board of Directors shall have the consent of not less than six persons before they can be carried out.

The Director General and the Assistant Director General shall jointly manage the affairs of the Board of Directors and shall both sign all the documents of the Board.

In the absence of either the Director General or the Assistant Director General, their respective Governments may appoint another Director to officiate as the Director General or Assistant Director General (in the case of the Director General, by one of the Chinese Directors, and in that of the Assistant Director General, by one of the Russian Directors).

7. The Railway shall establish a Board of Auditors, to be composed of five persons, namely, three Russian Auditors, who shall be appointed by the Union of Soviet Socialist Republics, and two Chinese Auditors, who shall be appointed by China.

The Chairman of the Board of Auditors shall be elected from among the Chinese Auditors.

8. The Railway shall have a Manager, who shall be a citizen of the Union of Soviet Socialist Republics, and two Assistant Managers, one to be a citizen of the Union of Soviet Socialist Republics and the other to be a citizen of the Republic of China.

The said officers shall be appointed by the Board of Directors, and such appointments shall be confirmed by their respective Governments.

The rights and duties of the Manager and Assistant Managers shall be defined by the Board of Directors.

9. The Chiefs and Assistant Chiefs of the various Departments of the Railway shall be appointed by the Board of Directors.

If the Chief of a Department is a national of the Union of Soviet Socialist Republics, the Assistant Chief of the Department shall be a national of the Republic of China, and if the Chief of a Department is a national of the Republic of China, the Assistant Chief shall be a national of the Union of Soviet Socialist Republics.

10. The employment of persons in the various departments of the Railway shall be in accordance with the principle of equal representation between the nationals of the Union of Soviet Socialist Republics and those of the Republic of China.

(NOTE.—In carrying out the principle of equal representation the normal course of life and the activities of the Railway shall in no case be interrupted or injured, that is to say, the employment of the people of both nationalities shall be based in accordance with experience, personal qualification and fitness of the applicants.)

11. With the exception of the estimates and budgets, as provided in Section 12 of Article I of the present Agreement, all other matters, on which the Board of Directors cannot reach an agreement, shall be referred to the Governments of the Contracting Parties for a just and amicable settlement.

12. The Board of Directors shall present the estimates and budgets

of the Railway to a joint meeting of the Board of Directors and the Board of Auditors for consideration and approval.

13. All the net profits of the Railway shall be held by the Board of Directors and shall not be used pending a final settlement, in a joint Commission, of the question of its distribution between the two Contracting Parties.

14. The Board of Directors shall make a complete revision, as soon as possible, of the Statutes of the Chinese Eastern Railway Company approved on December 4, 1896, by the Czarist Government, in accordance with the present Agreement and, in any case, not later than four months from the date of the constitution of the Board of Directors.

Pending their revision, the aforesaid Statutes in so far as they do not conflict with the present Agreement and do not prejudice the rights of sovereignty of the Republic of China, shall continue to be observed.

15. As soon as the conditions of redemption by China of the Chinese Eastern Railway are settled by both Contracting Parties, or as soon as the Railway reverts to China upon the expiration of the time limit as stipulated in Section 2 of Article I of the present Agreement, all parts of this Agreement concerning the same shall cease to have any effect.

Article II. Navigation

The Governments of the two Contracting Parties agree to settle, on the basis of equality, reciprocity and the respect of each other's sovereignty, the question relating to the navigation of all kinds of their vessels on those parts of the rivers, lakes, and other bodies of water, which are common to their respective borders, the details of this question to be regulated in a Commission of the two Contracting Parties within two months from the date of signing of this present Agreement.

In view of the extensive freight and passenger interests of the Union of Soviet Socialist Republics on the River Sungari up to and including Harbin, and the extensive freight and passenger interests of China on the lower Amur River into the sea, both Contracting Parties agree on the basis of equality and reciprocity to take up the question of securing the said interests in the said Commission.

Article III. Boundaries

The Governments of the two Contracting Parties agree to redemarcate their boundaries through a Commission to be organized by both Parties, and pending such redemarcation to maintain the present boundaries.

Article IV. Tariff and Trade Agreement

The Governments of the two Contracting Parties agree to draw up a Customs tariff and conclude a Commercial Treaty in a Commission to be organized by said parties on the basis of equality and reciprocity.

Article V. Propaganda

The Governments of the two Contracting Parties mutually pledge themselves not to permit within their respective territories the existence and (or) activities of any organization of groups whose aim is to struggle by acts of violence against the Government of either Contracting Party.

The Governments of the two Contracting Parties further pledge themselves not to engage in propaganda directed against the political and social systems of either Contracting Party.

Article VI. Commissions

The Commissions as provided in the Articles of this Agreement shall commence their work within one month from the date of signing this Agreement, and shall complete their work as soon as possible and not later than six months. This does not apply to those Commissions whose time limits have been specified in the respective articles of this Agreement.

Article VII.

The present Agreement shall come into effect from the day of signature.

In witness whereof, the respective Plenipotentiaries have signed the present Agreement in duplicate in the Russian, Chinese and English languages, and have affixed thereto their seals.

In case of dispute, the English text shall be accepted as the standard.

Done at the City of Mukden, this Twentieth day of September, One thousand nine hundred and twenty-four, which corresponds to the Twentieth day of the Ninth month of the Thirteenth year of the Republic of China.

> (*Seal*) CHEN TSIAN.
> (*Seal*) LUI JUN-HUAN.
> (*Seal*) JUN SHI-MIN.
> (*Seal*) N. C. KOUZNETSOFF.

DECLARATION I

The Government of the Union of Soviet Socialist Republics and the Government of the Autonomous Three Eastern Provinces of the Republic of China hereby declare that immediately after the signing of the Agreement of September 20, 1924, between the Governments of the two Contracting Parties, the Government of the Autonomous

Three Eastern Provinces of the Republic of China will hand over to the Government of the Union of Soviet Socialist Republics the consular buildings formerly belonging to the Tsarist Government.

In faith whereof the Plenipotentiaries of the two Contracting Parties have signed the present Declaration in duplicate in the Russian, Chinese and English languages and have affixed thereto their seals.

In case of dispute, the English text shall be accepted as the standard.

Done at the City of Mukden, this Twentieth day of September, One thousand nine hundred and twenty four, corresponding to the Twentieth day of the Ninth month of the Thirteenth year of the Republic of China.

Declaration II

The Government of the Union of Soviet Socialist Republics and the Government of the Autonomous Three Eastern Provinces of the Republic of China mutually declare that after the signing of the Agreement of September 20, 1924, between the Governments of the two Contracting Parties, if there are at present any Chinese in any employ of the Government of the Union of Soviet Socialist Republics which by their presence and/or activity constitute a menace to the interests of the Autonomous Three Eastern Provinces of the Republic of China or if there are at present in the employ of the Government of the Autonomous Three Eastern Provinces of the Republic of China former Russian subjects, which constitute by their presence and/or activity a menace to the interests of the Union of Soviet Socialist Republics, the respective Governments shall communicate to the other Party a list of names of such persons and shall instruct the respective authorities to take measures necessary to put an end to the activities or the employment of the aforesaid persons.

In witness whereof the Plenipotentiaries of the two Parties have signed the present Declaration in duplicate in the Russian, Chinese and English languages and have affixed thereto their seals.

In case of dispute, the English text shall be accepted as the standard.

Done at the City of Mukden, this Twentieth day of September, One thousand nine hundred and twenty-four, corresponding to the Twentieth day of the Ninth month of the Thirteenth year of the Republic of China.

THE SOVIET-JAPANESE CONVENTION OF
JANUARY 20, 1925

Regarding the basic principles of inter-relations between the Union of Soviet Socialist Republics and Japan.

The Union of Soviet Socialist Republics and Japan, desiring to firmly establish mutual good-neighbourly relations and economic co-operation, decided to conclude a convention regarding the basic principles of such relations and have for this purpose appointed their respective representatives, namely:

> The Central Executive Committee of the Union of Soviet Socialist Republics appointed:
> LEV MIKAILOVICH KARAKHAN, Ambassador to China.
> His Majesty, the Emperor of Japan appointed:
> KENKITI YOSHIZAVA, Envoy Extraordinary and Minister Plenipotentiary in China, Djushia, Chevalier, First Class Order of 'Holy Treasure',

who upon presenting to each other their respective credentials, these being found to be in proper and correct form, agreed upon the following:

Article I. The High Contracting Parties agree that with the coming into force of the present convention diplomatic and consular relations are established between them.

Article II. The Union of Soviet Socialist Republics agrees that the treaty concluded in Portsmouth on September 5, 1905, remains in full force.

It is agreed that all treaties, conventions and agreements outside of the above-mentioned Portsmouth Treaty entered into between Japan and Russia up to November 7, 1917, will be revised at the conference which is to take place subsequently between the Governments of the Contracting Parties, and that they may be changed or cancelled as will be called for by the changed circumstances.

Article III. The Governments of the High Contracting Parties agree that with the coming into effect of the present convention they will take up the revision of the Fishing Treaty of 1907, taking into consideration those changes which might have taken place in the general conditions since the said Fishing Treaty was concluded.

Until such a revised treaty is concluded, the Government of the

Union of Soviet Socialist Republics will adhere to the practice established in 1924 in regard to the leasing of fisheries to Japanese subjects.

Article IV. The Governments of the High Contracting Parties agree that with the coming into effect of the present convention they will take up the matter of concluding a treaty regarding trade and shipping in accordance with the principles set forth below, and that until such a treaty is concluded the general relations between the two countries will be regulated by these principles:

1. Citizens and subjects of each of the High Contracting Parties in accordance with the laws of each country will have the right of (*a*) full freedom of entry, movement and stay in the territory of the other party, and (*b*) constant full protection of the safety of life and property.

2. In accordance with the laws of the country, each of the High Contracting Parties gives on its territory, to citizens or subjects of the other party, to the widest possible extent and on conditions of reciprocity, the right of private ownership, as well as freedom to engage in trade, shipping, mining and other peaceful occupations.

3. Without prejudice to the right of each Contracting Party to regulate by its own laws the system of international trade in that country, it is understood that neither Contracting Party will apply against the other party in particular, any prohibitive measures, limitations or taxation, which might act as obstacles to the development of economic or other intercourse between the two countries; and both countries propose to grant to the trade, shipping and industry of each country, in so far as possible, the privileges of the most favoured country.

The Governments of the High Contracting Parties further agree from time to time, as circumstances may demand, to enter into negotiations to conclude special agreements regarding trade and shipping for the purpose of regulating and cementing the economic relations between the two countries.

Article V. The High Contracting Parties solemnly confirm their desire and intention to live in peace and amity with each other, conscientiously to respect the undisputed right of each State to arrange its own life within the limits of its own jurisdiction at its own desire, to refrain and restrain all persons in their governmental service, as well as all organizations receiving any financial support from them, from any open or secret action, which may in any way whatsoever threaten the peace or safety of any part of the territory of the Union of Soviet Socialist Republics or of Japan.

It is further agreed that neither of the High Contracting Parties will permit on the territory under its jurisdiction the presence of:

(*a*) Organizations or groups claiming to be the Government of any part of the territory of the other party, or,

(b) Foreign subjects or citizens, in regard to whom it has been established that they actually carry on political work for these organizations or groups.

Article VI. In the interests of the development of economic relationship between the two countries, and taking into consideration the needs of Japan with respect to natural resources, the Government of the Union of Soviet Socialist Republics is ready to grant to Japanese subjects, companies and associations, concessions for the exploitation of mineral, timber and other natural resources in all parts of the territory of the Union of Soviet Socialist Republics.

Article VII. The present convention is subject to ratification. Such ratification by each of the High Contracting Parties should be notified as soon as possible through the diplomatic representatives in Peking to the Government of the other party, and from the date of the last of such notifications this convention comes into full force.

The formal exchange of ratifications will take place in Peking within the shortest possible time.

In testimony whereof the respective representatives have signed the present convention in duplicate, in English, and have affixed their seals thereto.

Drawn up in Peking, this Twentieth day of January, in the year One thousand nine hundred and twenty-five.

(*Signed*) L. KARAKHAN.

(*Signed*) K. YOSHIZAVA.

PROTOCOL (A)

The Union of Soviet Socialist Republics and Japan, upon signing this date the convention regarding the basic principles of interrelations between them, found it desirable to regulate certain questions in connection with the above convention, and through their respective representatives have agreed upon the following stipulations:

Article I. Each of the High Contracting Parties binds itself to turn over to the other party the immovable and movable property belonging to the Embassy and Consulate of that party and actually situated in the territory of the first party.

In the event that it is found that the land occupied by the former Russian Government in Tokio is situated in such a way as to interfere with the plans for laying out the City of Tokio or serving the public needs, the Government of the Union of Soviet Socialist Republics will be ready to consider the proposals, which may be made by the Japanese Government with the view of eliminating such difficulties.

The Government of the Union of Soviet Socialist Republics will give to the Japanese Government all reasonable facilities in the choice of suitable sites and buildings of a Japanese Embassy and Consulates in the territory of the Union of Soviet Socialist Republics.

Article II. It is agreed that all questions regarding debts to the Government or subjects of Japan in connection with State loans or treasury bonds issued by the former Russian Governments, namely, the Imperial Russian Government and its successor—the Provisional Government—are left for decision in subsequent negotiations between the Government of the Union of Soviet Socialist Republics and the Japanese Government.

It is intended that in regulating these questions, the Government and subjects of Japan, all conditions being equal, will not be placed in a less favourable position than that which the Government of the Union of Soviet Socialist Republics will concede to the Government or citizens of any other country on the same questions.

It is also agreed that all questions relating to claims of the Government of one party against the Government of the other party, or of citizens of one party to the Government of another, are left to be regulated at the subsequent negotiations between the Government of the Union of Soviet Socialist Republics and the Japanese Government.

Article III. In view of the fact that climatic conditions in northern Sakhalin prevent immediate transportation home of the Japanese troops now stationed there, these troops will be completely evacuated from the said region by May 15, 1925.

This evacuation must commence as soon as climatic conditions permit, and in each and all of the districts in northern Sakhalin thus evacuated by Japanese troops will immediately afterwards be restored full sovereignty of corresponding authorities of the Union of Soviet Socialist Republics.

Details regarding the transfer of administration and winding up the occupation will be arranged in Alexandrovsk between the Commander of the Japanese army of occupation and representatives of the Union of Soviet Socialist Republics.

Article IV. The High Contracting Parties mutually declare that at the present time there exists no treaty or agreement regarding military alliance or any other secret agreement concluded by either of them with any third party, which might constitute a violation of or threat to the sovereignty, territorial rights or national safety of the other Contracting Party.

Article V. The present protocol will be considered ratified with the ratification of the convention regarding the basic principles of the inter-relations between the Union of Soviet Socialist Republics and Japan as signed this date.

In witness whereof the respective representatives have signed the present protocol in duplicate in English and affixed their seals thereto.

Drawn up in Peking, this Twentieth day of January, in the year One thousand nine hundred and twenty-five.

(*Signed*) L. KARAKHAN.
(*Signed*) K. YOSHIZAVA.

PROTOCOL (B)

The High Contracting Parties have agreed upon the following basic stipulations for concession agreements to be concluded during the period of five months from the date of complete evacuation of northern Sakhalin by Japanese troops, as provided by Article III of Protocol (A), signed this date by representatives of the Union of Soviet Socialist Republics and of Japan.

1. The Government of the Union of Soviet Socialist Republics agrees to give to Japanese concerns recommended by the Japanese Government concessions for the exploitation of fifty per cent of the area of every oil field in northern Sakhalin, mentioned in the memorandum presented to the representatives of the Union of Soviet Socialist Republics on August 29, 1924. In order to ascertain the area which is to be leased to Japanese concerns for such exploitation, each of the mentioned oil fields is to be divided into checker board squares, from fifteen to forty dessiatins each, the Japanese being given such a number of these squares as will represent fifty per cent of the entire area; it being understood that the squares thus to be leased to the Japanese should not as a rule be adjacent, but should include all wells which are now being drilled or worked by the Japanese. As regards the remaining unleased oil lands mentioned in the same memorandum, it is agreed that should the Government of the Union of Soviet Socialist Republics decide to offer these lands, in full or in part, on concessions to foreigners, Japanese concerns will enjoy equal chances in regard to such concessions.

2. The Government of the Union of Soviet Socialist Republics will grant to Japanese concerns recommended by the Japanese Government the right, for a period of from five to ten years, of carrying on exploration work on the oil fields along the eastern shore of northern Sakhalin over an area of one thousand square versts, which must be allotted within a year from the date of the conclusion of concession agreements, and if, as a result of such exploration work by the Japanese, oil should be located, a concession for the exploita-

tion of fifty per cent of the oil field area thus established will be granted to the Japanese.

3. The Government of the Union of Soviet Socialist Republics agrees to grant to Japanese concerns recommended by the Japanese Government concessions for the exploitation of coal deposits on the western shore of northern Sakhalin over a definite area, which is to be established by concession contracts. The Government of the Union of Soviet Socialist Republics further agrees to grant to Japanese concerns concessions for coal mining in the Dui district over an area to be established in the concession contracts. As regards coal fields situated outside the definite area mentioned in the two previous sentences, it is also agreed that should the Government of the Union of Soviet Socialist Republics decide to offer them on concession to foreigners, Japanese concerns will be given equal rights in regard to such concessions.

4. The period of the concessions for the exploitation of oil and coal fields, as set forth in the previous paragraphs, is to be established for forty to fifty years.

5. As payment for the above-mentioned concessions, Japanese concessionaires will turn over annually to the Government of the Union of Soviet Socialist Republics—in the coal fields, from five to eight per cent of the gross output; in the oil fields, from five to fifteen per cent of the gross output. It is proposed that in the event of striking oil gushers, the payment may be increased to forty-five per cent of the gross production.

The percentage of production thus to revert as payment will be finally determined in the concession contracts, it being subject to change in accordance with the scale of annual production by a method to be established in the above-mentioned contracts.

6. The said Japanese concerns shall have the right to cut timber necessary for the needs of the enterprise, and to erect various structures to facilitate communication and transportation of materials and products. The details in connection therewith will be stipulated in the concession contracts.

7. In view of the above-mentioned rental, and taking into consideration the unfavourable conditions in which the enterprises will be placed owing to the geographical position and other general conditions in the said regions, it is agreed that there will be a duty-free import and export of all articles, materials and products necessary for such enterprises or produced in the latter, and that the enterprises will not be subject to such taxation or limitations as would actually make profitable exploitation impossible.

8. The Government of the Union of Soviet Socialist Republics will provide for the said enterprises all reasonable protection and facilities.

9. The details in connection with the above-mentioned articles will be stipulated in the concession contracts.

The present protocol is to be considered ratified with the ratification of the convention regarding the basic principles of inter-relations between the Union of Soviet Socialist Republics and Japan as signed this date.

In witness whereof the respective representatives have signed the present protocol in duplicate in English, and have affixed thereto their seals.

Drawn up in Peking, this Twentieth day of January, in the year One thousand nine hundred and twenty-five.

(Signed) L. KARAKHAN.
(Signed) K. YOSHIZAVA.

Upon signing this day the convention regarding the basic principles of inter-relations between the Union of Soviet Socialist Republics and Japan, the undersigned representative of the Union of Soviet Socialist Republics had the honour to declare that the recognition by his Government of the validity of the Portsmouth Treaty of September 5, 1905, in no way signifies that the Government of the Union shares with the former Tsarist Government the political responsibility for the conclusion of the said treaty.

Peking, January 20, 1925.

(Signed) L. KARAKHAN.

KHARBAROVSK CONVENTION

On December 22, 1929, M. Simanovsky, representing the Moscow Foreign Office, and Mr. Tsai Yun-shing, representing the Chinese Republic, signed the following protocol in settlement of the Chinese Eastern Railway dispute.

1. Preliminary conditions of the Government of the U.S.S.R. understood by both parties in full conformity with the telegram of Mr. Litvinov of November 27 and the Nikolsk-Ussuriisk Protocol of December 3 as restoration of the situation existing prior to the conflict and based upon the Mukden and Peking Agreements.

All outstanding questions which have arisen during the period of joint Soviet Chinese Management of the Railway are to be solved at the forthcoming conference. Accordingly the following measures are to be immediately carried out:

(a) Restoration, on basis of the old agreement of the activity of the Management of the Chinese Eastern Railway and resumption by Soviet members of the management of their duties. Henceforth the Chinese Chairman of the Management, and Soviet Vice-Chairman of the Management must act only jointly in conformity with Article 6 of the Soviet-Mukden Agreement.

(b) Restoration of the former proportion of offices held by Soviet and Chinese citizens and reinstatement (or immediate appointment of new candidates, should such be recommended on the Soviet side) of Soviet citizens, officers, chiefs and assistant chiefs of departments.

(c) Orders and instructions on the Chinese Eastern Railway issued on behalf of Management and Administration of Chinese Eastern Railway beginning on July 10, 1929, are considered invalid unless properly confirmed by the local management and administration of the road.

RELEASE OF PRISONERS

2. All Soviet citizens without exception arrested by Chinese authorities after May 1, 1929, and in connection with the conflict,

373

immediately to be released without sub-division into any categories, including Soviet citizens arrested during the search of the Harbin Consulate on May 27, 1929.

The Government of the U.S.S.R. also immediately release all Chinese citizens without exception arrested in connection with the conflict, and interned Chinese soldiers and officers.

3. All workers and employees of the Chinese Eastern Railway, citizens of the U.S.S.R., discharged or resigned, beginning July 10, to be given the right and opportunity immediately to return to positions held prior to discharge and to receive money owing them from the Chinese Eastern Railway.

Those discharged and resigned who fail to utilize this right must immediately be paid full wages, pension dues, etc., owing to them. Vacancies may be filled only by a proper order of the lawful management and administration of the Chinese Eastern Railway, and all former Russian citizens, non-citizens of the U.S.S.R. employed by the Chinese Eastern Railway during the conflict must be summarily and immediately discharged.

4. Chinese authorities immediately to disarm the Russian White Guards detachments and deport from the Three Eastern Provinces their organizers and inspirers.

RESTORATION OF CONSULATES

5. Leaving open the question of resumption of full diplomatic and consular relations between the U.S.S.R. and China until the Soviet-Chinese Conference, both parties consider possible and necessary the immediate restoration of Soviet Consulates in the territory of the Three Eastern Provinces and Chinese Consulates at respective points of the Soviet Far East. In view of the fact that the U.S.S.R. Government declared on May 21, 1929, that 'Since the Chinese authorities have proved by all their actions their clear unwillingness and inability to reckon with the generally accepted principles of International Law and customs, it on its part does not henceforth regard itself bound by these principles in relation to Chinese representation in Moscow and Chinese Consulates in Soviet territory, and that this representation and these Consulates will no longer enjoy the extraterritoriality to which International Law entitled them,' and that both parties intend to restore consular relations between them on a basis conforming with the principles of International Law and customs, the Mukden Government declares that it undertakes to assure the Soviet Consulates in the territory of the Three Eastern Provinces full inviolability and all privileges to which

International Law and customs entitled them, and will, of course, refrain from any action violating this inviolability and these privileges. On its part the Government of the U.S.S.R. discontinues the special régime established by it between May 21, 1929, and the rupture of relations for Chinese Consulates, and grants these Consulates, which are to be restored by virtue of the first clause of this point, in the territory of the Soviet Far East, all privileges and the full inviolability to which International Law and customs entitle them.

RESUMPTION OF COMMERCE

6. With restoration of Consulates, opportunity immediately is given for the resumption of normal activity of all Soviet business organizations existing before the conflict within the Three Eastern Provinces.

Similar opportunity is offered to restore Chinese commercial enterprises which existed within the U.S.S.R. and whose operations were discontinued in connection with the Chinese Eastern Railway conflict.

The question of commercial relations between the two countries as a whole to be settled at the Soviet-Chinese Conference.

7. The question of real guarantees of observance of agreements and the interests of both sides are to be solved at the forthcoming conference.

8. The Soviet-Chinese Conference to regulate all outstanding questions to be held at Moscow on January 25, 1930.

9. The peaceful situation on the frontiers of China and the U.S.S.R. to be restored immediately with the subsequent withdrawal of troops by both sides.

10. This protocol comes into force from the moment of its signature.

Appendix B

PROVISIONAL COMMERCIAL AGREEMENT BETWEEN THE U.S.S.R. AND SINKIANG PROVINCE

THE Provincial Government of Sinkiang of the Republic of China and the U.S.S.R., in view of their adjoining territories and historical economic relations and the desire repeatedly expressed to develop their trade relations, have hereby agreed pending the conclusion of a formal Commercial Treaty between the Republic of China and the U.S.S.R., upon the following terms: The U.S.S.R. have concluded an agreement as follows:

I. It is agreed that merchandise as well as travellers from Sinkiang Province to the U.S.S.R., or *vice versa*, shall hereafter effect passage through the frontier points, Irkeshtan, Holkutz, Bakhti and Dzimunai in accordance with the existing laws and regulations of the Republic of China and the U.S.S.R.

II. The Provincial Government of Sinkiang desires that the Government of the U.S.S.R. should permit merchants of Sinkiang to import into the U.S.S.R. any amount of various products of Sinkiang to be sold to the national commercial bureaus of the Soviet Union, without having first to obtain special permits for the act. This does not, however, include products whose importation is forbidden by the existing laws of the Soviet Union.

III. The Provincial Government of Sinkiang agrees to allow the commercial bureaux of the U.S.S.R. and its citizens the privilege to carry on trade in the areas of Kashgar, Ili, Tacheng, Altai and Tihwa as well as the right to appoint from the above-named areas representatives or commissioners to proceed to Yarkent, Turfan, Karashar, Khotan and Aksu to enter into sale and purchase contracts of trade with the local merchants or commercial houses and to enforce the execution of the same.

For the purpose of putting this trade with the Soviet Union on a regular basis, the Provincial Government of Sinkiang agrees to permit employees of the commercial bureaux of the U.S.S.R. and its citizens the privilege of free travelling, in accordance with the existing laws and regulations, to and from the various representatives as well as places where such commercial bureaux are situated.

IV. The Provincial Government of Sinkiang desires that the Government of the U.S.S.R. should allow its commercial bureaux and citizens when they enter into sale and purchase contracts with merchants or commercial houses of Sinkiang, freely to arrange the terms as regards price, transportation, and terms of contract and to register such items with the government bureaux in accordance with the existing laws of China. The Provincial Government of Sinkiang declares that the date limit for registration shall not exceed five days, in accordance with the existing practice in Sinkiang. In case of dispute, the Provincial Government of Sinkiang undertakes that government offices under its jurisdiction shall investigate the contracts or agreements held by either side, and to enforce fair and just fulfilment of such contracts in accordance with the existing laws of China.

V. The Provincial Government of Sinkiang agrees not to impose higher or heavier Customs dues or taxes on the commercial bureaux of the Soviet Union or its citizens than such as are paid by Chinese merchants or business houses, in accordance with the existing laws of China, either at the present or at any future time. Should business taxes or similar levies be introduced at some future time, in accordance with the existing laws of China, commercial bureaux of the Soviet Union or its citizens shall pay such taxes or levies along with Chinese merchants or business houses.

VI. With the object of promoting the national economy of Sinkiang, the Provincial Government of Sinkiang desires that the Government of the Soviet Union should supply in full in the nature of a business deal various machineries for the development of Sinkiang, such as industrial, electrical, agricultural and transportation machines, also to provide necessary technicians, in the same nature, for the reconstruction of Sinkiang, and to train Chinese technicians for the same purpose. It is requested that the Soviet Government should give appropriate assistance in the improvement of agriculture, cattle raising, etc., in connection with the national economy of Sinkiang.

VII. With the object of promoting the national economy of Sinkiang, the Provincial Government of Sinkiang desires that the Soviet Government should allow free passage through territories of the U.S.S.R. of such products of Sinkiang into China proper or of such products of China proper into Sinkiang, as are given in the appended list. This list shall be made out by a special commissioner appointed by the Provincial Government of Sinkiang with the Soviet Consul-General at Urumchi, on the basis of developing commercial relations between Sinkiang and the U.S.S.R., not later than November 15 of the present year. Said list may be revised yearly to suit conditions necessary to the national economy of Sinkiang and the Soviet Union.

The Provincial Government of Sinkiang desires that the Soviet Government should allow free passage through its territories of such articles as are needed by the former, but not for purposes of trade, either from China proper into Sinkiang or from Sinkiang into China proper or from a third country with which the Soviet Union has commercial agreements already concluded or to be concluded in the future.

The Provincial Government of Sinkiang acknowledges the receipt from the Soviet Government of a written document stating that, should any article to be transported through the territories of the U.S.S.R. be prohibited by existing laws, passage of such would not be permitted. The above specified clauses are concluded with the aim and purpose of developing mutual economic relations, to which the Provincial Government of Sinkiang signifies agreement, and shall take effect herewith.

ANNEX I

For the purpose of developing trade between Sinkiang and the U.S.S.R., the Provincial Government of Sinkiang has ordered the Sinkiang Customs to make a uniform rate of dues on all merchandise of import and export between Sinkiang and the U.S.S.R. in order to facilitate the mutual development of trade.

ANNEX II

In order to promote the facilities for trade between the Soviet Union and Sinkiang, the Government of the U.S.S.R. proposes to establish at Urumchi, Kashgar, Ili and Tacheng, Soviet financial bureaux to take charge of the trade and financial affairs of the Soviet commercial bureaux or intercourse with Chinese merchants or business houses. Said financial bureaux will also accept commissions from Chinese merchants or business houses. The financial bureaux are entitled to charge certain amounts upon mutual consent, for the execution of such commissions.

ANNEX III

For the purpose of facilitating passenger traffic and transportation of goods, the Government of the U.S.S.R. desires that the Provincial

Government of Sinkiang will agree, six months after the opening of the pass at Dzimunai, to the closure of the pass at Irkeshtan, so that merchandise already in transit and intended to pass through the pass at Irkeshtan may be enabled to arrive at its destination.

ANNEX IV

The Provincial Government of Sinkiang considers it necessary to regulate telegraphic communications between Sinkiang and the U.S.S.R. For this purpose there should be direct connection of the cable between Tacheng and Bahkti. At the same time, direct wireless communication between Sinkiang and the U.S.S.R. should also be established. The procedure and conditions for the materialization of such arrangements shall be made by the Chinese Commissioner for Foreign Affairs in Sinkiang and the Soviet Consul-General at Urumchi.

AGREEMENT BETWEEN MANCHUKUO AND THE UNION OF SOVIET SOCIALIST REPUBLICS FOR THE CESSION OF THE NORTH MANCHURIA RAILWAY, MARCH 23, 1935

Article I. The Government of the Union of Soviet Socialist Republics shall cede to the Government of Manchukuo all the rights they possess concerning the North Manchuria Railway (Chinese Eastern Railway), in consideration of which the Government of Manchukuo shall pay to the Government of the Union of Soviet Socialist Republics the sum of one hundred and forty million (140,000,000) yen in Japanese currency.

Article II. All the rights of the Government of the Union of Soviet Socialist Republics concerning the North Manchuria Railway (Chinese Eastern Railway) shall pass to the Government of Manchukuo upon the coming into force of the present Agreement, and at the same time the North Manchuria Railway (Chinese Eastern Railway) shall be placed under the complete occupation and the sole management of the Government of Manchukuo.

Article III. 1. Upon the coming into force of the present Agreement, the senior members of the administration of the North Manchuria Railway (Chinese Eastern Railway) who are citizens of the Union of Soviet Socialist Republics shall be released from their duties. The said senior members of the administration of the Railway shall hand over all the archives, records, papers and documents of whatever description in their charge to their respective successors in the new administration of the Railway.

It is understood that the term the 'senior members of the administration of the North Manchurian Railway (Chinese Eastern Railway)' employed in the present Article indicates:

(a) All the members of the Board of Directors and of the Audit Committee.

(b) The General Manager and Assistant Manager of the Administration.

(c) The Assistant Chief Controller.

(d) All the Managers and Sub-Managers of the departments of the Board of Directors, the Audit Committee, the Control and the Administration. All agents for commission, engineers for commission. All the senior agents, advisers and chiefs of the sections and sub-sections.

2. With the aim of ensuring the normal functioning of the railway, the Government of the Union of Soviet Socialist Republics agree to place at the disposal of the new administration the following persons from among the senior members of the administration of the Railway who are citizens of the Union of Soviet Socialist Republics as advisers for one month from the date of the coming into force of the present Agreement.

(a) The General Manager of the Administration.

(b) The Manager of General Affairs Office of the Administration.

(c) The Manager of the Motive Power Department of the Administration.

(d) The Chief of the Financial Department of the Administration.

(e) The Manager of the Commercial Department of the Administration.

3. At any time after the coming into force of the present Agreement, the Government of Manchukuo may dismiss any or all of the following persons:

(a) All the chiefs of railway sections, stations and depots.

(b) The chiefs of all the following auxiliary enterprises of the Railway:

    A. Forest concessions and lumbering.

    B. Coal mines.

    C. Power stations.

    D. Printing plants.

    E. Auxiliary enterprises of the Commercial Department.

    F. Nursery and greenhouses in Harbin.

    G. Main workshops of the Ways Department.

    H. Wool washing works and hydro-loading works.

    I. Water works in Harbin.

    J. Soft drinks factory.

    K. Saw mill.

    L. Gradations of beans.

    M. Waste-cleaning works.

    N. Grand Hotel.

    O. Health resorts and sanatoria.

    P. Hospitals and clinics.

    Q. Library.

    R. Economic Bureau.

4. The persons referred to in Section 1 of the present Article shall have the right to remain in Manchukuo and to retain their railway lodgings for one month after the coming into force of the present Agreement.

The persons referred to in Section 2 of the present Article shall have the right to remain in Manchukuo and to retain their railway lodgings for two months after the coming into force of the present Agreement.

Those persons who have been dismissed by virtue of Section 3 of the present Article shall have the right to receive their regular salary for one month from the date of their dismissal. They shall have the right to remain in Manchukuo and to retain their railway lodgings for two months from the date of their dismissal.

Article IV. The Government of Manchukuo shall succeed to the assets and liabilities of the North Manchuria Railway (Chinese Eastern Railway) in accordance with the list of assets and liabilities of the North Manchuria Railway as on December 31, 1933, presented by the Delegation of the Government of the Union of Soviet Socialist Republics on March 22, 1934, to the Delegation of the Government of Manchukuo through the Minister for Foreign Affairs of Japan, as supplemented by the lists which were made on March 17 and March 21, 1935, in order to show the changes sustained by the assets and liabilities included in the first list from the date of the first list up to the date of the last list and also to show the new assets and liabilities which have arisen on and after January 1, 1934.

It is agreed that the provisions of Section 4, Article IX of the Agreement on General Principles for the Settlement of the Questions between the Union of Soviet Socialist Republics and the Republic of China signed at Peking on May 31, 1924, and those of Section 3, Article I, of the Agreement between the Government of the Union of Soviet Socialist Republics and the Government of the Autonomous Three Eastern Provinces of the Republic of China signed at Mukden on September 20, 1924, shall remain in force.

Article V. The Government of the Union of Soviet Socialist Republics shall have the right to maintain the following property for the use of their Consulate General in Harbin in the form of a permanent and rent-free lease:

(*a*) The land and buildings now occupied by the said Consulate General:

    Locality: Yio-Ching-Kai, Chin-Chia-Kang.
    Area: 14,873·68 square metres.
    Buildings: Office No. 1049: 2,174·90 square metres.
               Residence No. 1047: 685·37 square metres.
               Residence No. 1048: 1,447·61 square metres.
               Garage and its annex, No. 1051: 245·88 square metres.
               Guard-room, No. 1052: 38·90 square metres.

(*b*) The land and building now occupied by the officials of the said Consulate General:

Locality: Hai-Cheng-Kai, Chin-Chia-Kang.
Area: 2,530 square metres.
Building: No. 934: 258·51 square metres.

The following property shall be leased rent free and *sine die* to the Consul General of the Union of Soviet Socialist Republics in Harbin on the day of the coming into force of the present Agreement, and shall immediately thereafter be placed and remain under the occupation and management of the community of the citizens of the Union of Soviet Socialist Republics in Harbin to be used solely for the purposes prescribed hereunder:

(a) The IVth School of the North Manchuria Railway (Chinese Eastern Railway), situated at No. 35 Shang-Wu-Kai, Tao-Li, Harbin, with all the buildings and property to be found there, to be used for the elementary and secondary education of the said community.

(b) The land known under No. 949, at the corner of Kao-Shi-Kai and Ching-Cha-Kai, Tao-Li, Harbin, with all the buildings on it, which are to be used in the future as a hospital.

Within one month from the date of the coming into force of the present Agreement, a library shall be selected, for the use of the above-mentioned IVth School, from the books of the North Manchuria Railway (Chinese Eastern Railway) Library in Harbin, by mutual agreement between the local authorities of Manchukuo and the Consul General of the Union of Soviet Socialist Republics in Harbin. The books so selected shall be transferred to the said School.

Article VI. The properties occupied by the North Manchuria Railway (Chinese Eastern Railway) which are claimed by the Government of the Union of Soviet Socialist Republics as belonging to them and not to the Railway, and the properties existing in the territory of the Union of Soviet Socialist Republics which are claimed by the Government of Manchukuo as belonging to the North Manchuria Railway (Chinese Eastern Railway), are regarded as having been mutually renounced by respective Governments in favour of the other Government, and neither Government shall in future raise against the other Government any demand concerning the said properties.

The above provisions shall not apply to the properties (buildings and their sites and other railway properties) of the Transbaikal Railway now existing in Manchouli, and the properties of the Ussuri Railway now existing at Suifenho, which are actually occupied respectively by the said two railways and shall remain their property under their management.

Article VII. Out of the sum of one hundred and forty million (140,000,000) yen in Japanese currency referred to in Article I of the present Agreement, the sum of forty-six million seven hundred thousand (46,700,000) yen shall be paid in cash in accordance with the provisions of Article VIII of the present Agreement, and the settlement for the remaining sum of ninety-three million three hundred thousand (93,300,000) yen shall be effected in the form of payments made by the Government of Manchukuo for goods delivered to the Government of the Union of Soviet Socialist Republics in accordance with the provisions of Article IX of the present Agreement.

Article VIII. Out of the sum of forty-six million seven hundred thousand (47,700,000) yen to be paid in cash in accordance with the provisions of Article VII of the present Agreement, the sum of twenty-three million three hundred thousand (23,300,000) yen shall be paid simultaneously with the signing of the present Agreement.

The remaining sum of twenty-three million four hundred thousand (23,400,000) yen as well as the simple interest at the rate of three per cent per annum is to be paid by the Government of Manchukuo to the Government of the Union of Soviet Socialist Republics in the form of Treasury Bonds of the Government of Manchukuo. The said Treasury Bonds are to be issued of the following amounts, and mature on the dates indicated hereunder: Six million three hundred and seventy-six thousand five hundred (6,376,500) yen maturing on December 23, 1935; six million two hundred and forty-four thousand eight hundred and seventy-five (6,244,875) yen maturing on September 23, 1936; six million one hundred and thirteen thousand two hundred and fifty (6,113,250) yen maturing on June 23, 1937; five million nine hundred and eighty-one thousand six hundred and twenty-five (5,981,625) yen maturing on March 23, 1938. The Treasury Bonds of the Government of Manchukuo mentioned above are to be issued in favour of the Government of the Union of Soviet Socialist Republics and are to be delivered by the Representatives of the Government of Manchukuo to the Representative of the Government of the Union of Soviet Socialist Republics simultaneously with the signing of the present Agreement, and shall be paid at the Industrial Bank of Japan, Ltd.

In case the exchange rate of the yen in terms of the Swiss franc calculated on the basis of the respective exchange rates of the yen and the Swiss franc in London on the date before the day of payment of any of the second and subsequent instalments provided for in the present Article should be lower or higher by eight per cent or more in comparison with the exchange rate of the yen in terms of the Swiss franc as calculated on the basis of the respective exchange rates of the yen and the Swiss franc in London on the date of the coming into force of the present Agreement, the amount of the said instalment shall be increased or reduced, as the case may be, so that the value in Swiss francs of the instalment shall be the same as it is on the date of the coming into force of the present Agreement.

In case the present gold parity of the Swiss franc (one Swiss franc being equivalent to nine thirty-firsts of one gramme of fine gold) should be altered, or in case the convertibility of the Swiss franc into gold should be suspended, the following method shall be adopted in place of the method provided for in the preceding paragraph.

In case the weight of fine gold whose value, when calculated on the basis of the price of gold and the exchange rate of the yen in London on the day before the date of payment of any of the second and subsequent instalments provided for in the present Article, is equal to the amount of the instalment, should be less or more by eight per cent or more in comparison with the weight of fine gold whose value, when calculated on the basis of the price of gold and the exchange rate of the yen in London on the date of the coming into force of the present Agreement, is equal to the said instalment, the amount of the instalment shall be increased or reduced, as the case may be, so that the value in fine gold of the instalment shall be the same as it is on the date of the coming into force of the present Agreement.

Article IX. The settlement for the sum of ninety-three million three hundred thousand (93,300,000) yen, to be effected in the form of payment made by the Government of Manchukuo for the goods delivered to the Government of the Union of Soviet Socialist Republics, as provided for in Article VII of the present Agreement, shall be executed in the following manner:

1. The Trade Representation of the Union of Soviet Socialist Republics in Japan will make contracts for the purchase of goods produced or manufactured in Manchukuo or Japan, with the sub-jects or juridical persons of either of these two countries, up to the sum of ninety-three million three hundred thousand (93,300,000) yen indicated in Article VII within the period of six months from the date of the coming into force of the present Agreement. The delivery of the goods thus purchased shall be effected to the Trade Representation in Japan by the above-mentioned subjects or juri-dical persons within the period of three years from the date of the coming into force of the present Agreement in accordance with the terms of the contracts concerned, it being understood that the goods so delivered in the course of each of the six equal periods of six months constituting the said three years shall not exceed in value the sum of thirty-one million one hundred thousand (31,100,000) yen, and that the total amount of the goods delivered in the course of each of the three equal periods of one year con-

stituting the said three years shall not exceed in value the sum of thirty-one million one hundred thousand (31,100,000) yen.

2. The terms of payment for the goods shall be arranged in such a way that for each such period of six months in the course of the said three years the Government of Manchukuo shall make payment not exceeding the sum of fifteen million five hundred and fifty thousand (15,550,000) yen for the delivery of the goods mentioned in the foregoing Section and in case any balance of that sum shall for any reason remain unpaid at the end of any such period of six months, such balance shall be paid off during the next six months and so on, so that the whole sum of ninety-three million three hundred thousand (93,300,000) yen shall be paid off by the end of the said three years.

3. It is agreed that should the above-mentioned contracts not be concluded within the period of six months after the coming into force of the present Agreement, the Trade Representative shall have the right to make such contracts after the expiration of the said period of six months, and further that, should any of the parties other than the Trade Representation to the contracts concluded in accordance with the foregoing provisions of the present Article fail to carry out such contracts or to fulfil such contracts in a proper manner for which reason these contracts are abrogated, the Trade Representation shall in each case have the right to conclude fresh contracts with other subjects or juridical persons of Manchukuo or Japan, in which case the latter contracts may provide for the payment for and delivery of the goods to be effected after the three years' term above-mentioned.

4. The contracts mentioned in the present Article shall be concluded either c.i.f. or f.o.b. at the choice of the Trade Representation and shall provide for payments in cash for goods by the Government of Manchukuo.

5. When the Trade Representation have concluded a contract for the purchase of goods with the subjects or juridical persons of Manchukuo or Japan, the Trade Representation shall give the Financial Attaché to the Legation of Manchukuo in Japan a résumé of the contract, mentioning the names of the parties to the contract, the description, place of origin and quantity of the goods, the total amount of the sums to be paid, the date and place of delivery of the goods and of the payment therefor, as well as any other terms of the payment and delivery, including any provisions for payment in advance. The said résumé shall be attested by both parties to the contract. Besides this, so far as circumstances permit, certificates of origin issued by any chamber of commerce and industry in Manchukuo or Japan in respect of the goods, or by any other organization authorized to issue such certificates by the Govern-

ment of either of these two countries, shall be presented to the Financial Attaché by the seller of the goods.

The Financial Attaché, upon receipt of the résumé of the contract, provided its contents do not conflict with the provisions of the present Article, shall notify, not later than within seven days thereafter, the Trade Representation and the seller of the goods concerned to the effect that the Government of Manchukuo undertake to effect payment for the goods in conformity with the said résumé of the contract.

For the purpose of obtaining a settlement of his accounts the seller of the goods shall hand to the Trade Representation the document entitling the Trade Representation to dispose of the said goods (bills of lading, invoices, etc.).

The Financial Attaché, upon receipt of the notification given by the Trade Representation to the effect that the delivery of the goods referred to in the résumé of the contract has been accomplished, shall issue a cheque to order drawn with the Industrial Bank of Japan, Ltd., as payer, the seller of the goods as payee, and the price of the goods as its face amount, and shall deliver it to the seller on the date of payment, and, in case the presentation of the certificates of origin of the goods above referred to shall have been prevented at the time of presentation of the résumé of the contract, against such certificates. The seller of the goods shall give a receipt for the said cheque. Payment in advance to the seller of the goods may be effected in a similar manner by the Financial Attaché in conformity with the résumé of the contract against the advice of the Trade Representation to the effect that such payment shall be made.

6. It is understood that in the present Article the term 'goods manufactured in Manchukuo or Japan' indicates goods manufactured within either of the said two countries from raw materials imported from any other countries as well as from raw materials produced in either, and that the term 'juridical persons of Manchukuo or Japan' indicates the juridical persons which are or may be incorporated in accordance with the law of Manchukuo or Japan respectively.

Article X. 1. Three months' notice shall be given to each of the employees of the North Manchuria Railway (Chinese Eastern Railway) other than those included in the provisions of Article III of the present Agreement, who are citizens of the Union of Soviet Socialist Republics and whom the Government of Manchukuo may desire to dismiss from reasons of convenience on the part of the Government of Manchukuo after the coming into force of the present Agreement.

2. Employees of the North Manchuria Railway (Chinese Eastern Railway) who are citizens of the Union of Soviet Socialist Republics

and who may be dismissed shall have the right to remain in Man-chukuo for two months after their dismissal in order to dispose of their personal affairs.

3. Employees of the North Manchuria Railway (Chinese Eastern Railway) who are citizens of the Union of Soviet Socialist Republics' shall continue in the full enjoyment of their rights in movable and immovable properties in accordance with the laws of Manchukuo.

4. Employees of the North Manchuria Railway (Chinese Eastern Railway) who are citizens of the Union of Soviet Socialist Republics shall enjoy the full right to dispose of their property in accordance with the laws of Manchukuo and to carry their property out of Manchukuo either in its original form or in its money equivalent in any foreign currency.

5. Employees of the North Manchuria Railway (Chinese Eastern Railway) who are citizens of the Union of Soviet Socialist Republics and who have retired through dismissal or of their own accord and who leave for territory of the Union of Soviet Socialist Republics within two months after their retirement, shall be granted the privilege of free transport over the North Manchuria Railway (Chinese Eastern Railway) for themselves, their families and their personal household effects either to the station of Manchuli or to the station of Suifenho, at their own option.

Article XI. 1. The various descriptions of retiring allowances and payments—(discharge allowances and other sums due to employees in respect of service on the railway, employees' savings in the Relief Savings Association and the payments additional thereto on the part of the railway including interest, pensions and block grants in accordance with the regulations of the Relief Savings Association, as well as pensions and compensations for personal injuries accord-ing to the 'Regulations of 1912 relating to the indemnification of persons who have met with accidents ')—to employees of the North Manchuria Railway (Chinese Eastern Railway) who are citizens of the Union of Soviet Socialist Republics and who may be dismissed or may retire of their own accord after the coming into force of the present Agreement, so far as such allowances and payments are in respect of the period before the coming in force of the present Agreement, shall be individually reckoned and paid out in accor-dance with the regulations of the North Manchuria Railway (Chinese Eastern Railway) in force up to the date of the coming into force of the present Agreement, as modified by the provisions of the present Article.

(NOTE.—Discharge allowances for the period up to November 11, 1930, are to be paid according to the rates existing up to November 11, 1930.)

2. Employees who are citizens of the Union of Soviet Socialist

Republics and who are dismissed or retire of their own accord after the coming into force of the present Agreement shall be considered as employees who have been dismissed as the result of the abolition of offices, so far as concerns the calculation of the various descriptions of retiring allowances and payments.

3. Discharge allowances and other payments relative to service concerning the railway, and compensations for injuries sustained in such service, as well as savings and the prescribed interest thereon, shall be paid within a fortnight from the day of dismissal or retirement, provided that in respect of persons who shall be dismissed, half the amount of such savings shall be paid within two months from the date of the notice of such dismissal.

The block grants to persons who have been in the service of the railway for less than ten years, as well as payments additional to savings together with the prescribed interest thereon, shall be paid in four equal instalments within two years from the date of dismissal or retirement. The first instalment shall be paid within a fortnight, and the second instalment at the end of a year after the date of dismissal or retirement, and the third and the fourth instalments shall be paid at the end respectively of six and twelve months after payment of the second instalment. As regards the last three of these instalments, the Government of Manchukuo shall issue bonds for the amounts due drawn up in the names of the respective persons and maturing on the dates prescribed above. These bonds shall be delivered to the respective recipients simultaneously with the payment of the first instalment above referred to, and shall not be transferred thereafter to any other person.

Persons who have been in the service of the railway for ten years or more shall be deemed entitled to pensions without undergoing the examination of their working efficiency, and the said pensions, instead of being paid annually, shall be paid in a block grant, that is to say, a sum of eight and a half times the sum payable annually in respect of a pension shall be paid to the recipient in four equal instalments in the course of two years, in accordance with the provisions of the preceding paragraph.

(NOTE 1.—The examination of the working efficiency of employees who have been in the service of the railway for less than ten years will be effected according to the regulations of the North Manchuria Railway (Chinese Eastern Railway) in force up to the date of the coming into force of the present Agreement.)

(NOTE 2.—Pensions for personal injuries instead of being paid annually shall be paid in block grants, that is to say, a sum eight and a half times the sum payable annually shall be paid to the recipient in the same manner as for persons who have been in the service of the railway for ten years or more.)

4. Employees of the North Manchuria Railway (Chinese Eastern Railway) who are in debt to the railway shall have the sum of their indebtedness deducted from the various descriptions of retiring allowances and other payments due to them.

5. The various descriptions of retiring allowances and payments shall be paid in the currency of Manchukuo at the exchange rate against the rouble of the North Manchuria Railway (Chinese Eastern Railway) existing at the date of the coming into force of the present Agreement and applied by the said railway for settlements with their employees. The recipients of these retiring allowances and payments shall be allowed to remit the money they have received to other countries after having converted it into foreign currency.

6. The various descriptions of retiring allowances and payments and the bonds of the Government of Manchukuo shall be paid or delivered to the legal recipients direct, but persons who have returned to the territory of the Union of Soviet Socialist Republics can empower the Consul General of the Union of Soviet Socialist Republics in Harbin or any other person to receive them. Persons who have given such authority shall at the same time inform the North Manchuria Railway (Chinese Eastern Railway) to that effect.

7. Those persons who have retired before the coming into force of the present Agreement and are now being paid pensions, shall continue to receive the pensions as previously in accordance with the regulations of the North Manchuria Railway (Chinese Eastern Railway) in force up to the date of the coming into force of the present Agreement, irrespective of whether the said regulations shall remain in force, be modified or abrogated thereafter. In this case Section 5 of the present Article shall be applied as regards the exchange rate against the rouble of the North Manchuria Railway (Chinese Eastern Railway) and, in case the legal recipients should be returning or should have returned to the territory of the Union of Soviet Socialist Republics, as regards remittances to other countries.

8. The sums which are to be paid out by the Administration or the Relief Savings Association of the North Manchuria Railway (Chinese Eastern Railway) to employees who are citizens of the Union of Soviet Socialist Republics and of which neither the legal recipients nor their proxies or successors have demanded payment up to the date of the coming into force of the present Agreement, shall be disposed of in accordance with the regulations of the North Manchuria Railway (Chinese Eastern Railway) in force up to the date of the coming into force of the present Agreement.

9. Employees who have been dismissed or have retired after the coming into force of the present Agreement shall, during a period

of one month from the date of their dismissal or retirement, retain their full rights with regard to their railway lodgings under the same conditions as before.

Article XII. It is understood that the term 'North Manchuria Railway (Chinese Eastern Railway)' includes all the rights, enterprises and properties appurtenant thereto.

Article XIII. The Governments of Manchukuo and the Union of Soviet Socialist Republics, with a view to promote and facilitate the intercourse and traffic between the two countries, shall conclude, within three months from the date of the coming into force of the present Agreement, a separate agreement which will provide for the settlement of questions concerning the conveyance of passengers, luggage and goods in transit, direct service for passengers, luggage and goods, between railway stations of the Union of Soviet Socialist Republics and those of the North Manchuria Railway (Chinese Eastern Railway), and also, technically, conditions permitting, direct services without reloading of goods between the Ussuri Railway and the North Manchuria Railway (Chinese Eastern Railway) via the station of Suifenho.

Within the period of the said three months, the two Governments shall conclude another separate agreement which will provide for telegraphic connection between the telegraphic lines hitherto operated by the North Manchuria Railway (Chinese Eastern Railway) and those of the Union of Soviet Socialist Republics.

Article XIV. The present Agreement shall come into force on the date of its signature.

PROTOCOL OF MUTUAL ASSISTANCE BETWEEN THE U.S.S.R. AND THE MONGOLIAN PEOPLE'S REPUBLIC

The Governments of the U.S.S.R. and the Mongolian People's Republic, in view of the constant friendship existing between their countries since the liberation in 1921 of the territory of the Mongolian People's Republic with the help of the Red Army from the White Guard Troops, which were connected with the military forces that invaded the territory of the U.S.S.R., and being inspired by the desire to support the task of peace in the Far East and to assist the further strengthening of their friendly relations, have decided to fix in the form of this Protocol the gentlemen's agreement, existing since November 22, 1934, which provides for mutual support by all means in every way to avert and to prevent the menace of a military attack of a third country on the U.S.S.R., or the Mongolian People's Republic; for this reason this Protocol is to be signed.

Article I. In case of the menace of an attack on the territory of the U.S.S.R. or the Mongolian People's Republic from a third country, the Governments of the U.S.S.R. and M.P.R. pledge themselves to discuss together immediately the situation created and to take all those steps, necessary to protect the safety of their territories.

Article II. The Governments of the U.S.S.R. and the M.P.R. pledge themselves in case of a military attack on one of the Contracting Parties, to render mutually any assistance including military assistance.

Article III. The Governments of U.S.S.R. and the M.P.R. consider it as a matter of fact, that troops of one of the Contracting Parties, which are by mutual agreement on the territory of the other party in order to carry out the obligation, stated in Articles I or II, will be withdrawn from the respective territory immediately the need is over—similarly to the withdrawal in 1926 of the Soviet troops from the territory of the M.P.R.

Article IV. This Protocol has been drawn up in duplicate in the Russian and Mongolian languages, and both texts are to be considered as authentic. It shall come into effect from the day of its signature and will remain in force for ten years from this date.

Signed by

Plenipotentiary Representative of the U.S.S.R. in the M.P.R. (V. Tairov.)

President of the Minor Khural of the M.P.R. (Amor.)

President of the Council of Ministers and Minister of Foreign Affairs of the M.P.R. (Gendun.)

Signed at Urga, 12 March, 1936.

TREATY OF NON-AGGRESSION BETWEEN THE REPUBLIC OF CHINA AND THE UNION OF SOVIET SOCIALIST REPUBLICS

The National Government of the Republic of China and the Government of the Union of Soviet Socialist Republics, animated by the desire to contribute to the maintenance of general peace, to consolidate the amicable relations now existing between them on a firm and lasting basis, and to confirm in a more precise manner the obligations mutually undertaken under the Treaty for the Renunciation of War signed in Paris on August 27, 1938, have resolved to conclude the present Treaty and have for this purpose appointed as their plenipotentiaries, that is to say:

> His Excellency the President of the National Government of the Republic of China:
> DR WANG CHUNG-HUI, Minister for Foreign Affairs.
> The Central Executive Committee of the Union of Soviet Socialist Republics:
> MR. DIMITRI BOGOMOLOFF, Ambassador Extraordinary and Plenipotentiary to the Republic of China,

who having communicated their full powers, found in good and due form, have agreed upon the following Articles:

Article I. The two High Contracting Parties solemnly affirm that they condemn recourse to war for the solution of international controversies, and that they renounce it as an instrument of national policy in their relations with each other, and in pursuance of this pledge, they undertake to refrain from any aggression against each other either individually or jointly with one or more other Powers.

Article II. In the event that either of the two High Contracting Parties should be subjected to aggression on the part of one or more third Powers, the other High Contracting Party obligates itself not to render assistance of any kind, either directly or indirectly, to such third Power or Powers at any time during the entire conflict, and also to refrain from taking any action or entering into any agreement which may be used by the aggressor or aggressors to the disadvantage of the party subjected to aggression.

Article III. The provisions of the present Treaty shall not be so interpreted as to affect or modify the rights and obligations arising,

394

in respect of the High Contracting Parties, out of bilateral or multi-lateral treaties or agreements of which both High Contracting Parties are signatories and which were concluded prior to the entering into force of the present Treaty.

Article IV. The present Treaty is drawn up in duplicate in English. It comes into force on the day of signature by the above-mentioned Plenipotentiaries and shall remain in force for a period of five years. Either of the High Contracting Parties may notify the other, six months before the expiration of the period, of its desire to terminate the Treaty. In case both parties fail to do so in time, the Treaty shall be considered as being automatically extended for a period of two years after the expiration of the first period. Should neither of the High Contracting Parties notify the other, six months before the expiration of the two-year period, of its desire to terminate the Treaty, it shall continue in force for another period of two years, and so on successively.

In witness whereof the respective Plenipotentiaries have signed the present Treaty, and have affixed thereunto their seals.

Done at Nanking, the Twenty-first day of August, 1937.

WANG CHUNG-HUI.

D. BOGOMOLOFF.

Appendix C

YALTA SECRET AGREEMENT

(Entered into by Marshal Joseph Stalin, former Prime Minister Winston Churchill, and the late President Roosevelt on February 11, 1945, and published on February 11, 1946, simultaneously in Washington, London and Moscow.)

THE leaders of the three great Powers—the Soviet Union, the United States of America, and Great Britain—have agreed that in two or three months after Germany has surrendered and the war in Europe has terminated, the Soviet Union shall enter into the war against Japan on the side of the Allies on conditions that:

Firstly, The *status quo* in Outer Mongolia (The Mongolian People's Republic) shall be preserved;

Secondly, The former rights of Russia violated by the treacherous attack of Japan in 1904 shall be restored, viz.:

(*a*) The southern part of Sakhalin as well as all the islands adjacent to it shall be returned to the Soviet Union;

(*b*) The commercial port of Dairen shall be internationalized, the pre-eminent interests of the Soviet Union in this port being safeguarded and the lease of Port Arthur as a naval base of the U.S.S.R. restored;

(*c*) The Chinese Eastern Railroad and the Southern Manchurian Railroad which provided outlet to Dairen shall be jointly operated by the establishment of a joint Sino-Soviet Company, it being understood that the pre-eminent interests of the Soviet Union shall be safeguarded and that China shall retain full sovereignty in Manchuria;

Thirdly, The Kurile islands shall be handed over to the Soviet Union.

It is understood that the agreement concerning Outer Mongolia and the ports and the railroads referred to above all require the concurrence of Generalissimo Chiang Kai-shek. The President will take measures in order to obtain this concurrence on advice from Marshal Stalin.

The Heads of the three Great Powers have agreed that these

claims of the Soviet Union shall be unquestionably fulfilled after Japan has been defeated.

For its part the Soviet Union expresses its readiness to conclude with the National Government of China a pact of friendship and alliance between the U.S.S.R. and China in order to render assistance to China with its armed forces for the purpose of liberating China from the Japanese yoke.

(Signed) JOSEPH V. STALIN.

FRANKLIN D. ROOSEVELT.

WINSTON CHURCHILL.

February 11, 1945.

TREATY OF FRIENDSHIP AND ALLIANCE BETWEEN THE REPUBLIC OF CHINA AND THE UNION OF SOVIET SOCIALIST REPUBLICS[1]

The President of the National Government of the Republic of China, and the Presidium of the Supreme Soviet of the Union of Soviet Socialist Republics,

Desirous of strengthening the friendly relations that have always existed between China and the U.S.S.R. through an alliance and good neighbourly post-war collaboration,

Determined to assist each other in the struggle against aggression on the part of enemies of the United Nations in this world war and to collaborate in the common war against Japan until her unconditional surrender,

Expressing their unswerving aspiration to co-operate in the cause of maintaining peace and security for the benefit of the peoples of both countries and of all the peace-loving nations,

Acting upon the principles enunciated in the Joint Declaration of the United Nations of January 1, 1942, in the Four Power Declaration signed in Moscow on October 30, 1943, and in the Charter of the International Organization of the United Nations,

Have decided to conclude the present Treaty to this effect and appointed as their Plenipotentiaries:

> The President of the National Government of the Republic of China:
>> His Excellency DR. WANG SHIH-CHIEH, Minister of Foreign Affairs of the Republic of China,
>
> The Presidium of the Supreme Soviet of the Union of Soviet Socialist Republics:
>> His Excellency MR. V. M. MOLOTOV, the People's Commissar of Foreign Affairs of the U.S.S.R.,

Who, after exchanging their full powers, found in good and due form, have agreed as follows:

Article I. The High Contracting Parties undertake in association with the other United Nations to wage war against Japan until final victory is won. The High Contracting Parties undertake mutually

---

[1] Translation of the text of the Treaty which was published as *White Book of the Ministry of Foreign Affairs*, No. 67, November 1945.

to render to one another all necessary military and other assistance and support in this war.

Article II. The High Contracting Parties undertake not to enter into separate negotiations with Japan and not to conclude, without mutual consent, any armistice or peace treaty either with the present Japanese Government or with any other government or authority set up in Japan which do not renounce all aggressive intentions.

Article III. The High Contracting Parties undertake after the termination of the war against Japan, to take jointly all measures in their power to render impossible a repetition of aggression and violation of the peace by Japan.

In the event of one of the High Contracting Parties becoming involved in hostilities with Japan in consequence of an attack by the latter against the said Contracting Party, the other High Contracting Party shall at once give to the Contracting Party so involved in hostilities all the military and other support and assistance with the means in its power.

This Article shall remain in force until such time as the Organization, 'The United Nations', may on request of the two High Contracting Parties be charged with the responsibility for preventing further aggression by Japan.

Article IV. Each High Contracting Party undertakes not to conclude any alliance and not to take part in any coalition directed against the other High Contracting Party.

Article V. The High Contracting Parties, having regard to the interests of the security and economic development of each of them, agree to work together in close and friendly collaboration after the coming of peace and to act according to the principles of mutual respect for their sovereignty and territorial integrity and of non-interference in the internal affairs of the other High Contracting Party.

Article VI. The High Contracting Parties agree to render each other every possible economic assistance in the post-war period with a view to facilitating and accelerating reconstruction in both countries and to contributing to the cause of world prosperity.

Article VII. Nothing in this Treaty shall be so construed as to affect the rights or obligations of the High Contracting Parties as members of the Organization 'The United Nations'.

Article VIII. The present Treaty shall be ratified in the shortest possible time. The exchange of the instruments of ratification shall take place as soon as possible in Chungking.

The present Treaty shall come into force immediately upon its ratification and shall remain in force for a term of thirty years.

If neither of the High Contracting Parties has given notice, a year before the expiration of the term, of its desire to terminate the

Treaty, it shall remain valid for an unlimited time, each of the High Contracting Parties being able to terminate its operation by giving notice to that effect one year in advance.

IN FAITH WHEREOF the Plenipotentiaries have signed the present Treaty and affixed their seals.

Done at Moscow, this Fourteenth day of the Eighth month of the Thirty-fourth year of the Republic of China, corresponding to the Fourteenth day of August, 1945, in duplicate, in the Chinese and Russian languages, both texts being equally authoritative.

The Plenipotentiary of the President of the National Government of the Republic of China.	*The Plenipotentiary of the Presidium the Supreme Soviet of the U.S.S.R.*
(L. S.) WANG SHIH-CHIEH.	(L. S.) V. MOLOTOV.

Exchange of Notes

(I) SOVIET NOTE TO THE CHINESE PLENIPOTENTIARY

YOUR EXCELLENCY,

With reference to the Treaty of Friendship and Alliance signed to-day between the Republic of China and the U.S.S.R., I have the honour to put on record the understanding between the High Contracting Parties as follows:

1. In accordance with the spirit of the aforementioned Treaty, and in order to put into effect its aims and purposes, the Government of the U.S.S.R. agrees to render to China its moral support as well as aid in military supplies and other material resources, such support and aid to be entirely given to the National Government as the Central Government of China.

2. In the course of conversations regarding Dairen and Port Arthur and regarding the joint operation of the Chinese Changchun Railway, the Government of the U.S.S.R. regarded the Three Eastern Provinces as part of China and reaffirmed its respect for China's full sovereignty over the Three Eastern Provinces and recognized their territorial and administrative integrity.

3. As for the recent developments in Sinkiang the Soviet Government confirms that, as stated in Article V of the Treaty of Friendship and Alliance, it has no intention of interfering in the internal affairs of China.

If Your Excellency will be so good as to confirm that the understanding is correct as set forth in the preceding paragraphs, the present Note and Your Excellency's reply thereto will constitute a part of the aforementioned Treaty of Friendship and Alliance.

I avail myself of this opportunity to offer Your Excellency the assurances of my highest consideration.

(*Signed*) V. Molotov.

Reply

Your Excellency,

I have the honour to acknowledge receipt of Your Excellency's Note of to-day's date reading as follows:

' With reference to the Treaty of Friendship and Alliance signed to-day between the Republic of China and the U.S.S.R., I have the honour to put on record the understanding between the High Contracting Parties as follows:

' 1. In accordance with the spirit of the aforementioned Treaty, and in order to put into effect its aims and purposes, the Government of the U.S.S.R. agrees to render to China its moral support as well as aid in military supplies and other material resources, such support and aid to be entirely given to the National Government as the Central Government of China.

' 2. In the course of conversations regarding Dairen and Port Arthur and regarding the joint operation of the Chinese Changchun Railway, the Government of the U.S.S.R. regarded the Three Eastern Provinces as part of China and reaffirmed its respect for China's full sovereignty over the Three Eastern Provinces and recognized their territorial and administrative integrity.

' 3. As for the recent developments in Sinkiang the Soviet Government confirms that, as stated in Article V of the Treaty of Friendship and Alliance, it has no intention of interfering in the internal affairs of China.

' If Your Excellency will be so good as to confirm that the understanding is correct as set forth in the preceding paragraphs, the present Note and Your Excellency's reply thereto will constitute a part of the aforementioned Treaty of Friendship and Alliance.'

I have the honour to confirm that the understanding is correct as set forth above.

I avail myself of this opportunity to offer Your Excellency the assurances of my highest consideration.

(*Signed*) Wang Shih-chieh.

(II) Chinese Note to the Soviet Plenipotentiary

Your Excellency,

In view of the desire repeatedly expressed by the people of Outer Mongolia for their independence, the Chinese Government declares that after the defeat of Japan should a plebiscite of the Outer Mongolian people confirm this desire, the Chinese Government will recognize the independence of Outer Mongolia with the existing boundary as its boundary.

The above declaration will become binding upon the ratification of the Treaty of Friendship and Alliance between the Republic of China and the U.S.S.R. signed on August 14, 1945.

I avail myself of this opportunity to offer Your Excellency the assurances of my highest consideration.

(*Signed*) Wang Shih-chieh.

Reply

Your Excellency,

I have the honour to acknowledge receipt of Your Excellency's Note reading as follows:

' In view of the desire repeatedly expressed by the people of Outer Mongolia for their independence, the Chinese Government declares that after the defeat of Japan should a plebiscite of the Outer Mongolian people confirm this desire, the Chinese Government will recognize the independence of Outer Mongolia with the existing boundary as its boundary.

' The above declaration will become binding upon the ratification of the Treaty of Friendship and Alliance between the Republic of China and the U.S.S.R. signed on August 14, 1945.'

The Soviet Government has duly taken note of the above communication of the Government of the Chinese Republic and hereby expresses its satisfaction therewith, and it further states that the Soviet Government will respect the political independence and territorial integrity of the People's Republic of Mongolia (Outer Mongolia).

I avail myself of this opportunity to offer Your Excellency the assurances of my highest consideration.

(*Signed*) V. Molotov.

AGREEMENT BETWEEN THE REPUBLIC OF CHINA AND THE U.S.S.R. CONCERNING THE CHINESE CHANGCHUN RAILWAY

The President of the Republic of China and the Presidium of the Supreme Soviet of the U.S.S.R., desiring to strengthen the friendly relations and economic bonds between the two countries on the basis of the full observation of the rights and interests of each other, have agreed as follows:

Article I. After the Japanese armed forces are driven out of the Three Eastern Provinces of China the main trunk lines of the Chinese Eastern Railway and the South Manchurian Railway from Manchuli to Suifenho and from Harbin to Dairen and Port Arthur united into one railway under the name of 'Chinese Changchun Railway' shall be in joint ownership of the U.S.S.R. and the Republic of China and shall be operated by them jointly.

There shall be joint ownership and operation only of those lands acquired and railway auxiliary lines built by the Chinese Eastern Railway during the time of Russian and joint Sino-Soviet administration and by the South Manchurian Railway during the time of Russian administration and which are designed for direct needs of these railways as well as the subsidiary enterprises built during the said periods and directly serving these railways. All the other railway branches, subsidiary enterprises and lands shall be in the complete ownership of the Chinese Government.

The joint operation of the aforementioned railway shall be undertaken by a single management under Chinese sovereignty and as a purely commercial transportation enterprise.

Article II. The High Contracting Parties agree that their joint ownership of the Railway shall be in equal shares and shall not be alienable in whole or in part.

Article III. The High Contracting Parties agree that for the joint operation of the said Railway the Sino-Soviet Company of the Chinese Changchun Railway shall be formed. The Company shall have a Board of Directors to be composed of ten members of whom five shall be appointed by the Chinese Government and five by the Soviet Government. The Board of Directors shall be in Changchun.

Article IV. The Chinese Government shall appoint one of the

Chinese Directors as President of the Board of Directors and one as the Assistant President. The Soviet Government shall appoint one of the Soviet Directors as Vice-President of the Board of Directors, and one as the Assistant Vice-President. Seven persons constitute a quorum. When questions are decided by the Board, the vote of the President of the Board of Directors shall be counted as two votes.

Important questions on which the Board of Directors cannot reach an agreement shall be submitted to the Governments of the two High Contracting Parties for consideration and settlement in an equitable and friendly spirit.

Article V. The Company shall establish a Board of Auditors which shall be composed of six members of whom three are appointed by Chinese Government and three appointed by the Soviet Government. The Chairman of the Board of Auditors shall be elected from among the Soviet Auditors, and Vice-Chairman from among the Chinese Auditors. ' When questions are decided by the Board the vote of the Chairman shall be counted as two votes. Five persons shall constitute a quorum.

Article VI. For the administration of current affairs the Board of Directors shall appoint a Manager of the Chinese Changchun Railway from among Soviet citizens and one Assistant Manager from among Chinese citizens.

Article VII. The Board of Auditors shall appoint a General-Comptroller from among Chinese citizens and an Assistant General-Comptroller from among Soviet citizens.

Article VIII. The Chiefs and Assistant Chiefs of the various departments, Chiefs of sections, station masters at important stations of the Railway shall be appointed by the Board of Directors. The Manager of the Railway has the right to recommend candidates for the above-mentioned posts. Individual members of the Board of Directors may also recommend such candidates in agreement with the Manager. If the chief of a department is a national of China, the assistant chief shall be a national of the Soviet Union, and vice versa. The appointments of the chiefs and assistant chiefs of departments and chiefs of sections and station masters shall be made in accordance with the principle of equal representation between the nationals of China and nationals of the Soviet Union.

Article IX. The Chinese Government will bear the responsibility for the protection of the said Railway.

The Chinese Government will also organize and supervise the railway guards who shall protect the railway buildings, installations and other properties and freight from destruction, loss and robbery, and shall maintain the normal order on the Railway. As regards the duties of the guards in execution of this Article, they well be determined by the Chinese Government in consultation with the Soviet Government.

Article X. Only during the time of war against Japan the Railway may be used for the transportation of Soviet troops. The Soviet Government has the right to transport by the above-mentioned Railway for transit purpose military goods in sealed cars without Customs inspection. The guarding of such military goods shall be undertaken by the railway guards and the Soviet Union shall not send any armed escort.

Article XI. Goods for through transit and transported by the Chinese Changchun Railway from Manchuli to Suifenho or vice versa and also from Soviet territory to the ports of Dairen and Port Arthur or vice versa shall be free from Chinese Customs duties or any other taxes and dues, but on entering Chinese territory such goods shall be subject to Chinese Customs inspection and verification.

Article XII. The Chinese Government will ensure, on the basis of a separate agreement, that the supply of coal for the operation of the Railway will be fully secured.

Article XIII. The Railway shall pay the same taxes to the Government of the Republic of China as are paid by the Chinese State railways.

Article XIV. Both High Contracting Parties agree to provide the Board of Directors of the Chinese Changchun Railway with working capital the amount of which will be determined by the Statutes of the Railway.

Profits and losses in the operation of the Railway shall be equally divided between the two Parties.

Article XV. For the working out in Chungking of the Statutes of joint operation of the Railway each of the High Contracting Parties undertakes within one month of the signing of the present Agreement, to appoint three representatives. The Statutes shall be worked out within two months and reported to the two Governments for their approval.

Article XVI. The determination, in accordance with the provisions in Article I, of the properties to be included in the joint ownership and operation of the Railway by China and the U.S.S.R. shall be made by a Commission to be composed of three representatives each of the two Governments. The Commission shall be constituted in Chungking within one month after the signing of the present Agreement and shall terminate its work within three months after the joint operation of the Railway shall have begun. The decisions of the Commission shall be reported to the two Governments for their approval.

Article XVII. The term of this present Agreement shall be thirty years. After the expiration of the term of the present Agreement, the Chinese Changchun Railway with all its properties shall be transferred without compensation to the ownership of the Republic of China.

Article XVIII. The present Agreement shall come into force from the date of its ratification.

Done at Moscow, this Fourteenth day of the Eighth month of the Thirty-fourth year of the Republic of China, corresponding to the Fourteenth day of August, 1945, in duplicate, in the Chinese and Russian languages, both texts being equally authoritative.

The Plenipotentiary of the President of the National Government of the Republic of China.

(*Signed*) WANG SHIH-CHIEH.

The Plenipotentiary of the Presidium the Supreme Soviet of the U.S.S.R.

(*Signed*) V. MOLCTOV.

AGREEMENT ON DAIREN

In view of a Treaty of Friendship and Alliance having been concluded between the Republic of China and the U.S.S.R. and of the pledge by the latter that it will respect Chinese sovereignty in the control of all of Manchuria as an integral part of China; and with the object of ensuring that the U.S.S.R.'s interest in Dairen as a port of entry and exit for its goods shall be safeguarded, the Republic of China agrees:

1. To declare Dairen a free port open to the commerce and shipping of all nations.

2. The Chinese Government agrees to apportion in the mentioned port for lease to U.S.S.R. wharves and warehouses on the basis of a separate agreement.

3. The administration in Dairen shall belong to China. The harbour-master and deputy harbour-master will be appointed by the Manager of the Chinese Changchun Railway and in agreement with the Mayor. The harbour-master shall be a Soviet national, and the deputy harbour-master shall be a Chinese national.

4. In peace time Dairen is not included in the sphere of efficacy of the naval base regulations, determined by the Agreement on Port Arthur of August 14, 1945, and shall be subject to the military supervision or control established in this zone only in case of war against Japan.

5. Goods entering the free port from abroad for through transit to Soviet territory on the Chinese Changchun Railway and goods coming from Soviet territory on the said Railway into the free port for export, or materials transported from Soviet territory to meet the requirement of the harbour equipment in the free port, shall be free from Customs duties. Such goods shall be transported in sealed cars.

Goods entering other parts of China from the free port shall pay the Chinese import duties, and goods going out of other parts of China into the free port shall pay the Chinese export duties as long as they continue to be collected.

6. The term of the present Agreement shall be thirty years.

7. The present Agreement shall come into force from the date of its ratification.

IN FAITH WHEREOF the Plenipotentiaries have signed the present Agreement and affixed thereto their seals.

Done at Moscow, this Fourteenth day of the Eighth month of the Thirty-fourth year of the Republic of China, corresponding to the Fourteenth day of August, 1945, in duplicate, in the Chinese and Russian languages, both texts being equally authoritative.

The Plenipotentiary of the President of the National Government of the Republic of China.

(L. S.) WANG SHIH-CHIEH.

The Plenipotentiary of the Presidium the Supreme Soviet of the U.S.S.R.

(L. S.) V. MOLOTOV.

PROTOCOL RELATIVE TO THE AGREEMENT ON DAIREN

1. At the request of the U.S.S.R. the Chinese Government leases to the U.S.S.R. free of charges one half of all port installations and equipment. The term of lease shall be thirty years. The remaining half of port installations and equipment shall be reserved for the use of China. The expansion or re-equipment of the Port shall be made by agreement between China and the U.S.S.R.

2. It is agreed that the sections of the Chinese Changchun Railway running from Dairen to Mukden that lie within the region of the Port Arthur naval base, shall not be subject to any military supervision or control established in this region.

The Plenipotentiary of the President of the National Government of the Republic of China.

(*Signed*) WANG SHIH-CHIEH.

The Plenipotentiary of the Presidium the Supreme Soviet of the U.S.S.R.

(*Signed*) V. MOLOTOV.

AGREEMENT ON PORT ARTHUR

In conformity with, and for the implementation of, the Treaty of Friendship and Alliance between the Republic of China and the U.S.S.R., the High Contracting Parties have agreed as follows:

Article I. With a view to strengthening the security of China and of the U.S.S.R. against further aggression by Japan, the Government of the Republic of China agrees to the joint use by the two countries of Port Arthur as a naval base.

Article II. The precise boundary of the area provided in Article I is described in the Annex and shown in the map. (See Annex.)

Article III. The High Contracting Parties agree that Port Arthur, as an exclusive naval base, will be used only by Chinese and Soviet military and commercial vessels.

There shall be established a Sino-Soviet Military Commission to handle the matters of joint use of the above-mentioned naval base. The Commission shall consist of two Chinese and three Soviet representatives. The Chairman of the Commission shall be appointed by the Soviet side and the Vice-Chairman shall be appointed by the Chinese side.

Article IV. The Chinese Government entrusts to the Soviet Government the defence of the naval base. The Soviet Government may erect at its own expense such installations as are necessary for the defence of the naval base.

Article V. The Civil Administration of the whole area will be Chinese. The leading posts of the Civil Administration will be appointed by the Chinese Government, taking into account Soviet interests in the Area.

The leading posts of the Civil Administration in the city of Port Arthur are appointed and dismissed by the Chinese Government in agreement with the Soviet military command.

The proposals which the Soviet military commander in the said Area may address to the Chinese Civil Administration in order to safeguard security and defence will be fulfilled by the said Administration. In case of disagreement, such cases shall be submitted to the Sino-Soviet Military Commission for consideration and decision.

Article VI. The Government of the U.S.S.R. has the right to maintain in the region mentioned in Article II, its army, navy and air forces and to determine their location.

Article VII. The Government of the U.S.S.R. also undertakes to establish and maintain lighthouses and other installations and signs necessary for the security of navigation of the Area.

Article VIII. After the termination of the present Agreement all the installations and public property installed or constructed by the U.S.S.R. in the Area shall revert without compensation to the Chinese Government.

Article IX. The term of the present Agreement shall be thirty years. The present Agreement shall come into force from the date of its ratification.

IN FAITH WHEREOF the Plenipotentiaries of the High Contracting Parties have signed the present Agreement and affixed thereto their seals. The present Agreement is made in duplicate, in the Chinese and Russian languages, both texts being equally authoritative.

Done at Moscow, this Fourteenth day of the Eighth month of the Thirty-fourth year of the Republic of China, corresponding to the Fourteenth day of August, 1945.

The Plenipotentiary of the President of the National Government of the Republic of China.	*The Plenipotentiary of the Presidium the Supreme Soviet of the U.S.S.R.*
(L. S.) WANG SHIH-CHIEH.	(L. S.) V. MOLOTOV.

ANNEX

With respect to the boundary of the Area of the naval base provided in Article II of the Agreement on Port Arthur, there shall be drawn a line starting from a point to the south of Hou-shan-tao Bay on the western coast of the Liaotung Peninsula, and thence running eastward across Shih-ho Station and Tsou-chia-jui-tze to the eastern coast of the said Peninsula. All the land situate to the south of this line shall constitute the land area of the naval base, the city of Dairen being excepted.

On the water to the west of the Area provided by the Agreement in the Liaotung Peninsula, all the islands situate to the south of a line connecting a point at lat. 39° N., long. 120° 49′ E. and a point at lat. 39° 20′ N., long. 121° 31′ E., and thence running northeastward towards Pu-lan-tien until it meets on its south the starting point of the boundary line on land are included in the Area of the naval base.

On the water to the east of the Area in the Liantung Peninsula, all the islands situate to the south of a line starting from the terminal point of the boundary line on land, thence running eastward across a point at lat. 39° 20′ N., long. 123° 08′ E., and thence south-eastward to a point at lat. 39° N., long. 123° 16′ E. are included in the Area of the naval base. (Attached hereto is a Russian map scaled 1 : 500,000.)

The boundary of the Area shall be determined on the spot and marked with boundary signs on land, and, if necessary, also on the water by a Sino-Soviet Mixed Commission. Land and sea maps shall be drawn by the Commission, with detailed descriptions attached, the land map to be scaled 1 : 25,000 and the sea map, 1 : 300,000.

The date for the said Commission to commence its work shall be determined by the two Contracting Parties.

The descriptions and the maps showing the boundary of the Area so prepared by the said Commission shall be subject to the approval of the Governments of the two Contracting Parties.

(*Initialed*). SHIH-CHIEH.   (*Initialed*) V. M.

AGREEMENT REGARDING RELATIONS BETWEEN THE CHINESE ADMINISTRATION AND THE COMMANDER-IN-CHIEF OF THE SOVIET FORCES AFTER THE ENTRY OF SOVIET TROOPS INTO THE THREE EASTERN PROVINCES OF CHINA DURING THE PRESENT JOINT MILITARY OPERATIONS AGAINST JAPAN

The President of the National Government of China and the Presidium of the Supreme Soviet of the Union of Soviet Socialist Republics,

Desirous that relations between the Chinese Administration and the Commander-in-Chief of the Soviet forces after the entry of Soviet troops into the Three Eastern Provinces of China during the present joint military operations against Japan should be governed by the spirit of friendship and alliance existing between the two countries,

Have agreed on the following:

1. After the Soviet troops enter the Three Eastern Provinces of China as a result of military operations, the supreme authority and responsibility in all matters relating to the prosecution of the war will be vested, in the zone of operations for the time required for the operations, in the Commander-in-Chief of the Soviet forces.

2. A Chinese National Government representative and staff will be appointed for the recovered territory, whose duties will be:

   (a) To establish and direct, in accordance with the laws of China, an administration for the territory cleared of the enemy;

   (b) To assist in the establishment of co-operation between the Chinese armed forces, both regular and irregular, and the Soviet forces in recovered territory;

   (c) To ensure the active co-operation of the Chinese Administration with the Commander-in-Chief of the Soviet forces and, specifically, to give the local authorities directions to this effect, being guided by the requirements and wishes of the Commander-in-Chief of the Soviet forces.

3. To ensure contact between the Commander-in-Chief of the Soviet forces and the National Government representative a Chinese military mission will be appointed to the Commander-in-Chief of the Soviet forces.

4. In the zones under the supreme authority of the Commander-in-Chief of the Soviet forces, the Chinese National Government authorities in the recovered territory will maintain contact with the Commander-in-Chief of Soviet forces through the Chinese National Government representative.

5. As soon as any part of the liberated territory ceases to be a zone of immediate military operations, the Chinese National Government will assume full authority in the direction of public affairs and will render the Commander-in-Chief of the Soviet forces every assistance and support through its civil and military authorities.

6. All persons belonging to the Soviet forces on Chinese territory will be under the jurisdiction of the Commander-in-Chief of the Soviet forces. All Chinese, whether civilian or military, will be under Chinese jurisdiction. This jurisdiction will also extend to the civilian population on Chinese territory even in the case of offenses against the Soviet armed forces, with the exception of offenses committed in the zone of military operations under the jurisdiction of the Commander-in-Chief of the Soviet forces, such cases coming under the jurisdiction of the Commander-in-Chief of the Soviet forces. In disputable cases the question will be settled by mutual agreement between the Chinese National Government representative and the Commander-in-Chief of the Soviet forces.

7. With regard to currency matters after the entry of Soviet troops into the Three Eastern Provinces of China, a separate agreement shall be reached.

8. The present Agreement comes into force immediately upon the ratification of the Treaty of Friendship and Alliance between China and the U.S.S.R. signed this day. The present Agreement is made in duplicate in the Chinese and Russian languages, both texts being equally authoritative.

Done at Moscow, this fourteenth day of the Eighth month of the Thirty-fourth year of the Republic of China, corresponding to the Fourteenth day of August, 1945.

The Plenipotentiary of the President of the National Government of the Republic of China.

(L. S.) WANG SHIH-CHIEH.

The Plenipotentiary of the Presidium of the Supreme Soviet of the U.S.S.R.

(L. S.) V. MOLOTOV.

MINUTES

At the fifth meeting held on July 11, 1945, between Generalissimo

Stalin and Dr. T. V. Soong, the question of the withdrawal of Soviet troops from Chinese territory after the participation by the U.S.S.R. in the war against Japan was discussed.

Generalissimo Stalin would not like to have a clause in the arrangement governing the entry of Soviet troops into Manchuria which provides for the withdrawal of Soviet troops within three months after the defeat of Japan. However, he said that after the capitulation of Japan the Soviet troops would commence to withdraw within three weeks.

Dr. Soong asked how long it would take to complete the withdrawal. Generalissimo Stalin said he thought the withdrawal could be completed in not more than two months.

Dr. Soong further asked whether the withdrawal would be definitely completed within three months. Generalissimo Stalin stated that three months would be the maximum for the completion of the withdrawal.

This Fourteenth day of the Eighth month of the Thirty-fourth year of the Republic of China, corresponding to the Fourteenth day of August, 1945.

(*Initialed*) SHIH-CHIEH.   (*Initialed*) V. M.

Appendix D

SINO-SOVIET TREATY OF FRIENDSHIP, ALLIANCE AND MUTUAL ASSISTANCE

THE Presidium of the Supreme Soviet of the Union of Soviet Socialist Republics and the Central People's Government of the People's Republic of China,

Filled with determination jointly to prevent, by the consolidation of friendship and co-operation between the Union of Soviet Socialist Republics and the People's Republic of China, the rebirth of Japanese imperialism and a repetition of aggression on the part of Japan or any other State which should unite in any form with Japan in acts of aggression;

Imbued with the desire to consolidate lasting peace and universal security in the Far East and throughout the world in conformity with the aims and principles of the United Nations Organization;

Profoundly convinced that the consolidation of good-neighbourly relations and friendship between the Union of Soviet Socialist Republics and the People's Republic of China meets the fundamental interests of the peoples of the Soviet Union and China,

Resolved for this purpose to conclude the present Treaty and appointed as their plenipotentiary representatives:

The Central People's Government of the People's Republic of China:

CHOU EN-LAI, Prime Minister of the State Administrative Council and Minister of Foreign Affairs of China.

The Presidium of the Supreme Soviet of the Union of Soviet Socialist Republics:

ANDROI YANUARYEVICH VYSHINSKY, Minister of Foreign Affairs of the Union of Soviet Socialist Republics,

Who after exchange of their credentials, found in due form and good order, agreed upon the following:

Article I. Both High Contracting Parties undertake jointly to take all the necessary measures at their disposal for the purpose of preventing a repetition of aggression and violation of peace on the part of Japan or any other State which should unite with Japan, directly or indirectly, in acts of aggression. In the event of one of the High Contracting Parties being attacked by Japan or States allied with it, and thus being involved in a state of war, the other High Contracting Party will immediately render military and other assistance with all the means at its disposal.

The High Contracting Parties also declare their readiness in the spirit of sincere co-operation, to participate in all international actions aimed at ensuring peace and security throughout the world, and will do all in their power to achieve the speediest implementation of these tasks.

Article II. Both the High Contracting Parties undertake by means of mutual agreement to strive for the earliest conclusion of a peace treaty with Japan, jointly with the other Powers which were allies during the Second World War.

Article III. Both High Contracting Parties undertake not to conclude any alliance directed against the other High Contracting Party, and not to take part in any coalition or in actions or measures directed against the other High Contracting Party.

Article IV. Both High Contracting Parties will consult each other in regard to all important international problems affecting the common interests of the Soviet Union and China, being guided by the interests of the consolidation of peace and universal security.

Article V. Both the High Contracting Parties undertake in the spirit of friendship and co-operation and in conformity with the principles of equality, mutual interests, and also mutual respect for the State sovereignty and territorial integrity and non-interference in internal affairs of the other High Contracting Party—to develop and consolidate economic and cultural ties between the Soviet Union and China, to render each other every possible economic assistance, and to carry out the necessary economic co-operation.

Article VI. The present Treaty comes into force immediately upon its ratification; the exchange of instruments of ratification will take place in Peking.

The present Treaty will be valid for thirty years. If neither of the High Contracting Parties gives notice one year before the expiration of this term of its desire to denounce the Treaty, it shall remain in force for another five years and will be extended in compliance with this rule.

Done in Moscow on February 14, 1950, in two copies, each in the Russian and Chinese languages, both texts having equal force.

Signed:

By authorization of the Central People's Government of the People's Republic of China—CHOU EN-LAI.

By authorization of the Presidium of the Supreme Soviet of the Union of Soviet Socialist Republics—A. Y. VYSHINSKY.

AGREEMENT ON THE CHINESE CHANGCHUN RAILWAY, PORT ARTHUR AND DAIREN

The Presidium of the Supreme Soviet of the Union of Soviet Socialist Republics and the Central People's Government of the People's Republic of China state that since 1945 radical changes have occurred in the situation in the Far East, namely: Imperialist Japan suffered defeat; the reactionary Kuomintang Government was overthrown; China has become a People's Democratic Republic, and in China a new People's Government was formed which has united the whole of China, carried out a policy of friendship and co-operation with the Soviet Union and proved its ability to defend the state independence and territorial integrity of China, the national honour and dignity of the Chinese people.

The Presidium of the Supreme Soviet of the Union of Soviet Socialist Republics and the Central People's Government of the People's Republic of China maintain that this new situation permits a new approach to the question of the Chinese Changchun Railway, Port Arthur and Dairen.

In conformity with these new circumstances, the Presidium of the Supreme Soviet of the Union of Soviet Socialist Republics and the Central People's Government of the People's Republic of China have decided to conclude the present agreement on the Chinese Changchun Railway, Port Arthur and Dairen.

Article I. Both High Contracting Parties have agreed that the Soviet Government transfers gratis to the Government of the People's Republic of China all its rights in the joint administration of the Chinese Changchun Railway, with all the property belonging to the Railway. The transfer will be effected immediately upon the conclusion of a peace treaty with Japan, but not later than the end of 1952.

Pending the transfer, the new existing position of the Soviet-Chinese joint administration of the Chinese Changchun Railway remains unchanged; however, the order of filling posts by representatives of the Soviet and Chinese sides, upon the coming into force of the present Agreement, will be changed, and there will be established as alternating filling of posts for a definite period of time (Directors of the railway, Chairman of the Central Board, and others).

As regards concrete methods of effecting the transfer they will be agreed upon and determined by the Government of both High Contracting Parties.

Article II. Both High Contracting Parties have agreed that Soviet troops will be withdrawn from the jointly utilized base of Port Arthur and that the installations in this area will be handed over to the Government of the People's Republic of China immediately upon the conclusion of a peace treaty with Japan, but not later than the end of 1952, with the Government of the People's Republic of China compensating the Soviet Union for expenses incurred in the restoration and construction of installations effected by the Soviet Union since 1945.

For the period pending the withdrawal of Soviet troops and the transfer of the above installations, the Governments of the Soviet Union and China will appoint an equal number of military representatives for organizing a joint Chinese-Soviet Military Commission which will be in charge of military affairs. in the area of Port Arthur; concrete measures in this sphere will be determined by the joint Chinese-Soviet Military Commission within three months upon the coming into force of the present Agreement and shall be implemented upon the approval of these measures by the Governments of both countries.

The civil administration in the aforementioned area shall be in the direct charge of the Government of the People's Republic of China. Pending the withdrawal of Soviet troops, the zone of billeting of Soviet troops in the area of Port Arthur will remain unaltered in conformity with the new existing frontiers.

In the event of either of the High Contracting Parties being subjected to aggression on the part of Japan or any State which should unite with Japan, and as a result of this being involved in military operations, China and the Soviet Union may, on the proposal of the Government of the People's Republic of China and with the agreement of the Soviet Government, jointly use the naval base of Port Arthur in the interests of conducting joint military operations against the aggressor.

Article III. Both High Contracting Parties have agreed that the question of Port Dairen must be further considered upon the conclusion of a peace treaty with Japan.

As regards the administration in Dairen, it fully belongs to the Government of the People's Republic of China.

All property now existing in Dairen provisionally in charge of or under lease to the Soviet side, must be taken over by the Government of the People's Republic of China. For carrying out work involved in the receipt of the aforementioned property, the Government of the Soviet Union and China appoint three representatives from each side for organizing a joint commission which in the course of three months after the coming into force of the present Agreement shall determine the concrete methods of transfer of property, and after approval of the proposals of the Joint Commission by the Governments of both countries will complete their implementation in the course of 1950.

Article IV. The present Agreement comes into force on the day of its ratification. The exchange of instruments of ratification will take place in Peking.

Done in Moscow on February 14, 1950, in two copies, each in the Russian and Chinese languages, both texts having equal force.

Signed:

By authorization of the Central People's Government of the People's Republic of China—CHOU EN-LAI.

By authorization of the Presidium of the Supreme Soviet of the Union of Soviet Socialist Republics—A. Y. VYSHINSKY.

AGREEMENT ON GRANTING CREDITS TO THE CHINESE PEOPLE'S REPUBLIC

In connection with the consent of the Government of the Union of Soviet Socialist Republics to grant the request of the Central People's Government of the People's Republic of China on giving China credits for paying for equipment and other materials which the Soviet Union had agreed to deliver to China, both Governments have agreed upon the following:

Article I. The Government of the Union of Soviet Socialist Republics grants the Central People's Government of the People's Republic of China credits, calculated in dollars, amounting to 300 million American dollars, taking thirty-five dollars to one ounce of fine gold.

In view of the extreme devastation of China as a result of prolonged hostilities on its territory, the Soviet Government has agreed to grant credits on favourable terms of one per cent annual interest.

Article II. The credits mentioned in Article I will be granted in the course of five years, as from January 1, 1950, in equal portions of one-fifth of the credits in the course of each year, for payments for deliveries from the U.S.S.R. of equipment and materials, including equipment for electric power stations, metallurgical and engineering plants, equipment for mines for the production of coal and ores, railway and other transport equipment, rails and other material for the restoration and development of the national economy of China.

The assortment, quantities, prices and dates of deliveries of equipment and materials will be determined under a special agreement of the Parties; prices will be determined on the basis of prices obtaining on the world markets.

Any credits which remain unused in the course of one annual period may be used in subsequent annual periods.

Article III. The Central People's Government of the People's Republic of China redeems the credits mentioned in Article I, as well as interest on them, with deliveries of raw materials, tea, gold, American dollars. Prices for raw materials and tea, quantities and dates of deliveries will be determined on the basis of prices obtaining on the world markets.

Redemption of credits is effected in the course of ten years in equal annual parts—one-tenth yearly of the sum total of received credits not later than December 31, 1954, and the last on December 31, 1963.

Payment of interest on credits, calculated from the day of drawing the respective fraction of the credits, is effected every six months.

Article IV. For clearance with regard to the credits envisaged by the present Agreement the State Bank of the U.S.S.R. and National Bank of the People's Republic of China shall open special accounts and jointly establish the order of clearance and accounting under the present Agreement.

Article V. The present Agreement comes into force on the day of its signing and is subject to ratification. The exchange of instruments of ratification will take place in Peking.

Done in Moscow on February 14, 1950, in two copies, each in the Russian and Chinese languages, both texts having equal force.

Signed:

By authorization of the Central People's Government of the People's Republic of China—CHOU EN-LAI.

By authorization of the Government of the Union of Soviet Socialist Republics—A. Y. VYSHINSKY.

BIBLIOGRAPHY

ABEND, HALLETT, *Chaos in China*, New York, 1939

ARNOT, R. PAGE, *Soviet Russia and Her Neighbours*, New York, 1927

ASAKAWA, K., *The Russo-Japanese Conflict*, New York, 1904

BADDELEY, JOHN F., *Russia, Mongolia, China*, 2 vols., London, 1919

BANTYSH-KAMENSKY, D. N., *Diplomaticheskoie Sobranie Diel Mezhdu Rossiiskim Kitaiskm Gosudarstvami, s. 1616-1792* (in Russian)

BARSUKOV, IVAN, *Graf N. N. Muraviev Amurski*, Moscow, 1891 (in Russian)

BAU, M. J., *The Foreign Relations of China*, New York, 1921

BELL, JOHN, *Travels from St. Petersburg in Russia to Diverse Parts of China*, 2 vols., London, 1763

BELOFF, MAX, *The Foreign Policy of Soviet Russia*, London, vol. I, 1947, vol. II, 1949

BLAND, J. O. P., *Recent Events and Present Politics in China*, Philadelphia, 1912

BOULGER, D. C., *Life of Yakub Beg*, London, 1878
    Sir A. S. Macartney, 1908
    Life of Gordon, 2 vols., London, 1896
    England and Russia in Central Asia, 2 vols., London, 1879
    Central Asian Question, London, 1885

BROWN, ARTHUR JUDSON, *The Mastery of the Far East*, New York, 1919

BUCK, JOHN LOSSING, *Land Utilization in China*, 1945

BYRNES, JAMES F., *Speaking Frankly*, New York, 1947

CAHEN, GASTON, *Historie des Relations de la Russie avec la Chine Sous Pierre le Grand, 1689-1730*, Paris, 1912
    Some Early Chinese Relations, Shanghai, 1914

Carnegie Endowment of International Peace, Outer Mongolia, Pamphlet No. 41, Washington, D.C., 1921

CARRUTHERS, A. D. M., *Unknown Mongolia*, London, 1914

CHAMBERLAIN, WILLIAM HENRY, *Soviet Russia*, London, 1930
    Russia's Iron Age, London, 1935

CHANG CHIH-TUNG, *Compiled Petitions to the Throne* (in Chinese)

CHANG TAO-SHING, *International Controversies over the Chinese Eastern Railway*, The Commercial Press, Shanghai, 1936

CHANG YUNG-FU, *Soviet-Chinese Questions*, The Commercial Press, Shanghai, 1937 (in Chinese)

CHEN FU-KWANG, *Sino-Russian Relations during Ching Dynasty*, Kunming, China, 1947 (in Chinese)

CHEN KUNG-LU, *The Modern History of China*, The Commercial Press, Shanghai, 1935 (in Chinese)

CHEN PAO-WEN, *History of Sino-Russian Relations*, The Commercial Press, 1928 (in Chinese)

CHEN TSUNG-TSOU, *Recent History of Outer Mongolia*, Shanghai, 1922 (in Chinese)

CHIANG KAI-SHEK, *China's Destiny*, 1943 (in Chinese)

CHIANG TING-FU, *A Collection of Recent Chinese Diplomatic Documents*, vols. I and II, Shanghai, 1931 (in Chinese)

CHIN CHIAO-TZU, *Modern Chinese Diplomatic History* (in Chinese)

China Year Book, 1924, 1938, 1939

CHU, C. L., *The Last Ten Years of Russo-Chinese Relations, 1926* (in Chinese)

CLYDE, PAUL HIBBERT, *International Rivalries in Manchuria*, Ohio, 1928
> *The Far East, New York*, 1948

Constitution of the U.S.S.R., Moscow, 1936

CO-OPERATIVE PUBLISHING SOCIETY OF FOREIGN WORKERS IN THE U.S.S.R., *The Soviet Union in the Struggle for Peace*, Moscow, 1936.

CORDIER, HENRI, *Historie des Relations de la Chine avec les puissances occidentales, 1860-1900*, 3 vols., Paris, 1901

COSTIN, W. C., *Great Britain and China, 1833-1860*, London, 1937

CREEL, GEORGE, *Russia's Race for Asia*, New York, 1949

CROLY, H. D., *Willard Straight*, New York, 1924

CULBERTSON, ELY, *Must we Fight Russia?* Philadelphia, 1946

CURZON, LORD, *Russia in Central Asia in 1889*

DALLIN, DAVID J., *Soviet Russia's Foreign Policy, 1939-1942*, New Haven, 1942
> *The Real Soviet Russia*, 1944
> *Soviet Russia in the Far East*, 1948
> *The Rise of Russia in Asia*, 1949

Davis, Sir John Francis, *China*, 2 vols., London, 1852. Selected and translated from the Italian by Fortunato Prandi, Memoire of Father Ripa, during thirteen years' residence at the Court of Peking in the service of the Emperor of China (beginning of the eighteenth century), London, 1846

Dennis, Alfred L. P., *The Foreign Policies of Soviet Russia*, 2 vols., 1924

Die Diplomatischen Akten des Auswartigen Amtes, 1871-1914, Berlin, 1926, vol. XXXII, Chapter 250, *Der Amerikanische Vorstoss für Internationalisierung der mandschurischen Eisenbahnen und Deutschlands Stellungsnahme Dezember 1909 bis Juli 1910.* Chapter 251, *Das Russisch-Japanische Mandschureiabkommen Vom 4 Juli 1910*

Die Internationlen Beziehungen im Zeitalter des Imperialismus Dokumente aus den Archiven der Zarischen und der Provisorischen Regierung, Berlin, 1931-1936, 2 vols.

Dillon, E. J., *The Eclipse of Russia*, New York, 1918

Dunn, Edward, *The Truth About Outer Mongolia*, Shanghai, China, 1935

Fairbank, J. K., *The United States and China*, Harvard, 1948

Fischer, Louis, *The Soviets in World Affairs*, 2 vols., 1930

Fisher, H. A. L., *A History of Europe*, 3 vols., London, 1935

Fleming, Peter, *News from Tartary*, London, 1936

Foreign Relations of the United States, Russia, 1918, 3 vols., 1931-1932

'Foreigner', *Russia, Europe and the East*, London, 1885

Forman, Harrison, *Report from Red China*, 1946
    Changing China, 1948

Fraser, John Foster, *The Real Siberia*, London, 1902

Gelder, Stuart, *The Chinese Communists*, London, 1946

Gerard, Auguste, *Ma Mission en Chine, 1893-1897*, Paris, 1918

Gilbert, Rodney, *The Unequal Treaties*, London, 1929

Gilmour, James, *Among the Mongols*, London, 1888

Grierson, Philip, *Books on Soviet Russia, 1917-1942*, London, 1943

Gunther, John, *Inside Europe*, 1936
    Inside Asia, 1939

Hedin, Sven, *Big Horse's Flight*, 1936
    The Silk Road, 1938

Herimann, A., *Atlas of China*, New York, 1935

Ho CHIU-TAO, *The Strategy of Conquering the Russians* (in Chinese)

Ho HAN-WEN, *The History of Russo-Chinese Relations*, Shanghai, 1935 (in Chinese)

Hoo, C. T., *Les Bases Conventionalles des Relations Modernes entre la Chine et la Russie*, Paris, 1918

HOSIE, ALEXANDER, *Manchuria: Its People, Resources and Recent History*, London, 1904

HOWORTH, H. H., *History of Mongols*, 5 vols., London, 1876

HSIAO, I-SAN, *History of the Manchu Dynasty*, 2 vols., Shanghai (in Chinese)

HSU SHUHSI, *How the Far Eastern War was Begun*, Shanghai, 1938

HUC, M., *The Chinese Empire*, London, 1859

IDES, E. Y., *The Three Years' Land Travels of His Excellency E. Ysbrandt Ides from Moscow to China*, London, 1705

IVANOVSKY, I. A., *Collection of Treaties*, 1890 (in Russian)

JAO SUNG-SUN, *History of Russo-Chinese Relations*, 1926 (in Chinese)

JONES, F. C., *Manchuria Since 1931*, London, 1949

KEETON, GEORGE W., *China, the Far East and the Future*, London, 1943

KENNAN, GEORGE, *E. H. Harriman: A Biography*, New York, 1922

KERNER, ROBERT J., *Russian Expansion to America*, 1931

KORFF, S. A., *Russia's Foreign Relations*, 1922

KUROPOTKIN, A. N., *The Russian Army and the Japanese War*, London, 1909

LANG, LAURENT, *Journal of Residence at the Court of Peking*, 1763

LANSDELL, H., *Chinese Central Asia*, 2 vols., 1893

LATTIMORE, OWEN, *Manchuria, Cradle of Conflict*, 1932
    Inner Asian Frontier of China, New York, 1940
    Solution in Asia, Boston, 1945
    The Situation in Asia, Boston, 1949

LAWTON, L., *Empires of the Far East*, 2 vols., London, 1912

Letters Captured from Baron Ungern, Washington Conference, 1921

LEVINE, J. D., *Letters from the Kaiser to the Tsar*, 1920

LI UNG BING, *Outlines of Chinese History*, Shanghai, 1914 (in Chinese)

LINEBARGER, PAUL M. A., *The China of Chiang Kai-shek*, Boston, 1941

LIU KWEI-HAN, *The Past and Future of Outer Mongolia* (in Chinese)

LOBANOV-ROSTOVSKY, A., *Russia and Asia*, 1933

MACMURRAY, J. V. A., *Treaties and Agreements With and Concerning China, 1894-1919*, 2 vols., Washington, D.C., 1919

MARTIN, H. MONTGOMERY, *China—Social, Commercial and Political*, 2 vols., London, 1847

MIDDLETON, DREW, *A Report on Soviet Russia*, 1948

MITCHELL, KATE, and HOLLAND, W. L., *Problems of the Pacific*, 1939 Institute of Pacific Relations, New York, 1940

MOORE, HARRIET L., *Soviet Far Eastern Policy, 1931-45*, Princeton, 1945

MORSE, H. B., and MACNAIR, H. F., *Far Eastern International Relations*, New York, 1931

MORSE, H. B., *The Trade and Administration of the Chinese Empire*, Shanghai, 1908
  The International Relations of the Chinese Empire, 3 vols., London, 1910-18

NORINS, MARTIN R., *Gateway to Asia: Sinkiang*, New York, 1944

OLIVER, FRANK, *Special Undeclared War*, London, 1939

OLUFSEN, A. F. O. H., *The Second Danish Pamir Expedition*, 1903

OSSENDOWSKI, FERDINAND, *Beasts, Men and Gods*, London, 1926

OTSUKA, *Red Influence in China*, 1936

OUDENDYK, WILLIAM, *Ways and By-ways of Diplomacy*, 1939

PAN SU, *Far Eastern Policy of Soviet Russia*, Shanghai, 1927 (in Chinese translated from Japanese)

PASVOLSKY, LEO, *Russia in the Far East*, New York, 1922

PAVLOVSKY, MICHEL N., *Chinese Russian Relations*, 1948

Peking Gazette (in Chinese)

PLATONOV, S. F., *History of Russia*, London, 1925

POTEMKIN, V. P., *Istroiia Diplomatii*, 3 vols., Moscow, 1941-6 (in Russian)

RAVENSTEIN, ERNST GEORGE, *Russia on the Amur*, 1861

ROBERTSON, DANIEL T., *Manchuria*, Edinburgh, 1913

ROMANOV, B. A., *Rossiia v Mandzhurii*, Leningrad, 1928 (in Russian)

ROMANOVSKY, *Notes on the Central Asiatic Question*, Calcutta, 1870

ROSEN, R. R., *Forty Years of Diplomacy*, 2 vols., New York, 1920

SHERWOOD, ROBERT E., *The White House Papers of Harry L. Hopkins*, 2 vols., 1949

SKRINE, F. H., *Expansion of Russia, 1815-1900*, Cambridge, 1915

SMITH, BEDELL, *Moscow Mission, 1946-1949*, New York, 1949

SNOW, EDGAR, *Red Star Over China*, 1937
   Scorched Earth, 1941

SOLOVEV, SERG. MIKH., *History of Russia*, 5 vols., 1911 (in Russian)

SOOTHILL, W. E., *China and the West*, London, 1925

Soviet Contemporary Materials, Japan, 1932 (in Japanese)

SPECTOR, IVAN, *Russia: A New History*, London, 1935

STEIN, G., *The Challenge of Red China*, 1945

STIMSON, HENRY L., *The Far Eastern Crisis*, New York, 1936

STITTINIUS, EDWARD, *Roosevelt and the Russians: The Yalta Conference*, New York, 1949

SUN CH'I-YI, *Russo-Chinese Negotiations* (in Chinese)

TEICHMAN, SIR ERIC, *Journey to Turkistan*, London, 1937
   Affairs of China, London, 1938

The Illustrated Encyclopœdia of Sinkiang, 116 vols. (in Chinese)

TIMKOWSKI, GEORGE, *Travels of the Russian Mission through Mongolia to China in the year 1820-21*, London, 1827

Treaties, Conventions, etc., Between China and Foreign States, 2 vols., Shanghai (in both Chinese and English)

TSENG CHI-TZE, MARQUIS, *Compiled Letters and Essays* (in Chinese)
   Compiled Petitions to the Throne (in Chinese)

TSO CHUNG-TANG, *Compiled Letters and Documents* (in Chinese)
   Compiled Petitions to the Throne (in Chinese)

TSO SUNG-SEN, *Historical Materials of the Recent Century in China*, 2 vols., Shanghai (in Chinese)

TU LI-SHEN, *Narrative of the Chinese Embassy to the Khan of the Torgat Tatars in the Years 1712, 1713, 1714 and 1715*, translated from the Chinese by Sir George Thomas Staunton, London, 1821

ULAR, ALEXANDER, *A Russo-Chinese Empire*, 1904

United States Relations with China, State Department, Washington, D.C., 1949

UTLEY, FREDA, *China at War*, London, 1939

VADTAEV, R. A., *Russia and China*, 1900 (in Russian)

VERNADSKY, GEORGE, *Political and Diplomatic History of Russia*, 1937

VESPA, AMLETO, *Secret Agents of Japan*, London, 1939

VLADIMIR (Pseudonym), *Russia on the Pacific and the Siberian Railway*, London, 1899

WALLACE, DONALD MACKENZIE, *Russia*, 1912

WANG, C. C., *Whither Manchuria?*, 1932
    The Sale of the Chinese Eastern Railway, 1933

WANG TAO-FU, *Diplomatic Documents in the later part of the Ching Dynasty*, Peiping, 1932 (in Chinese)

WANG YUNG-SHENG, *Sixty Years of China and Japan*, 7 vols., Tientsin, 1932 (in Chinese)

WANG YUN-WU, *Russo-Chinese Relations and the C.E.R.*, 1933 (in Chinese)

WEIGH KEN-SHEN, *Russo-Chinese Diplomacy*, 1928

WELLES, SUMNER, *The Time for Decision*, 1946

WELLS, WILLIAM S., *The Middle Kingdom*, 2 vols., New York, 1879

WILLKIE, WENDELL L., *One World*, New York, 1943

WILLOUGHBY, W. W., *Foreign Rights and Interests in China*, 2 vols., Baltimore, 1920

WITTE, COUNT SERGIE YULIEVITCH, *The Memoirs of Count Witte*, New York, 1921

WOODHEAD, H. G. W., *The Truth About the Chinese Republic*, New York, 1925

WRIGHT, G. H., *Asiatic Russia*, 2 vols., 1902

WU, AITCHEN K., *A Study on the Soviet Constitution*, Shanghai, 1937 (in Chinese)
    Turkistan Tumult, London, 1940

WU YON-SAN, *Russo-Japanese Relations*, 1938 (in Chinese)

YAKHONTOFF, VICTOR A., *Russia and the Soviet Union in the Far East*, 1932
    The Chinese Soviets, 1934

YAVDYNSKY, J. A., *The Chinese Eastern Railway in Contemplation of Law*, Shanghai, 1934

YOUNGHUSBAND, F. E., *The Heart of a Continent, 1884-1894*, London, 1896

INDEX